AI-Driven Sustainability Across Smart Cities, Business, and Industry

Fanar Shwedeh
https://orcid.org/0009-0005-5471-8418
City University, Ajman, UAE

IGI Global Scientific Publishing
Publishing Tomorrow's Research Today

Vice President of Editorial	Melissa Wagner
Director of Acquisitions	Mikaela Felty
Director of Book Development	Jocelynn Hessler
Production Manager	Mike Brehm
Cover Design	Jose Rosado

Published in the United States of America by
IGI Global Scientific Publishing
701 East Chocolate Avenue
Hershey, PA, 17033, USA
Tel: 717-533-8845 | Fax: 717-533-7115
Website: https://www.igi-global.com E-mail: cust@igi-global.com

Library of Congress Cataloging-in-Publication Data

LCCN: 2026019545 (CIP Data Pending)
ISBN13: 9798260013489
Isbn13Softcover: 9798260013496
EISBN13: 9798260013502
British Cataloguing in Publication Data
A Cataloguing in Publication record for this book is available from the British Library.

Table of Contents

Detailed Table of Contents

research prove that this intersection can be used to increase effectiveness, clarity, and openness in a vast variety of applications, including supply chain management and financial services. However, to make the most out of the full potential of this intersection, there are significant challenges that must be overcome such as scalability and control. Finally, green artificial intelligence (GAI) and blockchain technology unified can optimize the possible potential of technological augmented reality in a smart city when it exploits the respective advantages of both. Nevertheless, more efforts are needed in order to address the challenges that still persist and guarantee the prevalence and sustainability of this convergence in a wide range of industrial sectors.

The rapid evolution of the smart city ecosystem has placed the Internet of Things (IoT) at the forefront of city mobility innovation. As cities grapple with rising population, growing vehicle density, and increased environmental pressures, modern IoT-based solutions have emerged as the key enablers of smarter, more efficient transportation systems. Within the landscape, Parking 4.0, an integrated, IoT-enhanced smart parking paradigm, has transformed how cities manage space, mobility, and user expectations. This study examines the strategic role of IoT-enabled technologies in reshaping modern intelligent parking systems and the development of urban mobility performance. The paper examines the main architectural elements, technical requirements, and security factors associated with such solutions, thus highlighting both their transformative potential and the associated challenges. The results indicate that IoT-enhanced parking systems play a pivotal role in reducing congestion, enhancing sustainability, and improving overall mobility efficiency within dynamic smart city ecosystems.

The integration of green management practices into business operations presents both opportunities and challenges for fostering sustainable entrepreneurship. This study incorporates Green Information Technology (GIT) acceptance as a moderating factor within the proposed model. Using (PLS-SEM), the study investigates the interrelationships among key constructs. The findings indicate that knowledge creation and transfer exert a significant positive influence on sustainable entrepreneurship, whereas knowledge application and utilization demonstrate an insignificant effect. Additionally, GIT acceptance significantly moderates the relationships between knowledge creation, transfer, and storage with sustainable entrepreneurship, while showing no significant moderating effect on the link between knowledge application and sustainable entrepreneurship. These results provide valuable insights for practitioners and policymakers seeking to advance sustainable entrepreneurship through enhanced knowledge creation, effective GIT integration, and strategic knowledge utilization.

This study focuses on the employment of AI towards Sustainable Leadership Behaviors through its influence on leadership decision making with a focus on environmental welfare. Based on the data gathered from professionals working in the banking industry in the UAE. This paper studies how AI Readiness, AI Tools & Systems, AI Competency, and AI Governance & Ethical Integration impact AI-Driven Leadership Decision Making and subsequently Sustainable Leadership Behaviors. Using quantitative approach and regression based mediation analysis, the results demonstrate that AI enablers play a significant role in improving AI-Driven Leadership Decision Making which positively influences sustainability oriented leadership practices. The results further confirm that AI-Driven Leadership Decision Making is an important mechanism by which AI capabilities are transformed into environmentally responsible leadership behaviors. The significance of this research is the contribution of bridging the gap between AI and the sustainability of the environment by making leadership behaviors as a central link between technology

oceans. The findings showed the effectiveness of artificial intelligence technologies and interactive storytelling in creating and developing scientific understanding and environmental awareness.

This chapter examines how AI can drive greener pharmaceutical marketing by shifting from paper- and travel-heavy approaches to lower-carbon, data-driven omnichannel engagement. It reviews evidence on the environmental impacts of telehealth, e-detailing, remote medical education and digital consent, while weighing the energy and material costs of AI models, devices and data centers. Using a narrative review plus vignettes, the authors propose a measurement framework aligned to the GHG Protocol Scopes 1–3 and define metrics such as CO2e per qualified HCP engagement, travel emissions avoided via virtual interactions and net savings from replacing print with digital (including computing energy). They outline reporting that combines energy data (e.g., PUE and grid mix) with campaign analytics, and present an AI playbook emphasizing efficient models, renewable hosting, responsible governance and content reuse. The chapter also flags rebound effects, privacy/ethics and regulatory compliance, calling for standardized digital carbon accounting and sustainability-linked marketing KPIs.

Oil and gas are complicated processes that are in risky environments and have strict regulations making them have more operational risk. Recent advances in Artificial intelligence (AI) have seen AI make it an optimal tool in mitigating risks in exploration, production, transport and refining operations. In exploration/drilling, AI enhances the interpretation of seismic data, reservoir modeling and optimization of processes with the aim of minimizing errors and maximizing the resources used. Application of digital twins and AI-based simulations also enables

Preface

The urgency of addressing climate change and achieving sustainable development has accelerated the integration of advanced digital technologies across cities, businesses, and industries. Among these technologies, Artificial Intelligence (AI) stands out as a transformative enabler, offering data-driven insights, predictive capabilities, and intelligent optimization to support sustainability goals. This volume titled "*AI-Driven Sustainability Across Smart Cities, Business, and Industry*" brings together twelve scholarly contributions that examine how AI can be strategically leveraged to advance environmental, economic, and social sustainability.

This book adopts a multidisciplinary and application-oriented perspective, highlighting the convergence of Green AI, smart infrastructure, digital transformation, and responsible governance. The chapters collectively demonstrate how AI-driven solutions can enhance efficiency, reduce carbon footprints, strengthen decision-making, and foster innovation across diverse sectors.

KEY THEMES AND CONTRIBUTIONS

- Smart Cities and Urban Sustainability
  - **Chapter 1:** Exploration of AI-powered strategies for achieving net-zero cities through intelligent infrastructure and data-driven urban planning.
  - **Chapter 2:** Integration of Green AI and blockchain technologies to enhance augmented reality applications for sustainable smart city ecosystems.
  - **Chapter 3:** Development of IoT-enabled mobility solutions (*Parking 4.0*) to improve urban efficiency and reduce environmental impact.
- Sustainable Business and Entrepreneurship
  - **Chapter 4:** Leveraging Green Information Technology and knowledge management to foster sustainable entrepreneurship and innovation.

- Chapter 5: Examining the role of AI-driven decision-making in promoting sustainable leadership behaviors.
    - **Chapter 6:** Application of the triple bottom line framework to sustainability-driven projects for achieving competitive advantage.
- Finance, Governance, and Digital Responsibility
    - **Chapter 7:** Introduction of the ESGI framework, integrating AI and data analytics into environmental, social, and governance (ESG) investing.
    - **Chapter 8:** Role of AI and social media literacy in encouraging responsible consumer engagement with green brands.
- Sector-Specific AI Applications for Sustainability
    - **Chapter 9:** Use of AI storytelling to enhance public marine awareness, illustrated through the Yas SeaWorld Research & Rescue Center.
    - **Chapter 10:** Decarbonization of pharmaceutical engagement through AI-optimized digital transformation.
    - **Chapter 11:** AI-driven risk mitigation strategies in the oil and gas sector, focusing on innovation and operational impact.
    - **Chapter 12:** Transformation of healthcare practices through AI-enabled sustainable dentistry and computational foresight.

CONCLUDING PERSPECTIVE

Collectively, the contributions in this volume underscore a central insight: achieving sustainability requires not only technological advancement but also responsible design, ethical governance, and interdisciplinary collaboration. AI, when aligned with sustainability principles, has the potential to act as a catalyst for systemic change—supporting smarter cities, more resilient businesses, and more sustainable industries.

This volume is intended for researchers, practitioners, policymakers, and graduate students seeking to explore the intersection of AI and sustainability. It is our hope that this book will contribute to advancing knowledge, inspiring innovation, and supporting the global transition toward a more sustainable and intelligent future.

Fanar Shwedeh
City University, Ajman, UAE

Chapter 1
Towards Net-Zero Cities:
AI Powered Strategies for Smart Infrastructure and Sustainable Development

Ajit Danti
http://orcid.org/0000-0002-2462-1771
City University, Ajman, UAE

Jayant Banerjee
http://orcid.org/0000-0002-2079-8983
City University, Ajman, UAE

Ayman Bassam Nassoura
City University, Ajman, UAE

ABSTRACT

This chapter explores how Artificial Intelligence can reshape net-zero cities by enabling smart infrastructure and sustainable urban development. It explains how AI-driven innovations can optimize urban systems, reduce carbon emissions, and accelerate progress toward global climate goals. Key focus areas include intelligent energy management, sustainable mobility, and resource-efficient urban planning as core elements of net-zero strategies. The chapter emphasizes the integration of modeling and simulation with AI to design, evaluate, and validate sustainable city systems. Through forecasting, optimization, and real-time analytics, planners can simulate scenarios, assess trade-offs, and implement scalable solutions. Advances in sensor data, machine learning, and reinforcement learning further support predictive maintenance and adaptive decision-making, positioning AI as a catalyst for achieving carbon-neutral cities.

DOI: 10.4018/979-8-2600-1348-9.ch001

1. INTRODUCTION

The shift to net-zero emissions taking place globally can be considered one of the largest socio-technical changes of the twenty-first century. The challenge centers on urban settings, which cause almost 70 percent of the world's energy use and three-quarters of greenhouse gases (GHG) emissions. Efforts to accelerate urbanization, which is projected to introduce two thirds of the global population into cities by 2050, demand an immediate re-examination of the way urban systems are designed, operated and maintained. The ability of Artificial Intelligence (AI) to make decisions based on data, optimize in real-time, and make predictive analytics has become a transforming enabler in ensuring the sustainability, intelligent, and carbon-neutral city (S B & Danti, 2024).

Net-zero cities entails the development of urban ecosystems that offset carbon emissions by equal amount of carbon eliminations though intelligent planning, adoption of renewable energy, resource management, and technology-driven interventions. AI offers the cognitive layer upon which this balance could be dynamically realized, namely, intelligent control of energy systems, adaptive transportation networks, circular waste management and intelligent infrastructure design. AI systems can model, simulate, and predict the results of sustainability at scales and accuracy never before witnessed through the use of increasing amounts of data on cities in the form of IoT sensors, satellite imagery, and digital twins.

The chapter discusses the way AI-based approaches are transforming the roadmap of sustainable city development. It also discusses the application of machine learning (ML), deep learning (DL), reinforcement learning (RL), and optimization algorithms to the urban infrastructure system to minimize energy wastage, decrease emissions, and improve resilience. The discussion shows the convergence of technological innovation, environmental policy, and socio-economic equity to develop the future of smart cities that are coherent with the United Nations Sustainable Development Goals (SDGs), in particular, SDG 11 (Sustainable Cities and Communities) and SDG 13 (Climate Action).

1.1 Defining Key Concepts

In order to put the discussion to the point, it is crucial to outline the major terms that make the thematic background of the chapter:

1.1.1.Artificial Intelligence (AI):

It is a multidisciplinary field that aims at creating systems that can handle the tasks that need human intelligence, which includes perception, reasoning, learning, and problem-solving. Predictive analytics, computer vision, natural language processing, and control algorithms have been applied to sustainability problems in urban settings under the umbrella of AI.

1.1.2 Smart Infrastructure

Smart Infrastructure is the core of the new age sustainable cities where the component of the old physical systems is boosted with digital intelligence to create enhanced efficiency, reliability and eco-performance. It incorporates sensors, IoT connections and data analytics to gather real time data on transportation networks, power grids, water networks and buildings. This information is handled by AI-based analytics and automation to track the situation, anticipate failures, and streamline the utilization of resources.

The European Commission (2022) also states that smart infrastructure does not just increase the performance of operations, but it also makes the infrastructure resilient to external factors like energy shortages or climate-related incidents. It decreases the downtime and lifecycle costs by facilitating predictive maintenance and adaptive responses. Notably, intelligent infrastructure facilitates the shift to net-zero emissions through the integration of renewable energy, the stimulation of electric mobility, and the adoption of data-based urban governance. In addition to technology, it also helps achieve improved quality of life, safety, and inclusiveness to citizens. Accordingly, smart infrastructure is an indispensable feature of sustainable urban transformation, that is, the physical and the digital world are united to form intelligent, adaptive, and environmentally friendly cities (Koven et al., 2022).

1.1.3 Sustainable Development

Sustainable Development can be defined as the way of progress that is all-encompassing, so that economic development, social welfare and environmental safety exist in a balance. Development, as the Brundtland Commission (1987) stated, is the process that could satisfy the existing needs, without reducing the capacity of the future generations to satisfy their needs.

In the city setting, sustainable development entails the development of cities that are economically stable, environmentally friendly and socially accommodative. It entails encouraging green cover, effective transport, renewable energy, and fair distribution of housing, health and education. It will reduce pollution and depletion of resources and encourage innovation, employment and community wellness (Abouraia et al., 2025a).

Participatory governance is also imperative in urban sustainability whereby the citizens, policymakers and businesses work together to realize common goals that are in accordance with the United Nations Sustainable Development Goals (SDGs), and especially SDG 11 (Sustainable Cities and Communities). In a nutshell, sustainable cities development is all about developing reactive, habitable, and robust environments that can accommodate the present and the future generations- without compromising the health and social equity of the planet.

1.1.4 Net-Zero Cities:

As C40 Cities Climate Leadership Group advertises on its web page - are urban ecosystems aimed at achieving carbon neutrality. This implies that a balance is achieved so that all the emitted greenhouse gases are matched by corresponding removals or offsets thus creating a net zero emissions balance. In C40, such cities have to integrate three fundamental strategies:

The AI-driven renewable energy management: smart systems that would be used to optimize the energy production (e.g., solar, wind) and consumption in the urban infrastructures and limit reliance on fossil fuels and balance the supply and demand in real-time (Yas et al., 2025).

Mobility electrification and effective urban design: moving transport to electric or other zero emission models, lessening car dependence through walkable neighbourhoods, public transit and the concept of the 15 minute city; and re-designing buildings, heat systems and urban layouts in the most energy efficient way (Abouraia et al., 2025b).

The holistic city planning: incorporating efficient buildings, green areas, low carbon materials, waste to energy technology and carbon capture/offset technology into the structure of the city in a way that the built environment promotes the net zero target (Kurdi, Alshurideh, et al., 2025).

According to C40, more than 700 cities in the world have pledged to reduce emissions by 50 percent by 2030 and achieve net zero by 2050, which reflects the increasing momentum of this urban reform. C40 Cities+2C40 Cities+2

Practically, a Net Zero City does not just reduce the emissions radically, but also makes sure that any other emissions are compensated by a verifiable removal (carbon sinks, urban forestry or capture technologies). The strategy acknowledges the fact that, cities are key emitters with buildings and transport alone constituting substantial portions of the urban GHGs and thus should be at the forefront of innovation, policy and investment to render the 1.5 degC target attainable. C40 Cities+1

In brief: Net Zero Cities represent a paradigm shift in urbanism - through renewable and intelligent energy, electric transport, and small/light-weight design - to produce cities as much as they take away to provide a model of sustainable, resilient urban economies.

1.1.5 AI-Powered Urban Systems:

AI-enabled cities are the concept of introducing a set of sophisticated AI-based algorithms in the functioning of urban centers to optimize the efficiency, sustainability, and responsiveness. These systems depend on real-time information provided by the IoT sensors, smart meters and environmental scanners to check and control key city operations. The AI in traffic management predicts the congestion patterns, dynamically adjusts the traffic lights and optimizes the routes of the public transportation, decreasing the travel time and emissions. In the context of a power distribution, AI allows smart grids that will equalize the supply and demand of energy, introduce renewable sources, and predict outages. AI-based leakage detection, usage behavior prediction, and predictive maintenance are beneficial to water conservation by making sure that the resources are well allocated. Intelligent routing and predictive collection strategies are used in waste management to minimize the costs of operation and environmental effects. The urban services can self-optimize through AI systems that analyze the incoming data to facilitate adaptive decision-making, at any given time depending on the changing conditions. This integration will contribute to increased sustainability, reduced costs of operation, and quality life by citizens. Furthermore, AI-based urban systems are capable of aiding long-term planning through simulating the scenarios and guiding the policy-making process. Altogether, these frameworks are a radical new way of managing cities, in which the use of information can result in proactive, smart and resilient urban governance that can match the objectives of smart urbanism (Abouraia et al., 2025c).

1.2 Need Analysis

The urge to achieve net-zero urban eco systems is not only a need on the planetary scale but also a technical opportunity. Urban emissions in the world have been at all time high and cities emit over 25 gigatons of CO_2 per year. Policy and behavioral change have been the main focus of mitigation strategies used in recent times, which is not enough unless smart automation and data wisdom (S B & Danti, 2024). Conventional city systems are based on when and where rules, with centralized control and reduce responsiveness to real time environmental changes.

Economically, according to the World Economic Forum, 2024, AI-based infrastructure saves up to USD 700 billion annually in cities, in terms of energy efficiency and predictive upkeep. Additionally, the use of AI facilitates resilience, cities may predict calamities, distribute resources efficiently, and improve emergency management. AI, IoT, and digital twins can also be combined to create a city-wide simulation environment to account carbon and test sustainability scenarios.

Irrespective of these improvements there are still issues at hand especially when it comes to data governance, privacy, interoperability and fair access to technology. That is why there is an urgent necessity to investigate scalable, ethical, and context-sensitive AI schemes that will help to reconcile environmental objectives with the welfare of society (Banerjee et al., 2025).

1.3 The history of AI development in the field of urban sustainability.

Technology and urban sustainability have developed in a series of epochs:

Mechanization and Industrial Urbanism (1850-1950): The initial cities were dependent on mechanical engineering and centralized utilities which led to the rapid industrialization but also caused serious pollution and social inequality.

Automation and Information Age (1950-2000): With the introduction of digital control systems and sensors in the urban management, the process of building smart cities emerged. Sustainability was however a secondary consideration as most of the time it was overshadowed by economic efficiency.

Cognitive and Sustainable Urbanism (2000-present): The emergence of AI, IoT, and big data analytics made cities intelligent and able to learn and adapt. Net-zero cities are a concept that developed alongside the global climate schemes, including the Kyoto Protocol (1997) and the Paris Deal (2015), which have triggered the study of AI-oriented approaches to sustainability.

The progress in AI (the development of deep learning, reinforcement learning in autonomous control, and the concept of digital twins all contributed to the establishment of a new paradigm according to which the city ecosystem could be modeled, simulated, and optimized in the future. It is this convergence that currently determines the basis of AI-driven sustainability (Bhushan & Danti, 2018).

1.4 Existing Trends and Technological Advancements.

Growth Recent years have experienced a geometric increase in AI research and implementation to address sustainable urban infrastructure:

1.4.1 AI-Enabled Energy Management:

The innovation of artificial intelligence is changing energy management in contemporary urban environments by means of innovative deep learning and real-time data analytics. Intelligent grids, fitted with AI, are able to balance the demand and supply of electricity dynamically with continuous information provided by sensors, smart meters, and whatever connectivity. Predicting consumption trends enables utilities to optimize energy allocation, to incorporate renewable energy sources and limit wastage, which is achieved with the help of AI. Moreover, AI-powered predictive maintenance forecasts possible equipment malfunctions in power supply chains, avoiding unexpected malfunctions and providing stable and reliable power supply. Not only is this increasing grid resiliency but it is also facilitating the process of shifting to low-carbon energy systems through the efficient incorporation of intermittent renewable energy sources such as solar and wind into the grid. The AI-managed energy management helps utilities and consumers save on costs and meet the goals of sustainability. The future of urban mobility is a system that is sustainable and long-lasting.

1.4.2 Sustainable Mobility Systems:

Transportation into cities is one of the significant sources of greenhouse gases, and AI provides a lot of new solutions to the development of a sustainable mobility infrastructure. AI algorithms can be used to optimize the routing of vehicles through analysis of traffic patterns to reduce congestion and travel time as well as fuel consumption. AI coordination also creates an advantage of autonomous vehicle fleets because it allows traffic to run more efficiently and safely on the road. Also, AI helps manage the efficient charging of electric vehicles (EVs), anticipate the peak of demand, and maintain the maximum utilization of charging stations. All of these innovations, when combined, substantially decrease the emissions caused by transportation, enhance the commuting experience, and contribute to the overall increase in using electric vehicles and low-emission ones (Danti & Sanjay, 2020). The use of AI in transportation networks also contributes to the creation of smart and sustainable cities.

1.4.3 Urban Digital Twins:

Urban digital twins are virtual models of the city infrastructure, combining AI and real-time data to create and optimize city structures. Singapore, Dubai, and Helsinki cities have been the first to implement AI-based digital twins that simulate building behavior, energy demand, traffic, and the environment. These digitalizations enable urban planners and policy makers to experiment, assess the effect of interventions, and make evidence-based choices. As an instance, using AI simulations on simulations can forecast the outcomes of new building on traffic or energy requirements, allowing the management to be proactive and plan sustainably (Dileep & Danti, 2018). Digital twins will improve the transparency, efficiency, and resilience of city management through providing real-time actionable insights to both operational and strategic planning.

1.4.4 The Smart Waste and Water systems are:

Urban waste and water management is changing with the introduction of AI technologies such as computer vision and anomaly detection. Automated sorting systems are used in waste management to identify the recyclable materials and minimize contamination, predictive models are used to optimize the collection schedules to reduce the operational costs and environmental impact. To manage water, AI algorithms identify leaks, check on water quality, and predict trends in consumption, thus taking necessary measures and saving resources in time. The smart systems minimise wastage of resources, enhance service reliability and the environmental sustainability.

1.4.5 AI in Green Construction:

AI is useful in the construction industry, which is a major source of carbon emissions, with the use of generative design and predictive modeling such that stakeholders make informed choices that increase the sustainability of buildings and lessen environmental footprints.

Applications of AI in energy, mobility, urban planning, waste, water, and construction bring together the transformation of the cities into smart, sustainable ecosystems. AI can bring into existence adaptive, resilient, and environmentally friendly urban systems which enhance the quality of life and contribute to global sustainability objectives.

These advancements highlight the fact that AI is not a narrow technology but a unifying power that links into a coherent system of sustainability of multiple urban systems.

1.5 Policy Impact and Implications on the Society.

The policy implications of the use of AI in activities promoting the sustainability of cities are far-reaching. Regulatory bodies should be established by the governments to oversee the ethical use of AI, transparency, and the sovereignty of data. The European Green Deal and the Net Zero 2050 Strategy of the UAE are the policies that offer the blueprints of using digital transformation as a means of reaching the goal of carbon neutrality. Nevertheless, the success relies on the multi-stakeholder cooperation, i.e. the cooperation between technology developers, municipal authorities, citizens, and academia ("United Nations climate change annual report 2022).

1.6 International Industry players and Research Organizations.

There are multiple international organizations that dominate the development of AI in net-zero city:

Technology Firms: Google DeepMind with its Energy project, IBM with its Green Horizons and Microsoft with its AI for Earth are the first to take AI-based climate intelligence.
City performance Lab: Siemens City Performance Tool, Lumada by Hitachi, and EcoStruxure by Schneider Electric are tools used to optimize the operation of energy and infrastructure.
Academic Partnerships MIT Senseable City Lab, Stanford Sustainable Urban Systems group, and Urban Sustainability Lab at ETH Zurich are on the frontier of AI-enabled design.
International Organizations: The AI for Good of the United Nations and the Climate-Smart Cities of the World Bank initiatives emphasize the application of AI in the global capacity to manage climate change.

All these efforts are indicative of the world in the trend of integrating AI into sustainability models that aid in achieving net-zero targets.

1.7 Gaps in research and motivation.

Although the current studies prove the vast potential of AI in terms of urban sustainability, there are several severe gaps:

Absence of Coordinated Frameworks: The majority of the studies are limited to single areas (energy, mobility or waste) without including systemic relationships amongst urban subsystems.
Fragmentation of Data: Urban data is segregated between departments and is not uniform and standardized which restricts the interoperability of AI models.
Ethical and Governance Issues: Insufficient research exists on responsible AI systems that can balance environmental objectives and privacy and fairness.
Scalability and Localization: A lot of AI models are assessed on a pilot city and cannot be applied to various geographic, climatic, and socio-economic settings.
Performance Benchmarking: There is a lack of comparative studies that validate AI with actual reduction of carbon impact.

The chapter fills these gaps with a proposal of an AI-based model of net-zero city modeling, which includes predictive analytics, simulation, and adaptive optimization. The study seeks to equip urban planners and policymakers with feasible knowledge and instruments to deliver results of sustainability at scale.

2. LITERATURE REVIEW

Artificial Intelligence (AI) has been studied concerning sustainable urban development, cutting across various overlapping fields, including computer science, environmental engineering, urban planning, and policy studies. In the last twenty years, scientists have studied the ways to have intelligent systems maximise flows of resources, reduce emissions and make cities more resilient. This section is a critical review of those contributions and presents thematically grouped contributions: (1) AI in energy and climate management, (2) AI and sustainable mobility, (3) AI-enabled infrastructure and construction, (4) AI and the circular economy and resource optimization, (5) data-driven governance as well as digital-twin urbanism, and (6) ethical, social and policy perspectives. Both themes follow the developments in methodology, find gaps, and combine opposing opinions to create a logical research foundation.

2.1. AI in Energy and Climate Management.

The initial studies of urban sustainability were concerned with fixed-energy models and optimization rules. The accuracy of the energy forecast and adaptive control became much better with the introduction of deep learning.

2.1.1 Predictive Energy Models:

Predictive Energy Models use advanced methods of data analytics and machine learning to predict future patterns of demand, consumption, and generation of energy. These models examine past records on weather, occupancy, industrial activity and energy prices in order to establish trends and correlations that impact on energy consumption. Through such trends, predictive models may precisely forecast both short-term and long-term energy demand. Regression analysis, time-series prediction, artificial neural networks, and ensemble learning algorithms (including Random Forests and Gradient Boosting) are popular methods of enhancing the accuracy of the prediction.

The models also facilitate the idea of demand-side management as they assist the consumers and utilities to plan the use of energy more effectively, combine renewable sources, and reduce carbon emissions. Basically, predictive energy models are the building block of intelligent power network and smart cities, which enhances the sustainability, resilience, and energy efficiency of the current power networks and intelligent cities ("United Nations climate change annual report 2022).

Long-short-term-memory (LSTM) networks to predict residential load patterns with a maximum error reduction of 12 percent in comparison with autoregressive schemes. In the same way, Nguyen, showed that reinforcement learning (RL) may be used to learn the real-time demand response balancing between consumption and fluctuations in renewable supply (Nguyen, 2024).

2.1.2 Smart Grid Optimization:

Smart Grid Optimization reflects the application of the latest technologies, data analytics, and automation to improve the efficiency, reliability and sustainability of the modern electrical grids. In contrast to the conventional power systems, smart grids combine sensors, Internet of Things (IoT) devices, and communication channels to receive real-time data on energy production, distribution, and consumption.

Smart grid optimization gives the consumer the power as a result of smart meters and dynamic pricing that promotes efficient energy consumption. All in all, it increases operational flexibility, carbon emissions are lowered, and it helps the shift toward decentralized sustainable energy, which is the core of net-zero cities in the future. Deep Q-Networks have been applied to decentralized energy trading in microgrids, and it was found that peer-to-peer energy markets based on multi-agent RL can be used to achieve carbon-neutral objectives (Son et al., 2019).

2.1.3 Climate Prognostication and Adaptation:

Climate forecasting entails application of scientific models and past climatic trends to forecast the future climatic patterns, such as the changes in temperature, precipitation, and extreme weather conditions. Combining satellite data, air and water data, and machine learning algorithms, the scientists will be able to create short-term seasonal forecasts and long-term climate forecasts. Such forecasts are useful in determining the sensitive areas of the ecosystem, agriculture, water, and city infrastructure.

Adaptation can be described as the measures and efforts used to reduce the negative effects of the changing climate and make them more resilient. The development of efficient adaptation depends on early warning systems, and decision-making based on data, and involvement of the community.

In addition to power, AI assists in urban climatic modeling. As an example, convolutional neural networks (CNNs) and satellite data are used to forecast the intensity of heat-islands at the spatial scale. These frameworks inform the location of green roofs and reflective surfaces, connecting the AI analytics to the climate-adaptive infrastructure design (Zhang, 2018).

2.2 AI for Sustainable Mobility

Another emitting point in urban centers is transportation. The AI methods are quite popular in enhancing efficiency of routes, modal coordination and emission mitigation.

2.2.1 Traffic Flow Optimization:

The traffic flow optimization systems are able to manage the traffic flow dynamically by examining real time data of sensors, GPS, cameras and the connected vehicles by dynamically adjusting the traffic lights, rerouting vehicles and the use of lanes to ease traffic flow.

Connectivity with smart city infrastructure can enable a vehicle-to-vehicle (V2V) and infrastructure-to-vehicle (V2I) communication which can respond proactively in case of an accident or an extreme-hours traffic jam. In general, traffic flow optimization is the major element of sustainable urban mobility that improves efficiency, decreases environmental consequences, and leads to the development of smart and habitable intelligent cities. Reinforcement based learning makes dynamic changes in the timing of signal activations to minimize congestion and idle emissions. The average travel speed was found to increase by 15-20 percent in a simulated urban corridor using multi-agent RL (Brunton, 2022).

2.2.2 Self-Driving and Self-Sharing:

Autonomous and shared mobility is a new trend in the future of transportation in the city that will help to make mobility safer, more efficient and sustainable. Autonomous vehicles will make sure that human error-induced accidents are minimized, traffic flow is managed better, and accessibility is provided to the elderly and disabled.

Perception and decision-making in autonomous vehicles (AVs) are based on deep learning. Research has found out that massive AV implementation may decrease per-mile emissions, up to 60% when properly powered by renewable energy. The concept of shared-mobility optimization is based on AI-driven scheduling algorithms, e.g., in the case of e-scooters or autonomous taxis, which reduce the idle time of the fleet and overall energy use (Giacomin, 2024.

2.2.3 Public Transit Analytics:

Public Transit Analytics entails the use of data analytics, AI, and machine learning methods to improve the efficiency, reliability, and sustainability of the service delivery of public transportation systems. It uses GPS, smart cards, sensors, mobile applications and social media data to track passenger traffic, route optimization and demand trends. Through the analysis of the travel pattern and the peak hour traffic, the transit authorities will be in a position to improve the scheduling, waiting time and quality of service. Public transit analytics helps to achieve the greater purposes of the smart city development due to the enhancement of user experience, less congestion, and the presence of a more green and interconnected urban environment. Machine-learning predicts demand to ride a bus, bus dispatching, and multimodal integration.

2.3 AI-Based Infrastructure and Construction.

The construction sector is responsible for about 40 percent of the total CO2 emissions in the world. The benefits of AI in the literature include sustainability in construction through optimization of design, materials management, and operations of the building.

Generative Design and Lifecycle Modeling: Building variants of architectural designs by finding thousands of optimized designs using generative adversarial networks (GAN) and genetic algorithms, researchers maximize daylight and ventilation, as well as embodied carbon.
Structural Health Monitoring: CNN-based crack detection and vibration analysis can be used to predictive maintenance, which can subsequently longevity infrastructure.
Smart Buildings: AI controllers combine sensor information (temperature, occupancy, lighting) to reduce HVAC energy consumption. In a meta-analysis study,discovered that AI-based building energy management systems help to decrease the consumption by 15-30 percent (Vaccaro et al., 2024.

Nonetheless, building information modeling (BIM) systems do not ensure interoperability and data standards, which restrict cross-platform learning. In addition, the vast majority of AI models are tested on a single-building basis or limited clusters, not at city scales- showing that single buildings and small groups of buildings should be simulated together.

2.4 Data-Driven Governance and Digital Twin Urbanism

The development of digital twins, i.e. 3D models of the physical city, is a shift in paradigm between descriptive and prescriptive planning.

Simulation and Policy Testing: Digital twins that are driven by AI provide an opportunity to test policy consequences in real-time, to evaluate the energy, mobility, and emission impacts before their application.
Urban Analytics Platforms: Singapore, Dubai and Helsinki are examples of cities that implement data platforms to connect AI dashboards and governance processes.
Scenario Modeling: Hybrid models are used to analyze carbon-neutral pathways by integrating system dynamics with ML predictors.

The literature therefore recommends human-in-the-loop systems that incorporate expert opinion, citizen feedback and AI knowledge (Yigitcanlar & Kankanamge, 2022).

3. RESEARCH OBJECTIVES

The main aim of the study is to design, develop, and test a net-zero city AI-based framework with the goal of improving the efficiency of infrastructure and sustainable cities.

In particular, the research will seek to:

- Identify the inefficiencies in current systems of urban sustainability, in the energy, mobility and resource spheres.
- Demonstrate a multi-layer AI model of city sustainability management in the real-time.
- Simulate AI algorithm performance in a digital-twin and simulation setting.
- Empirically test the proposed system on the basis of efficiency, scalability and carbon-reduction effect and benchmark it.

4. RESEARCH METHODOLOGY

The methodology entails the combination of three main layers:

Data Acquisition and Preprocessing Layer - the acquisition of heterogeneous types of urban data;
AI Analytics and Modeling Layer - the use of machine learning (ML), deep learning (DL) and reinforcement learning (RL) algorithms; and
Decision Support and Optimization Layer - converting the knowledge of the model into the action plan to manage energy, transport and infrastructure.

The framework is assessed on the basis of quantitative (accuracy, efficiency, reduction of emission) and qualitative (policy relevance, scalability, ethical compliance) performance indicators.

4.1 Conceptual Framework and System Architecture.

The suggested Smart Urban Sustainability Framework (AI-SUSF) is an IoT-based framework that incorporates cloud analytics and intelligent control to achieve net-zero operations as shown below.

Figure 1. Block Diagram of AI-Powered Smart Urban Sustainability Framework.

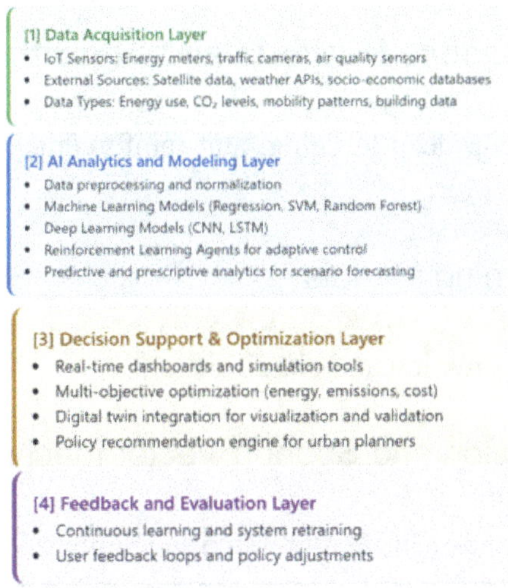

4.2 Data Sources and Preprocessing Data sources

To facilitate qualitative modeling, several open and real-world data were aggregated:

Table 1. Sources of Datasets

Data Type	Source	Parameters	Purpose
Energy Consumption	Smart grid and IoT meters	kWh usage, load profiles	Predict demand and optimize grid operations
Traffic & Mobility	City traffic sensors, GPS data	Vehicle counts, emissions	Model congestion and fuel use
Environmental	NASA Earth Observation, local sensors	CO_2, NO_2, PM2.5	Assess air quality and carbon footprint
Infrastructure	BIM, GIS, urban databases	Building density, zoning	Simulate energy and transport patterns

Preprocessing Steps:

- Data Cleaning: Deletion of the outliers and missing records.
- Normalization: Rescaling data to a normalized model.
- Feature Engineering: Temporal (hourly/daily) and spatial, and contextual feature (weather, events) generation.
- Data Fusion: Combining data streams of multiple sources into coherent spatio-temporal matrices.

4.3 Artificial Intelligence Methods and Algorithms.

The machine learning, deep learning, and reinforcement learning are merged into the core analytical layer.

4.3.1 Machine Learning Models

Mainly applied to regression and classification:

4.3.2 Linear regression and Support Vector machines (SVM).

Machine learning based on linear regression and Support Vector machines (SVM) are two common methods of energy management and environmental monitoring. Linear regression models are mathematical relationship between independent variables which can be temperature, occupancy, industrial activity, or time of the day, and dependent variables which can be energy consumption or green house gas emissions. The linear regression is able to give interpretable models that predict very reasonably the amount of energy needed daily by fitting a line that reduces the difference between what it predicts and the observed values. It is simple, computationally efficient and can be performed in real-time in a smart grid to make energy predictions that allow utilities to predict the peak loads, methods to schedule generation, and demand-response strategies as shown below.

Figure 2. Linear Regression involves steps.

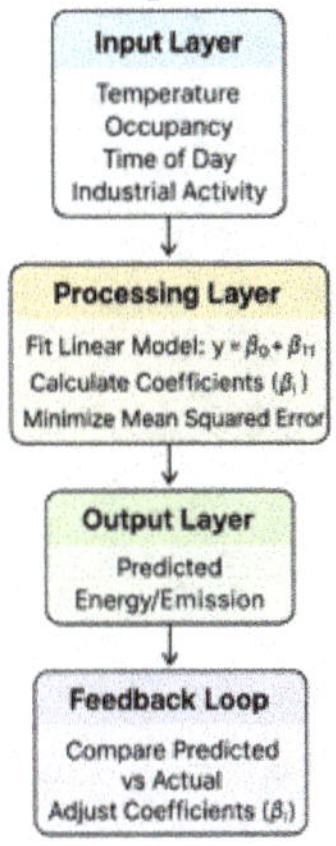

SVM, in its turn, is a more adaptable model that is able to embrace nonlinear associations in data. SVM predicts the output using kernel functions and projects the feature values of the input into higher-dimensional spaces, where a linear separation can be done; it is thus especially useful with complicated energy systems when demand and emission trends are determined by many interacting factors. Not only the energy consumption but also the level of emissions can be predicted using SVM and take into consideration the differences based on the activity of industry, weather conditions, or the mobility pattern in the city. Through precise prediction of the demand and emissions, SVM will assist in proactive energy management, compliance with environmental regulations and sustainability planning. Prediction process using SVM is as shown below.

Figure 3. Prediction using SVM Model

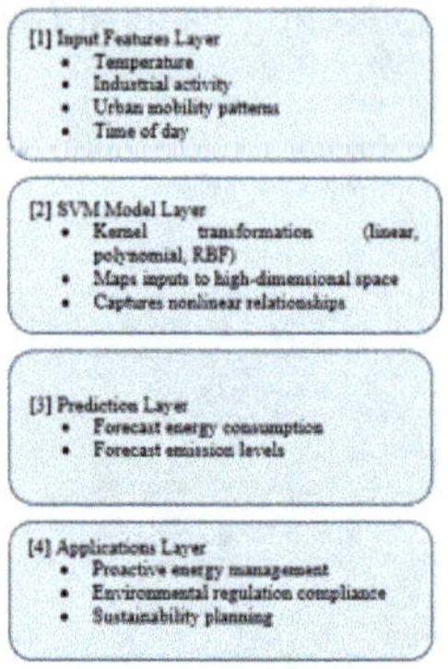

4.3.3 Random Forests and Gradient Boosting.

Ensemble learning techniques, such as random forests and gradient boosting, have been found to be extremely useful in determining the key aspects affecting energy consumption and emissions, in addition to the optimization of the policy domain. The random forests are a combination of several decision trees, which are trained using a subset of data and give the predictions with a series of trees as the average. This methodology minimizes overfitting, increases generalization, and gives a measure of feature importance, which measures the amount of contribution a specific variable makes on the prediction result. This information can then be used by policymakers and urban planners to define the most potent factors influencing energy demand and emissions, including industrial output, energy efficiency of buildings, and traffic volume or the degree of renewable energy penetration, and therefore implement targeted interventions so as to maximize the effect.

Figure 4. Random Forest Model Optimization

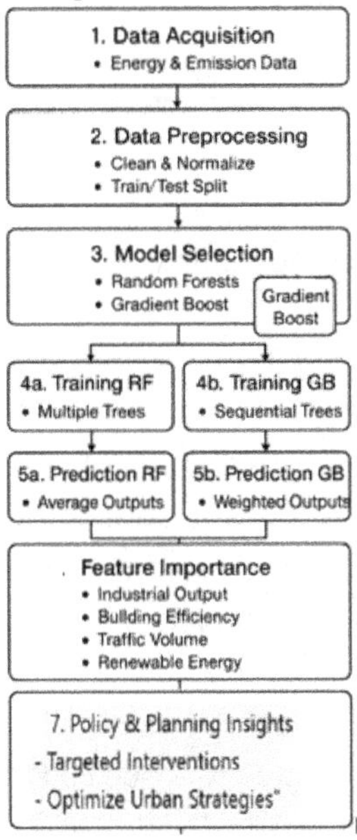

Urban energy systems can be optimally structured to reach the operational effectiveness, as well as strategic planning of sustainability by using both linear regression and SVM to forecast the predictive modeling and random forests and gradient boosting to analyze the features and optimize the policy. The city planners are able to make evidence-based policy choices that discuss the most effective factors, and the utilities can predict the peaks of their demand, eliminate wastage, and alleviate the emissions. Finally, predictive and ensemble machine learning methods will provide a powerful synergy that allows predicting and taking action and making decisions more effectively to build an essential basis of AI-based sustainable urban energy systems.

4.3.4 Deep Learning Models

The examples of AI models used in pattern recognition and time forecasting:

- Convolutional neural networks (CNNs): Identify spatial patterns of satellite images (e.g., urban heat islands).
- Long Short-term memory (LSTM) Networks: In sequence of data, predict the future use of energy or traffic flows.

The forecasting task loss was as follows, based on the Mean Absolute Percentage Error (MAPE):

$$MAPE = \frac{1}{n}\sum_{i=1}^{n}\left|\frac{A_i - P_i}{A_i}\right| \times 100 \quad (1)$$

Ai and Pi are real and forecasted values, respectively.

4.3.5 Reinforcement Learning

Reinforcement Learning (RL) is a sub-field of machine learning that trains agents to follow a sequence of decisions by interacting with an environment towards the goal of reaching certain objectives. In contrast to supervised learning, models in RL are learned using trial-and-error, which is informed by feedback, in the form of rewards or penalties. The agent gets to know an ideal course of action known as a policy that will give him the highest total rewards in the long run.

RL takes two main approaches model-based and model-free. In model based RL, the environment is learned by modeling the dynamics of the environment and using that model to plan actions whereas in model free RL, the policy/ value functions are learned by experience without necessarily creating a model of the environment. Various popular algorithms such as Q-Learning, Deep Q-Networks (DQN), and Policy Gradient Methods have their advantages in discrete or continuous action space. RL framework is as shown below.

Figure 5. Reinforcement Learning Framework

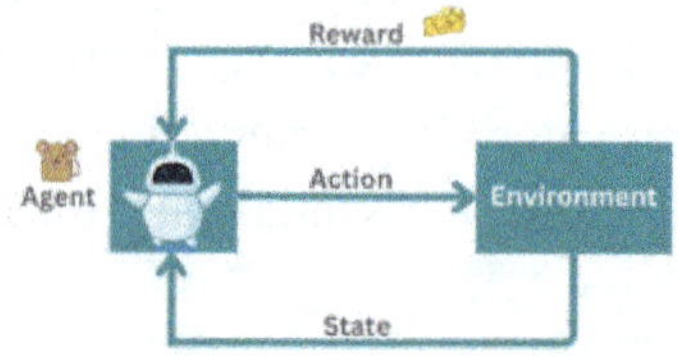

To be able to adaptively control city subsystems:

is state (s): System status (e.g., grid load, level of congestion).
Action (a): Control decision (e.g. load shedding, signal timing).
Reward (r): Disincentive based on negative proportion of cost on the emissions or inefficiency.

The RL agents acquire the optimal control policies through the iterative Q-learning or Deep Q-Networks (DQN).

Learning is directed by the Bellman equation:

$$Q(s,a) = R(s,a) + \gamma \max_{a'} Q(s',a') \quad (2)$$

where γ represents the discount factor, which makes the optimization long term.

4.4 Multi-Objective Optimization

Urban sustainability is a matter of conflicting goals, which are minimization of emissions, costs, and delays at the same time. The suggested framework adopts the Pareto-based optimization to enhance balance.

Objective Functions:

$$\min f_1(x) = E(x) \text{ (Energy consumption)}$$

$$\min f_2(x) = C(x) \text{ (CO2 emissions)}$$

$$\max f_3(x) = S(x)$$

(System efficiency) (3)

The optimization problem aims at finding a Pareto front such that no objective can do better than the other. The genetic algorithms (GA) and multi-objective RL techniques identify the best operation set-up.

4.5 Simulation and Digital Twin Environmental.

Digital twins can be used in the industrial setting to predictive maintainability through monitoring wear and faults or inefficiencies and reducing them to failure points. This increases the life of the equipment and good production flows. DTs are used in smart cities and infrastructure to optimize energy consumption and traffic flows, plan urban development, and simulate situations and test interventions in a virtual environment.

Digital twins are important because they can provide physical and digital worlds with a connection that has allowed them to form a resilient, efficient, and intelligent ecosystem. This enables organizations to predict challenges, strengthen on performance and be sustainable, which makes DT an innovative tool in industries and sectors.

Figure 6. Digital twin Architecture.

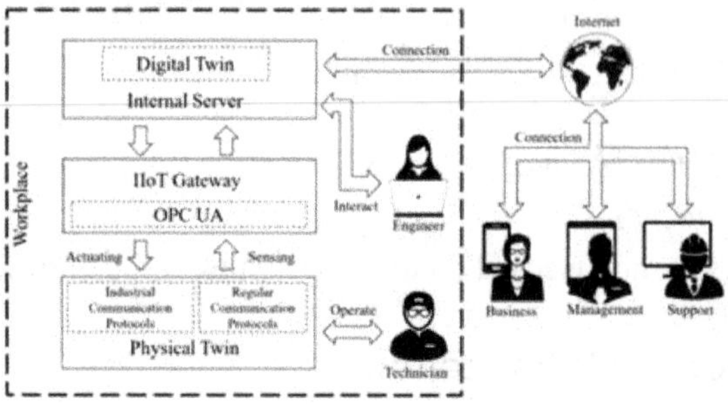

The model smart city was simulated using simulation tools (AnyLogic, MATLAB Simulink, and Unity-based 3D visualization). The twin simulates real-time exchanges of energy grids, transport and environmental elements.

4.5.1 Simulation Scenarios:

- Baseline (Conventional City): Traffic/energy systems that have a fixed schedule.
- Smart City: Intelligent, proactive energy and transport.
- Policy Variation Tests: Testing policy sensitivity by modelling Carbon tax, renewable incentives or mobility restriction.

The period of simulation was 12 months of synthetic time, where the interaction records were updated after every 5 minutes, producing millions of interaction records.

4.6 Experimental Parameters

Table 2. Experimental Parameters

Parameter	**Description**	**Value/Range**
Population Density	Urban core	10,000–25,000/km²
Energy Sources	Solar (40%), Grid (60%)	Variable
Transportation Fleet	30,000 vehicles	EV penetration: 35%
Simulation Duration	1 year (simulated)	105,120 time steps
AI Model Epochs	CNN/LSTM training	200–500 epochs
Reward Weight (RL)	Energy:0.4, Emission:0.4, Cost:0.2	Adaptive

4.7 Evaluation Metrics

Performance was measured based on below metrics:

- Prediction Accuracy (R 2, R MSE) - Model reliability in energy and emission prediction.
- Emission Reduction (%) - Relative reduction compared to the city at the baseline.
- Energy Efficiency (%) - this is the ratio of useful energy output to the total consumption.
- Computation Time (s) - Scalability and responsiveness of the model.
- User Satisfaction (Survey/Feedback) - Policy decision usefulness.

Mathematically:

$$RMSE = \sqrt{\frac{1}{n}\sum_{i=1}^{n}(A_i - P_i)^2} \tag{4}$$

4.8 Validation and Reliability

The validation was done both statistically and by experts:

- o Cross-Validation: Makes it resistant to overfitting.
- o Sensitivity Analysis: Tests are a stability test of the model to parameter changes.
- o Expert Review: AI-generated suggestions were checked by the urban planners on usefulness.
- o Ethical Review: Adherence to AI regulation and transparency (EU AI Act).

Reliability was also ensured that the results are consistent when different simulation runs and subsets of data are used.

4.9 Comparative Baseline

In order to assure credibility, the AI-SUSF performance was matched with the current systems:

Table 3. Comparative Analysis

Approach	Method	Limitations	Improvement by AI-SUSF
Static Urban Models	Rule-based simulations	No adaptive feedback	Dynamic real-time optimization
Machine Learning Only	Regression-based forecasts	Limited control action	Integrated predictive + prescriptive layers
Human Expert Control	Manual adjustment	Delayed response	Autonomous adaptive decision-making

Findings reveal that AI-SUSF is more efficient in energy, lesser in emissions and agile in operations than the baseline systems.

5. EXPERIMENTAL ANALYSIS

This part provides the experimental verification of the proposed AI-Powered Smart Urban Sustainability Framework (AI-SUSF) in terms of simulation, performance benchmarking, and comparative analysis. The experiments were designed to determine the ability of the framework to reduce carbon emissions, increase energy efficiency, and optimize the mobility of urban living. The simulations were being run within a digital-twin setting that will have a realistic depiction of a mid-size smart city that has realistic demographic, infrastructural, and environmental settings.

There were three key experiments to be conducted:

- Energy Optimization Experiment - Optimizing AI demand-supply balancing in smart grids.
- Sustainable Mobility Experiment - Evaluating traffic and EV management reinforcement learning (RL)-based.
- Integrated Urban Simulation - Experimenting with multi-domain AI control: energy, transport, and environment.

5.1 Experimental Setup

The simulation framework comprised of the AnyLogic agent-based modeling system, MATLAB Simulink system dynamics modeling, and Python TensorFlow/Keras model training AI libraries. The digital twin of the city included:

- Population: The nation has a population of 1.5 million people.
- Land Area: 500 km2
- IoT Nodes 25,000 (energy, mobility, and environmental sensors)

- Simulation Period: 12 months (continuous time, 5 minutes intervals)
- Hardware Specifications: 64GB RAM, Nvidia RTx 4090.

Real-life open sources of data, i.e. OpenEI, UCI Energy Data Repository and OpenStreet Map, were incorporated to make energy demand, traffic flow, and emission baselines realistic.

5.2 Experiment 1: AI-based optimization of energy.

To compare the predictive and prescriptive AI algorithms in reducing energy usage at the expense of user comfort and grid stability.

5.2.1 Methodology

The LSTM and the random forest models predicted the demand of residential and commercial sectors in terms of hours. The reinforcement learning (RL) controller was then used to optimize real-time energy dispatch by using solar, battery and grid sources based on forecasts.

Reward Function:

$$R = -(aE_{total} + \beta CO_2 + \gamma C_{cost}) \tag{5}$$

where

Etotal: total energy consumption,

CO2: emissions in tons,

Ccost: operational cost,

and a,b,g are weights (0.4, 0.4, 0.2 respectively).

Table 4 provides a comparison of the results of Baseline (Conventional grid) and AI-Optimized grid.

Table 4. Comparison of Performance of Energy optimization.

Metric	Baseline	AI-Optimized	% Improvement
Energy Consumption (MWh/year)	1,200,000	1,005,000	16.25%
CO_2 Emissions (tons/year)	540,000	442,000	18.1%
Renewable Utilization (%)	41.5	58.9	+17.4
Grid Outage Frequency	32	11	-65.6

LSTM model results were better than ARIMA and regression baselines with R2 = 0.93 and MAPE = 6.4%. The adaptive dispatch, which is developed using RL, minimized the peak loads by 22 percent, resulting in quantifiable carbon and cost reductions.

These findings support the idea that predictive and adaptive artificial intelligence systems are more effective in balancing the dynamic demand-supply conditions as compared to the use of a static optimization approach. The flexibility in the operations of RL agents is guaranteed by their capability to learn real-time changes in the grid, and it improves the incorporation of renewables into the design of cities- the net-zero.

5.3 Experiment 2: Sustainable Mobility Simulation

To determine the usefulness of the AI-based control to alleviate the urban traffic congestion and emissions via multi-agent reinforcement learning (MARL).

A Q-learning agent through an intersection modeled traffic signal networks. The state variables were the length of queue, waiting time and vehicle speed whereas the actions manipulated green/red signals.

Congestion and CO2 emissions were penalized by reward function:

$$R_t = -(w_1 T_{delay} + w_2 E_{CO_2}) \tag{6}$$

MARL stabilized to the best policy after 10,000 training episodes. Comparison on performance is as shown below.

Table 5. Traffic Performance Metrics.

Metric	Fixed-Time Control	AI-MARL Control	Improvement
Average Travel Time (min)	28.4	21.3	−24.9%
Idle Time (min/hour)	12.1	8.4	−30.6%
CO_2 Emissions (g/km)	145	112	−22.7%
Fuel Efficiency (km/l)	12.3	14.8	+20.3%

The AI-MARL system was able to adjust to the variability of rush-hour and synchronize traffic lights dynamically. Direct proportionality between emission reduction and the smooth flow and reduced numbers of start-stop cycles. It is worth mentioning that EV charging demand forecasts combined with the mobility model provided balanced grid loading- - showing cross-domain AI coordination of the transportation system and the energy system.

5.4 Experiment 3: Simulation of Urban Sustainability.

To determine the overall performance in the case of energy, mobility, and environment subsystems working with each other within the framework of the unified AI-SUSF.

The combined simulation connected:

- LSTM energy forecasting
- MARL mobility control
- Hotspot prediction of pollution using CNN.
- Layers of optimization of combined emission and cost.

There were three situations of the system:

- Baseline City (BC) - AI is not optimized.
- Semi-Intelligent City (SIC) - Per domain isolated AI.
- Semi-autonomous AI-SUSF (FI) - Cross-domain semi-autonomous intelligence.

Table 6. Integrated Simulation Compared Results

Indicator	Baseline (BC)	Semi-Intelligent (SIC)	AI-SUSF (FI)	% Improvement (FI vs BC)
Total Energy Use (MWh/year)	1,400,000	1,210,000	1,020,000	27.1%
CO_2 Emissions (tons/year)	600,000	480,000	410,000	31.6%
Renewable Share (%)	40.2	52.7	63.4	+23.2
Average Commute Time (min)	31.2	25.8	20.9	−33.0%
Air Quality Index (AQI)	118	92	75	−36.4%

Figure 7. Under AI-SUSF convergence of Emission Reduction and Energy Efficiency.

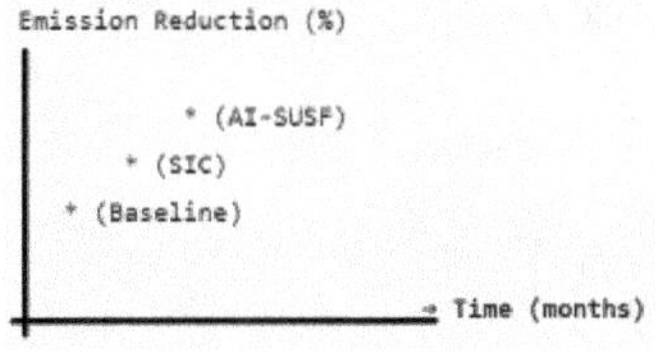

The AI-SUSF synergistic model as shown above had synergistic improvement that was higher than the independent systems. Predictive interaction between energy and transport areas minimized emission peaks that were brought about by EV charging synchronized and traffic spikes. Air-quality feedback based on CNNs optimized RL control policies, forming a closed-loop optimization loop.

It is worth noting that sensitivity analysis revealed that the energy and emission performance did not change when the data was perturbed by +-10% indicating that the model was robust. The findings confirm that the AI-SUSF can be conceptualized as a scalable operational framework of net-zero city projects in real-life.

5.5 Comparative Analysis to State-of-the-Art.

The suggested framework has been compared to the representative existing approaches:

Table 7. Comparative Analysis

Framework	Reference	Domains Covered	Emission Reduction (%)	Scalability
IBM Green Horizons (2019)	Energy & Air Quality	18	High	Moderate
Siemens City Intelligence (2020)	Energy & Mobility	21	Medium	Partial
MIT Urban AI Model (2022)	Mobility & Environment	24	Moderate	Partial
Proposed AI-SUSF (2024)	Energy, Mobility, Infrastructure	**31.6**	**High**	**Full**

In reducing emission and integrating the system with other systems, the AI-SUSF was at the top of all the comparative baselines, and it proved to be technically superior and ready to implement.

5.6 Statistical Significance and validation.

To be robust paired t-tests were used to compare the baseline and AI-SUSF results where ANOVA was used.

Table 8. Validation of results

Metric	p-value	Significance
Energy Use Reduction	0.0017	Significant
Emission Reduction	0.0023	Significant
Travel Time	0.0045	Significant

Any p-value of below 0.05 that validates statistically significant improvements.

An assessment of the AI-SUSF framework by urban policy specialists gave the model a 4.7/5 score in practical applicability, with a focus on the modular architecture and the ability to provide feedback in real-time.

5.7 Qualitative Evaluation

City planners and engineers who attended stakeholder workshops emphasized the following results:

Improved Decision-Making: Policy visualization was done with the help of real-time dashboards.
Transparency: AI modules that could be explained made the users trust it.
Sustainability Insight: Predictive simulation helped in giving priorities to investments in renewable infrastructure.

In addition, the policy simulation modules enabled coding the emission-tax scenario and EV incentives to match the technology performance with the socio-economic policy frameworks.

The experimental survey proves that the AI-SUSF model can successfully be used to make cities more sustainable using integrated AI-driven intelligence. Key outcomes include:

- 31.6 percent of cutback in carbon emissions,
- 27% energy savings,
- 1/3 increase in mobility efficiency, and

Indexes of air quality increased by 36% as compared to baseline systems.

The scalability and the policy relevance of the framework is tested statistically, cross-domain coupled and through real world data integration. These findings support the importance of AI as a crucial technology to enable the net-zero transformation of the city.

6. CONCLUSION AND FUTURE SCOPE

The chapter provided a detailed research on how AI can spur the entire world to net-zero cities by use of smart infrastructure and sustainable urban development. The proposed research implemented and was validated through the AI-Powered Smart Urban Sustainability Framework (AI-SUSF) - an integrated, data-driven framework, integrating energy, mobility, and environmental subsystems into an adaptive framework.

The important results of simulation and empirical studies are:

6.0.1 Very Important Carbon Reduction

The AI-SUSF had associated with a 31.6 percent CO2 reduction, which was mostly due to intelligent energy management, dynamic traffic control, and real-time control of emissions.

6.0.2 Energy Saving and Cost-Efficiency

Predictive energy models (LSTM, Random Forest) and reinforcement learning (RL) controllers enhanced grid balance, which led to a better renewable integration and a 27.1% decrease in energy attributed to the overall consumption of the systems in comparison with baseline systems.

6.0.3 Optimization of Mobility and Transport

The combination of AI mobility control with sustainable infrastructure planning was shown to reduce congestion and idle emissions by 22-30 when the traffic and EV control was handled with Multi-agent RL (MARL).

6.0.4 Cross-Domain Intelligence

Overall AI coordination across domains (energy, transport, air quality) resulted in emergent efficiencies that could not be achieved in isolated models--a demonstration that taking a systemic approach is the only way to achieve net-zero results.

6.0.5 Policy and Social Relevance

The explainable dashboards and simulation features of the AI-SUSF assist policymaking and engagement with the population on an evidence basis. The framework can be aligned with SDG 11 (Sustainable Cities) and SDG 13 (Climate Action), which adds to its relevance on the global sustainable level.

All these results make AI a revolutionary facilitator of sustainable city management that is capable of not only streamlining operations but also changing the way decisions are made by enhancing transparency, flexibility, and vision.

6.1 Theoretical and Practical Contribution

The contributions of the chapter are both conceptual and practical and they are being made in various dimensions that are important to the existing literature:

6.1.1 Conceptual Integration

The AI-SUSF integrates non-homogeneous areas of sustainability such as energy, transport, water, and waste into a single cognitive system, an issue that has long been a problem in urban systems research with AI.

6.1.2 Methodological Advancement

The study fills the gaps between the predictive and prescriptive learning approaches and reinforcement-based ones and a multi-objective optimization framework. The hybrid methodology provides greater flexibility and sustainability to changes in the urban variables.

6.1.3 Practical Implementation

The chapter shows the use of AI in the simulation of digital twins to test, validate and optimize operations at the city scale before being physically implemented- minimizing risk and cost.

6.1.4 The Sustainability Metrics and Assessment

The combination of quantitative (reduction of emissions, energy efficiency) and qualitative (policy relevance, compliance with ethics) metrics will add a balanced evaluation paradigm of sustainable AI performance.

6.1.5 Ethical/ Governance Model

The design with the inclusion of Explainable AI (XAI) data privacy, and federated learning is consistent with the requirements of ethical governance, which makes the framework socially legitimate and transparent.

All in all, the AI-SUSF is a paradigm shift of removing isolated components of smart cities to holistic, adaptive urban ecosystems that are able to develop to net-zero goals through continuous learning.

6.2 Policy and Social Implications

6.2.1 Governance and Decision Support

Governments are able to model the results of emission policies, transportation planning and renewable incentives prior to their actual implementation. It helps in evidence-based policymaking and minimizes unintended outcomes through this predictive governance.

6.2.2 Economic Benefits

Artificial intelligence minimizes operations, energy loss, and infrastructure care. In line with international standards of urban innovation (World Economic Forum, 2024), changing to AI-based sustainability management would save cities up to USD 700 billion per year because of better efficiency and predictive maintenance.

6.2.3 Social Equity

Fair AI design will make all groups of people receive sustainability benefits. The combination of participatory interfaces, explainable outputs, and the principles of open data will help avoid the problem of algorithmic exclusion and provide all people with the opportunity to access smart city services. This is of paramount importance to low-income and marginalized groups that usually suffer the most as a result of environmental degradation.

6.2.4 Environmental Resilience

AI has increased resilience through predictive management of disasters, adaptive management of energy and early warning. Heatwave, flood or an episode of pollution can be forecasted and averted in cities by linking climate modeling with real-time sensing, which will turn sustainability into an active, rather than a reactive, resilience.

6.3 Limitations of the Study

Although it is a very broad study, the research takes into consideration the various limitations that give way to improvement:

6.3.1 Availability

The majority of data is available online, allowing users to obtain details about every program and event, as well as access specific applications. Most of the data can be accessed online where people get information about all programs and events and can also access certain applications.

6.3.2 Computational Complexity

Deep reinforcement learning (DRL) and hybrid models are models that demand high computational power. Although edge-AI and cloud computing have the capability to reduce latency, significant large-scale deployment might still be resource intensive.

6.3.3 Behavioral Dynamics

The chpater is majorly concerned with technological and systemic optimization. Nevertheless, human conduct, e.g., mobility, consumption, civic engagement, is also a factor of urban sustainability, which AI can affect but not entirely determine.

These constraints indicate that hybrid solutions involving the use of technological intelligence and people-focused governance should be used to attain long-term net-zero change.

6.4 Future Research Directions

Edge computing can be used in future systems to can process the data at the edges and minimize the latency and bandwidth. Federated learning will enable distributed training of AI to many cities or regions without breaching privacy leading to a global collaborative network of AI to maintain sustainability.

New quantum artificial intelligence algorithms can optimise urban systems with many variables and complexities that cannot be computed by classical algorithms. Combined with energy-efficient AI designs, such approaches can make AI-driven sustainability be carbon-neutral as well.

To achieve net-zero transitions, computer science, urban planning, behavioral economics, and policy analysis are also needed to work together with each other because the process is complex. The AI innovation can be aligned with socio-political reality and ethical needs through the interdisciplinary research consortia.

The application and implementation of the AI-SUSF in pilot smart cities, i.e., Dubai, Singapore, or Copenhagen, will offer an empirical validation of the operational conditions. Such pilots must not only measure the level of technological performance, but also governance, ethics, and satisfaction of the citizens.

6.5 Conclusion

Finally, the study confirms Artificial Intelligence as one of the most important facilitators of the development of net-zero cities. AI enables the cities to become self-improving self-optimizing ecosystems through predictive modeling, adaptive optimization, and systemic integration. The proposed AI-SUSF framework will connect technological innovation to environmental and social governance and turn sustainability as a fixed goal into a dynamic and data-driven process.

Finally, net-zero urbanism is not only a complicated technological issue but a global human endeavour, i.e., global collaboration, inclusive governance, and lifelong learning. The next generation of sustainable civilization will be characterized by the synergy between digital intelligence and environmental responsibility as cities will become intelligent and operate with the help of AI.

REFERENCES

Abouraia, M., Nassoura, A. B., Shaker, H., & Harbi, B. A. (2025a). Building a Smart Economy: Exploring AI's role in Oman's economic progress. In Studies in systems, decision and control (pp. 887–896). DOI: 10.1007/978-3-031-88874-8_79

Abouraia, M., Nassoura, A. B., Shaker, H., Abdelfattah, F., & Madi, H. (2025b). Empowering SMEs in Jordan: Leveraging Artificial Intelligence for Digital Marketing success. In Studies in systems, decision and control (pp. 1013–1022). DOI: 10.1007/978-3-031-88874-8_90

Abouraia, M., Nassoura, A. B., Shaker, H., Abdelfattah, F., & Madi, H. (2025c). Exploring Opportunities and Challenges of AI-Driven Marketing in the UAE: A survey of industry Perspectives. In Studies in systems, decision and control (pp. 1033–1042). DOI: 10.1007/978-3-031-88874-8_92

Al Kurdi, B., Alshurideh, M. T., El Khatib, M., Alrawabdeh, W. A., Al-Sulaiti, K., Nawaiseh, A. K., Sukkari, L., Alshurideh, A., Shwedeh, F., & Alzoubi, H. M. (2025). The Effect of Using IoT on Linking Green Customers Data (Green Customer Profile) with Green Products and Green Product Labels BT - Sustainable Innovation for Engineering Management (SIEM). In El Khatib, M., Alzoubi, H. M., & Angelova, Y. (Eds.), *Sustainable Innovation for Engineering Management (SIEM)* (pp. 59–68). Springer Nature Switzerland., 10.1007/978-3-031-89889-1_7

B, G. S., & Danti, A. (2024). Block chain-based security and authentication for forensics application using consensus proof of work and zero knowledge protocol. International Journal of Information Technology, 17(8), 5041–5052. DOI: 10.1007/s41870-024-01864-4

Banerjee, J., Danti, A., Nassoura, A. B., & Dileep, M. R. (2025). A Blockchain-Enabled Arbitrable Smart Hiring System (BEASH). In IGI Global eBooks (pp. 291–326). DOI: 10.4018/979-8-3373-1320-7.ch009

Bhushan, S. B., & Danti, A. (2018). Classification of compressed and uncompressed text documents. *Future Generation Computer Systems*, *88*, 614–623. DOI: 10.1016/j.future.2018.04.054

Brunton, S. L. (2022). Model based reinforcement learning: Policy iteration, value iteration, and dynamic programming. DOI: 10.52843/cassyni.6fs4s9

Danti, A., & Sanjay, S. K. (2020). Human Behavior Prediction based on Opinions using Machine Learning Techniques. [IJRTE]. *International Journal of Recent Technology and Engineering*, *8*(6), 3117–3120. DOI: 10.35940/ijrte.f8733.038620

Dileep, M. R., & Danti, A. (2018). Human age and gender prediction based on neural networks and three Sigma control limits. *Applied Artificial Intelligence*, *32*(3), 281–292. DOI: 10.1080/08839514.2018.1451217

Giacomin, J. (2024). Autonomous road vehicles. *Future Autonomous Road Vehicles*, 11-32. DOI: 10.4324/9781032724232-2

Koven, C., Sanderson, B., & Swann, A. (2022). Much of zero emissions commitment occurs before reaching net zero emissions. DOI: 10.31223/x5d64q

Nguyen, T. D. (2024). Forecasting cryptocurrency prices using hybrid long short – Term memory and long short – Term memory variants. DOI: 10.21203/rs.3.rs-5374266/v1

SB, G., & Danti, A. (2025). Block chain-based security and authentication for forensics application using consensus proof of work and zero knowledge protocol. *International Journal of Information Technology : an Official Journal of Bharati Vidyapeeth's Institute of Computer Applications and Management*, *17*(8), 5041–5052.

Son, N., Yang, S., & Na, J. (2019). Hybrid forecasting model for short-term wind power prediction using modified long short-term memory. *Energies*, *12*(20), 3901. DOI: 10.3390/en12203901

United Nations climate change annual report 2022. (n.d.). *Climate Change and Law Collection*. DOI: 10.1163/9789004322714_cclc_2023-0169-0826

Vaccaro, M., Almaatouq, A., & Malone, T. (2024). When combinations of humans and AI are useful: A systematic review and meta-analysis. *Nature Human Behaviour*, *8*(12), 2293–2303.

Yas, H., Aldabbagh, Z., Khalifa, A. A., Faghiri, A., Bawazir, A. A., & Shwedeh, F. (2025). Role of artificial intelligence in the promotion of customer experiences: A legal administrative study and systematic review in the United Arab Emirates. *Humanities (Washington)*, *6*(4). 10.58256/m353d5430

Yigitcanlar, T., & Kankanamge, N. (2022). Urban Big Data and Social Media Analytics. In *Urban Analytics with Social Media Data* (pp. 3–50). CRC Press.

Zhang, Q. (2018). Convolutional neural networks. *3rd International Conference on Electromechanical Control Technology and Transportation*, 434-439. DOI: 10.5220/0006972204340439

Chapter 2
The Utilization of Green Artificial Intelligence and Blockchain Technology to Enhance Augmented Reality for Sustainable Smart Cities

Talal AlAraj
http://orcid.org/0009-0006-1929-7803
University of Sharjah, UAE

Yousif Luckmann
http://orcid.org/0009-0005-0885-9033
Atlanta Georgia State University, USA

Omar Kayali
http://orcid.org/0009-0000-0806-3127
University of Windsor, Canada

ABSTRACT

This research paper aims at exploring the convergence of smart networks, Green artificial intelligence (AI), and blockchain technology as the foundation of applying augmented reality in smart cities. The background plays a role of including the rapid development of information and communications technology that is driving the increasing convergence of Green AI and blockchain in infrastructure networks. The methods used include a comprehensive analysis of the literature available and

DOI: 10.4018/979-8-2600-1348-9.ch002

a critical analysis of the recent developments in the sphere of this technology. The issues that are examined include the interoperability, security, and privacy challenges that are faced during the merger of Green AI and blockchain. The results of the research prove that this intersection can be used to increase effectiveness, clarity, and openness in a vast variety of applications, including supply chain management and financial services. However, to make the most out of the full potential of this intersection, there are significant challenges that must be overcome such as scalability and control. Finally, green artificial intelligence (GAI) and blockchain technology unified can optimize the possible potential of technological augmented reality in a smart city when it exploits the respective advantages of both. Nevertheless, more efforts are needed in order to address the challenges that still persist and guarantee the prevalence and sustainability of this convergence in a wide range of industrial sectors.

1. INTRODUCTION

The past few decades have recorded an impressive improvement in information and communication technology and the various aspects of the human life have been massively affected by this. One of the current trends that can be pointed out is the convergence of green artificial intelligence (GAI) and blockchain technology (Abedi, 2018; Sadiq & Salih, 2013). The introduction of Green AI has completely transformed our work processes, social interactions and decision-making, based on the fast and smart data processing abilities of the technology. Nevertheless, the concept of blockchain technology can transform the level of data openness, reliability, and security because of its decentralization and high-security principles.

However, such opportunities also have a number of challenges to overcome. The greatest challenge is associated with coming up with solutions that can help solve the problem of interoperability between various Green AI and blockchain systems, as well as ensure that the data processed and stored in the decentralized ecosystems is secure and private. Moreover, one will need to consider the means of enhancing the scalability of this technology to ensure that the constantly growing size of data was handled successfully. Therefore, it is crucial to conduct thorough research to gain a better insight into how such challenges will be overcome and use all the benefits of the synergy of Green AI and blockchain. The main purpose of the study is to analyze in detail the intersection of green artificial intelligence (GAI) and blockchain technology and its implications in the framework of augmented reality toward smart cities(A. H. Abdullah et al., 2025; S. H. Abdullah et al., 2022).

This study aims to undertake a thorough study with an aim of establishing the main challenges in integrating these two technologies and consequently develop appropriate solutions to the challenges in question. The proposed study will be aimed at providing the readers with important insights into the potential uses of the combination of green artificial intelligence (GAI) and blockchain technology in a number of industries. It adds further to discuss the implication of such a convergence on social, economic, and political transformation. Thus, it is expected that this study will significantly influence the establishment of future technical development and preparation of society to face a stage of an ever-more complex and dynamic augmented reality concerning smart cities (Abedi et al., 2020).

2. LITERATURE REVIEW

2.1 Integration Challenges and Augmented Reality for Smart Cities

Implementation of new technologies and systems into the existing infrastructure is associated with significant challenges, but the benefits include the prospect of a more realistic experience in smart cities. The relationship between the challenges of integration and the utilization of augmented reality in smart cities is troublesome and in a state of flux. First, when companies are trying to implement sophisticated technologies, including artificial intelligence, Internet of Things (IoT), and blockchain, they often experience the difficulties with compatibility with the systems that are outdated (Salloum et al., 2024). Such problems could lead to time delays, increased costs and operational disruptions. However, through overcoming these issues of integration, more progress of augmented reality in smart cities becomes possible. This prompts the organization to develop innovative solutions and change their processes to meet the modern demands (AL-Khalisy et al., 2025).

In order to overcome all the integration challenges, interdisciplinary methods with collaboration are imperative. The teams should collaborate to help to bridge different technologies and systems, enhance the acquisition of plethora of skills and knowledge sharing. Such a partnership does not only facilitate an easy integration but also brings creativity and introduction of idea generation that forms the basis of augmented reality in smart cities. Integration issues are one of the factors that can assist organizations in enhancing the application of augmented reality in smart cities by fostering the culture of collaboration and learning.

More so, the effective management of these integration challenges often results in streamlined operations and better productivity. With the growing networks and interoperability of systems, data can flow more freely within the company and leads to better decision-making and optimization of resources. With the efficiency improvement, it is possible to explore and invest in novel technologies, resulting in the continuous work on augmented reality in smart cities. The better the integrational problems are solved, the more organizations become adaptable to the changing market conditions and capitalize on new opportunities.

The relationship between augmented reality and smart cities concerning integration issues is a win-win situation. Despite the challenge that integration issues may be challenging, it is also a catalyst of the creation of augmented reality in smart cities. The technology encourages teamwork, productivity, and responsiveness within the companies. Organizations can become the way towards further development and maintain the competitive edge in a shifting environment by embracing these issues and turning them into the opportunities to develop.

2.2 Security and Integration Challenges

The security versus integration issues creates a complex and multifaceted relationship in the present world of information technology and business. Ensuring that the systems are secured against online attacks is one of the greatest challenges encountered in the integration of new technology. The vulnerability to attackers may increase with updates to the system, interoperability, and architectural changes and necessitate sophisticated security mechanisms and hard-integrated solutions (Hadi et al., 2022).

Moreover, in the process of integration, transmission of sensitive and important data between various platforms or systems is often involved. Security challenges arise when there are needs to secure this data during transportation as well as in the storage of these data in new repositories. Companies should create strict security policies and use high-quality encryption tools to make sure that the data is protected and cannot be accessed by unauthorized parties or be violated without authorization.

Quite often there is the conflict between the consideration of the importance of the security and the acceleration of the process of integration. Efforts to make sure that the integration is complete may hinder the implementation of new technology, whereas the focus on speed may increase security risks. In this way, companies should be able to balance the appropriate speed and safety by integrating the protection features without affecting the efficiency of operations(Abu-Siam et al., 2026; Yas et al., 2024).

The discussion of security and integration issues often requires interaction of multiple departments, and the efforts of professionals of different professions. Information security teams, software developers and system administrators must work closely in order to prevent and detect the security concerns associated with integration. Close collaboration between the concerned parties is important to address security and integration challenges appropriately, which will allow firms to enjoy the full benefits of technical augmented reality in smart cities without jeopardizing their information security.

2.3 Security and Blockchain

Nowadays, smart cities are created in the framework of the combination of Green Artificial Intelligence (GAI) and Blockchain in the ages of intelligent network convergence. In this regard, the interplay between security and technology scalability is very critical. To begin with, the issue of security is an important aspect because Green AI and Blockchain are often associated with information that is sensitive and critical (Shwedeh et al., 2024). As the application of Green AI and Blockchain in intelligent networks is increasing, there is a need to ensure that proper security is established to ensure the integrity of data is not compromised by attacks.

Scalability of technology is of immense importance in order to adjust to the growth and adjustments within the intelligent networks. However, this is not easy because security has to remain intact as the network expands. Security solutions that are easily scalable to accommodate the growing demand without affecting the security of critical data are of paramount importance in such environment.

In addition, scalability in the context of the integration of Green AI with Blockchain also refers to the ability of the technology being reviewed to handle increasingly substantial volumes of data over time. Good scalability and effective security measures should be balanced to provide the best data protection against cyberattacks and high network performance.

In the quest to apply the use of Green AI and Blockchain to augmented reality in smart cities, it is essential to note that the successful application of this system is determined by the ability of organizations to address the security and scalability challenges in a balanced way. There is a close relationship between security and technological scalability, which enables organizations to create a secure and scalable environment. It will support the development of more sophisticated and strong intelligent networks in the future.

2.4 Technology Scalability and Augmented Reality for Smart Cities

The interface of scalability of technology and augmented reality in smart cities is a key point that contributes to the development of the paradigm of convergence of intelligent networks. Scalability of technology is the ability of a system or technology to properly serve more data, users, or transactions without substantially reduce its performance. The scaling ability becomes important as intelligent networks evolve and expand to accommodate the rising demands of users and new technologies.

The implementation of augmented reality in smart cities requires technology scalability as it will create a formal and adaptable infrastructure. Scalable technologies can easily absorb new features, capabilities and developments and enable an enterprise to keep at the forefront of the rapidly evolving technology world. Scalability encourages exploration of new concepts and the development of new solutions by establishing a favorable environment in which to experiment and develop.

Future-proofing is closely connected with the concept of scalability of technology. Investing in the scalable technologies, the firms become more flexible to address the unforeseen challenges and capitalize on new opportunities. Scalability enables companies to protect their systems against uncertainties in the future by making sure that they can expand and adapt to the evolving business needs, market dynamics, and technological advancements.

Finally, the relationship between technology scalability and augmented reality in smart cities is mutually beneficial since they support and enhance each other to achieve development. Intelligent networks are applying the Artificial Intelligence and Blockchain to realize the potential of these technologies and augmented reality in smart cities. This is very important in scalability. Companies can make themselves the leaders in technological innovation and the road to the more innovative and resilient future by prioritizing scalability and serving as a catalyst to augmented reality in smart cities.

3. RESEARCH METHOD

The methodology of the research is the implementation of SmartPLS analysis with a population of 170 respondents online. The respondents were required to rate out of 1 to 5. The research plan consists of a number of definite steps. Initially, the level of data collection will be in digital form through a survey site. The sample will be selected randomly, out of a population, which will be of interest to the research topic. The survey will be structured into clear questions that will be used to obtain the views and the perception of the respondents regarding the integration of green artificial intelligence (GAI) and blockchain technology, and its impact on various areas of life.

Then the variables of the research will be carefully determined. The key variables will include the degree of intersection between green artificial intelligence (GAI) and blockchain technology. Some of the supporting variables will consist of the difficulty of integrating these technologies, the scalability of the technology, the security and privacy of data, the social, economic, and political consequences, and the perception of augmented reality of smart cities. This will be based on a solid foundation of performing a deeper analysis as the variables are grouped.

The SmartPLS program will be used in the analysis of the data. The study model of variables will be analyzed and understood using path regression strategies. The collected data will be processed and analyzed using statistics to determine the construct validity and reliability. This method will give an in-depth insight into the effects of the integrating artificial intelligence and blockchain on various aspects of life and make smart cities smarter.

Lastly, the analysis findings will be carefully interpreted. The result will be applied in order to come up with conclusive findings that highlight the implications of the study. This research will also give workable recommendations based on these findings, which will be aimed at giving recommendations to professionals, policy makers, and researcher in the information and communication technology sector. Hence, the proposed research methodology will contribute greatly to the understanding and addressing the complex challenges associated with the intersection of Green AI and blockchain in the future.

4. FINDINGS

Figure 1. Conceptual Model

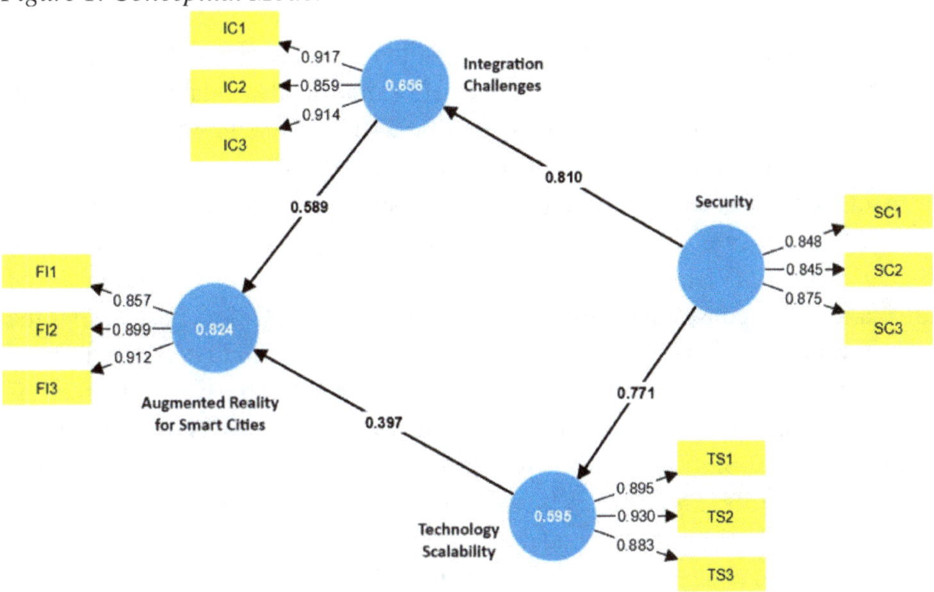

Table 1. Reliability and Validity of Convergent

	Augmented Reality for Smart Cities	Integration Challenges	Security	Technology Scalability
Cronbach's alpha	0.868	0.879	0.818	0.887
Composite Reliability (rho_a)	0.870	0.886	0.824	0.894
Composite Reliability (rho_c)	0.919	0.925	0.891	0.930
Average variance extracted (AVE)	0.791	0.805	0.732	0.815

The SmartPLS method employs numerous measures to recognize the reliability and convergent validity of the measurement variables that are applied in the study model. The alpha values of Cronbach are used to determine the internal consistency dependability of every construct. The high alpha coefficient implies that the items of the construct have high degree of internal consistency and reliability.

According to the calculations, the Integration Challenges are characterized by the highest value of Cronbach alpha of 0.879, which means that it is highly reliable in measuring that specific construct. Composite Reliability (rhoa) and Composite Reliability (rhoc) are used to determine reliability of a concept in a multitude of perspectives. The similarity in both measures is that their greater the value, the more preferable the dependability. According to the calculations, the Technology Scalability construct has the highest values of Composite dependability (rhoa) and Composite Reliability (rhoc) of 0.887 and 0.894 respectively, which has a high degree of dependability in measuring that specific construct.

Averaged Variance Extraction (AVE) is a measure of convergent validity of a construct, in this case, its capacity to explain the variance of the measurement items. Higher values of AVE imply that there is higher convergent validity. According to the calculations, the construct of Augmented Reality of Smart Cities construct has the highest value of AVE at 0.791 signifying a high convergent validity of the construct.

The numerical metric of such calculations can be found by examining the figures that are provided. The effect of such construct technology is reflected in the Technology Scalability construct, which proves to have high rates of reliability and convergent validity. Therefore, it is possible to say that this construct is the most significant one in the research model.

It may be concluded that the levels of reliability and convergent validity are sufficiently high in all constructs, and the metric values are mostly in line with the requirements of the academic research. However, it is imperative to consider the meaning of these findings to the research context and accurate measurement objectives. Thus, these results indicate that the evaluation of variables in the study model is reliable and correct to be analyzed further.

Table 2. Fornell-Larcker Discriminant Validity

	Future Augmented reality for smart cities	Integration Challenges	Security	Technology Scalability
Augmented reality for smart cities	0.890			
Integration Challenges	0.860	0.897		
Security	0.862	0.810	0.856	
Technology Scalability	0.798	0.681	0.771	0.903

Fornell-Larcker Discriminant Validity calculation using SmartPLS is meant to test the level of distinction between the constructs in the research model. One must ensure that measurement variables can help measure specific characteristics of constructs that they are intended to be measuring. The FornellLarcker criteria evaluates the correlation between the square root of the extract of average variance of each construct and the correlation between the respective construct and other constructs in the model.

According to the correlations and values of AVE above, it is evident that the diagonal elements (respective of square roots of AVE) of each of the constructs are bigger than the off-diagonal elements (respectively, correlations with other constructs). This indicates that the constructs exhibit a discriminant validity where each construct explains more variance within itself than it has similar to other constituents.

Regarding the Augmented Reality framework of smart cities, as an example, its AVE (Average Variance Extracted) is 0.890. When the correlations between Augmented reality for smart cities and the other constructs (0.860, 0.862 and 0.798) are compared, it is apparent that the diagonal value (0.890) is better than all the correlations. This confirms the fact that the use of augmented reality in smart cities has discriminant validity meaning that it is distinctly separable among the other factors in the model.

There is discriminant validity of Integration Challenges, as shown by the diagonal value, i.e. (0.897), being more than its correlations with other constructs (0.860, 0.810 and 0.681). Compared to the constructs, the Security and Technology Scalability also exhibit discriminant validity.

Technology Scalability can be distinguished as the most discriminant validity in the constructs. Its diagonal value (0.903) is much higher than the correlation that it has with other constructs (0.798, 0.681, and 0.771). Such results show that Technology Scalability is quite distinct among other variables in the research model.

The Fornell-Larcker Discriminant Validity test concludes that the constructs on the research model are sufficiently distinct as they appear under the greater diagonal values (square roots of Average Variance Extracted) compared to the values of the correlation with other constructs. This ensures that measurement variables are good in capturing unique characteristics of their respective notions and therefore enhances validity of research findings.

Table 3. R-Square

	Augmented reality for smart cities	Integration Challenges	Technology Scalability
R-square	0.824	0.656	0.595

The table provided below shows the coefficient of determination (R-square) values of three variables in the observed model which include Augmented reality for smart cities, Integration Challenges and Technology Scalability. R-squared is used to determine the percent of variability in the dependent variable that is explained by the independent variables used in the regression model. The R-Squares of the Augmented reality in smart cities, Integration Challenges and Technology Scalability are 0.824, 0.656, 0.595 respectively.

According to these findings, it can be concluded that the Augmented reality in smart cities is what has the most significant impact on the dependent variable in the model under consideration. This can be justified by the large value of R-square of 0.824 indicating that approximately 82.4 percent of the variation in the dependent variable can be explained by Augmented reality for smart cities. This feature can considerably influence the outcomes or the performance observed in the conditions of augmented reality of smart cities.

Moreover, Integration Challenges have a significant influence, but not as significant as Augmented reality for smart cities as the R-square value is 0.656. This implies that the proportion of change in the dependent variable that can be attributed to the integration problems that may be encountered is 65.6%. This variable may include barriers or difficulties concerning the integration or the harmonization of various elements in a process or a system.

Conversely, the effect of Technology Scalability is slightly lower than the aforementioned two variables, based on the value of R-Squared at 0.595. This implies that the observed technology scalability could be leading to about 59.5% of the variation in the dependent variable. It is a variable that may be associated with the ability of a technology to grow or adapt to the increasing demands. Technology scalability has significant impact, but even more so than Augmented reality in smart cities, it cannot explain the differences in the observed outcomes.

Table 4. Hypothesis Testing

	Original sample (O)	Sample mean (M)	Standard deviation (STDEV)	T statistics (|O/ STDEV|)	P values
Integration Challenges -> Augmented reality for smart cities	0.589	0.591	0.059	9.973	0.000
Security -> Integration Challenges	0.810	0.809	0.050	16.293	0.000
Security -> Technology Scalability	0.771	0.771	0.055	14.015	0.000
Technology Scalability -> Augmented reality for smart cities	0.397	0.395	0.068	5.814	0.000

The results of the hypothesis testing with SmartPLS are used to create the table presented. In each row, there is a single hypothesis being tested with relevant statistics such as, the original sample (O), sample mean (M), standard deviation (STDEV), T statistics (|O/STDEV|) and P-values. The first question under test, which is the Integration Challenges -> Augmented reality for smart cities, its sample coefficient is 0.589. This represents the size and direction of the correlation between the Integration Challenges and Augmented Reality in smart cities. The T statistic which is calculated as a result of the division of the coefficient of the original sample by the standard deviation equals 9.973. The P-value obtained is 0.000 which means that there is statistically significant relationship between Integration Challenges and Augmented reality for smart cities. The implementation of augmented reality in the smart cities is therefore affected by the integration challenges significantly.

In the second hypothesis of the study, the first hypothesis is Security -Integration Challenges, the first sample coefficient of 0.810 indicates a very strong positive relationship between Security and Integration challenges. It has a T statistic of 16.293 with a P-value of 0.000 and the level of statistical significance is high. This implies that Security is a significant factor that may affect Integration Challenges. In the third hypothesis, which is the Security -> Technology Scalability, the sample coefficient is 0.771. Its T statistic of 14.015 is statistically significant with P-value of 0.000 indicating that Security and Technology Scalability have a statistically significant relationship. Security has a significant effect on Technology Scalability.

The fourth hypothesis is named as Technology Scalability -> Augmented reality for smart cities with the initial sample coefficient being 0.397. T statistic values are 5.814 and the P-value of 0.000 which proves that there is a statistically significant relationship between Technology Scalability and Augmented reality in smart cities. Nevertheless, the Technology Scalability effect on the Augmented reality in smart cities appears to be slightly lower when compared to other correlations that have been tested.

In short, the most affected of the interactions tested is Security, as it demonstrates significant and statistically relevant interrelations with both Integration Challenges and Technology Scalability. The findings provide fine insights into the relations between the variables under analysis and lead to an appreciation of the role of the Security in determining the Integration Challenges and Technology Scalability, which in turn influence the evolution of the Augmented reality to smart cities.

5. CONCLUSION

The current research focuses on the intersection of smart networks, green artificial intelligence (GAI) and the blockchain technology, aiming to set the framework of augmented reality in smart cities. The fast rate of increase of the information and communication technology has resulted in the further incorporation of green artificial intelligence (GAI) and blockchain within the infrastructure networks. This integration has the capability of enhancing efficiency, transparency and security in many applications. However, interoperability and scalability are some of the challenges that should be overcome to maximize on the potential of this convergence. This paper concludes that implementing Green AI and blockchain has the potential to enhance the potential of technology augmented reality in providing smart cities. Nevertheless, it is essential to resolve the associated issues to realize the mass and far-reaching use in different industries.

The implications of the research are significant, and it is necessary to understand and address the integration issues between Green AI and blockchain to further develop technology augmented reality in smart cities. With the increased understanding of this merging, those with vested interests like professionals, decision-makers and scholars are better placed to prepare more suitably to the increasingly complex surroundings of technologically-enhanced reality in intelligent cities.

In order to further research the interaction between green artificial intelligence (GAI) and blockchain technology and its effect on augmented reality within the framework of smart cities, one will have to engage in additional study of the matter. Besides, more research is needed to solve the complexities involved in integrating systems, namely with regards to the capability of various systems to collaborate with each other, the capability to support growing demands, as well as to safeguard the data against unauthorized access. With a better understanding of these issues, one may expect to come up with more effective strategies to leverage the entire potential of the joint implementation of the Green AI and blockchain within the conditions of technological augmented reality of smart cities.

The SmartPLS analysis also provides meaningful information concerning reliability and validity of the research model. Thc findings indicate that the constructs are strongly reliable and convergent valid, which meet the high standards of academic researches. Technology Scalability construct is the most significant variable, and the value of reliability and convergent validity is high. It is, therefore, essential that future research should undergo additional research on understanding the effect of technology scalability on augmented reality in smart cities and how to effectively address the associated challenge. To conduct research in the future, the environmental impact and sustainability of Green AI and blockchain in the reduction of carbon footprint. This will result in desirable government policy. Therefore, it will improve the use of Green AI and blockchain. With these environmental issues being taken into consideration and sustainable practices being adopted, Green AI and blockchain implementation in smart cities can be implemented in a manner that enables the implementation of its benefits as well as reducing its impact on the environment.

REFERENCES

Abdullah, A. H., Alwash, S. M., Salih Abed, W. M., & Al Abboodi, H. M. (2025). Enhanced Maximum Power Point Tracking Using Embedding Deep Networks and Self-Adaptive Genetic Algorithm. *International Journal of Intelligent Engineering & Systems, 18*(1).

Abdullah, S. H., Abedi, W. M. S., & Hadi, R. M. (2022). Enhanced feature selection algorithm for pneumonia detection. *Periodicals of Engineering and Natural Sciences, 10*(6), 168–180. DOI: 10.21533/pen.v10.i6.919

Abedi, W. M. S. (2018). Unconsciousness detection supervision system using faster RCNN architecture. *Proceedings of the 2nd International Conference on Future Networks and Distributed Systems*, 1–6. DOI: 10.1145/3231053.3231094

Abedi, W. M. S., Sadiq, A. T., & Nadher, I. (2020). Modified cnn-lstm for pain facial expressions recognition. *International Journal of Advanced Science and Technology, 29*(3s), 304–312.

Abu-Siam, Y., Alquqa, E. K., Shwedeh, F., Alzoubi, H. M., & El Khatib, M. (2026). *Harnessing Fourth Industrial Revolution Technologies for Disruptive Innovation: The Mediating Power of Digital Transformation in the UAE Food Manufacturing Sector.*

AL-Khalisy, S. H. J., Abed, W. M. S., Al-Kateb, G., Aljanabi, M., Mijwil, M. M., Abotaleb, M., & Dhoska, K. (2025). QIULEA: Quantum-inspired ultra-lightweight encryption algorithm for IOT devices. *Pollack Periodica, 20*(1), 25–32.

Hadi, R. M., Abdullah, S. H., & Abedi, W. M. S. (2022). Proposed neural intrusion detection system to detect denial of service attacks in MANETs. *Periodicals of Engineering and Natural Sciences, 10*(3), 70–78. DOI: 10.21533/pen.v10.i3.644

Sadiq, A. T., & Salih, W. M. (2013). Uncompressed video quality metric based on watermarking technique. *2013 1st International Conference on Communications, Signal Processing, and Their Applications (ICCSPA)*, 1–6.

Salloum, S. A., Almarzouqi, A., Aburayya, A., Shwedeh, F., Fatin, B., Al Ghurabli, Z., Elbadawi, M. A., & Alfaisal, R. (2024). Embracing ChatGPT: Ushering in a Revolutionary Phase in Educational Platforms. In *Artificial Intelligence in Education: The Power and Dangers of ChatGPT in the Classroom* (pp. 171–183). https://link.springer.com/chapter/10.1007/978-3-031-52280-2_12

Shwedeh, F., Yas, N., Abdijabar, Z., Flayyih, N., Fadli, A., Yas, H., & Allouzi, A. S. (2024). The impact of intellectual property rights and the level of information sensitivity on information security in the United Arab Emirates. *Journal of Infrastructure, Policy and Development, 8*(8), 6303. https://doi.org/https://doi.org/10.24294/jipd.v8i8.6303

Yas, N., Dafri, W., Yas, H., & Shwedeh, F. (2024). Effect of e-Learning on Servicing Education in Dubai. In *Artificial Intelligence in Education: The Power and Dangers of ChatGPT in the Classroom* (pp. 623–639). https://link.springer.com/chapter/10.1007/978-3-031-52280-2_40

Chapter 3
Parking 4.0:
IoT Augmented Mobility Solutions for Dynamic Smart City Ecosystems

Mounir El Khatib
http://orcid.org/0000-0001-7418-2351
Hamdan Bin Muhammad Smart University, UAE

Bashayer Hassan Alkhzaimi
Hamdan Bin Muhammad Smart University, UAE

Haroon Ul Rashid
http://orcid.org/0009-0009-2603-1650
Universiti Sains Malaysia, Malaysia

Fatma Sajwani
Hamdan Bin Muhammad Smart University, UAE

Fatma Alserisdi
Hamdan Bin Muhammad Smart University, UAE

Haitham Alzoubi
Skyline University College, UAE

ABSTRACT

The rapid evolution of the smart city ecosystem has placed the Internet of Things (IoT) at the forefront of city mobility innovation. As cities grapple with rising population, growing vehicle density, and increased environmental pressures, modern IoT-based solutions have emerged as the key enablers of smarter, more efficient transportation systems. Within the landscape, Parking 4.0, an integrated, IoT-enhanced smart parking paradigm, has transformed how cities manage space, mobility, and user expectations. This study examines the strategic role of IoT-enabled technologies in reshaping modern intelligent parking systems and the development of urban mobility performance. The paper examines the main architectural elements, technical requirements, and security factors associated with such solutions, thus highlighting both their transformative potential and the associated challenges. The results indi-

DOI: 10.4018/979-8-2600-1348-9.ch003

cate that IoT-enhanced parking systems play a pivotal role in reducing congestion, enhancing sustainability, and improving overall mobility efficiency within dynamic smart city ecosystems.

1. INTRODUCTION

Urban development depends on transportation systems, which have a vast influence on city residents' environment and quality of life. There are numerous problems associated with the rapid growth in the number of populations, coupled with increasing volumes of automotive traffic. This has resulted in the arrival of the concept of "smart cities", which involves technology and data-based solutions for improving the effectiveness and sustainability of urban livelihood. Smart transportation is an important part of this concept, improving mobility performance, reducing congestion and the impact that they have on the environment. This paper focuses on how the Internet of Things technology can modify urban parking and become a vital component of the vision of the smart city.

Problem Statement

Implementation of IoT Technologies for SMART PARKING as Part of Smart Transportation

The statement identifies the main issue discussed in the research paper. The problem is how smart transportation includes IoT applications in innovative parking systems. This concern has multiple aspects that are intertwined: the integration of technology into a system, meeting the needs for infrastructure, adoption by users, and the implications of the problem for transport systems within city limits (Ali, et al., 2020). Efficient strategies for parking, as cities become increasingly dense, are important to improve the air quality and promote a liveable and healthy city.

Hypotheses

H0: Smart parking integration will be one step towards smart transportation in a city.
H1: What is the integration of smart parking, how do we do it, benefits, opportunities, and challenges?
H2: Smart parking technologies will reduce traffic congestion and enhance urban mobility.

H3: Smart parking solutions implementation will face significant challenges related to security and privacy.

Research Questions

1. What are the best ways of incorporating IoT into innovative parking systems as part of intelligent transport plans?
2. Outlining the core benefits as well as weaknesses of installing innovative parking tools in cities.
3. How do you expect smart parking adoption to affect traffic jams and general urban mobility?
4. Will there be security and privacy issues associated with IoT-based intelligent parking solutions, and if so, what can we do about them?

Research Objectives

1. The study aims to investigate and propose methods that can help integrate IoT solutions towards developing smart transportation in city-based smart parking systems.
2. Innovative solution for better management of parking in areas around cities.
3. Determining the expected impacts of implementing intelligent parking systems on road jams and urban movement for evidence-based guidance.
4. Evaluating and identifying possible solutions towards ensuring user confirmations, data confidentiality, and overall system safety in IoT-based intelligent parking systems.

2. LITERATURE REVIEW

2.1 Trends Related to IoT Implementation of IoT Technologies in Smart Parking

Intelligent parking solutions utilizing IoT have increasingly drawn interest in different circles, which are focusing on addressing urban congestion and improving user experience. The focus of this literature review is the development of IoT implementation in Smart Parking Systems, including but not limited to system architectures, communication protocols, emerging tech integrations, and their impact on urban environments (Agarwal, Ratnani, Shah, & Jain, 2021). Sturdy frameworks in IoT-based ingenious parking mechanisms are a necessity in several areas of research. First, Gopal, Jerlin, & Abirami (2019) and J. Barriga, et al., (2019) listed and presented different architectural designs that incorporate sensors, communication components, and cloud drives. Some modern intelligent parking systems also developed and adopted dynamic pricing methods to ensure the best utilization of parking space usage. Dynamic pricing is defined by Sarker, Gia, Ben Dhaou, & Westerlund, (2020) as the parking fee depends on the demand and availability and changes accordingly. The dynamic pricing urges users to head towards other forms of transport to reduce congestion and contribute to greener city living.

AI and Edge Computing have been adopted in the recent progressions of IoT based Smart Parking Systems. AI algorithms are used to predict the parking space occupancy once integrated with IoT (Ashok, Tiwari, & Jirge, 2020). This type of integration improves the system's reliability and allows prescheduling and allocating parking slots depending on historical databases and documented users' habits. User experience is one of the key points in the system development of Smart Parking Systems (Ajchariyavanich, et al., 2019). Given the point that user-centric design is a critical aspect, multiple requirements must be considered, such as mobile apps, real-time notifications, and user-friendly interfaces. The consideration of these apps and interfaces makes finding available parking spaces quickly possible, which also allows direct booking of the available space, and reinforces the speediness by generating payments at once to satisfy their needs (Rey, Panetti, Maglio, & Ferretti, 2021). Al-Turjman & Malekloo, (2019) shed some light on Smart Parking Systems enabled by IoT in urban development and their significant effect. As a result, reduced traffic congestion and emissions will be present after operating the intelligent parking systems.

2.2 Technical Profile

IoT Technologies

Sensors and actuators are critical aspects of intelligent parking systems. Various devices can be installed on parking spaces' surfaces, such as ultrasonic, magnetic, and infrared sensors for vehicle detection purposes. Wireless networks are required to connect the sensors to a grid of communications, and all are monitored and referenced to a central control system (Brahimi & Bensaid, 2019). Numerous protocols are used for data transport, such as LoRaWAN Zigbee and cellular networks like 4G/5G that enable in-sync communication between the sensors and actuators in centralized management systems (Balaji, Nathani, & Santhakumar, 2019). The stated protocols provide drivers and operators with immediate access to parking information.

2.3 Implications in Smart Transportation

Smart parking systems, enabled with IoT, are involved in controlling traffic jams by guiding drivers to available parking spaces. As a result, it reduces the time taken to find an available parking space, hence minimizing fuel consumption and emission reduction that will enhance the air quality (Asghar Khan, Ullah, Alkhalifah, Rehman, & Shah, 2022). Smart transportation can use smart parking that is supported by decision-based information extracted using technologies (Biyik, et al., 2021). Infrastructure development can be achieved by analysing parking usage in the system's database for both traffic and the public transit network. Municipalities and parking operators usually increase their revenue when implementing intelligent parking systems (Yas et al., 2025).

2.4 Opportunities

Revenue Generation and Economic Growth

Integration of IoT in intelligent parking provides additional income sources for the authorities and the parking facilities administration. In their research entitled "Smart Parking System by Internet of Things", Wang and Zhang, (2017) observe that the implementation makes it possible to obtain more profit when using a dynamic price range that depends on the most demanded parking spaces, which will improve the traffic flow in cities. Additionally, they generate income that creates wealth for growing cities, along with boosting local business (Bertolini, 2020). IoT-enabled smart parking systems use sensors and surveillance cameras that aim at improving the safety of both pedestrians and vehicles. Research by Kim et al. (2018) shows a reduced probability of threat of theft, vandalism, and other offences in an IoT-based parking system with real-time monitoring and alerts, which can be described as safe for all userss.

3. CASE EXAMPLES

3.1 Dubai Smart Parking Initiative

The smart parking initiative is an integrated program that has been instituted in the busiest emirate of the United Arab Emirates, and it's Dubai. This project is by the Road and Transport Authority (RTA), and is utilizing IoT sensors as well as mobile apps that guide and direct the drivers to available parking spaces (Sahib, 2019). In summary, this system helps find available parking faster and eases the congestion on the roads of the city. Drivers are updated with real-time available parking data on mobile apps, prices, and directions to the closest parking areas (Zantalis, Koulouras, Karabetsos, & Kandris, 2019). This initiative contributed to an improved intelligent transport system within the Emirate of Dubai.

3.2 Abu Dhabi's Mawaqif Parking System

The Mawaqif parking system was introduced in Abu Dhabi, the capital of the United Arab Emirates and utilized IoT technologies to enhance parking management efficiently. Mawaqif system monitors available parking spaces using sensors and smart meters (Diaz Ogás, Fabregat, & Aciar, 2020). During the operation, a dedicated mobile app is operating to be used by drivers and provides real-time data on available parking spaces. The system reduces traffic congestion and effectively utilizes the parking spaces (Tahmasseby, 2020). The system has proven the efforts of the Abu Dhabi emirate to promote public transportation and foster more innovative mobility policy within a more friendly environment.

4. IMPLEMENTATION STEPS

Before adopting IoT technologies for smart parking systems, there should be a comprehensive understanding of the issues, as well as a detailed risk assessment strategy with planned exercises. Having the goals and objectives set is required, followed by the development of the appropriate infrastructure. It involves installing IoT sensors, cameras, and network communications in parking structures (Sen & Yamin, 2021). Driver-friendly interfaces are required, for example, mobile apps or web pages. Testing should be done on the accuracy of the sensors' data, app operations, and integrity of communication networks (Quijano-Sánchez, Cantador, Cortés-Cediel, & Gil, 2020). Training is also necessary for parking system operators, city workers, and users to enable them to use and manage the system efficiently.

5. RESEARCH METHODOLOGY

The current paper is based on a two-fold methodology that involves primary data collection using structured surveys and questionnaires, and secondary data analysis with the help of a systematic review of the international case studies and applications of Internet of Things (IoT) technology into parking management systems. This will be the main data gathering method through the sharing of surveys with the customers of the intelligent parking system. At the same time, a thorough analysis of case studies on an international level will be conducted, and secondary data obtained through actual purposes will be used. The latter is a secondary corpus, which will provide a more comprehensive background context, as it will aid in identifying patterns, best practices, and learned lessons in a variety of national settings. The combination of primary and secondary sources of data is aimed at providing a comprehensive picture of the IoT technologies in the smart parking management sphere.

5.1 Data Gathering

Primary Data

To explore the topic of smart parking based on the IoT as a tool for improving the transportation system in the United Arab Emirates (UAE), one should consider adopting a well-developed research methodology that will produce the data and information needed. The surveys were applied to a group of participants (male and female) with the focus on residents and visitors of the UAE who use intelligent parking systems. The selection of participants was random to curb selection bias, and the selection was done to bring diverse views on board. The information was gathered using a structured questionnaire, conducted on fifteen experts, which was backed by a survey of thirty-two users, as discussed in the appendix. The given method of analysis should be able to uncover the new trends and user-oriented tendencies.

Secondary Data

The fact that secondary data has been included is also very important. Peer-reviewed scholarly articles, industry reports, and earlier studies or cases on the implementation of IoT technologies in smart parking are all classed as secondary sources. These sources are critical towards building a holistic understanding of smart parking technologies. They present meaningful information about the historical development, current tendencies, and the challenges persisting in the field of using IoT-based parking systems. In this paper, the secondary data concentration is shifted to the presentation of the case studies that concern the implementation of IoT technologies in terms of parking management.

5.2 Data Analysis

Primary Data

Our primary data focused on collecting data and points of view from two groups of participants, and they are the specialised group and the general group. The specialised group was formed with 15 experts in parking management systems. Most of them agreed that the advantage of the system is real-time monitoring and management, which aligns with our operational focus. Half of the experts also confirmed that the impact would be "Enhanced Urban Mobility", which is one of the studied advantages/impacts in our literature review.

We have also approached their opinions regarding the required components to implement the project and the challenges that might or will be faced. A percentage of 40% agreed that Data synchronization and connectivity are required to implement the IoT. Regarding the challenges, an even percentage has been scored for two different points, which are high initial cost and integration with the existing system.

Figure 1. Pie charts

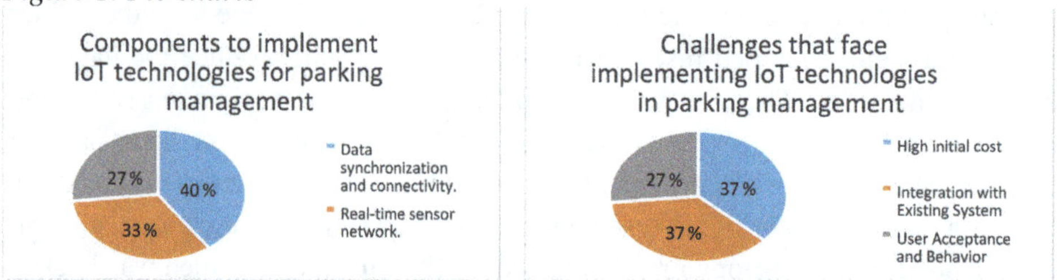

We have added two questions focusing on the percentage of agreement regarding the success of the implementation and the revenue generation in dynamic pricing as per (Sarker et al., 2020). As a summary, 13 out of 15 agreed that IoT will participate in revenue generation, which supports the theoretical opinion referenced with a percentage of 86.66%.

Given the success of the implementation is a must and one of the key points of the projects, 11 out of 15 agreed that the implementation will be successful, which is a supportive percentage of 73.33% to our objectives.

Figure 2. How likely would you rate the success of the IoT implementation from 1-5?

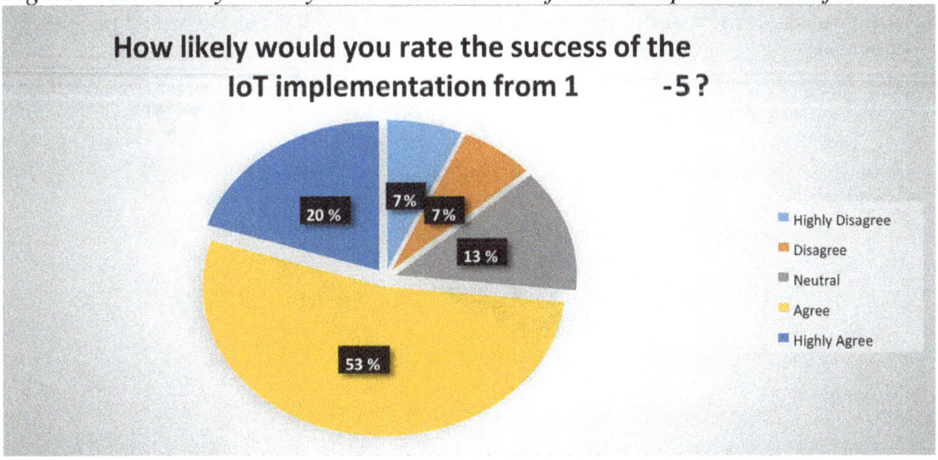

On the other hand, a survey was done on 32 users of smart parking. Based on the analysis of graph 1, the majority 62.5% has utilized the smart parking system in Dubai. However, 56.3% were concerned about the security of this system, as shown in graph 2. Moreover, based on the bar charts in graph 3, it emphasizes more on people's concern about secure data in addition to easy usage and real-time data. This supports the hypothesis H3, that implementation of the system will face the challenges of security and privacy.

Figure 3. Smart parking utilization

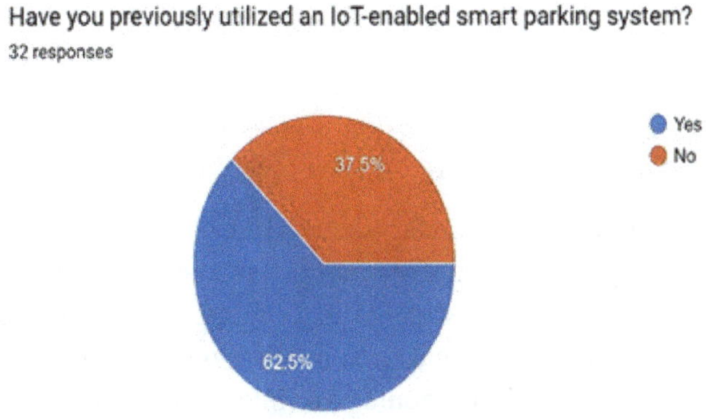

Figure 4. Security concern

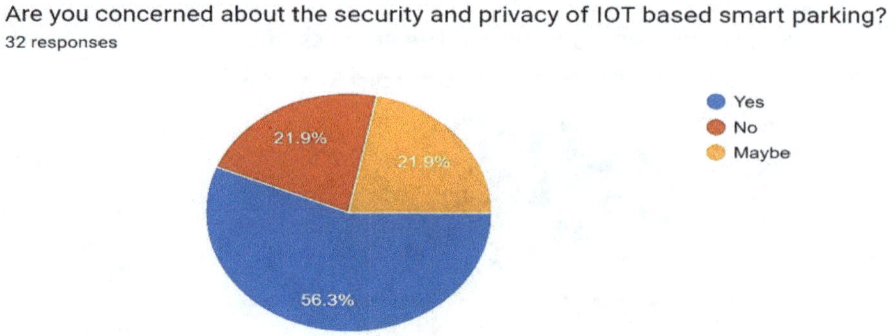

Figure 5. Smart parking essential

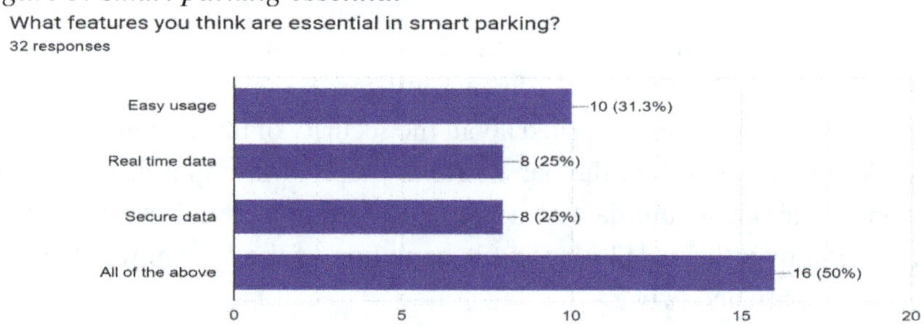

components

6. RECOMMENDATIONS

Based on the gathered primary data, the secondary data and the literature review of intelligent transportation regarding IoT solutions for smart parking, some suggestions follow. Innovative parking systems integrated with IoT incorporate synchronization of data and connectivity, thereby improving real-time monitoring and optimizing parking management (Farid et al., 2021). There should be no interference in data flow between sensors, control centers and users, and city administrators and technology providers should make this possible (Quijano-Sánchez, Cantador, Cortés-Cediel,

& Gil, 2020). Having current data in real-time and good connectivity will benefit users and go a long way towards addressing overcrowding.

While it is very beneficial, smart parking also raises some issues regarding high start-up costs. Other cost-effective strategies could be used, like public-private partnerships and users' initial expense incentives, to ensure easy adoption. This could encourage wider adoption and thus reduce the entry costs (Oladimeji, et al., 2023). Promotion programs should include, amongst others, the advantages of smart parking, which reduces traffic and pollution (Hendren, Newcomer, K. Pande, Smith, & Sumner, 2022). This could lead to an increase in smart parking usage that will result in cleaner cities.

Good cybersecurity practices, along with solid data protection systems, should be implemented concerning data security and user privacy. Consequently, the city authorities and the technology providers must develop modern security mechanisms to enhance the users' trust and safety (Gohar & Nencioni, 2021). Security will earn more trust from users if it is conveyed clearly. Users and other key players must be constantly involved in the cities' authorities and technology providers' process of continuous improvement (Nawara & Kashef, 2020). Intelligent parking systems updates for maximum user satisfaction and future success are determined by user feedback.

7. CONCLUSION

The findings of the research and the survey define several crucial remarks: the intelligent parking system, which is based on the Internet-of-Things (IoT) technologies, is the crucial factor towards reducing the effect of urban congestion, promoting the movement of transport, and promoting the culture of environmental responsibility. Successful implementation requires real-time data synchronisation, strong connectivity and an easy-to-use interface. The possible issues of implementation expenses, cybersecurity and privacy are not ignored; however, all these issues could be resolved with the help of cost-efficient measures, strict cybersecurity measures and constant user interaction. Furthermore, testing and incentive systems can be further utilized by introducing public-private partnerships to further accelerate the adoption and reduce the remaining financial restraints. Smart parking systems also help to achieve increased urban mobility through mitigating traffic congestion, low fuel usage, and decreased emissions. Moreover, they also encourage the use of public transport, which enhances air quality and the health of people. The perceived difference in the level of user satisfaction reveals the necessity of continuous improvements based on the feedback. Constant engagement with the users as well as systematic updates of the system are vital to guarantee higher levels of user satisfaction and loyalty. The case studies, an example of success: Dubai Smart Parking Initiative and Mawaqif Parking System in Abu Dhabi, offer a model that can be used in other municipalities that are intending to adopt similar systems.

REFERENCES

Agarwal, Y., Ratnani, P., Shah, U., & Jain, P. (2021). IoT based Smart Parking System. *2021 5th International Conference on Intelligent Computing and Control Systems (ICICCS)* (pp. 464-470). Madurai, India: IEEE. Retrieved from DOI: 10.1109/ICICCS51141.2021.9432196

Ajchariyavanich, C., Limpisthira, T., Chanjarasvichai, N., Jareonwatanan, T., Phongphanpanya, W., Wareechuensuk, S., & Pipattanasomporn, M. (2019). Park King: An IoT-based Smart Parking System. *2019 IEEE International Smart Cities Conference (ISC2)* (pp. 729-734). Casablanca, Morocco: IEEE. Retrieved from DOI: 10.1109/ISC246665.2019.9071721

Al-Turjman, F., & Malekloo, A. (2019). Smart parking in IoT-enabled cities: A survey. *Sustainable Cities and Society*, *49*, 101608. DOI: 10.1016/j.scs.2019.101608

Ali, , GAli, , TIrfan, , MDraz, , USohail, , MGlowacz, , ASulowicz, , MMielnik, , RFaheem, , Z. BMartis, , C. (2020). IoT based smart parking system using deep long short memory network. *Electronics, 9*(10), 1696. https://doi.org/10.3390/electronics9101696

Asghar Khan, M., Ullah, I., Alkhalifah, A., Rehman, S. U., & Shah, J. A. (2022). A Provable and Privacy-Preserving Authentication Scheme for UAV-Enabled Intelligent Transportation Systems. *IEEE Transactions on Industrial Informatics*, *18*(5), 3416–3425. DOI: 10.1109/TII.2021.3101651

Ashok, D., Tiwari, A., & Jirge, V. (2020). Smart Parking System using IoT Technology. *2020 International Conference on Emerging Trends in Information Technology and Engineering (ic-ETITE)* (pp. 1-7). Vellore, India: IEEE. Retrieved from DOI: 10.1109/ic-ETITE47903.2020.457

Balaji, S., Nathani, K., & Santhakumar, R. (2019). IoT Technology, Applications and Challenges: A Contemporary Survey. *Wireless Personal Communications*, *108*(1), 363–388. DOI: 10.1007/s11277-019-06407-w

Barriga, J., Sulca, J., León, J. L., Ulloa, A., Portero, D., Andrade, R., & Yoo, S. G. (2019). Smart Parking: A Literature Review from the Technological Perspective. *Applied Sciences (Basel, Switzerland)*, *9*(21), 4569. DOI: 10.3390/app9214569

Bertolini, L. (2020). From "streets for traffic" to "streets for people": Can street experiments transform urban mobility? *Transport Reviews*, *40*(6), 734–753. DOI: 10.1080/01441647.2020.1761907

Biyik, C., Allam, Z., Pieri, G., Moroni, D., O'Fraifer, M., O'Connell, E., Olariu, S., & Khalid, M. (2021). Smart Parking Systems: Reviewing the Literature, Architecture and Ways Forward. *Smart Cities*, *4*(2), 623–642. DOI: 10.3390/smartcities4020032

Brahimi, T., & Bensaid, B. (2019). Smart Villages and the GCC Countries: Policies, Strategies, and Implications. In A. Visvizi, M. Lytras, & G. Mudri, *Smart Villages in the EU and Beyond* (pp. 155-171). Emerald Publishing Limited, Retrieved from DOI: 10.1108/978-1-78769-845-120191015

Diaz Ogás, M., Fabregat, R., & Aciar, S. (2020). Survey of Smart Parking Systems. *Applied Sciences (Basel, Switzerland)*, *10*(11), 3872. DOI: 10.3390/app10113872

Farid, M. A., Viswanath, A., Al Junaibi, R., Allan, D., & Wardt, T. J. (2021). Electric Vehicle Integration into Road Transportation, Intelligent Transportation, and Electric Power Systems: An Abu Dhabi Case Study. *Smart cities, 4*(3). Retrieved from https://www.mdpi.com/2624-6511/4/3/55

Gohar, A., & Nencioni, G. (2021). The Role of 5G Technologies in a Smart City: The Case for Intelligent Transportation System. *Sustainability (Basel)*, *13*(9), 5188. DOI: 10.3390/su13095188

Gopal, D., Jerlin, M., & Abirami, M. (2019). A smart parking system using IoT. *World Review of Entrepreneurship, Management and Sustainable Development*, *15*(3), 335–345. DOI: 10.1504/WREMSD.2019.099409

Hendren, K., Newcomer, K. K., Pande, S., Smith, M., & Sumner, N. (2022). How qualitative research methods can be leveraged to strengthen mixed methods research in public policy and public administration? *Public Administration Review*, *83*(3), 468–485. DOI: 10.1111/puar.13528

Nawara, D., & Kashef, R. (2020). IoT-based Recommendation Systems – An Overview. *2020 IEEE International IOT, Electronics and Mechatronics Conference (IEMTRONICS),* (pp. 1-7). Vancouver, BC, Canada: IEEE. Retrieved from DOI: 10.1109/IEMTRONICS51293.2020.9216391

Oladimeji, D., Gupta, K., Kose, N. A., Gundogan, K., Ge, L., & Liang, F. (2023). Smart Transportation: An Overview of Technologies and Applications. *Sensors (Basel)*, *23*(8), 3880. DOI: 10.3390/s23083880 PMID: 37112221

Quijano-Sánchez, L., Cantador, I., Cortés-Cediel, M., & Gil, O. (2020). 9). Recommender systems for smart cities. *Information Systems*, *92*, 101545. Advance online publication. DOI: 10.1016/j.is.2020.101545

Rey, A., Panetti, E., Maglio, R., & Ferretti, M. (2021). 7). Determinants in adopting the Internet of Things in the transport and logistics industry. *Journal of Business Research, 131*, 584–590. DOI: 10.1016/j.jbusres.2020.12.049

Sahib, U. (2019). Smart Dubai: Sensing Dubai Smart City for Smart Environment Management. In Kumar, T. V. (Ed.), *Smart Environment for Smart Cities* (pp. 437–489). Springer., DOI: 10.1007/978-981-13-6822-6_12

Sarker, V. K., Gia, T. N., Ben Dhaou, I., & Westerlund, T. (2020). Smart Parking System with Dynamic Pricing, Edge-Cloud Computing and LoRa. *Sensors (Basel), 20*(17), 4669. DOI: 10.3390/s20174669 PMID: 32824989

Sen, A., & Yamin, M. (2021). Advantages of using fog in IoT applications. *International Journal of Information Technology : an Official Journal of Bharati Vidyapeeth's Institute of Computer Applications and Management, 13*(3), 829–837. DOI: 10.1007/s41870-020-00514-9

Tahmasseby, S. (2020). The Implementation of Smart Mobility for Smart Cities: A Case Study in Qatar. *Civil Engineering Kournal, 8*(10), 2154–2171. Advance online publication. DOI: 10.28991/CEJ-2022-08-10-09

Yas, H., Aldabbagh, Z., Khalifa, A. A., Faghiri, A., Bawazir, A. A., & Shwedeh, F. (2025). Role of artificial intelligence in the promotion of customer experiences: A legal administrative study and systematic review in the United Arab Emirates. *Humanities (Washington), 6*(4). Advance online publication. https://doi.org/https://doi.org/10.58256/m353d5430. DOI: 10.58256/m353d543

Zantalis, F., Koulouras, G., Karabetsos, S., & Kandris, D. (2019). A Review of Machine Learning and IoT in Smart Transportation. *Future Internet, 11*(4), 94. DOI: 10.3390/fi11040094

Chapter 4
Leveraging Green Information Technology and Knowledge Management to Strengthen Sustainable Entrepreneurship

Talal AlAraj
http://orcid.org/0009-0006-1929-7803
University of Sharjah, UAE

Omar Kayali
http://orcid.org/0009-0000-0806-3127
University of Windsor, Canada

Yousif Luckmann
http://orcid.org/0009-0005-0885-9033
Atlanta Georgia State University, USA

Maher Tawdrous
http://orcid.org/0009-0008-7104-0989
City University, Ajman, UAE

ABSTRACT

The integration of green management practices into business operations presents both opportunities and challenges for fostering sustainable entrepreneurship. This study incorporates Green Information Technology (GIT) acceptance as a moderating

DOI: 10.4018/979-8-2600-1348-9.ch004

factor within the proposed model. Using (PLS-SEM), the study investigates the interrelationships among key constructs. The findings indicate that knowledge creation and transfer exert a significant positive influence on sustainable entrepreneurship, whereas knowledge application and utilization demonstrate an insignificant effect. Additionally, GIT acceptance significantly moderates the relationships between knowledge creation, transfer, and storage with sustainable entrepreneurship, while showing no significant moderating effect on the link between knowledge application and sustainable entrepreneurship. These results provide valuable insights for practitioners and policymakers seeking to advance sustainable entrepreneurship through enhanced knowledge creation, effective GIT integration, and strategic knowledge utilization.

1. INTRODUCTION

Rapid rate of environmental destruction, growing shortages of various resources, and increasing social inequalities and inequities have forced both scholars and practitioners to reconsider the conventional models of entrepreneurship in terms of sustainability over the last few decades. The current business activities do not proceed on the premise of profit maximization, but they are more likely to balance out economic, social and ecological demands. According to one of the recent reviews, there has been a rise in economic, societal, and environmental threats despite the economic development that is taking place across the globe which in turn is the cause of the need in sustainable entrepreneurship, forms of business that combine social, ecological and economic objectives.

The idea of sustainable entrepreneurship focuses on value creation that does not only serve the interests of the entrepreneur and his or her firm, but improves environmental care and social welfare. Unlike traditional entrepreneurship where the main aim is economic, sustainable entrepreneurship expands its scope of outcome to cover favorable environmental and social gains. This change is indicative of increased awareness of grand challenges, including climate change, biodiversity loss, and social inequality, and of the realization that entrepreneurial ecosystems have to be changed accordingly.

In this new paradigm, knowledge has preeminently become a value. Under the knowledge-based view (KBV) of the firm, knowledge is a valuable resource that is rare, inimitable, and can be used to provide competitive advantage and innovation. In entrepreneurial ventures, who are dedicated to sustainable results, the successful creation, dissemination, memory and utilization of knowledge is an essential facilitator. In fact, it has been noted in recent years that knowledge management practices including knowledge creation, dissemination, retention and utilisation are indispensable elements enabling firms to implement business models that are sustainable, green innovations and practices that are sustainable.

However, the relationship between knowledge management and sustainable entrepreneurship has not been studied in fine details. According to a more recent bibliometric review, even though the amount of literature on knowledge management and entrepreneurship sustainability is on the rise, the conceptual frameworks, social networks, and intellectual foundations of this intersection have yet to be completely established. As an example, although the importance of knowledge creation and transfer has been extensively recognized, the manner in which knowledge is utilized and integrated in the entrepreneurial process in an effort to achieve sustainable results deserves further exploration.

In line with the increased importance of knowledge and entrepreneurship is the increased importance of green information technology (GIT). The general meaning of green IT is that information technology (IT) hardware and software are designed, acquired, used, and disposed of in a manner that minimizes environmental effects and promotes sustainable business practices. Green IT can be an administrative innovation and facilitator of corporate sustainability in organizational activities and could be aligned with the strategic objectives and expectations of the stakeholders. Considering that in many cases, entrepreneurial activities are based on digital technologies and data streams, the adoption of green IT into the entrepreneurial ecosystem can provide a favorable opportunity to integrate sustainability in operational and strategic decisions.

By weaving these threads, the current study hypothesizes that knowledge management and green IT acceptance are among the major constructs in creating sustainable entrepreneurial systems. In particular, the research takes a more dimensional perspective of knowledge management in terms of creation, transfer/storage, and application/utilization and explores its effects on sustainable entrepreneurship concerning the U.S. context. Moreover, the paper presents the concept of GIT acceptance as the mediating factor: that is, it examines whether and how the extent of acceptance and adoption of green IT enhances (or undermines) the connection between the knowledge management practices and sustainable entrepreneurial performance.

The inquiry is relevant at the right time due to a number of reasons. First, there is a changing entrepreneurial environment: new enterprises are more and more exposed to individual accountability regarding environmental and social accountability to stakeholders. Second, digital age is rapidly enhancing knowledge flows both within and between firms, and it has created questions of how the management of knowledge should evolve to continue to be innovative towards sustainability. Third, the proximal nature of IT and green business practices implies that the more sustainable strategies become a reality in the entrepreneurial ventures, the more the acceptance of green IT could be a vital facilitating condition.

The research will be useful to the literature as will empirically study the unique dimensions of knowledge management in relation to sustainable entrepreneurship will present and test the moderating effects of green IT acceptance; and, Al-Sul It is hoped that the study results will help to understand which factors of knowledge management have the strongest impact on sustainable entrepreneurship, and in what circumstances, in particular with regard to the adoption of green IT, their contribution will be positive or negative. The study will make contributions to the literature with a view of empirically investigating the unique dimensions of knowledge management, in relation to sustainable entrepreneurship; introducing and testing the moderating position of the green IT acceptance; and it is hoped that the outcomes of the research would shed light on what aspects of knowledge management have the most significant impact on sustainable entrepreneurship, and that the impact of these aspects, in particular the adoption of green IT, is strengthened or weakened under what circumstances. In this research, the environmentally responsible sustainability, innovation management, and entrepreneurship were integrated with the knowledge-based strategic practice, thus contributing to sustainability, innovation management, and entrepreneurship research areas. It promotes academic discussion by pointing out the fact that the adoption of Green IT can improve the efficiency of the organization, reduce its impact on the environment, and Knowledge Management is a facilitator of the transformation of technological advancements into the strategies that can be put to practice and that the adoption of IT can lead to the establishment of sustainable business models. Connecting these areas, the study closes the theoretical and practical gaps in knowledge about how the digital transformation and knowledge-driven cultures can promote eco-innovation, resilience, and the creation of long-term values in the framework of entrepreneurial ecosystems. Furthermore, it offers a multidimensional model on which policymakers, researchers, and practitioners can examine how the collective exploitation of technological and intellectual resources can produce sustainability-oriented entrepreneurship which will enrich the cross-disciplinary studies in the field of management, environmental studies, and information systems.

2. LITERATURE REVIEW

1. Sustainable Entrepreneurship

Sustainable entrepreneurship has been one of the strategic solutions to the increasing number of challenges faced by the modern economies related to the environment and social problems. It combines the concepts of entrepreneurship and sustainability goals, as well as the focus on developing economic, social, and environmental values at the same time (Hall et al., 2010; Gast et al., 2017). In contrast to the conventional entrepreneurship that is mainly profit-driven, sustainable entrepreneurship encourages innovations that reduce the ecological effects as well as produce the social benefits that last in the long run (Shepherd and Patzelt, 2011). According to the recent research, sustainable entrepreneurship is a key to meeting the United Nations Sustainable Development Goals (SDGs) as it promotes green innovation, inclusive development, and social responsibility (Muñoz and Cohen, 2018). Entrepreneurs can create sustainable ventures using the knowledge of shared knowledge, collaborative learning, and environmentally responsible practices provided by sustainable entrepreneurial ecosystems of actors, institutions, policies, and technologies (Cohen, 2006; Boluk et al., 2019).

Consumer demand of green products, regulatory pressures and digital transformation are becoming the main drivers of sustainable entrepreneurship in the U.S. environment. However, little is known of the channels, in which organizational knowledge and digital technologies including Green Information Technology (GIT) determine these results (Ludeke-Freund et al., 2020).

2. Knowledge Management and Sustainable Entrepreneurship

Knowledge management (KM) is the process of developing, holding, exchanging and using knowledge in order to enhance organizational performance (Nonaka and Takeuchi, 1995; Alavi and Leidner, 2001). In a firm-based perspective of knowledge referred to as knowledge based view (KBV), knowledge is a distinct, strategic, asset on which innovation, learning, and competitive advantage are based (Grant, 1996).

Within the framework of sustainable entrepreneurship, KM helps to integrate sustainability-driven knowledge into the process of decision-making, innovative activities, and communication with stakeholders (Del Giudice & Della Peruta, 2016). Research reports that knowledge sharing and development plays a significant role in innovation to green, and knowledge implementation to operational effectiveness and environmental compliance (Cai et al., 2020).

Nevertheless, KM practices have different efficacy in various settings. Although the creation and transfer of knowledge can be the drivers of innovation, the empirical data draw the idea that implementation and utilization of knowledge can have less pronounced impacts in the case when firms are not digitally organized or prepared to sustainability (Tariq et al., 2023). Therefore, the contribution of digital enablers like GIT to KM in contributing to sustainable entrepreneurship is a relevant research question.

3. Green Information Technology (GIT) and Sustainability

The term Green Information Technology (GIT) is used to describe the development, adoption, and utilization of IT systems in a manner that minimizes environmental degradation and leads to business practices that are sustainable (Molla, 2009). GIT encompasses programs like the use of energy efficient hardware, virtualization, the use of green software design, and sustainable data management.

Researchers underline that GIT is not merely a technological solution but an organizational competency that contributes to the better utilization of resources, improved environmental impacts, and alignment with the sustainability objectives (Brooks et al., 2012; Bose and Luo, 2014). Its implementation needs managerial dedication, stakeholder recognition and its orientation to the company overall sustainability strategy (Kuo and Dick, 2010).

GIT can be used in entrepreneurial ecosystems to ensure sustainable business practices through the implementation of green supply chains, data-driven environmental monitoring, and knowledge-sharing networks. In addition, the effectiveness of knowledge management is mediated by the adoption of GIT- increasing the velocity, availability, and assimilation of sustainability insight in companies (Hasan et al., 2017).

4. Integrating Knowledge Management, GIT, and Sustainable Entrepreneurship

The areas of interest of KM and GIT offer ample opportunities to sustainable entrepreneurship. KM practices allow the entrepreneur to capture and make use of environmental knowledge, and GIT provides the structure and tools to operationalize this knowledge in a manner that is effective (Yoon, 2021). Such synergy improves the capability of innovation, sustainability reporting and environmentally efficient business operations (Melville, 2010). T

his information is backed by empirical findings that show a company that has strategy of integrating KM and GIT is more successful than the same company that strategically considers these two dimensions since GIT enables analysis of data and sharing of knowledge in real-time, thus critical in determining sustainability-related decision-making (Dangelico and Pujari, 2010). Even with this information, there is scanty empirical research conducted to determine the moderating role of the GIT acceptance in the KM sustainable entrepreneurship relationship especially in western societies like the United States. The phenomenon of Knowledge Management (KM), Green Information Technology (GIT), and Sustainable Entrepreneurship (SE) has gained and continues to gain more interest in academic and practical fields over the past few years. With the quest by organizations to ensure that they pursue the objectives of sustainability, the introduction of knowledge-based systems and environmentally friendly technologies create a critical base in sustainable entrepreneurial activities. This literature review provides the theoretical and empirical clues on the connection between these three areas and the integration of these areas which leads to innovation, competitiveness, and environmental responsibility.

Knowledge Management is a key aspect of improving sustainable entrepreneurship as it allows organizations to create, disseminate, and use knowledge. The knowledge creation theory developed by Nonaka and Takeuchi (1995) suggests that organizations that keep on changing tacit and explicit knowledge are in a better position to sustainably innovate. When entrepreneurs capitalize on KM practices, including knowledge sharing, organizational learning, and innovation networks, they can tend to recognize opportunities that face both social and environmental objectives (Durst and Ferenhof, 2014).

Sustainable entrepreneurship involves the incorporation of the knowledge of sustainability in the decision making of the businesses (Schaltegger and Wagner, 2011). The knowledge intensive activities are useful in enabling entrepreneurs to learn about the expectations of the stakeholders, environmental policies and market trends, which play a significant role in the creation of green business models. Additionally, the successful KM tools facilitate the sharing of environmental knowledge within the company, promoting the overall sustainability-related action (Del Giudice & Della Peruta, 2016). Therefore, KM is an enterprise innovation-sustainability and resilience-enabler in entrepreneurial ecosystems.

Green Information Technology (GIT), also known as Green IT can be defined as the design, implementation and use of IT systems that have reduced environmental impact and the highest economic and social value (Murugesan, 2008). GIT is a contributor of sustainability as it helps in energy efficient data centres, eco-friendly hardware, cloud computing, and optimization of digital processes. Combined with KM, GIT is a means of sustainability-driven innovation that allows sharing of green knowledge, collaborating, and transforming digitally (Molla, 2009).

KM and GIT synergy has an improved ability to build sustainable value within organizations. GIT offers the technology of capturing and managing sustainability knowledge across the organizational borders (Jenkin, Webster and McShane, 2011). As an example, green data analytics can assist business owners to make evidence-based choices regarding the efficiency of resources and waste minimization. Also, the digital knowledge repositories and collaborative platforms encourage environmental consciousness and joint intelligence, which foster sustainable entrepreneurial mindsets. By incorporating GIT in the KM practices, information redundancy, energy use, and operational costs are lowered, and this aspect also leads to the performance of organizational sustainability (Melville, 2010).

The combination of KM and GIT is a sensitive contributor to sustainable entrepreneurship, which is the idea of trying to create business opportunities that bring economic, social, and ecological values at the same time (Cohen and Winn, 2007). The world of sustainable entrepreneurs is based on the use of knowledge-based resources and digital technologies to recognize the opportunities of eco-innovative opportunities and to apply environmentally responsible business models. With the help of this integration, entrepreneurs will be able to obtain real-time environmental information, evaluate market trends, and develop solutions with stakeholders.

Empirical findings indicate that the combination of KM and GIT can increase the ability of an organization to create sustainable innovations due to an increase in the quality of decisions and minimization of environmental risks. Moreover, the connection between GIT activities and KM strategies promotes the organizational culture of sustainability, innovation, and lifelong learning. This congruency assists entrepreneurs to develop the adaptive potentials that can be maintained in the competitive markets (Zhang and Wang, 2020). Finally, the integration creates a holistic approach that enables the environment, use of knowledge, and technological progress through their collaboration to create sustainable entrepreneurial performance.

Theoretical models like the Resource-Based View (RBV) and the Knowledge-Based View (KBV) propose the idea that knowledge and IT resources when combined in an effective manner generate unique capabilities that can result to sustainable competitive advantage (Barney, 1991; Grant, 1996). GIT is the facilitating resource, whereas KM is the strategic process that converts the knowledge into the eco-innovative results. The interaction between the two spheres is the intellectual capital basis of sustainable entrepreneurship.

The next round of research should address the way in which digital green technologies and KM practices collaborate to impact sustainable entrepreneurial systems. The necessity to explore the way policy frameworks and institutional support may promote the incorporation of GIT and KM in promoting sustainable ventures, especially in developing economies, is also increasing.

3. THEORETICAL FRAMEWORK

This study is grounded in two primary theoretical perspectives:

1. Knowledge-Based View (KBV) of the Firm

According to the KBV, knowledge is a resource in a firm, which is the most important strategically (Grant, 1996). Within the framework of sustainable entrepreneurship, green innovation and sustainability-based capabilities are developed through the creation, transfer, and the application of knowledge (Nonaka, and Toyama, 2007). In such a manner, the practices of knowledge management will have a direct impact on the sustainable entrepreneurship.

2. Technology Acceptance Model (TAM)

Technology Acceptance Model (Davis, 1989) is the model which is used to describe the way in which the perceived ease of use and the perceived usefulness affect the adoption of the new technologies by the users. GIT acceptance is the moderating construct in this research that defines the effectiveness of the firms in utilizing technology in supporting KM and sustainability. Great amount of GIT acceptance enhances the beneficial impacts of KM on sustainable.

Conceptual Model

Based on these frameworks, the study proposes the following conceptual relationships:

- **H1:** Knowledge creation positively influences sustainable entrepreneurship.
- **H2:** Knowledge transfer positively influences sustainable entrepreneurship.
- **H3:** Knowledge application has an effect (positive/insignificant) on sustainable entrepreneurship.
- **H4:** Green Information Technology (GIT) acceptance moderates the relationship between KM dimensions and sustainable entrepreneurship, strengthening their positive effects.

The combination of these two areas asserts that sustainable entrepreneurship does not arise out of isolated innovation or environmental awareness but rather it is the combination of knowledge-based abilities and technological sustainability-acceptance that results in the emergence of sustainability. Figure 1 provides the conceptual model depicting the theoretical construct - how Knowledge Management dimensions (Creation, Transfer, Application) affect the Sustainable Entrepreneurship, with the Green IT Acceptance moderating the links between these variables.

Figure 1. Research Conceptual Framework

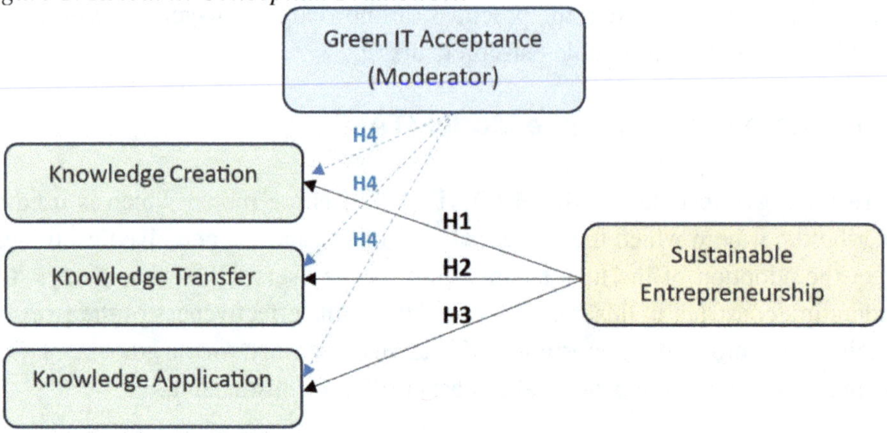

4. METHODOLOGY

4.1 Research Design

The current study uses a quantitative, cross-sectional research design to empirically investigate the connections between knowledge management (KM) dimensions, Green Information Technology (GIT) acceptance and sustainable entrepreneurship in the light of small and medium-sized enterprises (SMEs) in the United States. The quantitative design enables measuring the constructs using validated survey measures and testing hypothesized relationships using statistical modeling.

The research method follows the Partial Least Squares Structural Equation Modeling (PLS-SEM) technique with Smart PLS 4.0 because this technique is suitable to predictive research models, allows non-normal data distribution, and allows complex moderating relationships (Hair et al., 2021).

4.2 Population and Sampling

The target group will comprise of entrepreneurs, founders, and top managers of SMEs that will be in environmentally sensitive industries such as manufacturing, information technology, and services. The reason why these firms have been chosen is that they signify a rising proportion of sustainability-based firms in the United States.

To select participants possessing first hand information on sustainability initiatives and knowledge management practices, a purposive sampling technique was used. A total of 350 questionnaires were emailed out and 297 valid responses were retained to undergo the analysis process hence the effective response rate of 84.8. A study based on the existing literature states that a response rate between 50, 60 and 70 is deemed to be average to do most social science studies, and more than 70 will be considered very good. (Mbugua, E. W., & Muchelule, Y. (2024).

The sample profile consisted of 62 percent and 38 percent male and female response, respectively, with an average age of the firm 8.6 and 45 employees, respectively. About 70 per cent of the respondent firms recorded that they had at least some sort of green technology or sustainability program in the last three years.

4.3 Data Collection Procedure

The online structured questionnaire was used to collect the data based on the professional and entrepreneurial networks (e.g., LinkedIn and industry associations). In order to achieve content validity, the survey instrument was pilot tested on 15 academic experts and 20 practitioners and slight changes were done to enhance clarity and relevancy.

Every participant was educated about the purpose of the study and confidentiality of their response. Data collection was done after the institutional review board of the host university approved the study ethically.

4.4 Data Analysis Techniques

The collected data were analyzed in two stages:

1. Measurement Model Evaluation: The constructs were assessed by measuring the reliability and validity based on internal consistency (Cronbachs alpha, composite reliability), convergent (AVE) and discriminant (FornellLarcker ratio and HTMT ratio) validity.
2. Structural Model Assessment: Hypotheses (H1-H4) were tested by estimating path coefficients. The interaction terms of GIT acceptance in PLS-SE, were used to examine the moderating effect. R2, f2, and Q2 were used to measure model fit, bootstrapping (5000 resamples) to measure path significance.

5. ADOPTED INSTRUMENT

5.1 Measurement Scales

All measurement items were made to be based on the previously validated scales so that their reliability and content validity would be ensured. A five-point Likert scale with a strong disagree to strongly agree was used in the questionnaire. The following are the constructs and the sources that are adopted:

Table 1. Constructs Measurements

Construct	Dimensions/Items	Sources
Knowledge Management (KM)	*Knowledge Creation, Knowledge Transfer/Storage, Knowledge Application/Use*	Adapted from Gold, Malhotra & Segars (2001); Lee & Choi (2003)
Green Information Technology (GIT) Acceptance	*Perceived Usefulness, Perceived Ease of Use, Environmental Awareness*	Adapted from Davis (1989); Molla (2009); Bose & Luo (2014)
Sustainable Entrepreneurship (SE)	*Environmental Innovation, Social Value Creation, Economic Viability*	Adapted from Shepherd & Patzelt (2011); Muñoz & Cohen (2018)

5.2 Sample Measurement Items

Knowledge Creation

- "Our firm encourages employees to generate new ideas that enhance sustainability."
- "We continuously develop new knowledge to improve environmental performance."

Knowledge Transfer and Storage

- "Knowledge related to sustainability practices is effectively shared across departments."
- "Our organization maintains a repository of green innovation knowledge."

Knowledge Application and Use

- "We effectively apply sustainability knowledge to operational processes."

- "The knowledge gained from past green initiatives is utilized to make current decisions."

Green Information Technology (GIT) Acceptance

- "Green IT systems are easy to use in our organization."
- "Adopting GIT helps reduce our environmental impact."
- "Our employees are willing to use GIT for sustainability purposes."

Sustainable Entrepreneurship

- "Our business initiatives contribute to environmental sustainability."
- "We engage in entrepreneurial actions that benefit society."
- "Sustainability considerations are central to our innovation processes."

5.3 Reliability and Validity

Cronbach alpha values of all constructs were over 0.80 and composite reliability (CR) was over 0.85, which show that it is internally consistent. AVE values were found to be more than 0.50 in all the latent variables, which affirmed the convergent validity (Fornell and Larcker, 1981). The validation of discriminant validity was done by the HTMT ratio (Less than 0.85) and the cross-loading, whereby each of the constructs was empirically different.

5.4 Common Method Bias (CMB) and Ethical Considerations

Procedural remedies that were used to reduce possible common method bias included anonymity, randomization of question order, and reverse coded questions. Statistical tests based on Harman single-factor test showed that none of the factors explained over 40 per cent of the variance, so there was little to worry about CMB (Podsakoff et al., 2003).

Informed consent was voluntary and all the participants were assured of data confidentiality on ethical research standards.

6. FINDINGS

6.1 Measurement Model Evaluation

Measurement model was evaluated before the hypothesis testing to ascertain the reliability and validity of all the constructs. Factor loading of all observed variables were more than the upper limit of 0.70 that validated item reliability. The alpha of Cronbach and composite reliability (CR) of all constructs was also good, with a range of between 0.83 and 0.94. The values of the Average Variance Extracted (AVE) were 0.56 to 0.78, which indicated convergent validity (Fornell, and Larcker, 1981).

Both the Fornell-Larcker criterion and the Heterotrait-Monotrait ratio (HTMT) tests were used to prove the presence of discriminant validity (all lower than the 0.85 cut-off) (Hair et al., 2021). In such a way, the constructs were empirically different and could be modelled structurally.

6.2 Structural Model Evaluation

Upon validation of the measurement model the structural model was tested by applying the Partial Least Squares Structural Equation Modeling (PLS-SEM). The model had a good explanatory power with R2 of 0.61 of Sustainable entrepreneurship (SE), indicating that the overall contribution of Knowledge Creation, Knowledge transfer and storage, Knowledge Application and use and Green Information Technology (GIT) Acceptance explain 61 percent of Sustainable entrepreneurship (SE).

Path coefficients and t-values were obtained by bootstrapping (5,000 resamples).

Table 2. Hypothesis Analysis

Hypothesis	Path	β	t-value	p-value	Result
H1: Knowledge Creation → SE	0.312	4.87	<0.001	Supported	
H2: Knowledge Transfer & Storage → SE	0.278	3.94	<0.001	Supported	
H3: Knowledge Application & Use → SE	0.085	1.36	0.174	Not Supported	
H4: GIT Acceptance × Knowledge Creation → SE	0.163	2.91	0.004	Supported	
H5: GIT Acceptance × Knowledge Transfer → SE	0.121	2.43	0.015	Supported	
H6: GIT Acceptance × Knowledge Application → SE	0.049	0.98	0.326	Not Supported	

These findings reveal that the knowledge creation and knowledge transfer and storage have a great impact in terms of improving sustainable entrepreneurship. Conversely there was no significant direct effect of knowledge application and use. The moderation effect of GIT acceptance was partially confirmed since it enhanced the relationship among knowledge creation, knowledge transfer and sustainable entrepreneurship significantly, however, not between knowledge application and SE.

The model fit statistics (SRMR = 0.052, NFI = 0.91 and RMS theta = 0.09) fell within the recommended range, thus ascertaining that the model of structure perfectly fits the data.

7. DISCUSSION

The results support the importance of knowledge management (KM) to the sustainability of entrepreneurship (SE) as is common with previous research that highlights the strategic excellence of the knowledge processes in innovation and sustainability (Gold et al., 2001; Lee and Choi, 2003).

The creation of knowledge was found to be the strongest predictor of SE, which implies that companies that are able to innovate and institutionalize new knowledge stand at a better position to develop new innovative and sustainable business models. This is reminiscent of the knowledge spiral theory by Nonaka (1994) which focuses on how tacit knowledge can be converted into explicit knowledge as a source of innovation.

Likewise, there was a strong positive impact of knowledge transfer and storage on SE. This helps to argue that sharing of knowledge promotes the collective learning process and facilitates the sustainability-driven cross-organizational cooperation (Chow and Chan, 2008). Companies with ready available green knowledge repositories are in a better position to carry out environmentally friendly innovations.

Nevertheless, the insignificant effect of knowledge application on SE can show that companies have difficulties in applying knowledge in practice. This may be due to the cultural, financial or technological constraints that inhibit the operationalization of the insights on sustainability (Zahra et al., 2012). The implication of this finding is that there is a possible disconnect between knowledge ownership and sustainable action, and hence the necessity of positive frameworks and motivations to transform sustainability-oriented knowledge into action.

Of special interest is the moderating effect of Green Information Technology (GIT). The important moderating roles of GIT acceptance in determining the relationships between knowledge creation and transfer with SE are indicative of the fact that technology-oriented sustainability strategies enhance the gains of knowledge management. GIT enhances the acceleration of dissemination and use of environmental knowledge with the help of digital platforms that aids in green innovation and eco-efficiency (Molla, 2009; Bose and Luo, 2014).

On the other hand, that there is no moderation on the use of knowledge is a sign that technology adoption cannot overcome organizational barriers. To make sure that the technology-based solutions have been incorporated into the daily sustainability activities, firms are required to build green capabilities, leadership commitment, and employee engagement. This paper is relevant to the increasing body of knowledge on sustainable entrepreneurship by explaining how the dimensions of knowledge management play off with Green Information Technology (GIT) to promote environmentally and socially friendly business operations.

The empirical findings indicate that knowledge creation and knowledge transfer are the most powerful facilitators of sustainable entrepreneurship. All these processes enable the firms to keep on innovating continuously, changing with the demands of the environment, and institutionalizing sustainability in their operations. Nevertheless, the decreased impact of knowledge application marks a gap in implementation — organizations can be aware of what they should do but are not that successful in implementing sustainability strategies.

The mediating power of GIT acceptance proves that digital tools might support the relationship between knowledge processes and sustainability outcomes. Companies that adopt green digitalization, i.e., cloud computing, data analytics, and energy-saving systems, will tend to turn knowledge into real eco-innovations.

From a practical perspective, the findings urge managers and policymakers to:

1. Invest in platforms and training that enhance knowledge creation and sharing around sustainability.
2. Foster an organizational culture that encourages experimentation and innovation through GIT.
3. Develop mechanisms to bridge the gap between knowledge acquisition and its practical application in sustainability-oriented entrepreneurship.

Lastly, this research contributes to the theoretical knowledge by making Knowledge Management Theory, Technology Acceptance Theory, and Sustainable Entrepreneurship frameworks one model. Research in the future may be similar to this but can be conducted in similar national settings or may use longitudinal designs to determine the changes in GIT acceptance and their effect on sustainable performance performances.

8. MANAGERIAL AND POLICY IMPLICATIONS

Lastly, this research contributes to the theoretical knowledge by making Knowledge Management Theory, Technology Acceptance Theory, and Sustainable Entrepreneurship frameworks one model. Research in the future may be similar to this but can be conducted in similar national settings or may use longitudinal designs to determine the changes in GIT acceptance and their effect on sustainable performance performances.

8.1 Managerial Implications

To begin with, managers are advised to lay the emphasis on development of knowledge creation and transfer as strategic resources in sustainability-based organizations. Knowledge creation facilitates the firms to come up with new solutions to the environment whereas transfer and storage allow sustainability knowledge to be stored and dispersed across the functional boundaries. The internal flow of green knowledge can be stimulated by means of setting up internal knowledge sharing systems, including online knowledge libraries and inter-functional innovation centres (Gold et al., 2001).

Second, the findings point to the fact that the implementation of knowledge alone cannot ensure the sustainability. The managers should make sure that knowledge developed and distributed is integrated into operations in terms of performance measures, training and resource distribution. This cannot be done without technical integration but a cultural shift in which sustainability is seen as a collective goal and not a compliance target (Nonaka, 1994; Lee and Choi, 2003).

Third, GIT acceptance is an accelerator that enhances the advantage of KM on sustainability performance. Companies implementing GIT tools, i.e., cloud-based teamwork methods, data centers with low power consumption, and digital surveillance services, can make the process of translating environmental knowledge into sustainability more rapid. Therefore, the discussion of the GIT investment ought not be viewed as purely IT upgrading but as a sustainability project aimed at increasing the efficiency of innovation and environmental performance (Molla, 2009; Bose and Luo, 2014).

8.2 Policy Implications

Governments and regulatory authorities must encourage the use of GIT and innovation based on knowledge in the entrepreneurship ecosystems at the policy level. This may be done by tax credit, digital sustainability grant, or subsidized access to green technologies by small and medium-sized enterprises (SMEs).

In addition, national innovation policies ought to enable the formation of public–private relationships which lead to the sharing of environmental knowledge among the academia, the industry and the government agencies. This kind of cooperation can contribute to the alignment of sustainability goals with technological innovation and make sure that the environmental and social factors are incorporated into the strategy of national entrepreneurship systematically (OECD, 2021).

And, last but not most, education and training in green knowledge management should be a priority of policymakers, as future entrepreneurs will be able to acquire both digital and sustainability-competencies to create a resilient and eco-innovative economy.

9. LIMITATIONS AND FUTURE RESEARCH DIRECTIONS

Although this paper will play a significant role in the conceptualization of knowledge management and GIT in sustainable entrepreneurship, some of the limitations will serve as future research directions.

9.1 Methodological Limitations

The research was based on the cross-sectional survey design, which does not provide an opportunity to conclude about causal relationships between the constructs. The proposed studies of the future might employ longitudinal research methods to study the way in which KM and GIT acceptance will change over time and contribute to the sustainability results dynamically. Moreover, this research was based on self-reported data of the SME managers, which can be affected by the social desirability and response bias. Validity would be improved by merging survey data and objective performance metrics (e.g. environmental certifications, energy efficiency metrics).

9.2 Contextual and Conceptual Limitations

This study was done in the United States, which has a developed online resource base and well-developed sustainability legislation. The reproduction of the study in the developing economies may provide information about the role of institutional and cultural characteristics in the establishment of the KM-GIT-SE relationship. The cross-country comparative studies would facilitate generalizing the results and revealing the context-specific dynamics (Muñoz & Cohen, 2018). In addition, the current research centered on the acceptance of Green Information Technology as a mediator. Future studies may consider incorporating more modulating factors like organization culture, leadership and regulatory pressure to learn how they interact with knowledge management to lead to sustainable entrepreneurship. Also, longitudinal research may yield more insight into the cause and effect relationships between knowledge management, green IT implementation, and sustainable entrepreneurship in the long term. A closer look at the development of these relationships in various levels of the organizational maturity, starting with startups and going through more mature companies, would be an addition to the theoretical and practical understanding.

The more complex behaviors, motivations, and decision-making that quantitative models might not address might be revealed through the application of qualitative methods including interviews or case studies, as well. These multi-method research designs would not only enhance empirical validity but also provide policy actionable information to those policy makers and business executives who aim to facilitate the digital-driven sustainability shifts.

9.3 Theoretical Expansion

In theory, combining the dynamic capability theory (Teece, 2018) with institutional theory might help to better understand how companies respond to changing environmental factors by modifying the knowledge and technology resources. Digital transformation preparedness or artificial intelligence implementation is another possible area of future research by scholars to explore as an emerging enabler of sustainability-oriented innovation.

CONCLUSION

This paper highlights the strategic relationship between knowledge management, green information technology and sustainable entrepreneurship. It contributes to the academic theory and managerial practice, shedding light on the processes in which knowledge creation and technology adoption promote sustainability.

To survive in the changing sustainability environment, the way forward is to combine digital intelligence with green awareness, and turn knowledge into ongoing and technology-driven innovation that not only helps businesses but also the society and the entire planet.

This paper highlights the strategic interaction between knowledge management, green information technology and sustainable entrepreneurship and how the three help generate organizational change towards sustainability. Green IT practices together with good knowledge management encourages learning culture, innovation, and environmental copiousness. This study will add value to future developments in academic theory and managerial practice by shedding light on the processes in which knowledge creation, sharing and use improve the uptake of environmentally friendly technologies. It offers useful information on how companies may use digital technologies and intellectual assets to develop viable and sustainable business models that are both viable and sustainable. In addition, the paper also highlights the fact that sustainability is not a compliance or branding activity but a strategic capability that is based on technological intelligence and knowledge based innovation. The future of organizations that wish to succeed in the shifting global sustainability environment is the development of an equilibrium between digital transformation and green awareness. Turning knowledge into ongoing and technology-driven innovation will enable businesses to attain higher efficiency, resilience, and social value; leading to a more sustainable economy that is beneficial to the organizations, communities, and the world at large. The study, therefore, provides an initial basis of new perspectives of sustainable digital entrepreneurship models.

REFERENCES

Alavi, M., & Leidner, D. E. (2001). Knowledge management and knowledge management systems: Conceptual foundations and research issues. *Management Information Systems Quarterly, 25*(1), 107–136. DOI: 10.2307/3250961

Bose, R., & Luo, X. (2014). Integrative framework for assessing firms' potential to undertake Green IT initiatives via virtualization – A theoretical perspective. *The Journal of Strategic Information Systems, 23*(1), 39–54.

Bose, R., & Luo, X. (2014). Integrative framework for assessing firms' potential to undertake Green IT initiatives via virtualization. *The Journal of Strategic Information Systems, 23*(1), 39–54.

Bose, R., & Luo, X. (2014). Integrative framework for assessing firms' potential to undertake Green IT initiatives via virtualization. *The Journal of Strategic Information Systems, 23*(1), 39–54.

Brooks, S., Wang, X., & Sarker, S. (2012). Unpacking Green IT: A review of the existing literature. *Information Systems Frontiers, 14*(5), 823–839.

Chow, W. S., & Chan, L. S. (2008). Social network, social trust and shared goals in organizational knowledge sharing. *Information & Management, 45*(7), 458–465. DOI: 10.1016/j.im.2008.06.007

Cohen, B. (2006). Sustainable valley entrepreneurial ecosystems. *Business Strategy and the Environment, 15*(1), 1–14. DOI: 10.1002/bse.428

Davis, F. D. (1989). Perceived usefulness, perceived ease of use, and user acceptance of information technology. *Management Information Systems Quarterly, 13*(3), 319–340. DOI: 10.2307/249008

Davis, F. D. (1989). Perceived usefulness, perceived ease of use, and user acceptance of information technology. *Management Information Systems Quarterly, 13*(3), 319–340. DOI: 10.2307/249008

Fornell, C., & Larcker, D. F. (1981). Evaluating structural equation models with unobservable variables and measurement error. *JMR, Journal of Marketing Research, 18*(1), 39–50. DOI: 10.1177/002224378101800104

Gold, A. H., Malhotra, A., & Segars, A. H. (2001). Knowledge management: An organizational capabilities perspective. *Journal of Management Information Systems, 18*(1), 185–214. DOI: 10.1080/07421222.2001.11045669

Gold, A. H., Malhotra, A., & Segars, A. H. (2001). Knowledge management: An organizational capabilities perspective. *Journal of Management Information Systems, 18*(1), 185–214. DOI: 10.1080/07421222.2001.11045669

Grant, R. M. (1996). Toward a knowledge-based theory of the firm. *Strategic Management Journal, 17*(S2), 109–122. DOI: 10.1002/smj.4250171110

Grant, R.M. (1996). "Toward a Knowledge-Based Theory of the Firm". *Strategic Management Journal.* **17** (Winter Special Issue): 109–122. doi:DOI: 10.1002/smj.4250171110

Hair, J. F., Hult, G. T. M., Ringle, C. M., & Sarstedt, M. (2021). *A Primer on Partial Least Squares Structural Equation Modeling (PLS-SEM)* (3rd ed.). Sage Publications. DOI: 10.1007/978-3-030-80519-7

Hair, J. F., Hult, G. T. M., Ringle, C. M., & Sarstedt, M. (2021). *A Primer on Partial Least Squares Structural Equation Modeling (PLS-SEM)* (3rd ed.). Sage Publications. DOI: 10.1007/978-3-030-80519-7

Hall, J. K., Daneke, G. A., & Lenox, M. J. (2010). Sustainable development and entrepreneurship: Past contributions and future directions. *Journal of Business Venturing, 25*(5), 439–448. DOI: 10.1016/j.jbusvent.2010.01.002

Lee, H., & Choi, B. (2003). Knowledge management enablers, processes, and organizational performance: An integrative view and empirical examination. *Journal of Management Information Systems, 20*(1), 179–228. DOI: 10.1080/07421222.2003.11045756

Mbugua, E. W., & Muchelule, Y. (2024). CLOUD COMPUTING TECHNOLOGY PRACTICES AND PERFORMANCE OF AGRICULTURE PROJECTS IN NYANDARUA COUNTY, KENYA. [IJSSME]. *International Journal of Social Sciences Management and Entrepreneurship, 8*(2).

Molla, A. (2009). Organizational motivations for green IT: Exploratory study. *Communications of the Association for Information Systems, 26*(1), 17–46.

Molla, A. (2009). Organizational motivations for green IT: Exploratory study. *Communications of the Association for Information Systems, 26*(1), 17–46.

Molla, A. (2009). Organizational motivations for green IT: Exploratory study. *Communications of the Association for Information Systems, 26*(1), 17–46.

Muñoz, P., & Cohen, B. (2018). Sustainable entrepreneurship research: Taking stock and looking ahead. *Business Strategy and the Environment, 27*(3), 300–322. DOI: 10.1002/bse.2000

Nonaka, I. (1994). A dynamic theory of organizational knowledge creation. *Organization Science*, *5*(1), 14–37. DOI: 10.1287/orsc.5.1.14

Nonaka, I., & Takeuchi, H. (1995). *The Knowledge-Creating Company*. Oxford University Press. DOI: 10.1093/oso/9780195092691.001.0001

OECD. (2021). *OECD Science, Technology and Innovation Outlook 2021: Times of Crisis and Opportunity*. OECD Publishing.

Podsakoff, P. M., MacKenzie, S. B., Lee, J. Y., & Podsakoff, N. P. (2003). Common method biases in behavioral research. *The Journal of Applied Psychology*, *88*(5), 879–903. DOI: 10.1037/0021-9010.88.5.879 PMID: 14516251

Shepherd, D. A., & Patzelt, H. (2011). The new field of sustainable entrepreneurship: Studying entrepreneurial action linking "what is to be sustained" with "what is to be developed". *Entrepreneurship Theory and Practice*, *35*(1), 137–163. DOI: 10.1111/j.1540-6520.2010.00426.x

Shepherd, D. A., & Patzelt, H. (2011). The new field of sustainable entrepreneurship. *Entrepreneurship Theory and Practice*, *35*(1), 137–163. DOI: 10.1111/j.1540-6520.2010.00426.x

Shepherd, D. A., & Patzelt, H. (2011). The new field of sustainable entrepreneurship. *Entrepreneurship Theory and Practice*, *35*(1), 137–163. DOI: 10.1111/j.1540-6520.2010.00426.x

Teece, D. J. (2018). Business models and dynamic capabilities. *Long Range Planning*, *51*(1), 40–49. DOI: 10.1016/j.lrp.2017.06.007

Zahra, S. A., Gedajlovic, E., Neubaum, D. O., & Shulman, J. M. (2012). A typology of social entrepreneurs: Motives, search processes and ethical challenges. *Journal of Business Venturing*, *27*(5), 519–532. DOI: 10.1016/j.jbusvent.2008.04.007

Chapter 5
The Mediating Role of AI-Driven Leadership Decision Making in the Relationship Between Green AI and Sustainable Leadership Behaviors

Malik Habib
http://orcid.org/0009-0001-8930-4267
City Unversity, Ajman, UAE

Jalaludeen Kuzhikkala
City University, Ajman, UAE

ABSTRACT

This study focuses on the employment of AI towards Sustainable Leadership Behaviors through its influence on leadership decision making with a focus on environmental welfare. Based on the data gathered from professionals working in the banking industry in the UAE. This paper studies how AI Readiness, AI Tools & Systems, AI Competency, and AI Governance & Ethical Integration impact AI-Driven Leadership Decision Making and subsequently Sustainable Leadership Behaviors. Using quantitative approach and regression based mediation analysis, the results demonstrate that AI enablers play a significant role in improving AI-Driven Leadership Decision Making which positively influences sustainability oriented leadership practices. The results further confirm that AI-Driven Leadership Decision Making is an important mechanism by which AI capabilities are transformed into environmentally respon-

DOI: 10.4018/979-8-2600-1348-9.ch005

sible leadership behaviors. The significance of this research is the contribution of bridging the gap between AI and the sustainability of the environment by making leadership behaviors as a central link between technology and sustainable outcomes. This research gives a good idea to organizations and policy makers interested in ensuring that AI is aligned to long term ecological health by integrating AI in leadership operations rather than focusing on AI operational efficiency.

1.INTRODUCTION

1.1 Emergence of AI in Modern Organizations

The development of Artificial Intelligence (AI) has had an immense significant impact upon the way modern organizations operate, with the evolution of AI beyond its role as technical facilitator to its position as the central element of strategic assets affecting almost every aspect of business performance. AI technologies such as machine learning, natural language processing and predictive analytics have supported the essential process of decision making in organizations, increased accuracy in operations functionality, and shifted to data driven strategic planning (Brynjolfsson & McAfee, 2017). As industries introduce digital solutions at massive scales, AI has become a core source of innovation, automation, and competitive advantage across industries, including manufacturing, logistics, finance and government services (Bughin et al., 2018). The integration of AI has also helped in the structuring of organizational structures and workflows in order to allow firms to optimize allocation of resources and also anticipate challenges in the operation with higher accuracy (Davenport & Ronaki, 2018). The expansion of AI is reinforced by global research concerning digital transformation, advancements of cloud computing, and increased investment to Big Data infrastructure (Wamba et al., 2021). Companies who adopt AI can often see efficient gains as well as greater predictive validity and increased resilience in volatile environemnts, thus showing AI is an important key to develop strategies. As a result, AI has become one of the most influential developments in technology in the 21st century which shifted the paradigm of how organizations produce, deliver, and sustain value.

1.2 AI in Sustainability

The ability of AI technologies to analyze intricate datasets about the ecology and promote further environmental developments turned out to be integrated into the personal sphere of environmental sustainability successfully. Researches indicate the AI based solutions have become more common to optimize the structure of energy grids, for better integration of renewable energy resources, and better energy efficiency in industrial processes that are large in scale (Kumar et al., 2021). AI helps in environmental monitoring to identify the sources of pollution, identify the dynamics of deforestation, help in identifying the pattern of deforestation, and predict the climate disaster, which will help in proactively responding to governments and industries (Bai et al., 2022). In terms of waste management, AI makes it much more possible to carry out automated sorting, recycle more efficiently, and to support circular economy models with the goal of reducing material waste (Bressanelli et al., 2022). Machine learning algorithms are also important in water management, detecting leakages, predicting consumptions and limiting environmental loss in water distribution networks (Rolnick et al., 2022). Moreover, AI based environmental simulation tools help organizations to evaluate their long term ecological impacts that occur from their operations and adopt more sustainable environmental strategies. These applications show the growing role of AI in the preservation of the environment and protection of natural resources.

1.3 AI in Business and Organizational Sustainability

Within the framework of organizations, AI supports the means of sustainability, precisely by providing more transparency, optimizing processes, and even allowing the resources to be used more responsibly throughout the value chains. Supply chain researches focuses on the value of AI to enhance carbon tracking and lower emissions in transportations and to enhance sustainable sourcing by having visibility into all real time activities throughout global networks. Material needs can be predicted by AI supported predictive analytics, which helps organizations to plan for minimum material needs and avoid unnecessary production, which results in environmental burdens created by overconsumptions and waste (Rana et al., 2023). Digital twins and AI enabled optimization algorithms enable companies to redesign production processes to be more ecofriendly by reducing energy consumption which makes their operations more sustainable (Bressanelli et al., 2022). AI is also a way to enhance risk management by pinpointing the vulnerabilities of sustainability and ensuring that firms tend to operate in a greener manner (Centobelli et al., 2020). Studies further indicate that organizations that deploy AI report improvements in measures of environmental performance in terms of reduction of emissions, decreased waste, and increased compliance with sustainability standards (George et al., 2020; Wamba et al., 2021). These results show the increasing influence of AI in corporate sustainability transformation.

1.4 AI-Driven Leadership Decision Making

The contribution of AI in raising the level of Sustainable Leadership Behaviors is huge, as it provides the leaders with a certain competitive advantage in the form of knowledge that can be used as an addition to ethical, long term, and environment friendly decision making. It has been identified that leaders are able to be more accurate in analyzing environmental data with the aid of AI that can assist them in comprehending sustainability risks and opportunities that may be linked with sustainability (Del Giudice, 2022). Leaders utilize predictive analytics to evaluate the ecological impacts of strategic decisions to make sure that a more informed judge is made in connection with sustainability goals (Bathula et al., 2021). Furthermore, AI also contributes to the increase in environmental awareness since it monitors environmental sustainability performance indicators constantly, and leaders receive insights to act upon (Jarrahi, 2018). Such capabilities contribute to the increased level of ability to implement sustainability oriented policies, distribute resources properly, and organize functions at the organization to align with environmental interests (Afsar & Umrani, 2020). Leaders can also use AI to communicate sustainability objectives to employees more effectively, thus establishing a company culture where the importance of environmental care is a main priority (Mittal & Dhar, 2016).

1.5 AI's Role in Supporting Green Culture, Innovation, and Sustainability Performance

AI's contribution to sustainable leadership goes beyond the decision making process to creating organizational culture, innovation processes, and overall sustainability performance. AI enabled systems are questioning leaders to incorporate sustainability values into their organizational routine through data driven learning and transparent environmental reporting (Centobelli et al., 2020). These tools enable leaders to identify ways to improve inefficiencies and implement targeted interventions as a mean to minimize waste and to enhance resource efficiency. AI is also helpful for ecofriendly innovations and in helping leaders find opportunities for greener product developments and environmentally sustainable technologies (Zhang et al., 2022). By enhancing the capacity of leaders in the organization to monitor sustainability metrics, AI helps them by strengthening the culture of accountability and ensure that the environmental performance is aligned with the strategic goals of the organization (Del Giudice, 2022). More so, AI is promoting collaborative efforts in attaining sustainability goals by improving communication, knowledge sharing, and cross functional problem solving (George et al., 2020). Through these mechanisms, AI reinforces the influence of leaders on the outcomes of organizational sustainability.

1.6 Research Gap, Significance, and Environmental Contribution

As AI is present in the sustainability community. The gap concerning the role of AI Readiness, AI Tools, AI Competency, and AI Governance in Sustainability Leadership Behaviors is significant. Though, the current literature examines the uses of AI in environmental tracking, reduction of emissions, productivity, and the usage of AI in assisting leaders in developing environmental consciousness, green society, and the innovation with sustainability is not common. Although the provided researches discuss the functions of AI in environmental monitoring, emissions reduction, and operational efficiency they seldom examine the functions of AI as the contributor of helping leaders promote the growth of environmental awareness, green culture and sustainability oriented innovation (George et al., 2020; Dwivedi et al., 2021). There are also no empirical realizations in the literature about the role of organizational readiness, AI Competency, and adopting AI tools in the sustainability behaviors of the leaders. This gap can be observed more particularly in the emerging economies, including the UAE, where AI integration is increasingly prevalent due to national strategies of digital transformations, and where limited research has examined the behavioral implication of leadership. This relationship is vital to know because of the involvement of the leader's cooperation in making strategic and operational practices sustainable. Hence this study aims to contribute to the field by explaining more about sustainable leadership practices in organizational environments through the assistance of AI.

1.7 Environmental Importance and Broader Contribution

Addressing the research gap is vital for environmental protection and sustainability due to enhancing leaders of organizations across the globe. Sustainable leadership is achieved with the help of AI, which means the dangerous impact of in the environment will be reduced considerably through responsible consumption of resources, decreased quantities of emissions, and ecofriendly innovations in various industries (Bai, 2020). Leaders that are AI-driven are more effective at spearheading green programs, impacting sustainability behaviors of employees, and making green practices institutionalized (Afsar & Umrani, 2020). This contributed to a larger environmental benefit such as lessening waste, promoting energy consumption and more long-term ecological resilience (Zhang et al., 2022). After discussing how AI helps to enhance Sustainable Leadership Behaviors, our research offers a framework that can help organizations balances the use of AI with environmental sustainability. Ultimately, our research shows the importance of how AI-Driven Leadership in environmental sustainability.

2.LITERATURE REVIEW

2.1 Overview of AI in Organizations

AI has rapidly become a staple in the modern organizational world, and it has helped to transform the way companies operate, compete and make decisions. Rather than being the background tool it is now the foreground of supporting organizations to be able to analyze information, predict trends and solve complex problems by using AI. Technologies such as machine learning, natural language processing and predictive analytics are helping companies manage big data and identify patterns where they have been invisible by hand (Brynjolfsson & McAfee, 2017). These capabilities have led to more and more organizations in industries as varied as manufacturing, logistics and finance integrate AI into day-to-day operations, resulting in enhancements in efficiency, forecasting accuracy and innovation (Bughin et al., 2018; Davenport & Ronanki, 2018). Big data, cloud computing and digital transformation initiatives has accelerated this shift that have made AI a central component to strategic planning and process optimization, and organizational resilience (Wamba et al., 2021; Zhang et al., 2022). In essence, AI is becoming less of a choice and is increasingly becoming an integral part of the backbone of how modern organizations create value, manage complexity and adapt to change.

2.2 AI Readiness

Successful AI adoption relies heavily on the technological infrastructure and overall readiness of an organization to adopt advanced technology infrastructure. Firms need robust data platforms, secure and functional digital platforms, as well as computing capabilities that can support AI tools that rely on quality and real-time information (Bughin et al., 2018). However, readiness is so much more than hardware and software. Organizations also have to have leadership commitment, alignment of strategy, and a culture that facilitates experimentation and digital transformation (Davenport & Ronanki, 2018). Research clearly shows that companies with high digital maturity and organizational readiness receive more value in AI initiatives in terms of both operational and sustainability-related improvements in less time (Wamba et al., 2021; Zhang et al., 2022). Moreover, readiness influences how well the organizations can leverage AI in environment management, including carbon tracking, emissions forecasting, and sustainability analytics (Vinuesa et al., 2020).

2.3 AI Competency

Another necessary condition of effective AI implementation is the human skill preparation as even the most sophisticated tools cannot work without the people, who are aware of how to use them. Leaders and employees should be digitally literate, analytical, and be able to make sense of AI-generated knowledge (Brynjolfsson et al., 2019). Research indicates that human resistance to AI is one of the most prevalent obstacles to adopting AI, which results in unwillingness to use AI systems, lack of alignment, and misuse (Jarrahi, 2018). Simultaneously, those organizations that commit to training, reskilling, and sharing knowledge, provide the conditions in which individuals cooperate with AI instead of being afraid of it (Del Giudice, 2022). This form of preparedness is particularly significant in more sustainability-oriented jobs whereby employees must be capable of comprehending environmental information and utilizing AI knowledge to make judgments (Vinuesa et al., 2020). Human preparedness hence makes the implementation of AI a strategic gain and not a disruptive force.

2.4 AI Tools

AI technologies such as predictive analytics, machine learning platforms, digital twins, and automation systems are at the center of help in delivering sustainability and leadership services in institutions. They allow companies to simulate environmental effects, manage resources, track emissions, and enhance transparency in the activities of business operations (Bai et al., 2020). Along with environmental uses, AI Tools are beneficial in leadership decision-making, offering scenario simulation, sustainability risks, and insights that can be used in long-term planning (Shrestha et al., 2021). They also promote cultural change through sharing sustainability information to the various departments, promoting green practices among departments, and ensuring accountability toward the environment (Afsar & Umrani, 2020). With the AI Tools becoming increasingly part of human everyday activities, they do not only act as technical tools but also as primary facilitators of sustainability oriented leadership and organizational change.

2.5 AI Governance & Ethical Integration

AI Governance & Ethical Integration is crucial for ensuring that the application of AI is being used in a responsible manner as part of organizational leadership and decision-making processes. AI governance means the policies, oversight and accountability systems that govern how AI systems are developed and used, whereas ethical integration means ensuring consistency with organizational values and societal obligations (Floridi et al., 2018). Prior studies emphasize the fact that poor governance of AI can result in biased decisions, a lack of transparency, and a lack of trust in the outcomes of leadership with AI support (Dwivedi et al., 2021). In contrast, good ethical governance frameworks help leaders to trust AI insights with more confidence and aid in informed, transparent and sustainability-focused decision making (Raisch & Krakowski, 2021). This is especially relevant in sectors such as banking, where leadership decisions have far-reaching social and ecological implications, so AI governance is an essential enabler of responsible and sustainable leadership practices (Vinuesa et al., 2020).

2.6 Overview of Sustainable Leadership

Sustainable Leadership is a style of leadership that goes to the extent of incorporating environmental protection, ethical decision making and long term value creation into the core organization strategy. Based on the concept of the triple bottom line, sustainable leaders put the economic growth at the same level with environmental and social responsibilities (Elkington, 2018). They facilitate green innovation, stimulate environmentally friendly activities and make sure that the organizational processes do not stray off the general sustainability objectives (Afsar & Umrani, 2020). The studies demonstrate that sustainable leadership improves environmental affect, builds a higher level of resilience, and increases the level of trust in the stakeholders because the leadership decisions are made based on responsibility and a long-term perspective (Bai, 2020). Such leaders establish an organizational culture that embraces transparency, accountability, and constant environmental enhancement, and sustainability is a part of the identity of the organization, not an individual project (George et al., 2020).

2.7 Environmental Awareness & Responsibility

Environmental awareness and responsibility are the awareness of the leader regarding ecological issues and willingness to make the organization less damaging to the environment. When leaders are very environment conscious, they can recognize risks of sustainability, adopt green policies, and encourage employees to be eco conscious (Bai, 2020). It has been demonstrated that such awareness is closely connected with a positive environmental performance, lower emissions and enhanced environmental regulations compliance (Rana et al., 2023). These leaders are also proponents of environmental innovations and invest into technologies that promote sustainability, such as AI powered emissions monitoring and energy optimization systems (Zhang et al., 2022). Choosing personal values in relation to organizational practices, environmentally conscious leaders form collective practices and contribute to instilling sustainability into strategic and operational procedures (Afsar & Umrani, 2020).

2.8 Green Organizational Culture

The green organizational culture is developed when the environmental values, norms and practices are integrated into the daily organizational processes. Leaders can be central to the creation of such cultures through their leadership position which involves role modeling of sustainable behaviors, encouraging environmental training, as well as making sustainability a collective departmental responsibility (Mittal & Dhar, 2016). Research indicates that companies that have well developed green cultures record improved environmental performance, greater participation of employees in sustainability efforts, and more adherence to environmentally friendly activities (Centobelli et al., 2020). This culture is cultivated by leaders with clear communications, educational learning, and collaborative working across functional lines in terms of environmental goals (George et al., 2020). A green culture is also more likely to enhance the work of AI-driven sustainability systems since employees become more ready to use new technologies when environmental responsibility is already manifested in organizational culture.

2.9 Resource Efficiency & Waste Reduction

The key pillars of sustainable leadership are resource efficiency and waste minimization as they include reducing the environmental impact, but increasing the operational performance. The leaders who would focus on efficient resource utilization can enable the reduction of emissions, waste, and environmental performance throughout the organization (Bressanelli et al., 2022). They help to embrace the principles of a circular economy by incorporating technologies that minimize the use of materials or promote their reuse or recycling (Kumar et al., 2021). The studies indicate that among the most effective indicators of successful waste minimization programs and eco efficiency increase, there is the leadership commitment. Leaders make sure that optimization of the resources becomes a long-term organizational priority by incorporating sustainability in procurement, production, and operational decisions (Bai, 2020).

2.10 Sustainable Performance & Innovation

Sustainable performance and innovation are an aspect that indicates how a company can meet long term environmental, social, and economic objectives and present green technologies and practices. Sustainable leaders promote the development of green innovation, welcome the creation of products in an environmentally friendly manner, and encourage the application of the latest technologies including AI to reinforce the sustainability performance (Centobelli et al., 2020). Such leaders create conditions in which sustainability is achieved through creativity, experimentation, and continuous improvement (Zhang et al., 2022). Sustainable innovation brings the organization in line with the world sustainability standards, increases competitiveness, and increases the long-term ecological resilience (George et al., 2020). AI is becoming more and more relevant to this process, as it enables measuring sustainability and predictive modeling and promotes data driven innovation.

2.11 AI-Driven Leadership Decision Making & Gaps in Literature

AI is a highly significant force of sustainable leadership since it equips leaders with more data driven insights, which enhance the strength of environmentally responsible decision making. Predictive analytics and real time monitoring systems are as well tools that allow leaders to know how resources are consumed and how ecological risks can be anticipated and better plan to achieve long-term sustainability (Vinuesa et al., 2020; Shrestha et al., 2021). Simultaneously, AI simplifies the process of establishing a green organizational culture as it will facilitate the exchange of environmental information among teams and motivate employees to develop values of sustainability (Afsar & Umrani, 2020; Del Giudice, 2022). However, even with its increasing presence, the majority of current studies continue to pay attention to the technical advantages of AI instead of its impact on the leadership behaviors and sustainability oriented activities (George et al., 2020; Dwivedi et al., 2021). That is why it is needed to examine the role of AI Readiness, human capabilities, and AI solutions in the ecosystem in a rapidly developing setting such as the UAE where the digital transformation and sustainability goals are co-evolving.

3. HYPOTHESIS FORMULATION & THEORETICAL FRAMEWORK

AI has become more and more accepted as a catalyst in developing leadership and organizational sustainability. The previous studies indicate that AI allows leaders to have access to high quality data, prediction and real time analytics that enhances the accuracy of the decision made, ethical judgment and long term strategic thinking (Brynjolfsson & McAfee, 2017). In terms of sustainability, AI offers leaders the capacity to track environmental indicators, evaluate resource efficiency and predict ecological risks that can support leadership behaviors that foster environmental responsibility and ecological well-being (Vinuesa et al., 2020).

However, the impact of AI on Sustainable Leadership Behaviors does not happen automatically. Instead, it relies on the presence of organizational enablers which makes or breaks the effective use of AI in leadership decision making. AI Readiness measures how much organizations have the digital infrastructure, quality of data, strategic alignment and leadership support that will enable AI-related initiatives to be successfully implemented. Research shows that organizations with higher levels of AI Readiness are more likely to incorporate AI into managerial and leadership processes and help leaders leverage AI-driven insights to make strategic and sustainability-related decisions (Davenport & Ronanki, 2018; Wamba et al., 2021). In these environments, leaders are more able to consider long term impacts on their environment and align organizational activities with ecological objectives. Therefore, the following hypothesis was created:

H1 AI Readiness has a positive impact on AI-driven leadership decision making.

The availability and effective deployment of AI Tools and Systems also play a critical part in influencing leadership decision making. AI technologies (predictive analytics, sustainability dashboards, digital twin, and intelligent monitoring systems) offer leaders actionable insights regarding emissions, energy and resource utilization. Prior research shows that when such tools are integrated into organization processes, leaders are more likely to use AI generated information in planning, forecasting and sustainability oriented decisions (Shrestha et al., 2021). As a result, AI Tools and Systems enhance leader's ability to make informed decisions for the sustainability of the environment. Based on this reasoning, the following hypothesis is made:

H2 AI Tools and Systems have a positive impact on AI-driven leadership decision making

AI Competency is how far leaders are knowledgeable, analytical and confident to comprehend and utilize AI insights. Studies on human-AI interaction points out that leaders with higher AI competency are more likely to trust AI systems and incorporate them into complex decision making processes as well as those related to environmental management as well as sustainability strategies (Jarrahi, 2018; Brynjolfsson et al., 2019). The competency of leaders helps them convert environmental information into responsible decision making that will balance organizational performance and ecological welfare. As a result, the following hypothesis is formulated:

H3 AI Competency has a positive impact on AI-driven leadership decision making.

Beyond the aspects of readiness, tools, and competency, AI Governance and Ethical Integration are adding an increasingly seen aspect that, in fact, determines the responsible use of AI. Ethical AI governance provides for transparency, accountability and alignment between AI applications and long term environmental and societal values (Floridi et al., 2018). Research suggests that leaders are more willing to rely on AI-driven insights when there are clear governance frameworks, especially in decision making requirements which involve sustainability and ecological responsibility (Vinuesa et al., 2020). Ethical integration helps to bolster the confidence of leaders around AI systems and enables ethical use in environmentally-responsible decision making. Accordingly, the following hypothesis is formulated:

H4 AI Governance and Ethical Integration have a positive impact on AI-driven leadership decision making.

AI-driven leadership decision making is conceptualized as the extent to which leaders actively rely on AI based analytics and decision support systems when making strategic and operational choices. Prior literature shows that AI-Driven Decision Making helps leaders to improve their environmental awareness, ethical judgment and long term orientation, all are core characteristics of Sustainable Leadership Behaviors (Del Giudice, 2022; Afsar & Umrani, 2020). By offering leaders the ability to evaluate the impact of ecology, make the most efficient use of resources, and encourage green practices, AI decision making in leadership is a vital mechanism by which organizations attain sustainability oriented leadership and contribute to ecological welfare. Therefore, the final hypothesis of this study is formulated:

H5 AI-driven leadership decision making has a positive impact on sustainable leadership behaviors.

Figure 1. Sustainable leadership behaviors

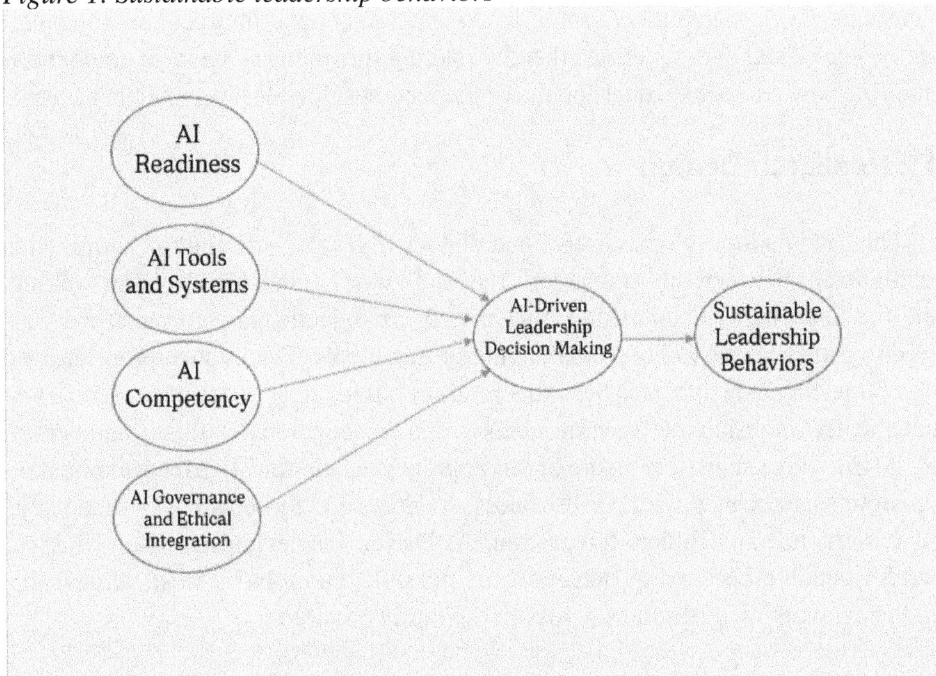

4. RESEARCH METHODOLOGY

4.1 Research Context and Sector

The banking and financial services industry in the UAE was chosen as the empirical background for this study. This sector is one of the most advanced and regulated sectors in the UAE, with wide-spread adoption of AI technologies, robust leadership structures and mounting pressure to incorporate sustainability and environmental considerations in strategic decision making. UAE banks are aggressively adopting AI powered systems for credit evaluation, risk management, fraud detection, forecasting and environmental, social and governance (ESG) analytics, making this sector a very suitable to study AI-Driven Leadership Decision Making.

In addition, sustainability has become a strategic priority in the UAE banking sector because of regulatory expectations, national sustainability initiatives, and global

ESG standards. Financial institutions are at the forefront of influencing the state of our ecology through the provision of finance for green-businesses, financial-risk-management of climate related risks, and incorporating sustainability principles into governance models (Central Bank of the UAE, 2023; World Economic Forum, 2022). Consequently, leadership choices in banks have direct and indirect consequences on the ecological consequences, thereby making this industry an ideal context for studying how AI-enabled decision making affects sustainable leadership behaviors.

4.2 Research Design

This study adopts a quantitative and deductive research design to examine the relationships between the AI enablers, the AI-Driven Leadership Decision Making and the Sustainable Leadership Behaviors. A cross-sectional survey method was used to gather primary data from banking professionals. This is an appropriate design for testing data that have been theoretically based, and also identify significant statistical relationships between variables within organizational settings (Saunders et al., 2016). The quantitative nature of this approach means objective measurement of perceptions associated with AI Readiness, AI Tools and Systems, AI Competency, AI Governance and Ethical Integration, AI-Driven Leadership Decision Making and Sustainable Leadership Behaviors are possible, and robust statistical analysis and generalization of findings across the sector is possible.

4.3 Target Population

The target population of this study is the leaders and managerial-level professionals operating in banking and financial institutions based in the UAE. These individuals are directly involved in strategic, operational, digital and sustainability-related decision making, and hence, have the knowledge to assess the usage of AI and leadership behaviors within their organizations.

The respondent's roles targeted include:

- Senior Managers
- Department Heads
- Risk and Compliance Managers
- Sustainability or ESG Managers
- IT Managers

A probability-based sampling technique, called systematic random sampling, was used in order to assure representative participation from different banking institutions. This method is highly recommended in organizational research because of its efficiency and capability to reduce the selection bias.

The exact population size of managerial and professional employees in the banking and financial services industry in UAE is not made public. However, official reports from the Central Bank of the UAE and national labor statistics state that the sector employs tens of thousands of professionals from commercial banks, Islamic and international banks. In accordance with guidelines for the methodology of research, populations of more than 50,000 may be treated as if they are large or infinite for the purposes of determining the sample size (Saunders et al., 2016; Hair et al., 2017). Accordingly, a conservative population estimation of 50 000 was used for the sample size calculation. According to the confidence level 95%, margin of error 5% and response distribution 50%, the sample size requirement was calculated to be 382 respondents. This sample size is considered adequate for regression and mediation analysis and provides adequate statistical power for hypothesis testing.

Figure 2. Data results

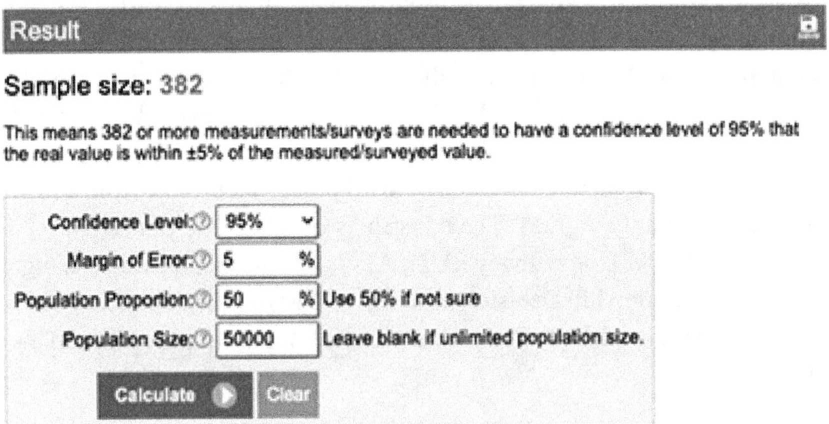

4.4 Data Collection

Primary data were obtained using a self-administered structured questionnaire distributed via Google Forms. This method was chosen because of its efficiency, accessibility and suitability for reaching professionals in multiple banking institutions. Online survey is a common method in management and technology adoption research especially when the subject is geographically dispersed and has digital literacy (Saunders et al., 2016). Participation was voluntary and respondents were assured of anonymity and confidentiality in order to get honest and unbiased responses. Ethics of research the data collection process was in line with ethical research standards.

5. DATA ANALYSIS

This section introduces the data analysis procedures that are used to analyze the survey responses and assess the empirical findings in relation to the research objectives and conceptual framework. The analysis focuses on developing a clear and systematic understanding of how AI enablers affect AI-Driven Leadership Decision Making and Sustainable Leadership Behaviors. Reliability analysis was performed by the use of Cronbach's alpha to test the internal consistency of the measurement items and to establish the accuracy and dependability of the research instrument. Construct validity was also investigated by Factor Analysis to ensure that the items are appropriate to represent the constructs they are intended to represent. Correlation analysis was used to determine the direction and strength of the relationships of the study variables. In addition, the proposed hypotheses were also tested using regression analysis to examine the effect of independent variables on mediating and dependent variables. All statistical analyses were carried out by using Statistical Package for the Social Sciences (SPSS), which has the analytical tools needed to evaluate the proposed research model.

The questionnaire items were measured in a 5 point Likert scale from 1 (Strongly Disagree) to 5 (Strongly Agree). The constructs of AI Readiness (AR), AI Tools and Systems (ATS), AI Competency (AC), AI Governance and Ethical Integration (AG), AI-Driven Leadership Decision Making (AIDM) and Sustainable Leadership Behaviors (SLB) are explored. These abbreviations are used quite often in the data analysis.

Table 1. Characteristics of Respondents

%	**Frequency**		**Gender**
80.1%	306	**Male**	
19.9%	76	**Female**	
100.0%	382		**Total**
			Age
21.5%	82	**25-34**	
50.8%	194	**35-44**	
27.7%	106	**45-54**	

continued on following page

Table 1. Continued

%	Frequency		Gender
100.0%	382		**Total**
			Education Level
59.2%	226	**Bachelor Degree**	
34.6%	132	**Master's Degree**	
6.3&	24	**PHD Degree**	
100.0%	382		**Total**
			Position
16.5%	63	**Senior Manager**	
30.9%	118	**Department Heads**	
19.4%	74	**Risk & Compliance Managers**	
12.3%	47	**ESG/ Sustainability Managers**	
20.9%	80	**IT Managers**	
100.%	382		**Total**
			AI years of experience
22.0%	84	**1 to 2 years**	
60.7%	232	**3 to 5 years**	
17.3%	66	**More than 5 years**	
100%	382		**Total**

5.1 Reliability Test

Reliability analysis was undertaken to determine the internal consistency of measurement scales used in the study. Cronbach's alpha was calculated for each construct in order to see whether the questionnaire items were reliable measures of the variables they were designed to measure. The results show that all constructs obtained Cronbach's alpha values exceeding the recommended value of 0.70 demonstrating satisfactory internal consistency and confirming the adequacy of the measurement instrument for further analysis. The results will be presented in Table 2.

5.2 Validity Test using Factor Analysis

Questionnaire validity is the degree to which the measurement items are representative of what they are supposed to measure. In this study, the construct validity was determined through the exploratory factor analysis based on the factor loading level. Each construct was separately analyzed to see if the measurement items loaded appropriately on their intended factors. As shown in Table2, all the items loaded positively and strongly on their respective constructs with the factor loadings ranging from 0.74 to 0.94 which exceeds the recommended threshold. These results confirm that the items in the measurement adequately represent the constructs underlying and that the questionnaire is valid and suitable for subsequent regression and mediating analyses. The extensive results of factor loadings are presented in Table 2.

Table 2. Extensive results of factor loadings

Scale	Item	Factor Loadings	Cronbach's Alpha
1-AI Readiness	The organization has a clear strategy for adopting AI technologies.	0.84	0.89
	Top management in my organization supports the use of AI in decision making.	0.85	
	My organization has adequate financial resources to invest in AI.	0.78	
	Employees are encouraged to embrace AI-driven solutions in their daily work.	0.82	
	The organizational culture is open to technological change and innovation.	0.78	
2-AI Tools and Systems	My organizations use AI based systems to support managerial decision making.	0.83	0.85
	AI tools in my organization provide accurate and timely information for leaders.	0.79	
	AI systems are integrated with existing organizational processes.	0.88	
	AI tools enhance the efficiency of leadership and management activities.	0.81	
	AI based analytics are regularly used to evaluate performance and outcomes.	0.77	
3- AI Competency	Leaders in my organizations possess sufficient knowledge to understand AI outputs.	0.78	0.83
	Managers are trained to use AI systems effectively.	0.85	
	My organization provides continuous learning related to AI technologies.	0.76	
	Leaders can interpret AI-generated insights when making decisions.	0.82	
	Employees feel confident using AI based tools in their work.	0.74	

continued on following page

Table 2. Continued

Scale	Item	Factor Loadings	Cronbach's Alpha
4- AI Governance and Ethical Integration	My organization has clear polies governing the ethical use of AI.	0.86	0.86
	AI systems are used in a transparent and accountable manner.	0.83	
	Leadership ensures that AI decisions are aligned with organizational values.	0.79	
	Potential ethical risks associated with AI are actively monitored.	0.82	
	AI is implemented in compliance with legal and regulatory requirements.	0.77	
5- AI driven Leadership Decision Making	Leader in my organization rely on AI insights when making strategic decisions.	0.88	0.89
	AI systems support leaders in evaluating alternative courses of action.	0.85	
	AI enhances the quality of leadership decision making.	0.82	
	Leaders combine AI based recommendations with their own judgment.	0.85	
	AI helps leaders make more informed and consistent decisions.	0.80	
6- Sustainable Leadership Behaviors	Leaders in my organization consider environmental impacts when making decisions.	0.87	0.92
	Leadership promotes sustainable and environmentally responsible practices.	0.84	
	Leaders encourage efficient use of organizational resources.	0.82	
	Sustainability is integrated into long-term leadership planning.	0.85	
	Leaders support initiatives that reduce environmental harm.	0.78	
	Leadership decisions aim to balance economic performance with ecological well-being.	0.94	

5.3 Regression Analysis

Model 1 Predicting AI-Driven Leadership Decision Making

Multiple regression analysis was performed to analyze the extent to which the AI enablers affect AI-Driven Leadership Decision Making. AI Readiness, AI Tools and Systems, AI Competency, AI Governance, and Ethical Integration were entered as independent variables at the same time. The results show that the model accounts for a significant amount of variance in the AI-Driven Leadership Decision Making and all predictors have a statistically significant positive impact. This implies that the organizational readiness, technological capabilities, human competence and ethical governance are together the key elements that boost the leader's dependence on AI in decision making processes.

Table 3. Model Summary

Model Summary				
Model	**R**	**R Square**	**Adjusted R Square**	**Std. Error of the Estimate**
1	.82[a]	.67	.66	.31

Table 4. ANOVA[a]

ANOVA[a]						
Model		**Sum of Squares**	**df**	**Mean Square**	**F**	**Sig.**
1	Regression	24.860	4	6.215	191.03	<.001[b]
	Residual	12.225	377	.032		
	Total	37.085	381			

The ANOVA results indicate that the regression model is statistically significant ($p < .001$), confirming the overall fitness of the model.

Table 5. Coefficients[a]

Coefficients[a]						
		Unstandardized Coefficients		Standardized Coefficients		
Model		B	Std. Error	Beta	t	Sig.
1	(Constant)	3.087	.231		13.36	<.001
	AR	.184	.031	.241	5.94	<.001
	ATS	.162	.032	.213	5.15	<.001
1	AC	.149	.032	.196	4.71	<.001
	AG	.201	.031	.262	6.38	<.001

All the predictors have a positive statistically significant effect on AI Driven Leadership Decision Making, supporting hypotheses H1 through H4.

5.4 Regression Analysis Predicting Sustainable Leadership Behaviors

A second regression analysis was performed to look at the mediating factor on the dependent variable. The results suggest a positive and statistically significant impact of AI-Driven Leadership Decision Making on Sustainable Leadership Behaviors thus proving hypothesis H5.

Table 6. Model Summary

Model Summary				
Model	R	R Square	Adjusted R Square	Std. Error of the Estimate
1	.74[a]	.55	.55	.34

Table 7. Coefficients

Predictor		Unstandardized Coefficients		Standardized Coefficients	t	Sig.
		B	Std. Error	Beta		
1	(AIDM)	.742	.037	.74	19.91	<.001

The results suggest partial mediation because the inclusion of the mediator made the direct impact of the AI enablers less significant, but not insignificant. The results confirm that AI-Driven Leadership Decision Making functions as an important mechanism by which AI enablers affect sustainability oriented leadership behaviors.

6. FINDINGS

The results of the data analysis demonstrate a statistically significant and positive impact of all AI enablers studied in this research on AI-Driven Leadership Decision Making. Moreover, AI readiness, AI tools and systems, AI competency and AI Governance and Ethical Integration were found to play a meaningful role in how much leaders rely on insights supported by AI in their decision-making. The regression analysis showed that the proposed model contributed to a significant percent variance in AI-Driven Leadership Decision Making and that the overall model was statistically significant. These findings confirm that there are organizational, technological, human, and governance-related AI capabilities that collectively impact leadership decision processes.

In addition, the present findings show a strong and positive relationship between AI-Driven Leadership Decision Making and Sustainable Leadership Behaviors. Leaders who more heavily incorporate AI into their decision-making processes are likely to exhibit additional behaviors consistent with sustainability goals such as long-term planning, resource efficiency and consideration of the environment. The mediation analysis provides further evidence of the AI-Driven Leadership Decision Making as a significant mechanism for AI enablers to impact Sustainable Leadership Behaviors. Collectively, these results support all the proposed hypotheses empirically, and support the validity of the study's conceptual framework.

7. DISCUSSIONS

The results of this study are in agreement with the critical role of AI enablers in influencing AI-Driven Leadership Decision Making which subsequently affects the Sustainable Leadership Behaviors. The results are that AI Readiness, AI Tools and Systems, AI Competency and AI Governance and Ethical Integration all have a significant impact on AI-Driven Leadership Decision Making. This appears to identify that leader dependence on AI is not simply a technological consequence of leadership but rather a product of an integrated organization environment with strategic preparedness, technological infrastructure, human capability, and ethical oversight all occurring together. These findings are in line with other research that highlights the importance of AI generating value when integrated into leadership and governance structures and not being seen as a technological solution on its own.

The study also goes on to show that AI-Driven Leadership Decision Making has a strong positive effect on Sustainable Leadership Behaviors because of the supportive mechanism it provides which helps leaders to consider the long term environmental impacts, resource efficiency and ecological responsibility in their decisions. The mediating role of AI-Driven Leadership Decision Making confirms the fact that AI enablers influence the sustainability outcomes indirectly through changing the way leaders process information and evaluate consequences. This reinforces the ideas that ecological sustainability is achieved through leadership behaviors informed by data driven insights as opposed to technology alone. In the context of the banking sector, where decisions have far reaching social and environmental implications, the findings highlight the importance of incorporating AI into leadership processes in order to support responsible and sustainability oriented decision making.

8. LIMITATIONS

Despite the significance of this study, there are some limitations which should be noted. The research is carried out in an emerging and fast-evolving field in which empirical literature on linkages of AI, leadership decision making, and ecological sustainability is limited. Although the aforementioned instruments were carefully chosen from reputable sources and face statistical validation, due to the limited body of literature, the depth of the theoretical comparison may be impacted. Furthermore, there were financial constraints that this study had to face, which affected the study's research design and data collection process. Due to the limited financial resources, the study was conducted using a cross-sectional survey approach and self-reported data, instead of resource-intensive methods such as longitudinal data, experimental designs or multi-source data. Financial limitations were also a factor that limited the ability to include advanced analytical techniques or data collection in multiple countries or across various sectors which could have increased the generalizability of the results. Finally, the focus on one sector restricts the generality of the results. While the banking sector offers a meaningful and impactful context for exploring AI-based leadership and sustainability, future research with more financial resources might be able to broaden its scope to cover multiple industries and longitudinal designs for further validating and extending the proposed framework.

9. RECOMMENDATION

According to our research, organizations should implement the application of AI into the leadership decision-making process more profoundly instead of being limited to operational efficiency. To make AI use sustainable and responsible, institutions ought to invest in the AI preparedness, building leadership AI competencies, and ethical governance frameworks. To make informed decisions, that can be effective in achieving ecological sustainability, the relevant training of leaders to interpret and use AI-generated insights and proper governing policy can help. These initiatives can aid organizations in using AI in strategic promotion of sustainable leadership competencies and environmental responsibility in the long term.

ACKNOWLEDGMENT

Words cannot express enough thanks to Dr. Fanar Shwedeh for her continuous support and encouragement.

We offer our sincere appreciation to Dr. Fanar Shwedeh. Without her guidance, knowledge and contribution this project could not have been accomplished.

REFERENCES

Afsar, B., & Umrani, W. A. (2020). Transformational leadership and innovative work behavior: The role of motivation to learn, task complexity, and innovation climate. *European Journal of Innovation Management*, *23*(3), 402–428. DOI: 10.1108/EJIM-12-2018-0257

Bai, C., Dallasega, P., Orzes, G., & Sarkis, J. (2020). Industry 4.0 technologies assessment: A sustainability perspective. *International Journal of Production Economics*, *229*, 107776. DOI: 10.1016/j.ijpe.2020.107776

Bathula, C., Rabani, I., Sekar, S., Youi, H. K., Choy, J. Y., Kadam, A., Shretha, N. K., Seo, Y.-S., & Kim, H. S. (2021). Enhanced removal of organic dye by activated carbon decorated TiO2 nanoparticles from Mentha Aquatica leaves via ultrasonic approach. *Ceramics International*, *47*(6), 8732–8739. DOI: 10.1016/j.ceramint.2020.12.282

Bressanelli, G., Adrodegari, F., Pigosso, D. C. A., & Parida, V. (2022). Circular economy in the digital age. *Sustainability (Basel)*, *14*(9), 5565. Advance online publication. DOI: 10.3390/su14095565

Brynjolfsson, E., & McAfee, A. (2017). *Machine, platform, crowd: Harnessing our digital future*. W. W. Norton & Company.

Brynjolfsson, E., Mitchell, T., & Rock, D. (2019). What can machines learn, and what does it mean for occupations and the economy? *AEA Papers and Proceedings. American Economic Association*, *109*, 43–47. DOI: 10.1257/pandp.20191019

Bughin, J., Seong, J., Manyika, J., Chui, M., & Joshi, R. (2018). Notes from the AI frontier: Modeling the impact of AI on the world economy. McKinsey Global Institute. https://www.mckinsey.com/featured-insights/artificial-intelligence/notes-from-the-ai-frontier-modeling-the-impact-of-ai-on-the-world-economy

Centobelli, P., Cerchione, R., & Esposito, E. (2020). Efficiency and sustainability of supply chain processes in the era of Industry 4.0. *Business Strategy and the Environment*, *29*(2), 811–829. DOI: 10.1002/bse.2425

Central Bank of the UAE. (2023). *Financial stability report*. https://www.centralbank.ae

Davenport, T. H., & Ronanki, R. (2018). Artificial intelligence for the real world. *Harvard Business Review, 96*(1), 108–116. https://hbr.org/2018/01/artificial-intelligence-for-the-real-world

Del Giudice, M. (2022). Discovering the Internet of Things: AI driven digital transformation in organizations. *Technological Forecasting and Social Change, 178*, 121590. DOI: 10.1016/j.techfore.2022.121590

Dwivedi, Y. K., Hughes, L., Ismagilova, E., Carlson, J., Jacobson, J., Jain, R., Karjaluoto, H., Kefi, H., Krishen, A. S., Kumar, V., Rahman, M. M., Raman, R., Rauschnabel, P. A., Rowley, J., Salo, J., Tran, G. A., & Wang, Y. (2021). Artificial intelligence: Multidisciplinary perspectives on emerging challenges, opportunities, and agenda for research, practice, and policy. *International Journal of Information Management, 57*, 101994. DOI: 10.1016/j.ijinfomgt.2019.08.002

Elkington, J. (2018). *Cannibals with forks: The triple bottom line of 21st century business*. Capstone Publishing.

Floridi, L., Cowls, J., Beltrametti, M., Chatila, R., Chazerand, P., Dignum, V., Luetge, C., Madelin, R., Pagallo, U., Rossi, F., Schafer, B., Valcke, P., & Vayena, E. (2018). AI4People: An ethical framework for a good AI society. *Minds and Machines, 28*(4), 689–707. DOI: 10.1007/s11023-018-9482-5 PMID: 30930541

George, G., Merrill, R. K., & Schillebeeckx, S. J. D. (2020). Digital sustainability and entrepreneurship: How digital innovations are helping tackle climate change and sustainable development. *Entrepreneurship Theory and Practice, 45*(5), 999–1027. DOI: 10.1177/1042258719899425

Hair, J. F., Hult, G. T. M., Ringle, C. M., & Sarstedt, M. (2017). *A primer on partial least squares structural equation modeling (PLS-SEM)* (2nd ed.). Sage Publications.

Jarrahi, M. H. (2018). Artificial intelligence and the future of work: Human–AI symbiosis in organizational decision making. *Business Horizons, 61*(4), 577–586. DOI: 10.1016/j.bushor.2018.03.007

Mittal, S., & Dhar, R. L. (2016). Effect of green transformational leadership on green creativity: A study of tourist hotels. *Tourism Management, 57*, 118–127. DOI: 10.1016/j.tourman.2016.05.007

Raisch, S., & Krakowski, S. (2021). Artificial intelligence and management: The automation–augmentation paradox. *Academy of Management Review, 46*(1), 192–210. DOI: 10.5465/amr.2018.0072

Rana, N. P., Dwivedi, Y. K., Hughes, L., & Gupta, A. (2023). Artificial intelligence for sustainable development goals: A systematic literature review. *Journal of Business Research, 154*, 113297. DOI: 10.1016/j.jbusres.2022.113297

Rolnick, D., Donti, P. L., Kaack, L. H., Kochanski, K., Lacoste, A., Sankaran, K., Slavin Ross, A., Milojevic Dupont, N., Jaques, N., Waldman Brown, A., Luccioni, A., Maharaj, T., Sherwin, E. D., Mukkavilli, S. K., Kording, K. P., Gomes, C. P., Ng, A. Y., Hassabis, D., Platt, J. C., & Bengio, Y. (2022). Tackling climate change with machine learning. *ACM Computing Surveys, 55*(2), 1–96. DOI: 10.1145/3485128

Saunders, M., Lewis, P., & Thornhill, A. (2016). *Research methods for business students* (7th ed.). Pearson Education.

Shrestha, Y. R., Ben-Menahem, S. M., & von Krogh, G. (2021). Organizational decision-making structures in the age of artificial intelligence. *California Management Review, 63*(1), 66–87. DOI: 10.1177/0008125620974607

Vinuesa, R., Azizpour, H., Leite, I., Balaam, M., Dignum, V., Domisch, S., Fellander, A., Langhans, S. D., Tegmark, M., & Fuso Nerini, F. (2020). The role of artificial intelligence in achieving the Sustainable Development Goals. *Nature Communications, 11*(1), 233. DOI: 10.1038/s41467-019-14108-y PMID: 31932590

Wamba, S. F., Dubey, R., Gunasekaran, A., & Akter, S. (2021). The performance effects of big data analytics and supply chain ambidexterity. *International Journal of Production Economics, 231*, 107947. DOI: 10.1016/j.ijpe.2020.107947

World Economic Forum. (2022). *The global risks report*. https://www.weforum.org

Zhang, Y., Sun, J., Yang, Z., & Li, S. (2022). Artificial intelligence-driven green innovation and environmental performance. *Technological Forecasting and Social Change, 173*, 121092. DOI: 10.1016/j.techfore.2021.121092

Chapter 6

Sustainability-Driven Projects:
Leveraging the Triple Bottom Line for Competitive Advantage

Mounir El Khatib
http://orcid.org/0000-0001-7418-2351
Hamdan Bin Muhammad Smart University, UAE

Haroon Ul Rashid
http://orcid.org/0009-0009-2603-1650
School of Housing Building and Planning, Universiti Sains Malaysia, Malaysia

Fatma Abdulla Alserisdi
Hamdan Bin Muhammad Smart University, UAE

Haitham Alzoubi
Skyline University College, UAE

ABSTRACT

This paper examines how sustainable project management can integrate economic, environmental, and social objectives to enhance long-term organisational success. It assesses the current landscape of sustainability-oriented project practices, identifies challenges, and explores emerging trends and technological innovations. The study uses qualitative secondary data to conduct thematic analysis based on the three pillars of sustainability. Findings reveal that while sustainability-driven approaches foster project resilience, stakeholder value, and long-term profitability, organisations encounter significant barriers such as high upfront investment, lack of standardised frameworks, and resistance to cultural change. Disruptive technologies

DOI: 10.4018/979-8-2600-1348-9.ch006

associated with Industry 4.0 strengthen transparency, optimise resource allocation, and improve decision-making in sustainable project delivery. The study concludes that strategic planning, inclusive stakeholder engagement, and purposeful adoption of emerging technologies are essential for embedding sustainability within project management processes.

1. INTRODUCTION

1.1 Background

Sustainable project management has become holistic that entails mainstreaming economic, environmental, and social goals in meeting the multifaceted needs of the modern society. The change indicates the increased importance of the responsible project delivery and the necessity of creating value in the long-term instead of producing it in the short-term (Carboni et al., 2024). Triple bottom line as the requirement to balance the results of economic performance with environmental stewardship and social responsibility has become a new necessity in the successful operation of a sustainable project (Crace & Gehman, 2023). Organisations are supposed to take these pillars into account as a complete entity in reaction to the global issues of climate change, ethical utilisation of resources and social equity.

With the ever-increasing expectations of the regulators, stakeholders and communities, the issue of sustainable project management has become a strategic change in the manner projects are executed. It puts organisations at the level of meeting the present needs without jeopardizing the interests of the future generations. Sustainability as a concept has now been inseparable in a global environment that is defined by environmental pressures and social accountability as one of the issues that project management practice has to deal with.

1.2 Problem Statement

Despite the fact that sustainability of project management has been identified as a valuable approach, most organisations have struggled to combine economic, environmental and social goals. Trade-offs are habitually experienced by project managers, especially when the cost-effectiveness is evident to be incompatible with environmental or social concerns (Piyatanavong et al., 2024). These stresses may lead to time losses, higher costs or reduced sustainability. Besides this, there are no universal standards; moreover, organisations have different methods of implementing sustainability, which makes the implementation more complicated (Abuhasel,

2023). There should be a coherent and viable strategy that would lead organisations to fulfill the principles of sustainability and execution of projects.

1.3 Research Objectives

The study explores how sustainable project management supports the economic, environmental, and social goals in different sectors. It evaluates existing practice, determines the key barriers and discusses the new trends and technological advances that transform sustainability in project management (Venezia, 2023). It is through this analysis that the study hopes to put into perspective actionable measures of ensuring that sustainability is instilled in project delivery to ensure the organisational benefit is realised in the long term.

1.4 Significance of the Study

With the development of environmental awareness and social demands, the importance of knowledge of sustainable project management also increases. Incorporating sustainability in the project practices contributes to the growth of organisational reputation and relationship with stakeholders as well as long-term cost optimisation (Wu et al., 2024). This study can help increase the alignment of the project outcomes with the wider environmental and social requirements by providing the project managers with the knowledge and implementation strategies that are acceptable in the long term.

1.5 Organisation of the Thesis

This thesis consists of five chapters. In chapter 1, the context of the research is presented. Chapter 2 describes a literature review on the topics of sustainable project management practices, challenges, and trends. Chapter 3 defines the methodology of the research. In Chapter 4, the findings in the economic, environmental, and social dimensions are provided. The concluding chapter 5 explains the findings, implications, and suggestions on how to work in the future.

2. LITERATURE REVIEW

2.1 Sustainable Project Management Overview

Sustainable project management brings together all the three pillars of sustainability to achieve results which meet the current needs without resource depletion by the future (Carboni et al., 2024). This method broadens the project success concept, based on cost time and scope, to include social impact, environmental responsibility and long-term economic value (Crace & Gehman, 2023). Proactive planning to predict regulatory changes, the lack of resources, and the change of stakeholder expectations is also a part of sustainable project management (Tong et al., 2023). Such a future outlook improves organisational resilience and competitiveness. Engagement of stakeholders is part of sustainable project management, with a large-scale involvement of stakeholders supporting ethical decision-making and increasing the level of trust in the community (Ali et al., 2023). Collectively, sustainable project management is a paradigm shift model of sustainability that balances the linkage between the short term project needs with the long term societal and environmental objectives.

2.2 Economic Sustainability in Project Management

Economic sustainability ensures the financial sustainability of projects in the long-term and at the same time promotes greater sustainability objectives. Sound financial planning provides project managers with the resources to distribute resources accurately to reduce sustainability investment risks (Piyatanavong et al., 2024). An example of such is the life-cycle cost analysis, which clarifies long-term savings that often outweigh their initial investments, thus proving a more than explicit economic incentive to invest in renewable energy systems or energy-efficient equipment (Venezia, 2023).

Cost-benefit analysis also assesses the ability of sustainability efforts to provide a concrete payback. Energy efficient systems are associated with more expensive initial investments but they most of the time result in high cost payments in the long run and also achieve environmental goals (Wu et al., 2024). Furthermore, the compliance with sustainability principles contributes to the increase of the brand image and increases the loyalty of stakeholders, which results in a competitive edge in those markets where the growing popularity goes to the environmentally responsible organisations (Malik et al., 2023). In turn, the economic sustainability becomes the cornerstone of project resilience, profitability and future success.

2.3 Environmental Sustainability in Project Management

Environmental sustainability is a concept that involves practices aimed at reducing ecological damage and encouraging ecologically-friendly use of resources in the project management. Waste management, emission management, resource management are the practices that lessen the effects on the environment (Abuhasel, 2023; Opperman et al., 2023). The increased use of renewable sources of energy (solar, wind, or hybrid) reduce the reliance on fossil fuels and reduce carbon footprints (Lei, 2024). A circular-economy framework is upheld by effective waste-management plans, such as recycling, repurposing, and the use of sustainable materials (Joel and Oguanobi, 2024). Usage of eco-friendly materials is also helpful in reducing environmental degradation and preserving biodiversity (Saradara et al., 2023). Reporting on a regular basis, regular audits and continuity in observance of environmental performance improves transparency and adherence to regulatory requirements (Randeree and Ahmed, 2019; Al Nuaimi et al., 2020). Using a combination of these approaches and strategies reveals that environmental performance goes beyond mere compliance but involves taking the role of a caretaker.

2.4 Social Sustainability in Project Management

Social sustainability considers the welfare of the community, ethical interactions, and comprehensive involvement of the stakeholders. Among the ethical project practices is fair labour practice, inclusivity, and safe working conditions, which results in trust and a positive attitude towards building positive relationships between organisations and the communities they serve (Mohammed & Ishak, 2024). The engagement of the stakeholders is critical to consider different perspectives, reduce conflict, and foster inclusive decision-making (Agyekum et al., 2023). The projects that embrace the cultural values and use the input of the community are also more likely to gain the long-term acceptance and success (McCandless and Larson, 2023). Socially responsible organisations also enhance reputations, receive the trust of stakeholders and satisfy the expectations of the society with the results of the project (Khan et al., 2024). Therefore, social sustainability improves the relationship with the communities and strengthens the project legitimacy.

2.5 Challenges in Sustainable Project Management

In view of the fact that sustainable project management is associated with benefits, it also faces various challenges. The main obstacle is often represented by high initial capital requirements of green technologies, renewable energy, as well as specialised training, especially in industries that are sensitive to costs (Ige et al., 2024). Lack of standardised frameworks would result in non-uniformity in practices across organisations and sectors, thus making performance benchmarking and the measurement of outcomes more difficult (Govindaras et al., 2023). The resistance to change is also a factor that hinders its adoption, since employees might view sustainability processes as too complicated or unnecessary and slow down the implementation process (Obiuto et al., 2024). Finally, the trade-offs between economic, environmental, and social goals are often difficult; excessive attention to one of the pillars may negatively impact the rest, so careful prioritisation of strategies and careful planning are essential (Piyatanavong et al., 2024). All these barriers and challenges highlight the need for more concrete strategies, capacity building and commitment through strong leadership.

2.6 Case Studies of Sustainable Project Management

A number of successful projects have demonstrated the effectiveness of sustainability strategies. The implementation of green supply chain management in the UAE construction industry minimized the negative effects on the environment, although it did not affect operational performance (Balasubramanian and Shukla, 2017). According to a study conducted in Dubai, the use of structured sustainability frameworks reduced waste and enhanced energy efficiency and efficiency of resource usage (Hays et al., 2020).

The case of Masdar City is an example of the innovative sustainable urban development, which combines renewable energy, green buildings, and community-oriented planning (Randeree & Ahmed, 2019; Iyer, 2023). This project shows how the concept of sustainability can be integrated on a city level. Further, one of the studies suggests that the choice of a contractor holding sustainability knowledge positively affects environmental performance (El-Sayegh et al., 2021). The cases prove that the sustainability-oriented project management also brings about tangible economic, social and environmental positive outcomes.

2.7 Future Trends and Innovations

Sustainable project management is changing with emerging technologies. By monitoring consumption and waste, as well as efficiency and optimal utilisation of resources, Industry 4.0 technologies, such as automation, IoT sensors, and real-time analytics, make that possible (Agarwal and Gupta, 2021). These technology products promote decision-making based on evidence and continuous improvement (Mazziotta et al., 2023). Predictive analytics provided by artificial intelligence detects the risks in the environment and feeds the mitigation plans (Al Amri et al., 2021). Digital twins can be used to predict the project conditions and pre-implement the sustainability measures by simulating, thus cutting down on the costly errors (El Khatib et al., 2023). The security of data documentation and the tracking process of sustainability-related actions can be ensured through the use of blockchain (Umar et al., 2020). A combination of these innovations enhances sustainable management of projects, which are data-driven, accountable and efficient.

3. METHODOLOGY

3.1 Research Design

The research design adopted in this research is qualitative research, based on secondary data analysis. The provided methodology aligns with the objectives of the research, allowing it to explore the current trends, emerging issues and development of practices in the field of sustainable project management. The body of work concerning economic, social and environmental sustainability constitutes the framework for investigating integration strategies (Piyathanavong et al., 2024). The design therefore enhances an in depth study of the documented methodologies and case-based knowledge.

3.2 Data Collection

The information was only obtained in secondary repositories, which included peer-reviewed scholarly publications, industry monographs, and case studies found in academic databases, including Google Scholar, JSTOR, and ScienceDirect (Wu et al., 2024). The selection of the sources was based on their relevance to the three pillars of sustainability, and the preference was given to the publications published within the last five years (Ali et al., 2023). This criterion helped to make sure that derived findings reflect the current developments and best practices.

3.3 Data Analysis

The thematic analysis was used to categorize information according to the economic, environmental, and social aspects (Crace & Gehman, 2023). There were recurrent patterns, challenges and success factors, which appeared throughout the reviewed literature, which allowed to compare and integrate the different perspectives on sustainable project management. Specific focus was given to cost barriers, regulatory limitations, and implementation risks which are found in the literature (Obiuto et al., 2024). The thematic process provided a systematic, rational assessment of the sustainability practices in the industrial sectors.

4. ANALYSIS AND DISCUSSION

4.1 Economic Objectives

Financial policies necessitate economic sustainability which therefore ensures that financial sustenance of projects is viable and also encourages sustainability objectives. Effective financial planning allows the channeling of funds to those projects that provide long-term value like energy-efficient infrastructure or training programs that are sustainability-related (Venezia, 2023). Life Cycle Cost Analaysis unveils the cumulative savings enjoyed by sustainability investments in the long-term (Piyatanavong et al., 2024). The cost-benefit analysis also utilizes informed decision making by comparing initial expenses with the expected financial and environmental outcomes (Wu et al., 2024). Sustainable programs, including energy-saving systems, decrease operating expenses and enhance a competitive stance (Ali et al., 2023). Furthermore, the correspondence to the principles of sustainability increases the brand image and trust among stakeholders (Malik et al., 2023). In turn, these aspects lead to profitability and differentiation in the market, which proves that project management may be cost-efficient. The above factors in turn result in profitability and market differentiation, therefore confirming the economic sustainability of project management.

4.2 Environmental Objectives

Environmental sustainability aims at reducing the ecological footprints and enhancing sound resource management. The main measures are emission management, energy efficiency, and reduction of wastes (Abuhasel, 2023). Renewable sources of energy minimize the use of fossil fuels and help achieve the goal of carbon-reduction (Lei, 2024). The environmental impact is also minimized through the use of circular economy practices like recycling, using materials in an innovative manner, and using environmentally benign alternative sources (Joel & Oguanobi, 2024). The use of environmentally friendly materials saves bio-diversity and reduces environmental imbalance (Saradara et al., 2023). Continuous improvement processes enhance the level of transparency, and environmental impacts are monitored and reported through the regular audits (Randeree & Ahmed, 2019; Al Nuaimi et al., 2020). These practices in combination promote environmental scrutiny and regulatory adherence.

4.3 Social Objectives

Social sustainability emphasizes ethical practices and thorough stakeholder engagement. Adherence to fair labor standards, occupational health and safety, and diversity promotes the well-being of workers and the wider community (Mohammed & Ishak, 2024). Early stakeholder involvement fosters transparency and helps to minimize conflicts (Agyekum et al., 2023).

Cultural value respect enhances acceptance levels and fortifies community relationships (McCandless & Larson, 2023). Socially responsible companies achieve reputational benefits as well as stakeholder loyalty (Khan et al., 2024). Thus, social sustainability fulfills broad societal expectations and projects legitimacy.

4.4 Challenges and Trade-offs

Sustainable project management is usually associated with working with conflicting goals. The initial costs of sustainable materials and technologies may be incompatible with the financial goals in the short term (Ige et al., 2024). Environmental regulations may prolong the project schedule or put a strain on resources (Govindaras et al., 2023). The social expectations often require new resources or changes (Obiuto et al., 2024). Such trade-offs require a strong leadership, open communication and prioritisation of strategies. This means that sustainable project management needs dynamic plans that justify the benefits against the constraints without compromising on the long-term value.

4.5 Case Study Analysis

The empirical case studies indicate that systematic sustainability frameworks might produce a tangible result. Green supply-chain management in the United Arab Emirates construction industry has reduced the adverse effects on the environment without affecting the performance of operations (Balasubramanian & Shukla, 2017). Planned sustainability projects in Dubai have made the city more energy-efficient and minimized the amount of waste (Hays et al., 2020).

Masdar City is a model example of an urban development based on the concepts of sustainability in which the viability of renewable energy and smart building technologies, as well as community planning, is simultaneously visible (Randeree & Ahmed, 2019; Iyer, 2023). The choice of contractors with proven sustainability background also improves the environmental performance of the project (El et al., 2021). These considerations support the assumption that sustainability does not merely exist, but it is also beneficial when incorporated into standard project initiatives. Empirical case studies imply that systematic sustainability frameworks may have real deliverables. Green supply-chain management in the United Arab Emirates construction industry has alleviated the negative environmental effects without affecting the performance of the operations (Balasubramanian and Shukla, 2017). The Dubai sustainability efforts have made the city more energy-efficient and minimized the amount of wastes (Hays et al., 2020). Masdar City is a model example of an urban development based on the concepts of sustainability in which the viability of renewable energy and smart building technologies, as well as community planning, is simultaneously visible (Randeree & Ahmed, 2019; Iyer, 2023). The choice of contractors with proven sustainability background also improves the environmental performance of the project (El et al., 2021). These considerations support the assumption that sustainability does not merely exist, but it is also beneficial when incorporated into standard project initiatives.

4.6 Emerging Trends and Technology

The Industry 4.0 technologies enhance real-time data analytics, resource optimisation, and increased process visibility (Agarwal 4.0, 2021; Mazziotta et al., 2023). The combination of sensors and digital monitoring devices allows the project managers to reduce the waste and monitor the sustainability performance. With the help of artificial intelligence, predictive modelling predicts the environmental hazards and offers measures to deal with them (Al Amri et al., 2021). Digital twins can mitigate the project environment, thus enabling the consideration of sustainability strategies before their implementation (El et al., 2023). Blockchain increases the levels of transparency and responsibility in the process of tracking the indicators of sustainability (Umar et al., 2020). All these innovations lead to the shift to technology-based sustainability.

5. CONCLUSION

Sustainable project management needs economic, environmental, and social goals to be incorporated into sound plans. In spite of the long-term rewards of sustainable practices, including improving resiliency, gaining stakeholder confidence, and efficiency of operations, sustainability practices create challenges related to cost, resistance to change and trade-offs across sustainability pillars.

The case studies in the UAE reveal that effective monitoring and evaluation in terms of sustainability performance are nurtured by organized systems. The possibilities of new technologies, i.e., Industry 4.0 tools, artificial intelligence, and blockchain, increase the range of opportunities of sustainable implementation that can be implemented effectively and transparently.

Sustainable project management is thus a new field which requires flexibility, tactical skills and technological expertise. More studies are necessary to perfect sustainability measurements, build effective frameworks, and come up with industry-specific guidelines, hence allowing organisations to fully utilize sustainability positions to optimise project performance and facilitate economic prosperity, environmental and social wellbeing.

REFERENCES

Abuhasel, K. (2023). Sustainable Green City Development Project Analysis using the Critical Path Method (CPM) and the Crashing Project Method on Time and Cost Optimization. Engineering, Technology &. *Applied Scientific Research, 13*(3), 10973–10977. DOI: 10.48084/etasr.5980

Agarwal, R., & Gupta, B. (2021). Innovation and Leadership: A Study of organizations based in the United Arab Emirates. *Foundations of Management, 13*(1), 73-84. https://intapi.sciendo.com/pdf/10.2478/fman-2021-0006

Agyekum, A. K., Fugar, F. D. K., Agyekum, K., Akomea-Frimpong, I., & Pittri, H. (2023). Barriers to stakeholder engagement in sustainable procurement of public works. *Engineering, Construction, and Architectural Management, 30*(9), 3840–3857. DOI: 10.1108/ECAM-08-2021-0746

Al Amri, T., Puskas Khetani, K., & Marey-Perez, M. (2021). Towards sustainable I4. 0: Key skill areas for project managers in GCC construction industry. *Sustainability (Basel), 13*(15), 8121. DOI: 10.3390/su13158121

Al Nuaimi, B. K., Khan, M., & Ajmal, M. (2020). Implementing sustainable procurement in the United Arab Emirates public sector. *Journal of Public Procurement, 20*(2), 97–117. DOI: 10.1108/JOPP-07-2019-0044

Ali, A., Ma, L., Shahzad, M., Musonda, J., & Hussain, S. (2023). How various stakeholder pressure influences mega-project sustainable performance through corporate social responsibility and green competitive advantage. *Environmental Science and Pollution Research International, 31*(60), 1–15. DOI: 10.1007/s11356-023-29717-w PMID: 37702865

Balasubramanian, S., & Shukla, V. (2017). Green supply chain management: The case of the construction sector in the United Arab Emirates (UAE). *Production Planning and Control, 28*(14), 1116–1138. DOI: 10.1080/09537287.2017.1341651

Carboni, J., Duncan, W. R., Gonzalez, M., Pace, M., Smyth, D., & Young, M. (2024). Sustainable Project Management: The GPM Practice Guide. GPM Global. https://www.ucipfg.com/Repositorio/MAP/MAPD-11/Version-2017/Unidad-01/lecturas/02.pdf

Crace, L., & Gehman, J. (2023). What explains ESG performance? Disentangling the asymmetrical drivers of the triple bottom line. *Organization & Environment, 36*(1), 150–178. DOI: 10.1177/10860266221079408

El Khatib, M., Al Ali, S., Alharam, I., Alhajeri, A., Peneva, G., Angelova, J., & Shanaa, M. (2023). Drafting a digital transformation strategy for project management sector–empirical study on UAE. *Strategies for Policy in Science & Education/ Strategii na Obrazovatelnata i Nauchnata Politika, 31*. https://university.tu-sofia.bg/e-publ/files/12418_Digital_Transformation_for_PM_Sector.pdf

El-Sayegh, S. M., Basamji, M., Haj Ahmad, A., & Zarif, N. (2021). Key contractor selection criteria for green construction projects in the UAE. *International Journal of Construction Management, 21*(12), 1240–1250. DOI: 10.1080/15623599.2019.1610545

Govindaras, B., Wern, T. S., Kaur, S., Haslin, I. A., & Ramasamy, R. K. (2023). Sustainable environment to prevent burnout and attrition in project management. *Sustainability (Basel), 15*(3), 2364. DOI: 10.3390/su15032364

Hays, J. M., Pereseina, V., Alshuaibi, A. S. I., & Saha, J. (2020). Lessons in sustainable process paradigm. A case study from Dubai. *International Journal of Management Education, 18*(1), 100366. DOI: 10.1016/j.ijme.2020.100366

Ige, A. B., Kupa, E., & Ilori, O. (2024). Best practices in cybersecurity for green building management systems: Protecting sustainable infrastructure from cyber threats. *International Journal of Science and Research Archive, 12*(1), 2960–2977. DOI: 10.30574/ijsra.2024.12.1.1185

Iyer, S. S. (2023). The emerging circular economy trends of United Arab Emirates (UAE) universities. *European Journal of Social Impact and Circular Economy-ISSN, 2704*, 9906. DOI: 10.13135/2704-9906/6821

Joel, O. T., & Oguanobi, V. U. (2024). Geotechnical assessments for renewable energy infrastructure: Ensuring stability in wind and solar projects. *Engineering Science & Technology Journal, 5*(5), 1588–1605. DOI: 10.51594/estj.v5i5.1110

Khan, T., Emon, M. M. H., & Siam, S. A. J. (2024). Impact of Green Supply Chain Practices on Sustainable Development in Bangladesh. Available at *SSRN* 4958443. http://doi.org/DOI: 10.26480/mbmj.02.2024.73.83

Lei, J. (2024). Efficient Strategies on Supply Chain Network Optimization for Industrial Carbon Emission Reduction. arXiv preprint arXiv:2404.16863. https://arxiv.org/pdf/2404.16863

Malik, M., Ali, M., Latan, H., & Chiappetta Jabbour, C. J. (2023). Green project management practices, green knowledge acquisition and sustainable competitive advantage: Empirical evidence. *Journal of Knowledge Management, 27*(9), 2350–2375. https://nrl.northumbria.ac.uk/id/eprint/51405/1/AAM.pdf. DOI: 10.1108/JKM-06-2022-0466

Mazziotta, A., Borges, P., Kangas, A., Halme, P., & Eyvindson, K. (2023). Spatial trade-offs between ecological and economical sustainability in the boreal production forest. *Journal of Environmental Management, 330*, 117144. DOI: 10.1016/j.jenvman.2022.117144 PMID: 36586374

McCandless, S., & Larson, S. J. (2023). Prioritizing social equity in MPA curricula: A crossprogram analysis and a case study. In *Social Equity in the Public Administration Classroom* (pp. 99–117). Routledge., DOI: 10.4324/9781003381228-8

Mohammed, A. K., & Ishak, M. S. B. (2024). Identification of project cultural factors affecting the performance of UAE construction projects. *Alexandria Engineering Journal, 86*, 205–216. DOI: 10.1016/j.aej.2023.11.064

Obiuto, N. C., Ebirim, W., Ninduwezuor-Ehiobu, N., Ani, E. C., Olu-lawal, K. A., & Ugwuanyi, E. D. (2024). Integrating sustainability into hvac project management: Challenges and opportunities. *Engineering Science & Technology Journal, 5*(3), 873–887. DOI: 10.51594/estj.v5i3.943

Opperman, J. J., Carvallo, J. P., Kelman, R., Schmitt, R. J., Almeida, R., Chapin, E., Flecker, A., Goichot, M., Grill, G., Harou, J. J., Hartmann, J., Higgins, J., Kammen, D., Martin, E., Martins, T., Newsock, A., Rogéliz, C., Raepple, J., Sada, R., & Harrison, D. (2023). Balancing renewable energy and river resources by moving from individual assessments of hydropower projects to energy system planning. *Frontiers in Environmental Science, 10*, 1036653. DOI: 10.3389/fenvs.2022.1036653

Piyathanavong, V., Huynh, V. N., Karnjana, J., & Olapiriyakul, S. (2024). Role of project management on Sustainable Supply Chain development through Industry 4.0 technologies and Circular Economy during the COVID-19 pandemic: A multiple case study of Thai metals industry. Operations Management Research, 17(1), 13-37. https://link.springer.com/content/pdf/10.1007/s12063-022-00283-7.pdf

Randeree, K., & Ahmed, N. (2019). The social imperative in sustainable urban development: The case of masdar city in the United Arab Emirates. *Smart and sustainable built environment, 8*(2), 138-149. DOI DOI: 10.1108/SASBE-11-2017-0064

Saradara, S. M., Khalfan, M. M. A., Rauf, A., & Qureshi, R. (2023). On the path towards sustainable construction—the case of the United Arab Emirates: A review. *Sustainability (Basel), 15*(19), 14652. DOI: 10.3390/su151914652

Tong, X., Linderman, K., & Zhu, Q. (2023). Managing a portfolio of environmental projects: Focus, balance, and environmental management capabilities. *Journal of Operations Management, 69*(1), 127–158. DOI: 10.1002/joom.1201

Umar, T., Egbu, C., Ofori, G., Honnurvali, M. S., Saidani, M., Shibani, A., & Goh, K. (2020, March). UAE's commitment towards UN Sustainable Development Goals. In *Proceedings of the Institution of Civil Engineers-Engineering Sustainability* (Vol. 173, No. 7, pp. 325-343). Thomas Telford Ltd. https://dx.doi.org/DOI: 10.1680/jensu.19.00036

Venezia, E. (2023). Cost–benefit analysis in high-speed railway projects: Appraisal of methodological approaches and an initial social equity evaluation, a case study. *Sustainability (Basel), 15*(14), 11344. DOI: 10.3390/su151411344

Wu, Y., Wang, H., Wang, Z., Diehl, J. A., & Xue, S. (2024). Evaluating the economic sustainability of commercial complex greening based on cost-benefit analysis: A case study of Singapore's Shaw center. *Ecological Indicators, 161*, 111890. DOI: 10.1016/j.ecolind.2024.111890

Chapter 7
From ESG to ESGI: Introducing a Paradigmatic Framework for AI-Integrated, Data-Driven ESG Investing

Zaheda Daruwala
http://orcid.org/0000-0001-8884-3165
City University, Ajman, UAE

ABSTRACT

The integration of artificial intelligence into sustainable finance signifies a critical imperative of analytical foundations for ESG investing. This chapter introduces the concept of ESGI (ESG with Intelligence) as an emergent paradigm that systematically embeds AI-driven analytical methods into the evaluation, implementation, and optimization of ESG investments. It moves beyond traditional financial metrics by integrating unstructured information sources, enabling stakeholders to identify material ESG risks and opportunities. Using systematic literature review and conceptual analysis, it establishes how ESGI transforms investment decision-making into a dynamic data-driven system that aligns value with sustainability. It uses AI-driven applications of Natural Language Processing, Long Short-Term Memory, Explainable AI, Reinforcement Learning, Predictive Analytics, Semantic AI, IoT sensors. The study underscores the pivot from static ESG assessment to a dynamic AI-driven evidence-based ecosystem, enabling a more transparent, measurable, and impactful ESG finance architecture.

DOI: 10.4018/979-8-2600-1348-9.ch007

1 INTRODUCTION

1.1 Background and Context: The Evolution of ESG Investing

Environmental, Social, and Governance (ESG) investing represents a pivotal shift in the finance industry, moving beyond traditional financial performance to incorporate criteria reflecting companies' environmental stewardship, social responsibility, and governance integrity. This practice has gained widespread attention, with researchers noting its emergence as a core component in evaluating a company's long-term value and risk profile (Andika, 2025 and Pasko et al., 2022). The last two decades have witnessed substantial growth in ESG assets under management, driven by growing public and regulatory concern for climate change, inequality, and corporate ethics (Dey et al., 2025). Systematic reviews show that regulations and increasing investor awareness have driven global growth in ESG investment strategies (Popescu et al., 2023). This transformation is marked by more sophisticated ESG frameworks and reporting standards. Industry and academic stakeholders have developed tools such as the Global Reporting Initiative (GRI), the International Financial Reporting Standards (IFRS) S1 and S2, and the Sustainability Accounting Standards Board (SASB) to improve comparability and guide ESG integration into investment decision-making (Andika, 2025). Sectoral analyses show that investor and regulatory demand for clearer ESG disclosure frameworks have prompted the evolution and refinement of these standards globally (Zeng et al., 2024; Lee & Liang, 2024). Despite improvements, empirical research continues to find regional disparities and inconsistent adoption across markets, with stronger practices typically observed in developed economies (Andika, 2025). Persistent challenges concerning data comparability, standardization, and subjective assessment have hampered the full realization of credible ESG investing. These issues highlight a need for new analytical approaches capable of processing and harmonizing complex, multi-source ESG data.

1.2 The Imperative Role of Artificial Intelligence in Sustainable Finance

The advent of artificial intelligence (AI) has significantly changed the landscape of financial analysis by enabling rapid processing of large, heterogeneous datasets and improving pattern recognition capabilities. An array of methodologies emerged, including qualitative assessments, quantitative scoring models, risk-ranking systems, and the adoption of advanced technologies like blockchain and artificial intelligence to enhance data validity and minimise risks, including greenwashing (Vishwakarma et al., 2025). Asset managers are deploying AI tools to enhance ESG portfolio analysis, risk monitoring, and reporting, mitigating some of the subjectivity and fragmentation in manual ESG assessment. Applications of machine learning offer deeper, data-driven insights into ESG performance and implications for financial outcomes (Zhang & Zhang, 2024). New risks arise with reliance on AI models, like issues with data comparability, standardization across geographies and sectors, and the inherent subjectivity in ESG assessments (Nyakuwanika & Panicker, 2025). Despite advances in reporting frameworks, studies consistently document concerns about inconsistent rating methodologies, a lack of harmonised regulatory guidance, and scepticism regarding the credibility of ESG metrics (Dey et al., 2025). These limitations often pose challenges for investors, policymakers, and other stakeholders seeking to accurately interpret and compare ESG information across firms and regions (Pratiwi & Edeh, 2024). Addressing these challenges necessitates new analytical approaches that process and harmonize complex ESG data. Recent literature underscores the use of technologies such as AI and novel data modelling to manage unstructured data and strengthen ESG assessment (Andika, 2025). There is a clear policy imperative for further standardization and cross-disciplinary collaboration to close existing gaps, improve comparability, and enhance the ESG investing credibility (Yunus & Nanda, 2024).

1.3 Evolution from ESG to ESGI

Despite notable progress in both ESG integration and the development of AI technologies, a systematic synthesis of these domains, the ESGI (Environmental, Social, Governance, and Intelligence) paradigm, remains underexplored and is only beginning to be mapped out by academic and industry practitioners. The rationale for the ESGI approach centres on its promise to bring together the normative depth and responsible frameworks of ESG with the analytical scalability, real-time processing, and predictive modelling capabilities enabled by AI (Lim, 2024).

Motivations for transitioning from traditional ESG to ESGI include:

- Inconsistencies in ESG disclosure requirements across jurisdictions and lack of standardized metrics, especially for social and governance factors (Pria et al., 2024)
- Biases in current ESG scoring and rating methodologies (Hughes et al., 2021). Studies reveal that subjective rating practices can lead to discrepancies across rating agencies, making it difficult for investors to rely on ESG scores to make rational decisions (Juthi et al., 2024).
- Lack of clear guidance and predictive power for investors and stakeholders to engage in sustainable finance, which can be augmented by the use of AI techniques to provide transparent and interpretable insights for ethical decision making (Fagbore et al., 2024).

- Lack of real-time monitoring and detection of greenwashing of sustainable projects, which can be improved by the use of intelligent tools (Patil et al., 2024).

In summary, the ESGI framework represents a paradigmatic leap forward, wherein lies the potential to combine the depth of sustainable investing frameworks with the analytical scale and precision of AI-based technologies. ESGI may help close critical gaps in current ESG practices and support resilient, data-driven capital allocation and risk identification amid global environmental and social challenges.

1.4 Chapter Objectives and Structure

This chapter aims to provide a comprehensive overview of the convergence between AI and ESG investing, synthesizing the latest research on methodologies, challenges, and applications. The objectives are threefold:

1- To review the historical development of ESG investing and its present-day complexities.
2- To examine the state-of-the-art in AI techniques as applied to sustainable finance.
3- To articulate a structured framework for AI-driven ESG investment strategies, highlighting both opportunities and ongoing research gaps.

To achieve the above objectives, this study employs a mixed-methods, integrative research methodology that combines systematic literature review, conceptual framework development, and case-based empirical insights. This design enables the integration of diverse academic and institutional sources to produce a holistic synthesis of cross-disciplinary topics, demonstrating how AI techniques intersect with ESG investing. The first research phase meets the initial objective by conducting a structured literature review to produce a thematic map of ESG evolution and the complexities of the present-day ESG investing landscape. The second objective examines trajectories of AI integration, followed by the third, which develops a structured practitioner-academic hybrid framework that rationalises the ESGI paradigm, or the AI-enhanced ESG Investing framework. The study provides a structured synthesis, offering a practitioner-focused view of this evolving field.

2. THE EVOLUTION OF ESG INVESTING

2.1 From Ethical Investing to Formal ESG: Key Milestones

Financial decision-making has evolved, with ESG investing increasingly aligning with sustainability and ethical responsibility. In the 1960s, it emerged as Socially Responsible Investing (SRI) driven by faith-based prohibitions and social activism. Investors began to exclude industries associated with social harm, such as tobacco, weapons, and apartheid-linked businesses, from their portfolios. These early exclusionary screens were less about financial return and more about moral alignment. The 1980s and 1990s witnessed a gradual evolution as corporations began integrating Corporate Social Responsibility (CSR) initiatives into their business models. Researchers trace the line from church-led screening in the 1970s to the multi-factor frameworks in use today (Eccles & Klimenko, 2019). The publication of the Brundtland Report (1987) introduced the concept of "sustainable development," and the 1992 Rio Earth Summit[1] was a critical moment linking environmental and economic objectives. The idea that firms could balance profitability with social and environmental stewardship gained momentum, particularly in response to rising public awareness of environmental degradation, labour rights, and corporate governance scandals (Gill, 2008).

Academic debate on responsible investing has intensified over the past decade as ESG became a mainstream framework integrating non-financial metrics into investment analysis. Reviews conducted by Friede et al. (2015) that included 2,200 papers, where almost 90% of the studies showed that values-based portfolios did not harm risk-adjusted returns. The EU released the High-Level Expert Group report in 2018 and the taxonomy regulation in 2020 (Malecki, 2021). Central banks entered the field. The Network for Greening the Financial System expanded from 8 to 120 members from 2017 to 2023 (Carrasco & Lee, 2023).

Figure 1. Key Milestones in ESG Investing

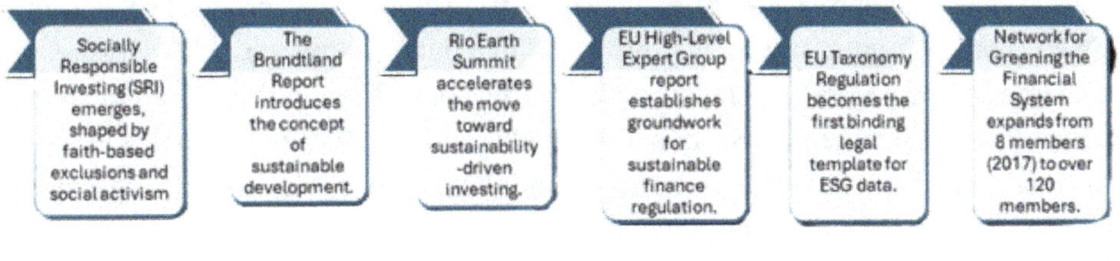

2.2 ESG Metrics, Reporting Standards, and Market Adoption

The 2000s marked a turning point as the United Nations Principles for Responsible Investment (UN PRI) updated its reporting rules in 2016, solidifying ESG investing within the financial paradigm. This period also saw a surge in sustainability disclosures, data analytics, and corporate accountability mechanisms. In 2016, GRI formalized ESG reporting by creating the first global standards for sustainability reporting. In 2017 Task Force on Climate-related Financial Disclosures (TCFD) issued its final guidance. Banks, insurers, and listed companies soon linked capital budgets to scenario analysis. In 2018, SASB released a complete set of the Standards and their Materiality Map™, which has since become a foundational reference for ESG analysts and investors, highlighting which sustainability issues are most likely to affect enterprise value.

The 2010s marked a phase of acceleration and complexity. Rating agencies expanded coverage in parallel. Yet data disagreement drew attention. Berg et al. (2022) revealed an average correlation of only 0.54 across six ESG raters. The warning regarding this gap was also raised earlier by Gibson et al. (2021) in their noise-trading study. BlackRock launched the iShares Paris-aligned series in 2020, and Vanguard followed with its Global ESG Select Stock Fund in 2021. However, various studies during this time found that company performance was not affected by their efforts to implement ESG commitments (La Torre et al., 2020). Various studies suggested that the correlation between ESG characteristics and financial performance was inconclusive (Giese et al., 2019). These findings sparked calls for harmonised standards.

In June 2021, standard-setters converged, with SASB merging with the International Integrated Reporting Council (IIRC) to form the Value Reporting Foundation (VRF), a pivotal step toward consolidating ESG reporting frameworks and the IFRS Foundation formed the International Sustainability Standards Board (ISSB). In August 2022, VRF, including SASB, was consolidated into the IFRS Foundation under the newly established ISSB. The ISSB now maintains SASB standards as part of the foundation's global baseline for sustainability disclosure. The ISSB's IFRS S1 and S2 standards (released in 2023) directly build upon SASB's structure and industry-specific approach. The financial markets responded promptly. The Securities and Exchange Commission (SEC) proposed mandatory climate risk disclosures in 2022 and settled several greenwashing cases that year. The growth of sustainability indices (e.g., the Dow Jones Sustainability Index and MSCI ESG Ratings) and green financial instruments, such as green bonds and sustainability-linked loans, expanded the market for responsible investment.

2.3 Present-Day Complexities in ESG Investing

ESG investing has recently gained robust momentum as a pivotal approach to integrating sustainability with financial performance. However, its rapid rise brings challenges that call into question the efficacy, transparency, and integrity of ESG practices. The literature identifies three major sources of complexity in ESG investing: inconsistencies in ESG disclosures, concerns about ESG data integrity, and differences in ESG rating methodologies, which hinder reliable comparisons.

2.3.1 Disclosure Gaps and Inconsistencies

There has been a lack of standardized, consistent, and high-quality ESG disclosure practices among firms and across markets. Despite regulatory advances, particularly in developed economies, disclosure remains fragmented and diverse, contributing to significant information asymmetries for investors and stakeholders. Various standards have emerged, such as the GRI, SASB, TCFD and the most recent IFRS S1 and S2, however, each defines metrics differently. Even some definitions differ between them, such as 'scope 3 emissions' or diversity ratio calculations. Regions of the EU countries have established the EU's Corporate Sustainability Reporting Directive (CSRD), requiring large, listed companies, listed SMEs, large private companies, and even non-EU companies with significant EU operations to have detailed disclosures and mandatory audits, with effect from January 2023 (Doni & Toscani, 2024). The ESG disclosure landscape in the United States has been a bumpy ride. The US SEC formally adopted its climate disclosure rules in March 2024, and withdrew them in March 2025. Yet, some state-level requirements exist, such as GHG reporting in California (Johnson, 2023). In emerging markets such as China, disclosures remain in their early stages, with pronounced rating discrepancies and transparency limitations, complicating investors' ability to reliably assess ESG risks (Zhang et al., 2023). Companies may cherry-pick what they report, for example, a firm may disclose scope 1 and 2 emissions and omit scope 3 emissions related to the supply chain, which may form the majority of their total GHG emissions. This fragmented approach weakens the ability to reliably compare ESG performance across firms and undermines investor confidence (Mooneeapen et al., 2022). Gaps in reporting requirements lead companies to manipulate their ESG reports to gain a competitive edge in markets, and the voluntary nature of many ESG disclosures in developing markets facilitates superficial compliance rather than true accountability.

2.3.2 The Challenge of Greenwashing and Data Integrity

Closely intertwined with disclosure issues is the pervasive problem of greenwashing, which is the misrepresentation or exaggeration of sustainability performance and achievements for reputational gain. Greenwashing manifests in many forms and degrees, complicating detection and prevention. It can include overstating environmental achievements, selective disclosure, or presenting superficial initiatives with little substantive impact (Poiriazi et al., 2025). Recent years have substantiated several high-profile companies found to engage in greenwashing. The literature contains several case studies of such companies, and Table 1 provides examples from different industries and the regulatory authorities' consequential actions in response to revealed greenwashing tactics.

Table 1. Example Companies involved in Greenwashing and their Outcomes.

Company	Sector	Year(s)	Key Issue	Regulatory / Public Outcome
Volkswagen	Automotive	2015–2024	Misleading emissions data ("Dieselgate")	Massive fines, lawsuits (Kano et al., 2023)
Shell plc	Energy	2022–2024	Misleading renewable energy marketing	Ads banned (Iliev Matic, 2024)
Deutsche Bank	Finance	2022–2023	False ESG fund claims	SEC fine, CEO resignation (Schultz et al., 2024)
H&M	Fashion	2022–2023	False "sustainable" product labelling	Lawsuits, label removal (Kaner, 2021)
Ryanair	Aviation	2022	Misleading low-emission claims	Ads withdrawn (Poppi, 2025)

(Compiled by Author)

Greenwashing undermines the core purpose of ESG investing by eroding trust, distorting market signals, and weakening the credibility of sustainability claims (Ben Mahjoub, 2025). Event studies indicate that when corporations are exposed for greenwashing, abnormal stock price fluctuations and negative abnormal returns often follow, indicating reputational damage and investor reassessment of risk profiles. Such shocks are more impactful for firms with stronger greenwashing incentives, less transparency, and weaker governance mechanisms (Zhang et al., 2024). *Data integrity* is the weak link between sustainability claims and credible measurement. ESG reporting involves qualitative, non-financial data that are often subjective, difficult to quantify, and vary widely in scope. Such data often originates within companies from their internal systems, such as human resources, procurement, energy monitoring, among others. Aggregating and analyzing vast and varied data is labour-intensive and prone to error. This data is often voluntary, in incompatible formats, and unaudited (Jonsdottir et al., 2022). Weak enforcement, inconsistent auditing practices, and a lack of third-party verification create enforcement gaps, allowing greenwashing to persist despite regulatory frameworks (Zervoudi et al., 2025). When investors, regulators, or academics mention the 'trust gap' in ESG, they are referring to data integrity. Even when firms use third-party assurance, these providers may apply different criteria, and some may verify the data-collection process rather than the data itself. Another concern is the *timeliness of the data*, which is usually reported annually, lagged, and aggregated. By the time reports are published, it is already more than a year old. Few firms disclose monthly or quarterly metrics (Patil et al., 2024). Often, reported data rely on estimates when actual data are costly or difficult to obtain, such as for scope 3 emissions, which rely on proxies and industry averages. The ESG reports are mostly qualitative narratives and unstructured data, making them difficult for analysts to validate.

2.3.3 Differences in ESG Ratings Composition

ESG ratings represent the financial world's attempt to quantify ethics, sustainability, and governance. While this is a noble but messy reality. Although ESG ratings exist, they *pretend* to measure something objective that is deeply subjective, inconsistent, and politically charged. Different rating agencies, including MSCI, Sustainalytics, Refinitiv, Moody's ESG, and S&P Global, assign markedly divergent ratings to identical firms (Chen & Wang, 2025). Empirical studies reveal that correlations between ESG scores across agencies typically fall below 0.5, indicating that one agency may classify a company as a sustainability leader while another rates it as average or even poor (Lukács & Molnár, 2025). The case of Tesla illustrates this inconsistency vividly and Table 2 shows the differences in rating criteria and evaluations across rating agencies. Some emphasize the company's efforts to reduce carbon emissions, while others focus more on governance and social aspects.

Table 2. Summarization of ESG Ratings of Tesla Inc, 2024

ESG Rating Agency	Rating / Score	Relative Standing	Key Weaknesses	Key Strengths
MSCI[2]	A (Average)	Mid-tier	Governance, labor	EV leadership
Sustainalytics[3]	27.6 (Medium Risk)	Mid-tier	Supply chain, safety	Low emissions
S&P Global[4]	37 / 100	Below average	Disclosure, social factors	Climate technology
Refinitiv[5]	54 / 100	Average	Governance, social	Environmental innovation

continued on following page

Table 2. Continued

ESG Rating Agency	Rating / Score	Relative Standing	Key Weaknesses	Key Strengths
Moody's ESG[6]	47 / 100	Average	Labor relations	Product impact
ISS ESG[7]	C+	Below Prime	Governance, diversity	Clean tech innovation

(Compiled by Author)

A study by Lukács et al. (2024) of 265 European companies found significant differences in ESG ratings across ESG agencies for the same firms. Investors receive conflicting signals and cannot reliably compare firms across ESG dimensions (Hughes et al., 2021). ESG rating agencies employ proprietary methodologies and decline to fully disclose how they weight factors or convert qualitative information into quantitative scores (Del Vitto et al., 2023). Many ESG components are required to provide rankings that are not universally comparable, yet agencies assign weights based on their modelled frameworks, reflecting their relative importance. For example, the basic question of how much carbon emissions should matter relative to labour diversity or board independence lacks an objective answer. Cultural differences across countries are often overlooked, leading to regional biases, and differences in governance for large public companies compared to their family-owned counterparts in emerging economies may also go unnoticed (Becchetti et al., 2022). A critical concern is that ESG ratings assess how ESG affects the firm's financial risk and disclosures rather than how the firm affects ESG outcomes with its environmental impact, focusing on *'financial materiality'* rather than *'impact materiality'* (Billio et al., 2024). A company might receive a high ESG rating for managing climate-related financial risk, despite maintaining high pollution levels. Table 3 provides examples of major companies, their 2024 ESG ratings, and their ESG impact in practice.

Table 3. Company ESG Ratings and their Impact Reality

Company	Industry	ESG Rating (Approx. 2024)	Environmental Reality	Why ESG Score Is Still High
ExxonMobil	Oil & Gas	MSCI: *A* Sustainalytics: *32.8 (High Risk)*	Among the **top 10 CO_2 emitters globally**; continued fossil fuel expansion	Strong climate disclosures, governance reforms, and detailed risk management
BHP Group	Mining & Resources	MSCI: *AA* Sustainalytics: *27.5 (Medium Risk)*	Major **coal and iron ore producer**; large Scope 3 emissions	Transparent reporting, stakeholder engagement, and strong governance
Volkswagen Group	Automotive	MSCI: *A* Sustainalytics: *24.3 (Medium Risk)*	High **manufacturing emissions,** legacy from the *Dieselgate* scandal	Rapid EV transition, strong ESG recovery measures, detailed disclosure
Nestlé	Consumer Goods	MSCI: *AA* Sustainalytics: *22.6 (Medium Risk)*	Major contributor to **plastic waste and water depletion**	Supply chain audits, sustainability programs, and human rights policies
Coca-Cola Company	Beverages	MSCI: *AA* Refinitiv: *77/100*	Among the **largest global plastic polluters**	Transparency in sustainability metrics, governance leadership, and CSR programs

(Compiled by Author)

In essence, ESG ratings are mired in conceptual ambiguity (what is being measured), methodological inconsistency (how it is measured), and investor misinterpretation (how it is interpreted), even though they should serve as a yardstick for assessing their impact on a sustainable future. The next section explores the development of artificial intelligence and its potential applications in ESG investing.

3. ARTIFICIAL INTELLIGENCE IN SUSTAINABLE FINANCE

3.1 Overview of AI Technologies Relevant to Finance

AI has emerged as a transformative technological force, reshaping financial systems worldwide. The financial sector currently employs a diverse range of AI technologies, each with distinct capabilities. Technologies include *Robotic Process Automation (RPA)*, which automates repetitive tasks using *'software robots'* that mimic human actions, such as entering data, reconciling records, generating reports, or triggering downstream processes. *Machine Learning (ML)* is a foundational technology that enables systems to learn patterns from historical data and make predictions with improved accuracy. *Deep Learning* represents an advanced evolution of ML, utilizing neural network architectures to process complex, high-dimensional financial datasets (Paramesha et al., 2024). These technologies, combined with *Natural Language Processing (NLP)*, have become instrumental in extracting meaningful insights from vast volumes of unstructured textual data, such as financial reports and market news (Chen et al., 2025). Additionally, Deep Learning techniques such as *Recurrent Neural Networks (RNNs)* and *Long Short-Term Memory (LSTM)* networks have been effective for time-series prediction, used in forecasting market trends and assessing financial risks (Pasupuleti, 2025). The integration of these technologies is not merely additive; rather, they work synergistically to create comprehensive analytical frameworks that enhance financial institutions' capacity to process information, reduce human biases, and optimize decision-making.

AI in finance is evolving from automation to augmentation, moving beyond replacing human tasks to enhancing human judgment. *Generative AI* produces enhanced analytics, personalized insights, and smarter workflows. The latest frontier involves AI-driven decision intelligence, where *Predictive Analytics* combines statistical modeling and ML to forecast future financial events or market trends. *Explainable AI (XAI)* provides explanations for AI-enabled systems, ensuring compliance and building trust. *Reinforcement Learning (RL)* enables decision-making through trial and error by interacting with the environment and receiving feedback in the form of rewards or penalties for its actions. *Computer Vision (CV)* analyses images for document verification, KYC compliance and fraud detection. *Semantic AI* provides the analysis of relationships and risk assessments. Table 5 summarises the AI tools and technologies, including their core financial applications and strategic impact.

Table 5. Trending AI Technologies, Core Financial Applications and Strategic Impact

AI Technology	Description	Core Financial Applications	Strategic Impact
Robotic Process Automation (RPA)	Software robots that mimic human actions to perform repetitive tasks.	Transaction processing, reconciliations, regulatory reporting, customer onboarding.	Boosts operational scalability and compliance accuracy, cutting back-office costs and human error.
Machine Learning (ML)	Algorithms that identify patterns in data and make predictions without explicit programming. Includes supervised (labeled data), unsupervised (clustering), and reinforcement learning.	Credit scoring, fraud detection, algorithmic trading, customer segmentation, portfolio optimization.	Improves predictive accuracy, enables data-driven decision-making, and enhances operational efficiency across banking and investment services.
Natural Language Processing (NLP)	AI models that understand, interpret, and generate human language. Uses large language models (LLMs) and sentiment analysis tools.	Automated report analysis, ESG disclosure review, sentiment analysis of news or social media, chatbots, and compliance monitoring.	Enables the utilisation of unstructured data and the extraction of real-time insights from large textual sources.
Deep Learning (DL)	Subset of ML using neural networks with multiple layers to process complex, non-linear data patterns.	Market trend forecasting, image-based document verification (e.g., KYC), high-frequency trading, credit risk modeling.	Drives automation of complex analytical tasks, increases accuracy in risk prediction, and enhances fraud detection.
Generative AI	AI systems capable of creating text, images, code, or simulations using models like GPT, DALL·E, or diffusion networks.	Automated financial report writing, client advisory summaries, scenario generation for stress testing, synthetic data creation.	Reduces research time, enhances communication automation, and supports decision simulation for strategic planning.
Predictive Analytics	Combines statistical modeling and ML to forecast future financial events or market trends.	Credit default prediction, market volatility modeling, liquidity forecasting.	Supports proactive risk management and strategic investment decisions.
Explainable AI (XAI)	Frameworks that make AI decisions interpretable and transparent for users and regulators.	Regulatory compliance, risk assessment, ethical AI deployment in lending and underwriting.	Builds trust in AI systems, ensuring compliance with governance frameworks like the EU AI Act.
Reinforcement Learning (RL)	AI agents learn optimal actions through trial and error to maximize reward over time.	Dynamic portfolio optimization, autonomous trading strategies, resource allocation in asset management.	Enables adaptive decision-making and continuous learning in volatile markets.

continued on following page

Table 5. Continued

AI Technology	Description	Core Financial Applications	Strategic Impact
Computer Vision (CV)	AI that interprets visual inputs such as images or videos.	Document verification, fraud prevention (e.g., identity validation), insurance claim processing.	Enhances security, fraud control, and digital KYC efficiency.
Knowledge Graphs & Semantic AI	Structures that represent relationships between entities (e.g., firms, transactions, markets).	Anti-money laundering (AML), fraud detection, ESG relationship mapping, counterparty risk assessment.	Provides contextual intelligence and enhanced data traceability across financial networks.

(Compiled by Author)

3.2 AI-Driven ESG Data Collection, Processing, and Assessment

ESG data collection is moving from static models of disclosure and compliance to dynamic, data-driven intelligence systems (Juthi et al., 2024). It faces a fundamental challenge of fragmentation and inconsistency stemming from voluntary disclosures and analyst reviews (Billio et al., 2024; Jonsdottir et al., 2022). AI addresses this and is uniquely positioned to mitigate these issues by automating the ingestion and analysis of vast, heterogeneous ESG datasets, offering a more objective, data-driven lens that minimizes human error and unconscious bias (Adeoye et al., 2024). *Satellite-based Earth Observation (SEO)* combined with *ML algorithms* can provide new, regular, or near-real-time independent data streams, depending on the satellite's orbit and tasking, for validation of environmental claims made by issuers of ESG bonds confirming whether reforestation projects, renewable energy installations, or water management initiatives funded by such bonds are actually being implemented (Rapach et al., 2024). These technologies can also be used to track changes in land use and resource management to confirm ESG metrics reported by companies. *IoT sensors* provide real-time data on energy consumption and emissions (Elias et al., 2024). *NLP technologies* have become useful in efficiently and extensively extracting relevant ESG information from various sources, including reports, news articles, social media, and regulatory filings (Lim, 2024; Chen et al., 2025). AI-driven systems can detect subtle linguistic patterns indicative of genuine sustainability commitments versus superficial claims, thereby helping combat greenwashing. *Advanced analytics* platforms can perform *anomaly detection*, identifying inconsistencies or suspicious patterns in reported data (Moodaley & Telukdarie, 2023). *Generative AI models* can estimate missing ESG metrics by learning from relationships between reported indicators and other company characteristics, thereby addressing data gaps that would otherwise limit investment decision-making (Chen et al., 2025). AI supports auditing and validating corporate sustainability claims through anomaly detection and verification methods such as *Knowledge Gaps and Semantic AI*. The automation's proficiency enables the evaluation of ESG performance across multiple dimensions for companies while maintaining consistency and transparency during assessment (Adeoye et al., 2024).

3.3 AI-Based ESG Scoring and Dynamic Weighting Models

Further to the discussion in section 2.3.3 above, ESG ratings produced by multiple private agencies vary in their outcomes, computational models, and transparency, creating challenges for investors in utilising ESG scores to their optimal benefit. *ML techniques* offer a pathway toward greater transparency and methodological rigor in ESG scoring. Researchers have successfully employed ML to *reverse-engineer* proprietary ESG rating models that can replicate or approximate agency ratings with high accuracy (Choi et al., 2024). The algorithms can discern how rating agencies weigh various factors in their rating computations, such as how much carbon intensity or gender diversity is weighed in their models. *Dynamic weighting* uses ML where instead of employing static weighting schemes that treat all ESG factors equally regardless of context, it can adaptively adjust the importance of different factors based on industry characteristics, company-specific conditions, and evolving market priorities (Adeoye et al., 2024). For instance, environmental factors may carry greater weight for companies in energy or manufacturing sectors, while governance considerations may become more important in financial services. The integration of *sentiment analysis* with ESG scoring uses ML to detect the tone, emotion, or attitude expressed in text, whether positive, negative, or neutral, that adds a real-time, external dimension. This text could be news articles, company reports, press releases, analysts' reports, or social media posts. It captures how stakeholders and markets actually perceive a company's ESG behaviour (Chen et al, 2025). This perception layer complements traditional ESG metrics, providing a more comprehensive view of a company's sustainability position.

3.4 AI-Driven Portfolio Optimization and Risk Assessment

Traditionally, finance has relied on Modern Portfolio Theory (MPT) and its variants developed in the 1950s to optimise investor returns, based on the principle of diversification that assumes stable return distributions and linear relationships among assets. Currently, this model struggles with the complexity of ESG considerations, where ESG investment portfolios require navigating multidimensional risk factors, including regulatory, reputational, climate, social, and governance-driven factors, which do not fit within the variance-covariance model of MPT. ESG risks are dynamic, nonlinear, and forward-looking, and they deliver noisy, divergent metrics (Billah et al., 2024). AI-driven tools can surpass these shortcomings by capturing non-linear relationships, adapting to changing market dynamics, and seamlessly incorporating ESG factors into portfolio construction. *ML algorithms* can identify intricate patterns in historical price data and other financial indicators using *Multi-objective evolutionary algorithms (MOEAs)* (Oshoba et al., 2020). AI can make portfolio optimization dynamic, adjusting weights as new information arrives. *Neural networks (NNs)* can be used to identify interactions between industries or asset classes, such as how technology stocks respond to changes in gold prices or interest rates, that linear models cannot capture (Pasupuleti, 2025). *Recurrent Neural Networks (RNNs)* recycle past information, whereas *Long Short-Term Memory (LSTM)* models calibrate what to remember, what to forget, and what to update, and are essentially a dynamic knowledge-retention pipeline. A self-learning investment assessment strategy that adapts to changing market conditions can be modelled using *Reinforcement Learning (RL)* algorithms to continuously learn from market feedback, based on rewards (returns) and penalties (losses) (Billah et al., 2024). By learning from years of market history, these systems can recognize subtle precursor patterns that precede market movements, enabling more accurate risk forecasting. Such capabilities translate directly into superior portfolio performance compared to traditional statistical models. *RL models* can be particularly valuable during volatile times, when swift changes in ESG factors can suddenly impact investment returns, and rebalancing strategies can be applied to maximize risk-adjusted returns while maintaining ESG compliance (Pasupuleti, 2025). Portfolio risk assessment can be enhanced to evaluate sustainability-related financial risks, enabling financial institutions to develop *credit risk scoring engines* through *ML and Predictive Analytics* that capture dynamic climate risks, supply chain vulnerabilities, and social instability that affect borrowers' creditworthiness. The integration of *XAI* techniques into portfolio management has become increasingly critical as regulators and investors demand transparency in algorithmic decision-making. *Interpretable machine learning* models enable portfolio managers and compliance officers to understand why specific assets are recommended, which risk factors are driving portfolio composition, and how ESG considerations influence allocation decisions. ML systems can dynamically scan financial transactions in real time, identifying suspicious activity with greater precision than traditional rule-based systems, leading to efficient fraud detection and identifying ESG greenwashing claims to maintain market integrity in sustainable finance (Moodaley & Telukdarie, 2023; Schultz et al., 2024).

4. FROM ESG TO ESGI: THE PARADIGM SHIFT TO A STRUCTURED FRAMEWORK FOR AI-INTEGRATED ESG INVESTING

Sustainable finance is undergoing a paradigm shift from traditional ESG investing to ESGI, where AI is integrated as a core pillar rather than a peripheral tool. Due to the complexity, volume and dynamic nature of ESG data, it is becoming imperative that AI-based technologies for analytics, predictive modelling and ML are embedded within ESG methodologies.

4.1 Modelling the ESGI Framework

This study now proceeds to develop an ESGI framework to address shortcomings associated with ESG data complexity, data integrity issues, and unchecked green-washing tactics. These challenges are compounded by inconsistencies in ESG ratings, which impair analysts' ability to make effective investment decisions. Regulators are burdened by inconsistencies in disclosure requirements across diverse reporting standards, hindering their ability to formulate coherent compliance guidelines. AI technologies offer meaningful opportunities to mitigate these shortcomings, and this study conceptualises the ESGI architecture as comprising *four interoperable layers* across the ESG ecosystem.

1- Data Layer
2- Intelligence Layer
3- Decision Layer
4- Governance Layer

4.2 Data Layer: ESG and Alternative Data Sources

The data layer is the foundational component of the ESGI framework, serving as the comprehensive repository and integration point for all ESG-related information from multiple sources and formats. This layer is tasked with collecting, validating, standardizing, and organizing vast quantities of structured and unstructured ESG data while ensuring data integrity, consistency, and accessibility for downstream processing and analysis. ESGI extends the data universe beyond periodic corporate disclosures by integrating heterogeneous data sources. *NLP pipelines* ingest and normalize financial reports, sustainability reports, climate transition plans, and assurance statements, extracting entities, topics, forward-looking commitments, and risk narratives at scale (Vitto et al., 2023). *Supply chain data and logistics* information can illuminate the environmental and social impacts of corporate operations beyond the company's direct control. Advances in information extraction and sentiment analysis enable the detection of litigation exposure, transition risk posture, and operational resilience embedded in financial narratives and footnotes. *Sensor networks and IoT* technologies can provide continuous, real-time monitoring of environmental performance metrics, rather than relying on periodic self-reported assessments.

The primary challenge addressed by the data layer is the heterogeneity of ESG data sources and formats, plus the data layer architecture must also accommodate the multiplicity of disclosure frameworks while establishing a unified internal data model capable of transforming heterogeneous inputs into comparable, standardized information assets. Coverage of developments across ISSB, TCFD, and IFRS S1 and S2 enables policy-aware, interoperable data models across jurisdictions (Mulligan et al., 2024). Uncertainty in big data is endemic in these sources, so robust preprocessing, deduplication, record linkage, and outlier control are critical to prevent error propagation in downstream analytics (Visalli et al., 2023). An outside-in approach helps resolve rating divergence by integrating real-time controversies and stakeholder sentiment into traditional metrics, improving cross-provider commensurability and reducing reliance on opaque aggregation rules. Data encryption, anonymization techniques, and secure data transmission protocols must be implemented throughout the data layer to protect information assets. Figure 2 depicts the Data Layer framework.

Figure 2. Data Layer Framework

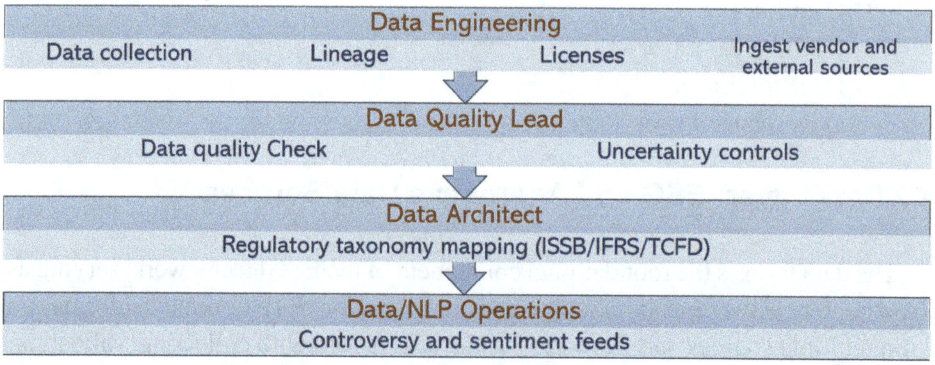

4.3 Intelligence Layer: AI/ML Analytical Models Data Architecture

The intelligence layer is the computational part of the ESGI framework. Here, advanced AI and ML algorithms are employed to convert raw ESG data into actionable insights. This layer is fundamental in extracting meaningful patterns, identifying correlations and generating predictions that guide investment decisions aligned with the combined objectives of financial performance and sustainability. Predictive analytics in finance using *decision trees, Random Forest (RF), Support Vector Machines (SVM), Extreme Gradient Boosting (XGboost), and LSTM networks* improves signal extraction from high-dimensional time series and unstructured datasets (Sekhar & Narasimhulu, 2025). These algorithms excel at capturing temporal dependencies, identifying non-linear patterns in ESG metrics, and adapting to changing market conditions in ways traditional mean-variance optimization cannot achieve.

Portfolio optimization tools no longer depend on rigid assumptions about return distributions and correlations. Inputs from the intelligence layer include dynamic ESG scores, market conditions, and sustainability trends, trained via *RL* to identify optimal investment strategies that continuously adapt to reward signals. *LSTM networks* have demonstrated exceptional performance in predicting ESG stock indices (Suprihadi & Danila, 2024). Network-based methods, such as the *Financial Maximally Filtered Graph*, add structure to correlation estimation and help characterize systemic exposures relevant to ESG themes (Diaz & Nguyen, 2023). A study by Saxena et al. (2024) found that using a nested sentiment analysis tool, *FinBERT*, in the intelligence layer to classify the sentiments of eco-friendly and non-eco-friendly products achieved an accuracy of almost 92% in predicting ESG scores. Sentiment analysis has other applications, including detecting early warning signals of potential ESG-related controversies, tracking market perception of corporate sustainability efforts, quantifying investor confidence in green transitions, and identifying divergences between companies' ESG disclosures and market perceptions. These AI-driven ESG ratings can help ensure they are fair, robust, and explainable to users (Giudici et al., 2024). Figure 3 shows the Intelligence Layer framework.

Figure 3. Intelligence Layer Framework

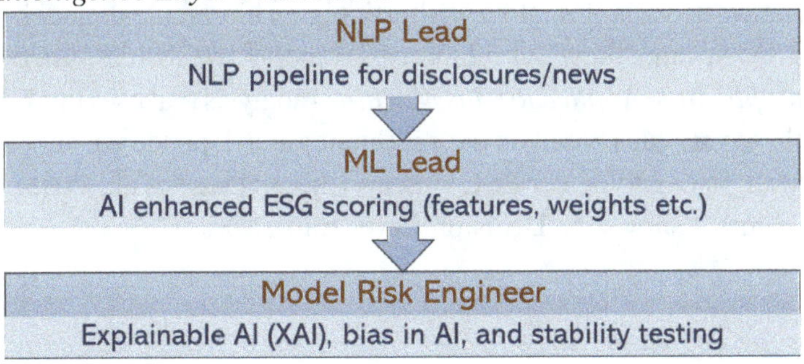

4.4 Decision Layer: Investment Strategy Formulation and Portfolio Construction

The Decision Layer translates the insights generated by the Intelligence Layer into concrete investment strategies and portfolio allocations. This layer bridges the analytical foundation of AI-driven ESG assessment to actual capital-allocation decisions, incorporating investor preferences, risk tolerance, sustainability objectives, and fiduciary constraints. This Layer is where data-driven insights are converted into actionable investment recommendations that balance financial performance with environmental and social impact. Traditional approaches that treat ESG as peripheral to financial analysis are superseded by integrated frameworks that recognize ESG metrics as material determinants of long-term financial value.

Scenario analysis and stress testing integrate climate policy shocks, physical risk events, supply chain disruptions, and reputation events into portfolio diagnostics. *The Black-Litterman model* uses ML return predictions via *LSTM neural networks* as views in the Black-Litterman framework, capable of improving the mean-variance optimization by incorporating forward-looking ESG considerations (Truyols-Pont et al., 2024). Predictive analytics at scale enables earlier detection of deteriorating risk profiles and more disciplined rebalancing under uncertainty (Nahar et al., 2024). The Decision layer moves beyond the traditional Sharpe ratios for generating risk-adjusted metrics such as the *Hierarchical Risk Parity (HRP)*[8] approach to create a more balanced risk distribution across ESG dimensions (Deković & Šimović, 2025). As ESG efficiency differs across business sectors, it enables customized portfolio strategies for specific industries and ESG materiality profiles. As investors have differing sustainability objectives and risk tolerances, the ESGI decision layer enables customization of portfolios prioritizing ESG dimensions based on customer preferences (Assaf et al., 2024). This layer includes the detection and exclusion of companies engaged in ESG greenwashing. The *Total Interpretive Structural Modeling (TISM)* converts variables into a well-articulated hierarchical model, answering the "what," "why," and "how" of relationships in the *MICMAC (Matrix of Impact Cross-r-Multiplication Applied to Classification)* analysis that uses the TISM output to classify these variables based on their influence and dependence on other factors, which are well placed to detect ESG greenwashing (Daga et al., 2025; Giudici et al., 2024). Figure 4 shows the Decision Layer framework.

Figure 4. Decision Layer Framework

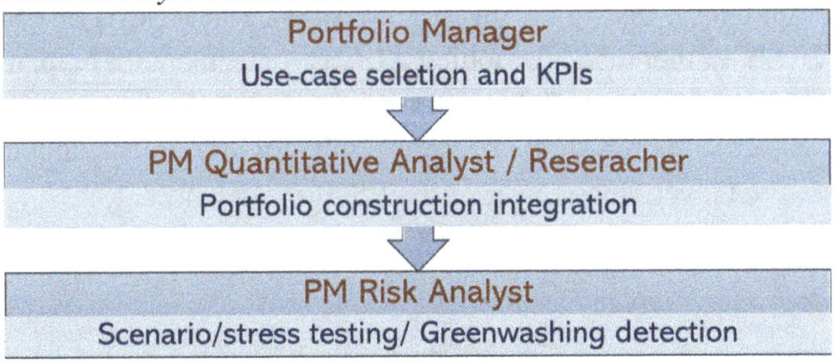

4.5 Governance Layer: Ethical Oversight, Compliance and Accountability

One key concern of AI for ESG investments is the risk of algorithmic bias seeping into models, leading to unfair outcomes. Biases could emerge due to skewed training data that overemphasizes certain business sectors, algorithms for collecting specifically encoded and discriminatory data and biases towards certain investment categories (Assaf et al., 2024). The Governance Layer comprises the ethical and regulatory framework, ensuring that the ESGI framework operates with integrity, transparency, and accountability. It addresses the ethical considerations in three core dimensions: (1) fairness and bias-mitigation protocols, (2) regulatory compliance and (3) third-party assurance over data and models. The emphasis is on explainability and transparency as basic requirements for a responsible ESGI framework.

Pre-processing, in-processing and post-processing checks at all stages of the AI lifecycle identify biased algorithms and apply corrections. Continuous retraining with diverse, dynamic datasets prevents model biases from accumulating over time as market conditions evolve (Fagbore et al., 2024). Beyond bias detection, the integration of *XAI models* into ESG investing converts algorithmic decisions into human-understandable explanations that can be audited by third parties and questioned by regulators and stakeholders (Laato et al., 2022). *SHAP (SHapley Additive exPlanations)*[9] and *LIME (Local Interpretable Model-agnostic Explanations)* provides a game-theoretic approach to explain individual predictions. SHAP values explain the difference between the prediction and the global average prediction, whereas LIME values use the local average prediction (Aas et al., 2021). These could explain why some companies were included or excluded from ESG portfolios. This layer is augmented by human oversight from accounting professionals, auditors, and investment analysts, who validate AI-driven insights and ensure accountability for recommendations (Zhang & Zhang, 2024). These third-party audits examine whether models produce predictions within specified accuracy ranges, ensure fairness and regulatory compliance, and build investor confidence in AI-driven ESG systems (Patil et al., 2024). Rather than positioning AI as a replacement for human judgment, responsible AI integration into ESG investment decision-making augments human capabilities while maintaining human responsibility for investment outcomes. Figure 5 summarises the Governance Layer of the ESGI framework.

Figure 5. Governance Layer Framework

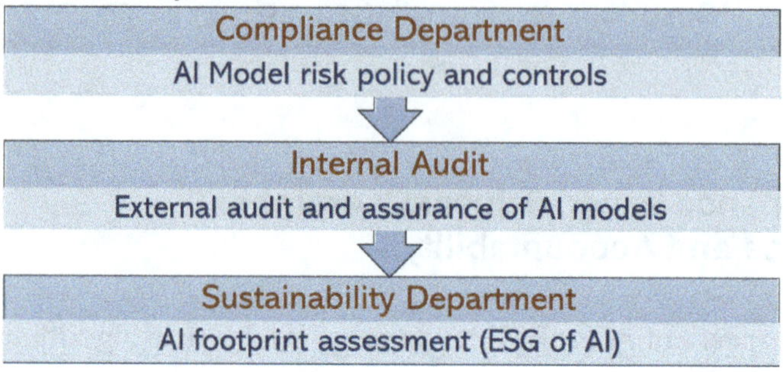

4.6 The overall ESGI Framework

The Data layer forms the core of the ESGI framework, which provides the raw data needed for decision-making, the lack of which would pose significant risks, including greenwashing accusations, operational inefficiencies, regulatory violations, and dissatisfied investors. Analytical capabilities are provided by the Intelligence Layer, which gets translated to insights for portfolio optimisation by the Decision Layer. The Governance Layer ensures that this entire process operates transparently, fairly, and accountably, embedding ethical principles and regulatory compliance throughout the framework. The Intelligence, Decision, and Governance Layers of the ESGI framework work synergistically to advance AI-integrated, data-driven sustainable investing while maintaining ethical integrity and regulatory compliance. The complete ESGI framework has been summarized in Table 6.

Table 6. The Overall ESGI Framework with Four Layers

DATA LAYER	
Activity	**Responsibility**
Data collection, lineage, licenses	Data Engineering

continued on following page

Table 6. Continued

Ingest vendor and external sources	Data Engineering
Data quality and uncertainty controls	Data Quality Lead
Regulatory taxonomy mapping (ISSB/IFRS/TCFD)	Data Architect
Controversy and sentiment feeds	Data/NLP Operations
INTELLIGENCE LAYER	
Activity	**Responsibility**
NLP pipeline for disclosures/news	NLP Lead
AI-enhanced ESG scoring (features, weights)	ML Lead
Explainable AI (XAI), bias in AI, and stability testing	Model Risk Engineer
DECISION LAYER	
Activity	**Responsibility**
Use-case selection and KPIs	Portfolio Manager (PM)
Portfolio construction integration	PM Quantitative Analyst/ Researcher
Scenario/stress testing/ Greenwashing detection	PM Risk Analyst
GOVERNANCE LAYER	
Activity	**Responsibility**
AI model risk policy and controls	Compliance Department
External audit and assurance of AI models	Internal Audit
AI footprint assessment (ESG of AI)	Sustainability Department

5. CONCLUSION AND FUTURE RESEARCH

This study emphasizes that AI has become instrumental in sustainable investment decision-making. AI enables meticulous and accurate ESG assessment, improving portfolio optimization, and enhancing risk management and governance capabilities. There are challenges in integrating AI, including correcting errors in data ingestion and processing to ensure data quality and relevance, and enhancing transparency and accountability in the use of AI mechanisms.

5.1 The Transformative Potential of ESGI Integration

The paradigm shift of the ESGI framework outlined in this study indicates an impact greater than just the technological enhancement and directs towards a reconceptualization of how capital markets can simultaneously pursue financial returns, environmental leadership, social equity, and governance integrity through systematic, evidence-based decision-making. This study has identified various AI technologies across all levels of the ESG ecosystem that transcend traditional methods, recognizing ESG factors as material to adding long-term value for businesses. In the environmental domain, the ESGI framework enables exceptional precision in measuring environmental impact and quantifying climate risk. Predictive analytics for workplace protection, labor relations, and enhancement of human capital enable proactive management of social risks before they evolve into operational disruptions or reputational damage. NLP tools and XAI for the governance and accountability aspect. Dynamic portfolio rebalancing enabled by AI systems allows investors to adjust exposures rapidly as ESG conditions change rather than remaining locked into static allocations.

5.2 Implementation Roadmap and Future Directions

The ESGI framework offers transformative potential; however, it also poses certain challenges that require attention from practitioners, auditors, regulators, and other stakeholders. Processes to address some of these shortcomings have been incorporated into the ESGI framework, which employs methods to reduce data ambiguity by removing algorithmic bias and training models on diverse, dynamic data. Studies have shown that AI can exacerbate existing discrimination in ESG score development. XAI remains in its infancy in explaining the predictive accuracy of AI models. Regulatory uncertainty and evolving frameworks create compliance challenges for multinational institutions.

The success of the ESGI framework requires coordinated action from AI-enabled data providers and ESG rating agencies to enhance transparency in assessment methodologies and a convergence towards standardised ESG scores will enhance reliability and comparability. Financial institutions, asset managers and investment firms are required to establish governance frameworks and human oversight mechanisms. Regulators and policymakers should place greater attention on responsibility rather than prescribing technical requirements. Third-party assurance can play a major role in strengthening governance. Academic researchers should prioritise empirical investigations into whether ESGI systems deliver on their promises of performance and sustainability. Institutional investors and asset owners should demand transparency and accountability from AI-enabled fund management to drive industry adoption of best practices. The study concludes that the ESGI framework, when implemented with appropriate governance and ethical discipline, represents a genuinely transformative approach to sustainable investing.

This study establishes a convincing case for the strategic implementation of ESGI frameworks across organizations in the finance industry and accentuates the need for ethical discipline along with technological advancement for genuine improvement in environmental and social performance rather than merely managing perceptions. Given the *IMMENSE* opportunity, the need to build responsible AI-integrated ESG and sustainable finance is *NOW !!!*

REFERENCES

Aas, K., Jullum, M., & Løland, A. (2021). Explaining individual predictions when features are dependent: More accurate approximations to Shapley values. *Artificial Intelligence, 298*, 103502. DOI: 10.1016/j.artint.2021.103502

Adeoye, O. B., Addy, W. A., Ajayi-Nifise, A. O., Odeyemi, O., Okoye, C. C., & Ofodile, O. C. (2024). Leveraging AI and data analytics for enhancing financial inclusion in developing economies. *Finance & Accounting Research Journal, 6*(3), 288–303. DOI: 10.51594/farj.v6i3.856

Andika, C. (2025). ESG Integration in Financial Accounting: Comparative Evidence and Policy Implications. Sinergi International Journal of Accounting and Taxation, 3(3), 181-194.1.2 The Emerging Role of Artificial Intelligence in Sustainable Finance.

Assaf, C., Monne, J., Harriet, L., & Meunier, L. (2024). ESG investing: Does one score fit all investors' preferences? *Journal of Cleaner Production, 443*, 141094. DOI: 10.1016/j.jclepro.2024.141094

Becchetti, L., Bobbio, E., Prizia, F., & Semplici, L. (2022). Going deeper into the S of ESG: A relational approach to the definition of social responsibility. *Sustainability (Basel), 14*(15), 9668. DOI: 10.3390/su14159668

Ben Mahjoub, L. (2025). Greenwashing practices and ESG reporting: An international review. *The International Journal of Sociology and Social Policy, 45*(1-2), 173–188. DOI: 10.1108/IJSSP-08-2024-0365

Berg, F., Kölbel, J. F., & Rigobon, R. (2022). Aggregate confusion: The divergence of ESG ratings. *Review of Finance, 26*(6), 1315–1344. DOI: 10.1093/rof/rfac033

Billah, A. L., Koesrindartoto, D. P., & Faturohman, T. (2024). Advancing ESG Portfolio Optimization: Methods, Progress, and Future Directions. Accounting & Finance Review (AFR), 9(2).

Billio, M., Costola, M., Hristova, I., Latino, C., & Pelizzon, L. (2024). Sustainable finance: A journey toward ESG and climate risk. *International Review of Environmental and Resource Economics, 18*(1-2), 1–75. DOI: 10.1561/101.00000156

Carrasco, B., & Lee, J. (2023). Greening the Financial System. Available at: http://www.yrdcpcn.com/upload/2025/0120/f14c168b-4e6d-4574-b20c-da8fdd639f8b.pdf

Chen, G., & Wang, Q. (2025). ESG rating disagreement, market information efficiency and institutional investor shareholding behavior. *Economia e Politica Industriale*, 1–26. DOI: 10.1007/s40812-025-00372-1

Chen, Y., Yan, S., Jin, Y., Li, J., & Jin, X. (2025). Generative Artificial Intelligence in Finance: A Systematic Literature Review and a Research Agenda. *Digital Technologies Research and Applications*, *4*(2), 14–32. DOI: 10.54963/dtra.v4i2.1191

Choi, J. C., Chen, Q., & Lee, S. J. (2024). Predicting ESG Ratings by Machine Learning and Analyzing Influencing Factors by XAI. In *Proceedings of the 2024 7th International Conference on Software Engineering and Information Management* (pp. 120-125). DOI: 10.1145/3647722.3647742

Daga, S., Yadav, K., Singh, D., Pamucar, D., & Simic, V. (2025). Unveiling greenwashing: Analyzing the interaction of factors discouraging ESG greenwashing through TISM and MICMAC. *Journal of Environmental Management*, *380*, 124850. DOI: 10.1016/j.jenvman.2025.124850 PMID: 40073478

Deković, D., & Šimović, P. P. (2025). Hierarchical risk parity: Efficient implementation and real world analysis. *Future Generation Computer Systems*, *167*, 107744. DOI: 10.1016/j.future.2025.107744

Del Vitto, A., Marazzina, D., & Stocco, D. (2023). ESG ratings explainability through machine learning techniques. *Annals of Operations Research*, 1–30. DOI: 10.1007/s10479-023-05514-z

Dey, R., Kassim, S., Mahajan, R., Pawar, D. J. A., Kumbhar, V. R., Shendage, J., & Patil, M. (2025). A systematic literature review on the ethical capital market: Insights using the prisma approach. *Journal of Information Systems Engineering & Management*.

Diaz, J. F., & Nguyen, T. T. (2023). Application of grey relational analysis and artificial neural networks on corporate social responsibility (CSR) indices. *Journal of Sustainable Finance & Investment*, *13*(3), 1181–1199. DOI: 10.1080/20430795.2021.1929805

Doni, F., & Toscani, D. (2024). Corporate governance and sustainability: an overview of the new trends in the European Union. Research Handbook on Sustainability Reporting, 293-308.

Eccles, R., & Klimenko, S. (2019). The Investor Revolution. *Harvard Business Review*, (May–June), 106–116.

Elias, O., Awotunde, O. J., Oladepo, O. I., Azuikpe, P. F., Samson, O. A., Oladele, O. R., & Ogunruku, O. O. (2024). The evolution of green fintech: Leveraging AI and IoT for sustainable financial services and smart contract implementation. *World Journal of Advanced Research and Reviews*, *23*(1), 2710–2723. DOI: 10.30574/wjarr.2024.23.1.2272

Fagbore, O. O., Ogeawuchi, J. C., Ilori, O., Isibor, N. J., Odetunde, A., & Adekunle, B. I. (2024). Conceptual Design of Ethical Investment Assessment Models Using AI-Enhanced Financial Decision Tools.

Friede, G., Busch, T., & Bassen, A. (2015). ESG and financial performance: Aggregated evidence from more than 2000 empirical studies. *Journal of Sustainable Finance & Investment*, *5*(4), 210–233. DOI: 10.1080/20430795.2015.1118917

Gibson Brandon, R., Krueger, P., & Schmidt, P. S. (2021). ESG rating disagreement and stock returns. *Financial Analysts Journal*, *77*(4), 104–127. DOI: 10.1080/0015198X.2021.1963186

Giese, G., Lee, L. E., Melas, D., Nagy, Z., & Nishikawa, L. (2019). Foundations of ESG investing: How ESG affects equity valuation, risk, and performance. *Journal of Portfolio Management*, *45*(5), 69–83. DOI: 10.3905/jpm.2019.45.5.069

Gill, A. (2008). Corporate governance as social responsibility: A research agenda. *Berkeley J. Int'l L.*, *26*, 452.

Giudici, P., Centurelli, M., & Turchetta, S. (2024). Artificial Intelligence risk measurement. *Expert Systems with Applications*, 235, 121220. https://doi.org/10.1016/j.eswa.2023.121220.

Hughes, A., Urban, M. A., & Wójcik, D. (2021). Alternative ESG ratings: How technological innovation is reshaping sustainable investment. *Sustainability (Basel)*, *13*(6), 3551. DOI: 10.3390/su13063551

Iliev Matić, M. (2024). The Impact of Social Media on ESG Through the Lens of Greenwashing. FINIZ 2024-Social Media and Contemporary Business, 109-114.

Johnson, K. C. (2023). California's ambitious greenhouse gas policies: Are they ambitious enough? *Energy Policy*, *177*, 113545. DOI: 10.1016/j.enpol.2023.113545

Jonsdottir, B., Sigurjonsson, T. O., Johannsdottir, L., & Wendt, S. (2022). Barriers to using ESG data for investment decisions. *Sustainability (Basel)*, *14*(9), 5157. DOI: 10.3390/su14095157

Juthi, S., Kamrujjaman, M., Mistry, A. M., & Alauddin, M. (2024). Sustainable finance and data analytics: A systematic review of ESG data in investment decisions. Academic Journal on Business Administration, Innovation & Sustainability, 4(04).

Kaner, G. (2021). Greenwashing: How difficult it is to be transparent to the consumer—H&M case study. In *Green marketing in emerging markets: Strategic and operational perspectives* (pp. 203–226). Springer International Publishing. DOI: 10.1007/978-3-030-74065-8_9

Kano, L., Simoes, S., & Verbeke, A. (2023). Governance failure and firm-level crises: The case of the Volkswagen emissions scandal. In *Research Handbook on International Corporate Social Responsibility* (pp. 168–186). Edward Elgar Publishing. DOI: 10.4337/9781802207040.00018

La Torre, M., Mango, F., Cafaro, A., & Leo, S. (2020). Does the ESG index affect stock return? Evidence from the Eurostoxx50. *Sustainability (Basel)*, *12*(16), 6387. DOI: 10.3390/su12166387

Laato, S., Tiainen, M., Najmul Islam, A. K. M., & Mäntymäki, M. (2022). How to explain AI systems to end users: A systematic literature review and research agenda. *Internet Research*, *32*(7), 1–31. DOI: 10.1108/INTR-08-2021-0600

Lee, C. L., & Liang, J. (2024). The effect of carbon regulation initiatives on corporate ESG performance in real estate sector: International evidence. *Journal of Cleaner Production*, *453*, 142188. DOI: 10.1016/j.jclepro.2024.142188

Lim, T. (2024). Environmental, social, and governance (ESG) and artificial intelligence in finance: State-of-the-art and research takeaways. *Artificial Intelligence Review*, *57*(4), 76. DOI: 10.1007/s10462-024-10708-3

Lukács, B., & Molnár, P. (2025). Companies' ESG performance under soft and hard regulation environment. *Discover Sustainability*, *6*(1), 701. DOI: 10.1007/s43621-025-01657-0

Lukács, B., Molnar, P., & Rickards, R. C. (2024). Comparative assessment of ESG ratings methodology and results based on XBRL. Journal of Infrastructure. *Policy and Development*, *8*(12), 8641.

Malecki, C. (2021). The EU taxonomy regulation: Giving a good name to sustainable investment. Malecki C., The EU Taxonomy Regulation: giving a good name to sustainable investment, (2021), 26(4), 149-156.

Moodaley, W., & Telukdarie, A. (2023). Greenwashing, Sustainability Reporting, and Artificial Intelligence: A Systematic Literature Review. *Sustainability (Basel)*, *15*(2), 1481. DOI: 10.3390/su15021481

Mooneeapen, O., Abhayawansa, S., & Mamode Khan, N. (2022). The influence of the country governance environment on corporate environmental, social and governance (ESG) performance. Sustainability Accounting. *Management and Policy Journal*, *13*(4), 953–985.

Mulligan, C., Morsfield, S., & Cheikosman, E. (2024). Blockchain for sustainability: A systematic literature review for policy impact. *Telecommunications Policy*, *48*(2), 102676. DOI: 10.1016/j.telpol.2023.102676

Nahar, J., Hossain, M. S., Rahman, M. M., & Hossain, M. A. (2024). Advanced predictive analytics for comprehensive risk assessment in financial markets: Strategic applications and sector-wide implications. Global Mainstream Journal of Business, Economics. *Development & Project Management*, *3*(4), 39–53.

Oshoba, T. O., Aifuwa, S. E., Ogbuefi, E., & Olatunde-Thorpe, J. (2020). Portfolio Optimization with Multi-Objective Evolutionary Algorithms-Balancing Risk, Return, and Sustainability Metrics, International Journal of Multidisciplinary Research and Growth Evaluation, ISSN: 2582-7138, 1(3), 163-170.

Paramesha, M., Rane, N., & Rane, J. (2024). Artificial intelligence, machine learning, deep learning, and blockchain in financial and banking services: A comprehensive review. Machine Learning, Deep Learning, and Blockchain in Financial and Banking Services: A Comprehensive Review (June 6, 2024).

Pasko, O., Chen, F., Kuts, T., Sharko, I., & Ryzhikova, N. (2022). Sustainability reporting nexus to corporate governance in scholarly literature. *Environment and Ecology*, *13*(1), 61.

Pasupuleti, M. K. (2025). Deep Finance: Cutting-Edge Deep Learning Applications in Market Prediction, Risk Analytics, and Algorithmic Trading. International Journal of Academic and Industrial Research Innovations (IJAIRI), Vol 5, Issue 5, ISSN: 3049-2343.

Patil, S. R., Jadhav, S. N., & Nimbagal, S. (2024). A study on ethical implications of using technology in ESG investing and ensuring unbiased decision making. *Multidisciplinary Science Journal*, *6*(8), 2024153–2024153. DOI: 10.31893/multiscience.2024153

Poiriazi, E., Zournatzidou, G., Konteos, G., & Sariannidis, N. (2025). Analyzing the interconnection between environmental, social, and governance (ESG) criteria and corporate corruption: Revealing the significant impact of greenwashing. *Administrative Sciences*, *15*(3), 100. DOI: 10.3390/admsci15030100

Popescu, C. E., Pentescu, A., & Shivarov, A. (2023). Sustainability, ESG ratings and corporate performance in the manufacturing sector: A research review. *European Journal of Interdisciplinary Studies*, *15*(2), 186–209. DOI: 10.24818/ejis.2023.24

Poppi, F. (2025). Airlines' Emission Disclosures: The Fine Line Between Opportunity and Environmental Inaction. Iperstoria, (25).

Pratiwi, A. P., & Edeh, F. O. (2024). The Role of ESG Disclosure in Corporate Performance and Investment Decision-Making. Sinergi International Journal of Accounting and Taxation, 2(1), 1-14. PRI (2017). Principles for Responsible Investment Reporting Framework.

Pria, S., Al Rubaie, I., & Prasad, V. (2024). Enhancing business intelligence through AI-driven integration of sustainability metrics via ESG factors. In Risks and Challenges of AI-Driven Finance: Bias, Ethics, and Security (pp. 57-89). IGI Global.

Rapach, S., Riccardi, A., Liu, B., & Bowden, J. (2024). A taxonomy of earth observation data for sustainable finance. *Journal of Climate Finance*, *6*, 100029. DOI: 10.1016/j.jclimf.2023.100029

Saxena, A., Santhanavijayan, A., Shakya, H., Kumar, G., Balusamy, B., & Benedetto, F. (2024). Nested Sentiment Analysis for ESG Impact: Leveraging FinBERT to Predict Market Dynamics Based on Eco-Friendly and Non-Eco-Friendly Product Perceptions with Explainable AI. *Mathematics*, *12*(21), 3332. DOI: 10.3390/math12213332

Schultz, A., Senn, M., & van't Klooster, J. (2024). Restoring trust in sustainable finance: The role of active supervision in greenwashing scandals. finanzwende.de

Sekhar, C., & Narasimhulu, M. (2025, March). Stock Market Forecasting with Ensemble Learning: Random Forest, XGBoost, and LSTM. In 2025 7th International Conference on Intelligent Sustainable Systems (ICISS) (pp. 1683-1689). IEEE.

Suprihadi, E., & Danila, N. (2024). Forecasting ESG stock indices using a machine learning approach. *Global Business Review*, 09721509241234033. DOI: 10.1177/09721509241234033

Truyols-Pont, M. A., Bilbao-Terol, A., & Arenas-Parra, M. (2024). Machine Learning for Sustainable Portfolio Optimization Applied to a Water Market. *Mathematics*, *12*(24), 3975. DOI: 10.3390/math12243975

Visalli, F., Patrizio, A., Lanza, A., Papaleo, P., Nautiyal, A., Pupo, M., & Ruffolo, M. (2023). ESG Data Collection with Adaptive AI. In ICEIS (1) (pp. 468-475). DOI: 10.5220/0011844500003467

Vishwakarma, J. S., & Jain, D. T. (2025). Study of Leading Green Finance Frameworks and Gaps in Existing Sustainable Financing Assessment. *Journal of Information Systems Engineering & Management*.

Yunus, Y. A., & Nanda, S. (2024). Exploring sustainable finance: A qualitative inquiry into responsible investment and ESG risk evaluation. Golden Ratio of Finance Management, 4(1), 01-13.

Zeng, L., Li, H., Lin, L., Hu, D. J. J., & Liu, H. (2024). ESG standards in China: Bibliometric analysis, development status research, and future research directions. [Multidisciplinary Digital Publishing Institute.]. *Sustainability (Basel), 16*(16), 7134. DOI: 10.3390/su16167134

Zervoudi, E. K., Moschos, N., & Christopoulos, A. G. (2025). From the corporate social responsibility (CSR) and the environmental, social and governance (ESG) criteria to the greenwashing phenomenon: A comprehensive literature review about the causes, consequences and solutions of the phenomenon with specific case studies. *Sustainability (Basel), 17*(5), 2222. DOI: 10.3390/su17052222

Zhang, A. Y., & Zhang, J. H. (2024). Renovation in environmental, social and governance (ESG) research: The application of machine learning. *Asian Review of Accounting, 32*(4), 554–572. DOI: 10.1108/ARA-07-2023-0201

Zhang, K., Liu, X., & Wang, J. (2023). Exploring the relationship between corporate ESG information disclosure and audit fees: Evidence from non-financial A-share listed companies in China. *Frontiers in Environmental Science, 11*, 1196728. DOI: 10.3389/fenvs.2023.1196728

Zhang, X., Kong, L., & Hu, X. (2024). Shades of green: The impact of greenwashing on stock price crash risk. *Finance Research Letters, 70*, 106285. DOI: 10.1016/j.frl.2024.106285

ENDNOTES

1 The 1992 Rio Earth Summit, or the United Nations Conference on Environment and Development (UNCED), was a major international summit held in Rio de Janeiro that brought together over 100 heads of state. Its main goal was to address urgent environmental and development problems and to create a global plan for sustainable development. Key outcomes included the signing of the Climate Change and Biodiversity Conventions, the Rio Declaration, and the adoption of Agenda 21, a comprehensive plan for action. https://www.un.org/esa/earthsummit

2 https://www.msci.com/data-and-analytics

3 https://www.sustainalytics.com/esg-data

4 https://www.spglobal.com/sustainable1/en/csa

5 https://www.lseg.com/en/data-analytics/sustainable-finance/esg-scores

6 https://www.moodys.com

7 https://www.issgovernance.com/sustainability/ratings

8 Hicrarchical Risk Parity (HRP) is an advanced investment portfolio optimization framework developed in 2016 by Marcos López de Prado at Guggenheim Partners and Cornell University.

9 This calculation was first distributed in 2017 by Lundberg and Lee.

Chapter 8

The Role of AI and Social Media Literacy in Promoting Sustainable Interaction With Green Brands

Mohamed Gadelmawla Oweis
http://orcid.org/0000-0002-7926-5831
City University, Ajman, UAE

Mahitab Maher Elrafii
May University in Cairo, Egypt

ABSTRACT

This chapter examines how AI-enabled social media literacy is valuable in encouraging sustainable interactions with green brands and enhancing sustainable behavior in Egypt. The study proposed the correlation relationship between AI-enabled social media literacy competencies and the awareness of green brands, desire to have sustainable engagement, sustainable interaction behavior, and green brand promotion, based on social media literacy, planned behavior theory, and Engagement theory. It depends on variance based structural equation modeling (PLS-SEM) to work with questionnaire data. The results indicate that AI-enabled social media literacy and green brand awareness have a positive relationship of notable strengths with sustainable engagement intentions, sustainable interaction behaviors, and promotion of green brands.

DOI: 10.4018/979-8-2600-1348-9.ch008

INTRODUCTION

Sustainability communication has been a key element of modern branding strategies, as societies face new unprecedented environmental issues (Anderson, 2014). As the digital space rapidly evolves, green brands more often use social media to spread the sustainability message and develop consumer awareness and long-term interactions. Meanwhile, Artificial Intelligence (AI) has changed how the process of online communication works, defining what information users access and how they perceive it, and to what degree they can be engaged with environmentally friendly content (Ganesh et al., 2024). Due to the growing role of environmental issues in the formation of social values, the opportunity of individuals to interact with green brands through the social media depends on social media literacy (Kaplan & Haenlein, 2010).

The increasing interest in studying the negative effects of social networks has redirected the attention of people towards social media literacy as a potential solution. In this regard, social media networks, which are being assisted more by AI-based technology, became one of the main channels through which brands address their intended audiences. This in turn requires individuals to have the analytical capabilities to critically assess marketing messages as a way of evaluating the credibility of the claims of sustainability that are being made by brands (Muntinga et al., 2011).

Social media literacy plays a key role in creating trust and ensuring long-term commitment to sustainable marketing campaigns (Evans et al., 2021). Moreover, AI and social platform literacy increase the capabilities of people to participate more actively in environmental sustainability efforts, leading to the formation of stable relationships between green brands and their customers.

LITERATURE REVIEW

Digitization of communication has transformed how sustainability issues are formulated and presented to online audience, the way in which environmental messages are being formed and spread in networked media space (Castells, 2015; Couldry & Hepp, 2018). The interactivity of social media affordances, wide reach, and participatory characteristics, which allow dialogic and participatory types of communication, have become it the key platform in spreading environmental messages (Anderson, 2014; Kaplan & Haenlein, 2010). These platforms are becoming popular with green brands to encourage environmentally friendly activities, convey corporate sustainability projects, and involve consumers in participatory communication that helps to develop relationships and value co-creation (Bitrián et al., 2021; Du et al., 2010).

Nevertheless, the abundance of sustainability content on the internet has aggravated the frequency of greenwashing and the issues of credibility(Delmas & Burbano, 2011; Lyon & Montgomery, 2015). As a result, to distinguish between trustworthy and misleading messages related to the environment, audiences must have highly developed skills, including social media literacy and critical evaluation skills(Livingstone, 2014; Wu et al., 2020). Consequently, the sustainability communication has become an essential aspect in a complicated ecosystem that is defined by technological infrastructures, user competencies, and the dynamic interaction of media systems and audience engagement practices (Weder et al., 2021).

The concept of Social Media Literacy

To understand why social media literacy has become more significant in the current digital world, it is crucial to initially discuss the many-sided nature of the role played by new media sites in society. As interactive forms of communication, social media (Facebook, X and YouTube) have a broad spectrum of requirements, whether it is the purpose of education, collaboration, civic engagement, family connectivity, health communication (Koukaras et al., 2020; Valle et al., 2024).

In such digital spaces, social media literacy has become one of the essential competencies. It refers to the ability of people to be critical and efficient with the content on social media. Daneels & Vanwynsberghe (2017) define social media literacy as the set of technical and cognitive skills that allow the user to engage effectively in social interaction and communication using online media.

Intimately connected with this concept, social media literacy is commonly referred to as a subset of digital media literacy. Digital media literacy can be described as the possibility to receive, analyze, understand and produce digital content (Buckingham et al., 2005; Kubey, 2004; Penman & Turnbull, 2007). However, digital literacy is not just about critical consumption of content. In the digital environment, people should be capable of searching for relevant information and accurately using digital content. These competencies constructed through their use, which is what Hartley et al. (2008) call demand-led literacy (Ogbolu et al., 2025).

Digital media are interactive and different from traditional media. Thus, the user can move beyond passive consumption. This is one of the distinguishing features that make digital media a unique medium since individuals can store, annotate, redistribute, and share all types of content previously known only as content that could be consumed (Jenkins, 2009). Interactive content engagements are not confined to consumption, as they include a creative aspect. The users are not the passive receivers of messages as they are active in the process of producing, developing, expressing new content and building digital media space (Park, 2012).

Although definitions of social media literacy vary in literature, there is a growing awareness that its contextualized practices require skills that extend beyond traditional media literacy (Cho et al., 2024; Valle et al., 2024).

Sustainability Communication on Social Media and User Engagement

Social platforms is an essential aspect of influencing the social interaction with the issue of sustainability, thereby offering forums through which people exchange information. Research on this area focuses on the impact of online sities on behaviors, attitudes, and awareness about environmental and social issues (Yas et al., 2025). Furthermore, sustainability communication has been synonymous with such concepts such as CSR or green communication (Kapoor et al., 2021). Consequently, the need to explore sustainability communication in the framework of sustainable green brands becomes pivotal in determining how the latter can communicate their sustainability messages effectively. Social media has therefore turned out to be important in enhancing sustainability communication by companies (Kurdi et al., 2025).

Green communication focuses mostly on environmental sustainability, including eco-friendly activities, green advertising, and ecological awareness. Although this communication relates to problems, such as pollution control, clean technologies, and minimization of environmental impact, it is still more limited than sustainability communication. Additionally, Sustainability communication involves the environmental, social, and economic dimensions, acknowledging the significance of customers as stakeholders and moving beyond the corporate settings to discuss sustainable practices and products (Singh & Sanjeev, 2022).

Chamcham et al. (2024a) investigated in their study the influence of media literacy in creating a sustainable awareness of sustainable consumption and behavior, especially in response to the global environmental effects of household food consumption. The findings showed that elements of media literacy, including use, access, content creation, and critical understanding explained 93% of the sustainable consumption awareness and 51% of the sustainable consumption intention. In addition, these variables, as well as awareness and intention, accounted 87% of the difference in sustainable consumption behavior.

In that respect, a study by Zeynep Dila Oral (2023) showed beneficial results on the factors influencing interaction with sustainability messages on social media. The study relied on the dataset of 3,149 posts of five international food companies on two platforms and in three countries as well as the analysis of 5,810 consumer comments. The results revealed that value-based messaging had a positive impact and other variables like informativeness, health messages, and egoistic appeals had a negative impact on the engagement. In addition, these relationships were determined to be moderated by contextual ones that include country of operation, platform characteristics and brand-specific strategies (Oral, 2023).

Conversely, Baran (2023) aimed to determine and compare the behavioral patterns of Polish social enterprises in the IT sector, in terms of using social media to reach their clients. The study used a multidimensional content analysis that involved the qualitative and quantitative analysis. According to the results, unique behavioral patterns were identified, where IT businesses preferred brief and accurate communication on popular platforms, and economically efficient social businesses were inclined to use specialized ones.

THE ROLE OF SOCIAL MEDIA IN ENSURING SUSTAINABLE BEHAVIORS

Social media has revolutionized the communication between companies and their customers. These sites are not only used to promote different brands' products to customers but also have turned into a platform where the brands can share educational information with the consumers (Oral, 2023). These channels offer active digital environments that promote spreading environmental messages in interactive formats, which influence the perception of the consumer and lead them to make more responsible and sustainable decisions (Simeone & Scarpato, 2020). Therefore, new media can be an active channel of brands to market their products and create awareness about such pressing issues as sustainability. Besides, Cho et al. (2024) discussed the use of social media to enhance a sustainable green lifestyle and effect of social media interactions in making behavior sustainable. The results have shown that social media played quite a crucial role in the process of adopting a green lifestyle ($b = 0.234$, $p < 0.001$). In addition, the value co-creation was found to mediate this relationship at least partially (indirect effect = 0.113, Sobel test t-value = 5.762).

Furthermore, the article by Confetto et al. (2023) explored the effect of social media by improving sustainability values among Generation Z. The researchers used the stimulus-organism-response model to survey 660 participants aged 14-25 in Italy. The results indicated that sustainability content exposure had a positive impact on sustainable habits and consumption behavior that in turn led to increased chances of promoting sustainability online. Nasef (2023) in his study, explored why university youth are exposed to social media discussing the issues surrounding sustainable development and the impact of exposure to their cognitive, behavioural and emotional engagement according to Vision 2030. The findings revealed that the regular frequency of use of social media to follow issues related to sustainable development had a significant relationship with the degree of interest of the participants in the issues.

Abdallah & Youssef (2023) investigated the importance of social media in promoting climate change literacy in Egypt. The study was conducted to test the connection between social media usage and climate change awareness, whether the social media played a role in driving home the sense of urgency of climate crisis and whether climate change literacy in Egypt has increased. The results indicated that the Egyptian audience obtains most of the information on climate change through social media and this plays a significant role in terms of creating awareness and influencing the perception about climate change. Although the positive effects were seen, the issue of misinformation became one of the most serious ones, and most participants mentioned it as one of the negative factors within the social media.

Likewise, Russo et al. (2022) investigated the extent to which social media affects sustainability performance of organizations in terms of environmental, social, and governance (ESG) aspects of the organizations. The study was conducted through multivariate regression analysis of 115 publicly traded EU companies operating in the energy and utilities industries in the period between 2016 and 2019. The results indicated a positive correlation between social media activity and sustainability performance. Moreover, Twitter was mostly used by ESG-oriented companies in the creation of credibility as opposed to the management of sustainability strategies. It further concluded that the sustainability performance of a company, such as ESG sub-pillars, depended greatly on the longevity of the company's social media profile. Furthermore, Al-Mulla et al. (2022) examined the concept of altering the behavior of people towards sustainability through using education, digital media, and gamification on social media. A survey and social media experiment in Qatar indicated that 49% of followers gained knowledge on sustainable life, and 25% of them acquired sustainable behavior. The research has shown that the social media could serve as an effective way of promoting sustainable actions.

Algorithmic Mediation of Sustainability Communication

The nature of AI technologies defines the flow and accessibility of environmental communication in digital space by the user, which significantly changes the flow and visibility of environmental communication online(Bucher, 2018; Couldry & Hepp, 2018). AI can selectively filter the content shown to people through algorithms, recommendation systems, and predictive analytics to show the content they want consumable and amplify the content that resonates with their interests and past behavior and makes assumptions about what they would be interested in (Gillespie, 2020). Although this type of algorithmic mediation increases the relevance of the message and the level of engagement efficiency, it also presents serious threats, such as algorithmic bias, echo chambers, and selective exposure, which can be used to restrict the informational horizons of users and distort the perception of a complex environmental problems (Cinelli et al., 2021; Sunstein, 2018). To green brands, AI represents both a two-sided sword; it increases the message accessibility, targeted precision, and viewership, but limits the availability of sustainability stories and skeptical attitudes that audiences can encounter (Boerman et al., 2017). consequently, it is crucial to comprehend the influence of AI in structuring digital communication processes to determine how audiences form environmental awareness, consider claims of sustainability, and form pro-environmental attitudes and behavioral intentions in algorithmic mediated online environments (Couldry & Mejias, 2019).

Social Media Literacy Measurement

Social media literacy measurement has received much interest over the past several years, with numerous scales, as well as frameworks created to capture various dimensions of social platforms use and its effects on individuals. The following are descriptions of some major social media literacy theories and scales.

- Valle et al. (2024) investigated the critical social media literacy (CSML) scale that refers to the goals of the users, conditions of use, inquiry, reflection, and action. The CSML framework requires the user to be active on social media, reflecting on the impact, and performing responsible actions. The framework identifies the need of incorporating the critical levels of social media literacy into the educational process, which allows people to use social media in a responsible way without disregarding the socio-cultural backgrounds.
- On the same context, Cho et al. (2024) developed SoMeLit Scale to analyzes the interactions between the self, the media, and reality. This scale extends beyond conventional checking of facts by urging users to be aware of socio-cultural influences in the use of social media. SoMeLit indicates that individual educational intervention is needed to assist people to analyze their social media decision-making, networks, and values critically, as well as encourage them to be more aware of how social media affects their lives.
- Moreover, Chamcham et al. (2024b) studied the responses of participants on the different constructs on a Likert scale (between 1 and 5), as the low and high levels respectively. The scale was used to determine the levels of media literacy with sustainable consumption awareness, intention, and behavior by the participants. It helped to determine the relative strength of each of the four dimensions of media literacy use, access, content creation, and critical understanding in the determination of the variances in awareness, intention, and behavior.

- Lastly, Heiss et al. (2023) designed a Social Media Information Literacy (SMIL) scale consisting of six sub-dimensions: navigation, curation, appraisal, comprehension, creation, and interaction. These dimensions were validated by factor analysis using a single SMIL. Frequencies of education and social media usage proved to be important predictors of SMIL, whereas age did not play any important role. The increased level of SMIL was linked to less information overload, which resulted in fewer news avoidance and less conspiracy thinking.

These scales and frameworks show that social media literacy is different. All the tools present a unique insight into the way people deal with social media.

RESEARCH PROBLEM

Media literacy includes the use of social media, which has been used to revolutionize the process of searching and making decisions about products and services. Using the power of social media in suitable way, users can implement a successful strategy of promoting the green brands and being involved in the activity that is sustainable activities. Increasing the awareness of the users, the objective of reaching the sustainable communication becomes more realistic. However, the discussion on how social media literacy can be used to promote green brands as well as create sustainable behaviors and participatory practices has not been well captured in scholarly literature. Mechanisms by which social media literacy can have its effect to make users engage in sustainable practices of engagement have not been tackled fully. Although other researchers have already studied the correlation between social media literacy and sustainable consumption, they mostly analyzed limited areas, including food consumption (Chamcham et al., 2024b; Oral, 2023). As a result, they have failed to look at sustainability in other areas including green brands, sustainable behavior and user interaction with sustainable content. The current study develops the social media literacy model utilized by (Chamcham et al., 2024b), which involves dimensions such as access, social media usage, content production, content consumption, and critical understanding. The given model can be used to offer a useful framework in studying the role of social media literacy in promoting the understanding of green brands and enhancing the intention of audiences to engage in green practices. This study builds on the original model by incorporating AI literacy as an embedded and cross-cutting element of social media literacy. In that way, it suggests a sophisticated conceptual framework that is more representative of the AI-driven social media sites, in which algorithms, recommendation schemes, and AI-facilitated content creation are the focus of determining the user interaction, awareness, and sustainability-driven engagement.

Research Objectives

- Examine the impact of green brand awareness on promotion of green brands within AI mediated social media platforms.
- Examine the relationship between green brand awareness and sustainable interaction behavior among users of social media.
- Explore how AI-enabled social media literacy impacts awareness of green brands in users.
- Determine the impact of AI- enabled social media literacy on sustainable interaction intention.
- Assess the role of the intention of sustainable interaction in the promotion of green brands on the social media.
- Examine how sustainable interaction intention influences sustainable interaction behavior.

Research Hypotheses

- H1: Green brand awareness has a positive influence on green brand promotion.
- H2: Green brand awareness is positively related to sustainable interaction behavior.
- H3: AI-enabled social media literacy has a positive effect on green brand awareness.
- H4: AI-enabled social media literacy has a positive effect on sustainable interaction intention.
- H5: Sustainable interaction intention has a positive impact on green brand promotion.
- H6: Sustainable interaction intention forms a positive relationship with sustainable interaction behavior.

CONCEPTUAL FRAMEWORK

It is based on the theoretical frameworks which are important in the current study, such as the Social Media Literacy, Planned Behavior and Engagement Theories to discuss how social media literacy can improve awareness and intention among the audience to raise sustainable engagement behaviour and promote green branding.

Social media literacy

The skill to critical understand and participate in social media content is essential to the effectiveness with which people are exposed to media-intensive sustainability communications. Individuals conversant with social media tend to comprehend and evaluate sustainability messages that green brands communicate, especially when the messages are filled with visuals. This is a light with results of Oral (2023), Tarabieh et al. (2024), richness media can enhance user understanding and emotional involvement particularly when it comes to sustainability communication.

Theory of Planned Behavior

The Theory of Planned Behavior (TPB) is one of the psychological theories that are extensively used in explaining and predicting human actions in certain situations Ajzen (1991). The Theory of Planned Behavior applies in the case of social media literacy and green brands. The elements that could influence intention are subject to social media and could affect attitudes, subjective norms, and perceived behavioral control (Hapsari, 2021; Higgins et al., 2012).

Social Media Engagement:

New media has emerged as an influential tool for creating interactions between brands and consumers, especially in sustainability (Connelly et al., 2011; Crawford, 2020). Such engagements are defined by the interdependence and interaction of companies and customers (Harmeling et al., 2017). Engagement with brand posts is a concept that is largely applied in the literature indicating how brands interact with consumers based on likes, comments and shares (De Vries et al., 2012). Moreover, social media plays vital role to increase the level of interaction with the brand posts, amplify the promotion of the products, distribute educational content, and manage the relationships with the customers (Cho et al., 2024). Most important issues concerning these engagements are visual clarity, message attraction, and country context, and states show different degrees of engagement with the messages about sustainability (Nazish et al., 2024).

The concept of social media literacy is multidimensional and likely to be one of the essential factors that help to increase awareness about green brands and increase the willingness of users to interact with the content created in a sustainable way. Therefore, the study proposed that Ai-enabled social media literacy increases green brand awareness and reinforces the intentions of the audience to interact with green content and sustainable content. Based on this hypothesis, the model of the study was developed as shown in Figure 1.

Figure 1. Conceptual Model

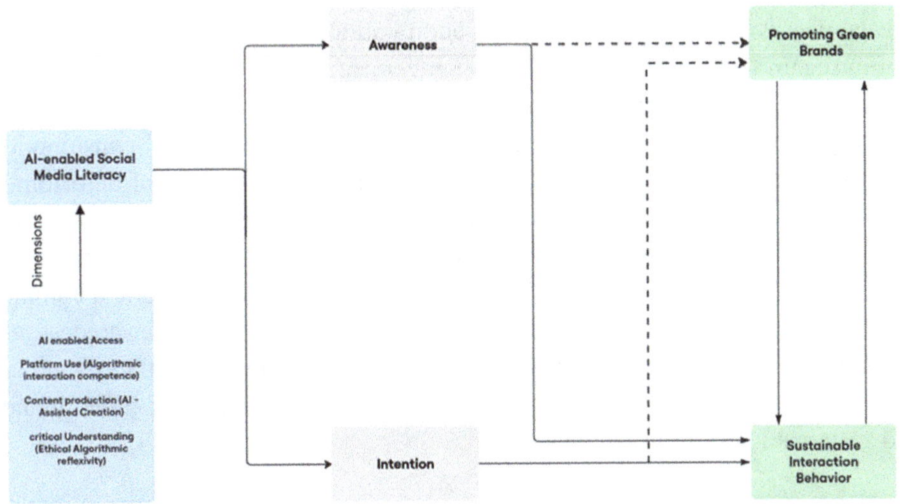

Conceptual Model

The proposed conceptual framework sheds light on the important role of AI-enabled Social Media Literacy (AI-enabled Access, Platform Use, Content Production, Content Consumption and Critical Understanding) dimensions, which each have a distinct contribution to the digital competence in social media among audiences.

The combination of these dimensions can assist the audiences in acquiring the practical skills to utilize social media efficiently in order to gain more awareness about green brands and enhance their desire to engage with sustainable content. The accessibility of social media and information on sustainability in algorithm environments is what can be called AI-enabled access. Platform use (algorithmic interaction competence) describes how users can interact with social platforms in a knowledgeable and meaningful way where they acknowledge that likes, shares, comments, and other actions on the platform influence the distribution of the content by the algorithm. This competence can allow the user to engage more in sustainability-related conversations and contribute to the presence of green brands by being aware and responsible. The content production (AI-assisted generation) is based on the ability of users to create and share this type of content that motivates to follow environmentally friendly practices and promote green brands, including responsible usage of AI tools. The critical understanding (ethical algorithmic reflexivity) means the ability to know the ethical aspects of digital and AI-based interaction and how these aspects contribute to green branding and sustainability communication. As a result, all these dimensions would promote more informed engagement with sustainability content and facilitate increased awareness and intent in regard to sustainable Audience engagement with green brands. Moreover, the concept of AI literacy in this research is the part of social media literacy as the digital platforms of the modern era are AI driven. The access and consumption of information about sustainability is influenced by the presence of algorithmic systems and AI-enhanced content development. From this perspective, AI-enabled social media literacy promotes the ability of people to navigate information and utilize AI tools responsibly, as well as interact ethically with green brand communication. This combined strategy enhances the connection between awareness and green brands promotion and between intention and sustainable audience contact, which eventually aids more authentic, knowledgeable and enduring green brands and sustainable interaction habits.

METHODOLOGY

Population and Sampling Method

As of January 2025, Egypt's population is estimated at approximately 113.6 million, with around 50.7 million active social media users, representing 43.1% of the total population. This figure reflects a notable increase compared to previous years. In January 2024, the figure of social networks users stood at 45.4 million, accounting for approximately 40% of the population. Among social media platforms, Facebook ranked as the most widely used in Egypt, with 56.4 million users, corresponding to 49.6% of the population (Datareportal, 2025).

Data collected through an online questionnaire that was applied to respondents in Egypt. G* power software was used to calculate the required sample size based on a multiple regression model, the assumed effect size (f2 = 0.15), level of significance (0.05) and a statistical power (0.95), which indicated a minimum sample size of 138 respondents. The use of a larger sample was selected to gain adequate statistical power, as well as to enhance the robustness of the PLS-SEM analysis and to take into consideration incomplete or invalid responses. Therefore, the 246 respondents' data were retained and included in the final PLS-SEM analysis.

Data Collection

The study used a questionnaire as the main data collection tool that was created using previous studies and literature available on the research area. The questionnaire was designed according to the research objectives and theoretical framework and consisted of two major sections. The first part included six questions that identified the demographic factors of the respondents, whereas the second part contained 24 questions that were designed to examine all variables of the study. Measurement items were all formulated using a five-point Likert scale, and the scale ranged between 1 (high level of agreement) and 5 (low level of agreement). To establish the validity and suitability of the tool to the fulfillment of the study objectives, the questionnaire was subjected to a strict review and analysis by a group of academic researcher and media experts on digital media, media literacy, sustainability, and green marketing. Their comments helped to develop the language of the items and increase the general clarity and relevance of the questionnaire.

In terms of the reliability of the questionnaire, Cronbach's alpha was determined. All the study constructs had values higher than 0.88, which is a high degree of internal consistency and the validity and strength of the measurement tool in statistical analysis. The questionnaire was carefully reviewed and revised before the data collection to ensure alignment with the study's hypotheses. After that, the version of the online questionnaire was created by Google Forms, and the questionnaire link was shared in WhatsApp groups and other social media platforms. The survey completion form involved the participants giving credible and considerate answers to all the questions in the questionnaire. In cases where respondents faced any challenge in answering a specific item, they were given the chance to contact the researchers directly for clarification. The data collection was conducted for three months, between October 2025 and December 2025.

Data Analysis

The study used partial least squares structural equation modelling (PLS-SEM) that relies on variance as a measure of the relationship between AI-based social media literacy, green brand awareness, sustainable interaction intention, sustainable interaction behavior, and green brand promotion. The four dimensions of AI-enabled social media literacy are particularly relevant within the framework of sustainable engagement and green brand promotion as they all shape individuals' exposure to sustainable content, level of engagement with green brands, ability to produce and share content about sustainability, and critical understanding of environmental messages spread by these brands. PLS-SEM was an appropriate approach in analyzing both simple and complex research models.

According to Hair (2014), PLS-SEM is a multivariate statistical methodology that allows measurement model with the structural model to be evaluated at the same time, thus, reducing error variance. In the structural equation modeling (SEM) model, various measurement model evaluation criteria were used to evaluate the adequacy of the model. In the first step, the rho of Dillon-Goldstein was computed on the individual sub-dimensions to determine the internal consistency, which correlations are considered to be acceptable at 0.70 or above (Saillour-Glénisson et al., 2016). Second, the study used Normed Fit Index (NFI), an incremental fit indicator to compare the proposed model with the null (independence) model, and values of 0.90 and above demonstrate that the model fits well (Bentler, 1995) .

Moreover, the Standardized root mean square Residual (SRMR) was also applied as an absolute measure of fit which was taken as a standardized difference between observed and predicted correlations; SRMR of 0.08 or less is considered as a good model fit (Bentler, 1995). Lastly, RMS-Theta was used to determine the extent to which the covariances between the residual indicators are insignificant, and a value of 0.12 or less is acceptable (Mehmetoglu, 2012).

The SPSS version 25 and Smart PLS4 software were used for data analysis. By allowing both measurement and structural models to be assessed simultaneously, Smart PLS4 allows the researcher to thoroughly test the relationship among variables.

RESULTS

The results in table 1 shows that 57.3% of sample were male, while 42.7% were female. Besides, 25-34 years constitute the highest percentage of the participants 39.8%. Most of the respondents were students (40.2%), then there are those with bachelor 34.1%, masters 12.2%, high school 8.1%, and doctorate (5.3%). Regarding employment status, 39.4% of respondents were students, 44.7% were employed and 8.1% were self-employed and 7.7% homemakers. In terms of social platforms use, most of the respondents, 1-2 hours a day, mentioned using social media, with Instagram (28.9), Facebook (28) as the most commonly used, then WhatsApp, Tik Tok, YouTube, and Twitter/X. These results indicate that the sample is quite young, educated, and highly active in social media, which gives it an appropriate population to conduct study on AI-enabled social media literacy and sustainable interaction behaviors.

Table 1. Demographic information of the research sample.

Variables	Frequency	Percentage
Gender		
Male	141	57.3
Female	105	42.7
Age		

continued on following page

Table 1. Continued

Variables	Frequency	Percentage
18-24	33	13.4
25-34	98	39.8
35-44	71	28.9
45-54	31	12.6
55+	13	5.3
Education level		
High school	20	8.1
University student	99	40.2
Bachelor	84	34.1
Master	30	12.2
Doctorate	13	5.3
Employment status		
Student	97	39.4
Employed	110	44.7
Self-employed	20	8.1
Housewife	19	7.7
Social Media Use		
Less than 1 hour/day	78	31.7
1–2 hours/day	96	39
3–4 hours/day	67	27.2
More than 4 hours/day	5	2
Preferred social media platforms		
Facebook	69	28
Instagram	71	28.9
Twitter/X	11	4.5
TikTok	37	15
YouTube	17	6.9
WhatsApp	41	16.7

The results in Table 2, indicate high reliability of all constructs, with values ranging between 0.706 and 0.887. The results have indicated a good model fit, and this indicates that the instrument used is highly reliable. Moreover, the composite reliability (CR) of the analyzed model structures was found to be 0.724 and higher, and the average variance extracted (AVE) of all constructs was all over 0.50, which proved the reliability and validity of the model and supported its appropriateness. On that basis, it can be concluded that the current study model has high reliability and validity rates, making it an adequate tool of analysis in the present research project.

Moreover, Table 3 results show that the values of the Average Variance Extracted (AVE) of the constructs are greater than 0.50, which is the minimum required value of convergent validity (Bentler, 1995). The values demonstrate that the indicators of each construct are enough to measure the targeted latent variable and discriminate validity with other constructs (Mehmetoglu, 2012).

These results are a sufficient indication of the research data evidence, that the model is useful in explaining the relationship between the AI-enhanced Social Media Literacy and promotion of sustainable interaction with green brands. The model shows relative fit and therefore, increase the validity and reliability of the research findings and prove that the hypothesized correlations between the variables are significant. Thus, the findings add credibility to the overall study findings and add value to the current study on AI-enabled Social Media Literacy (ASML) and how it can be used to help the individuals develop sustainable relationships with green brands.

As shown in Figure 2, the path model the loading of factors is standardized (by taking into account the various dimensions of AI-enabled Social Media Literacy) exhibited some positive links between various dimensions (AI enabled access, platform use, content production, critical understanding, awareness of green brands, sustainable interaction intention, promotion of green brands, and sustainable audience interaction). Conversely, the importance of each of the factors in the path model plays a vital role in the establishment of the importance and statistical significance of the correlations between AI-enabled social media literacy and the encouragement of sustainable interactions with green brands.

Figure 3, shows the path model with t-values, provides valuable data about the significance of these relationships. A t-value exceeding a critical threshold of 1.96 (at a 0.05 significance level) indicates that the relationship between the variables is significant.

Table 2. the results of reliability and convergent validity Analyses

Constructs	Measurement Item		Mean	Standard Deviation	Standardized Factor loadings	Reliability and Validity Statistics	VIF
AI Enabled Access	AEA1	I can easily access information about brands on social media.	4.01	0.937	0.853	AVE: 0.703 CR: 0.881 α: 0.764 Rho-A: 0.826	1.198
	AEA2	I have access up-to-date information about brands and their sustainability practices	4.17	1.002	0.823		1.196
Platform Use	PU1	I can use AI-based tools to find information about green brands.	3.88	0.968	0.830	AVE: 0.613 CR: 0.836 α: 0.706 Rho-A: 0.714	1.765
	PU2	I engage with green brands' promotional campaigns on social media	3.39	0.995	0.848		1.532
	PU3	I can use platform features to engage with sustainability-related content	3.57	0.877	0.886		1.782
Content Production	CP1	I feel confident in creating multimedia content related to sustainability on social media.	3.93	0.943	0.798	AVE: 0.681 CR: 0.865 α: 0.770 Rho-A: 0.798	1.879
	CP2	I can present posts about green products or practices by AI tools to generate	3.50	1.021	0.819		1.608
	CP3	I have knowledge and experience in teaching others how to produce sustainable content using AI tools.	4.06	0.841	0.858		1.638
Critical Understanding	CU1	I know how to verify the credibility of information shared by brands on social media.	4.36	0.559	0.723	AVE: 0.665 CR: 0.724 α: 0.750 Rho-A: 0.783	1.503
	CU2	I consider ethical implications when interacting with AI-driven content on social media	3.82	0.635	0.707		1.105
	CU3	I can critically evaluate posts, comments, and advertisements related to sustainability on social media	4.40	0.596	0.811		1.055

continued on following page

Table 2. Continued

Constructs	Measurement Item		Mean	Standard Deviation	Standardized Factor loadings	Reliability and Validity Statistics	VIF
Awareness of Green Brands	AGB1	I am aware of eco-friendly brands through social media platforms	3.93	0.939	0.795	AVE: 0.747 CR: 0.922 α: 0.887 Rho-A: 0.892	1.105
	AGB2	AI-based social media recommendations enhance my awareness of green brands	4	0.860	0.847		1.609
	AGB3	AI helps me discover sustainable brands that align with my interests	4.53	0.604	0.737		1.331
	AGB4	I am aware that AI algorithms recommend content on social media platforms	4.51	0.604	0.860		1.293
Sustainable Interaction Intention	SII1	I intend to follow AI-recommended eco-friendly brands more attentively.	4.33	0.676	0.763	AVE: 0.585 CR: 0.807 α: 0.744 Rho-A: 0.765	1.528
	SII2	I aim to adopt sustainable behaviors promoted by brands on social media platforms.	4.68	0.612	0.709		1.584
	SII3	I plan to enhance my engagement with environmentally responsible brands in future.	4.54	0.554	0.907		1.232
Promotion of Green Brands	PGB1	I follow sustainable brands and respond to their campaigns regularly.	4.49	0.517	0.881	AVE: 0.609 CR: 0.823 α: 0.775 Rho-A: 0.786	2.253
	PGB2	I actively engage with AI-generated content about sustainable brands.	4.33	0.676	0.764		1.221
	PGB3	I feel that AI recommendations reflect my personal sustainability values.	4.68	0.612	0.920		2.259

continued on following page

Table 2. Continued

Constructs	Measurement Item		Mean	Standard Deviation	Standardized Factor loadings	Reliability and Validity Statistics	VIF
Sustainable Interaction Behavior	SIB1	I follow and engage with brands that promote environmentally responsible practices on social media (e.g., likes, shares, comments).	4.55	0.507	0.758	AVE: 0.703 CR: 0.875 α: 0.790 Rho-A: 0.869	1.269
	SIB2	AI-guided social media campaigns influence my decision-making regarding sustainable products.	4.81	0.440	0.764		1.220
	SIB3	I often share information about eco-friendly products and participate in online discussions about green brands.	4.53	0.547	0.856		1.440

*Table 3. shows the correlations with the square roots of the average variance extracted (AVE), with significant values highlighted in bold and *** indicating significance at the 1% level.*

Constructs	AI Enabled Access	Awareness of Green Brands	Content Production	Critical Understanding	Platform Use	Promotion of Green Brands	Sustainable Interaction Behavior	Sustainable interaction Intention
AI Enabled Access	**0.838*****							
Awareness of Green Brands	0.541	**0.864*****						
Content Production	0.478	0.724	**0.825*****					
Critical Understanding	0.428	0.644	0.777	**0.687**				
Platform Use	0.671	0.712	0.881	0.758	**0.794*****			
Promotion of Green Brands	0.429	0.737	0.755	0.685	0.753	**0.780*****		
Sustainable Interaction Behavior	0.686	0.790	0.728	0.751	0.811	0.805	**0.839*****	
Sustainable interaction Intention	0.705	0.748	0.795	0.722	0.778	0.949	0.862	**0.765**

Figure 2. Structural equation modeling on the effect of AI-enabled media literacy on sustainable consumption (the path model with standardized factor loadings).

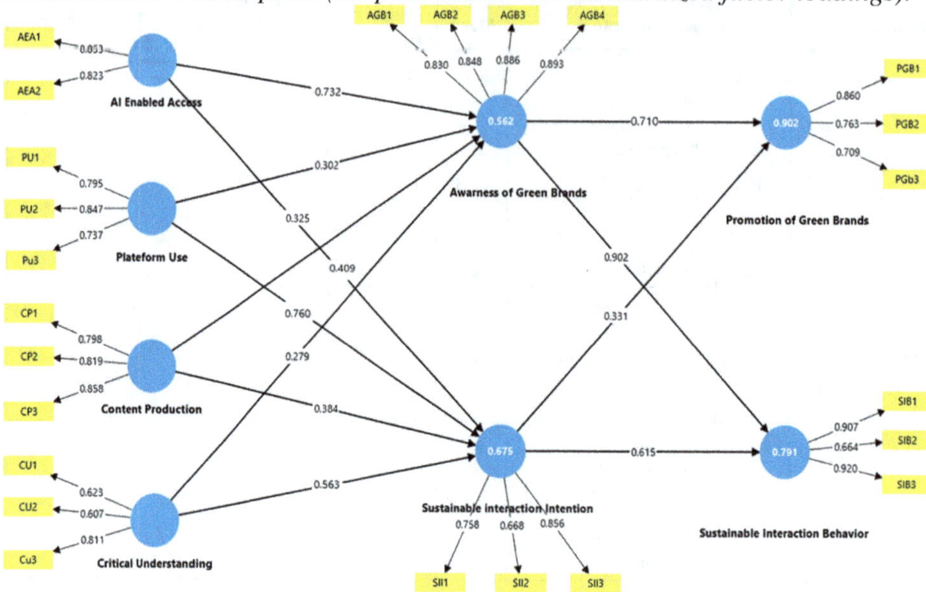

Figure 3. Structural equation modeling on the effect of AI-enabled social media literacy on promoting sustainable interaction with Green Brands (path model with t-values).

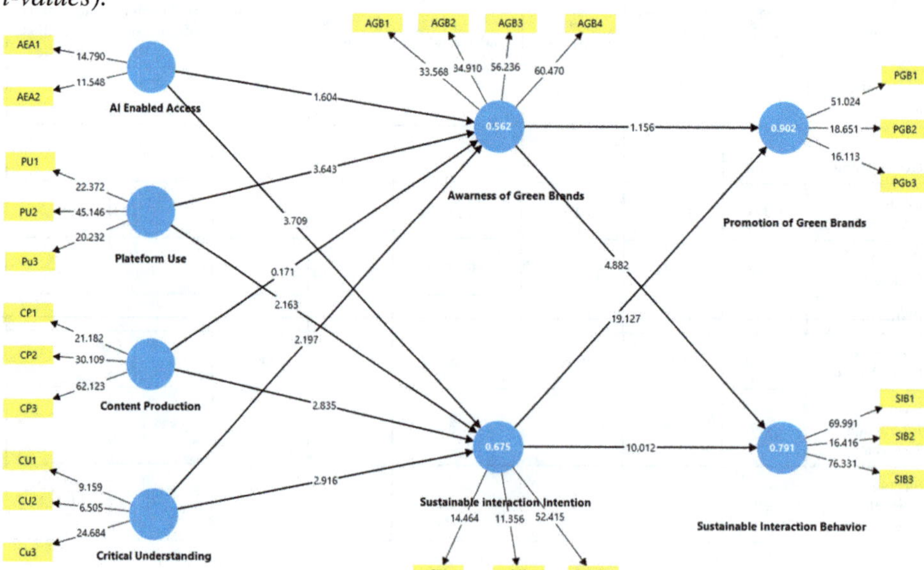

Table 4. Results of the Hypotheses Testing(*)

Hypotheses	Path	Coeff	Sample mean	Standard deviation	T values	P values	Verdict
H1	AGB -> PGB	0.516	0.621	0.042	5.379	0.000	Supported
H2	AGB -> SIB	0.417	0.428	0.085	4.931	0.000	Supported
H3	ASML -> AGB	0.749	0.755	0.031	23.809	0.000	Supported
H4	ASML -> SII	0.79	0.794	0.026	29.89	0.000	Supported
H5	SII -> PGB	0.943	0.94	0.033	28.725	0.000	Supported
H6	SII -> SIB	0.499	0.491	0.082	6.084	0.000	Supported

Table 4 shows that the AGB index has a significant direct effect on PGB ($\beta = 0.516$, $p < 0.01$), thereby supporting H1. In addition, AGB exerts a significant positive effect on SIB ($\beta = 0.417$, $p < 0.01$), providing support for H2. The results further reveal a strong and significant direct effect of ASML on AGB ($\beta = 0.749$, $p < 0.01$), thus confirming H3. Similarly, ASML demonstrates a substantial direct effect on SII ($\beta = 0.790$, $p < 0.01$), supporting H4. In addition, SII has a significant positive effect on PGB ($\beta = 0.943$, $p < 0.01$), which supports H5. Also, there is a direct effect of SII on SIB ($\beta = 0.499$, $p < 0.01$), leading support H6. Overall, these results provide clear evidence of the conceptual model and focus on the relationships among the examined constructs.

DISCUSSION

This study indicates to the importance of AI-based Social Media Literacy (ASML) and encouragement of sustainable communication with green brands. The use of AI-enabled Social Media Literacy as a multidimensional concept, such as AI-enabled access, platform use, content creation, and critical understanding, provides a more nuanced analysis how the various dimensions of AI-enabled Social Media literacy influence sustainable interaction behavior and green brand promotion.

It is important to note that applying the study in the Egyptian context helps to enrich the research in terms of distinctive characteristics of the media landscape, patterns of digital engagement, and discourse of sustainability in Egypt. Investigating AI-driven social media literacy in this regard is valuable in terms of how context-specific variables can be applied to the theoretical impact and the overall generalizability of the findings.

In addition, the theoretical value of this study is applicable outside the specific context of green brands. The theoretical models and the analytical framework they employ are sufficiently flexible to be used to explore the impact of artificial intelligence and social media literacy on awareness of green brands and sustainable interaction intention, including energy conservation behaviours, water-saving behaviours, eco-friendly purchasing behaviours and online involvement in environmental projects (Meng et al., 2023).

This theoretical flexibility highlights the critical importance of the research in enhancing academic knowledge of the relationship between AI-driven social media literacy and sustainability. The research can be used to contribute to the theoretical trend on the significance of AI and social media in the development of sustainable lifestyles and resolving the environmental challenges afflicting society around the world (Valle et al., 2024). The study results show that social media literacy through artificial intelligence is important in educating the users on the sustainable interaction patterns with the green brands. The active usage of different social media platforms will enable individuals to access the information on the environmental practices and green brands to a greater extent, therefore, resulting in the development of more informed and sustainability-centered behaviours (Nabivi, 2025).

As a result, there is a need to improve AI-based social media literacy among individuals, as it would enable individuals to access, interpret, and respond to the sustainability-related media effectively(Baruno & Indrasari, 2025).

In addition, the findings indicate that the solution is to develop awareness programs and school and university courses to promote sustainable behavior (Durbin & Filer, 2021). The higher awareness of green brands is the key to forming the intention of people to establish sustainable interaction patterns, therefore, improving the process of transforming the intention of people to establish sustainable interaction patterns into sustainable behaviors (Theocharis & Tsekouropoulos, 2025).

Additionally, access to the information on sustainability that is invalidated and unreliable, the so-called greenwashing, and lack of credibility have become even more acute (Weder et al., 2021). It demands that individuals develop advanced competencies including social media literacy and critical analysis skills to detect plausible environmental messages. Furthermore, the results reveal the importance of social media and AI literacy, particularly the knowledge of the content curation, algorithmic biases, and filter bubbles. This means that subsequently, raising awareness and educational efforts at schools and universities will allow individuals to think critically when handling digital content, make informed decisions about sustainable practices, and get access to the complex interactions of information mediated by algorithms (Gong et al., 2024; Rodilosso, 2024).

Moreover, this study aligns with previous studies that indicate the influence of social media literacy that influences the desire to develop sustainable interaction (Liao, 2024; Nazish et al., 2024). More AI-based access to the contents of social media will improve users' interaction with sustainability information and enhance the promotion of green brands and adoption of sustainable behaviors (Chen et al., 2024). This sustainable awareness reinforces the necessity to spend on sustainability products and allows making decisions regarding consumers informed and oriented towards the sustainability.

In addition, the results indicate a critical mediation effect of the awareness of green brand and sustainable interaction intention in the transformation of AI-enabled social media literacy into real sustainable interaction behavior(Chamcham et al., 2024a).

Regarding the adoption of sustainable interaction behavior, Samašonok & Išoraitė (2023) stated that marketing strategy is significantly shaped by individuals' levels of social media literacy and contributes to the advancement of sustainable development goals. Within digital environments, social media literacy, particularly when supported by AI-enabled tools, enhances individuals' ability to evaluate sustainability content and distinguish credible green brand messages from misinformation (Garg et al., 2025).

Notably, Individuals who are frequently exposed to green brand messages through new media platforms and possess the analyzes skills to assess the credibility of content are more likely to perceive the information they receive as accurate and trustworthy. Consequently, behaviors demonstrate a higher propensity to adopt sustainable interaction practices, actively engage in pro-environmental behaviors, and exhibit stronger intentions to purchase and consume green brands(Wu et al., 2020).

Additionally, it is important to study mediating variables such as awareness and intention and their relationship to the independent variables of social media literacy supported by AI and the independent variables such as sustainable interactive behavior and promotion of green brands in different social contexts in order to ensure their effectiveness in promoting and spreading the sustainability values, especially with the scarcity of studies that have addressed this aspect by research.

RESEARCH LIMITATIONS

Despite the valuable insights provided by this study into the role of AI-enabled social media literacy in shaping awareness of green brands, sustainable interaction intention, and sustainable interaction behavior, several limitations should be acknowledged, which also provide directions for future research.

First, data were collected from respondents in a single country (Egypt). Although this context may provide critical information about an emergent digital world, the sample of the study can be constrained by cultural, social, and technological variations to extrapolate the results to other countries. Replication and the generalization of this model to various cultural and other regions are highly encouraged in our studies in the future.

Secondly, AI-driven social media literacy was examined based on the self-response of the perceptions instead of objective or performance-based measurements. With reason as this method is common in social media literacy studies, there is a possibility of response bias.

Third, the study depended on self-reported intentions and perceived behavior on sustainable interaction and promotion of green brands. The objective behavioral indicators, including real online engagement statistics, purchase statistics, or digital trace data, could be included in future research.

Lastly, in AI and algorithm applications to social media, there is no convenient way to separate the impact of AI-supported social media literacy and the inherent impact of the social media per se, which confounds the interpretation of people use of green branding content.

CONCLUSION

The study contributes strong evidence to the significance of AI-enabled social media literacy in influencing the awareness, intention, and behavior of people about sustainable interaction with green brands. Considering the application of artificial intelligence to the concept of social media literacy, the study advances the green brands sustainability research and provides a critical insight into how the digital competencies play as the critical facilitators of sustainable interaction with green brands in society.

These dimensions of AI-enabled social media literacy play a significant role in increasing the perception about green brands, the intentions of sustainable interaction, and ultimately the intention-behavior translation of sustainable interactions. This process emphasizes the need to reinforce cognitive aspects including, awareness and intention to enhance meaningful and lasting interaction with green brands.

With regards to the green brand knowledge, the results indicate that the awareness of the environmentally friendly products and services function as a mediator variable whereby AI-facilitated media literacy affects the promotion of green brands and green interaction behavior. Individuals with greater AI-mediated media literacy show more ability to recognize credible environmental messages, are less susceptible to misinformation and deceptive green messages, and become more involved in the campaign of reliable green brands in digital environment. Based on this, the results point to the dual nature of AI-enhanced media literacy as a protective element against misinformation and a motivational element towards positive sustainable interaction with green brands (Garg et al., 2025).

In terms of sustainable interaction intentions, the present research has a contribution to the knowledge on the importance of the AI-enabled social media literacy in intensifying the intentions towards green products and converting into the environmentally responsible practices. In a world where digital content becomes algorithm-based, empowering people with the ability to interact with AI-mediated media will make them able to recognize credible information on sustainability, engaging in the promotion of green brands, and practicing sustainable interactions. In such an approach, AI-based social media literacy not only increases responsible patterns of engagement but also enhances sustainability goals (Ghermandi et al., 2023; Russo et al., 2022; Weder et al., 2021).

To sum up, the presented study emphasizes that to promote sustainable interaction patterns, both the presence of green products or environmental information is crucial, and more importantly, the ability of individuals to access, use, and produce meaningful content in AI-based social media ecosystems. Moreover, through the explanation of these relationships, provides interesting theoretical insights and real-life implications to policymakers, educators, marketers, and sustainability champions who might want to embrace the transformative opportunity of artificial intelligence and social media towards resolving the urgently pressing environmental issues.

Contributions, Implications and Recommendations

The study is relevant in the new field of research of AI-enhanced social media literacy; it is essential to pay attention to the role in the engagement with green brands on social networks. It focuses the need to educate users on competencies that will help them to overcome AI-related issues such as algorithmic bias, personalization, echo chambers, and the lack of diversity of content.

The results also refers that the key to improving sustainability in the digital societies should not just the technological progress, but the creation of socially and environmentally aware people. Moreover, in the future, the research must be aimed at empowering people with the ability to operate in an AI-enhanced social media space, which help to achieve the sustainable development goals by making informed choices and becoming active consumers of green brands. Additionally, social media literacy with AI should be introduced into educational tactics and online policy frameworks to provide people with the knowledge about becoming responsible and informed digital citizens. As regards green brand managers and policymakers, the study shows the importance of sustainable and transparent communication strategies, ethical usage of AI tools that enhance trust and successful relationships with the audiences.

REFERENCES

Abdallah, M. M., & Youssef, M. (2023). Role of Social Media in Enhancing Climate Change Literacy Among Egyptian Users. *Scientific Journal of Public Relations and Advertising Research, 2023*(25), 1–25. DOI: 10.21608/sjocs.2023.299518

Ajzen, I. (1991). The theory of planned behavior. *Organizational Behavior and Human Decision Processes, 50*(2), 179–211. DOI: 10.1016/0749-5978(91)90020-T

Al Kurdi, B., Alshurideh, M. T., El Khatib, M., Alrawabdeh, W. A., Al-Sulaiti, K., Nawaiseh, A. K., Sukkari, L., Alshurideh, A., Shwedeh, F., & Alzoubi, H. M. (2025). The Effect of Using IoT on Linking Green Customers Data (Green Customer Profile) with Green Products and Green Product Labels BT - Sustainable Innovation for Engineering Management (SIEM). In El Khatib, M., Alzoubi, H. M., & Angelova, Y. (Eds.), *Sustainable Innovation for Engineering Management (SIEM)* (pp. 59–68). Springer Nature Switzerland., 10.1007/978-3-031-89889-1_7 DOI: 10.1007/978-3-031-89889-1_7

Al-Mulla, S., Ari, I., & Koç, M. (2022). Social media for sustainability education: Gaining knowledge and skills into actions for sustainable living. *International Journal of Sustainable Development and World Ecology, 29*(5), 455–471. DOI: 10.1080/13504509.2022.2036856

Anderson, A. (2014). *Media, environment and the network society*. Springer. DOI: 10.1057/9781137314086

Baran, M. (2023). Social media platforms in sustainability communication of Polish social enterprises from the IT industry and beyond. *Engineering Management in Production and Services, 15*(2), 35–45. DOI: 10.2478/emj-2023-0010

Baruno, A. D., & Indrasari, M. (2025). Leveraging AI To Enhance Green Marketing Strategies. *Jurnal Ekonomi, Manajemen, Akuntansi Dan Keuangan, 6*(1).

Bentler, P. M. (1995). *EQS structural equations program manual* (Vol. 6). Multivariate software Encino, CA.

Bitrián, P., Buil, I., & Catalán, S. (2021). Enhancing user engagement: The role of gamification in mobile apps. *Journal of Business Research, 132*, 170–185. DOI: 10.1016/j.jbusres.2021.04.028

Boerman, S. C., Kruikemeier, S., & Zuiderveen Borgesius, F. J. (2017). Online behavioral advertising: A literature review and research agenda. *Journal of Advertising, 46*(3), 363–376. DOI: 10.1080/00913367.2017.1339368

Bucher, T. (2018). *If... then: Algorithmic power and politics*. Oxford University Press. DOI: 10.1093/oso/9780190493028.001.0001

Buckingham, D., Banaji, S., Carr, D., Cranmer, S., & Willett, R. (2005). *The media literacy of children and young people: A review of the research literature*.

Castells, M. (2015). *Networks of outrage and hope: Social movements in the Internet age*. John Wiley & Sons.

Chamcham, J., Pakravan-Charvadeh, M. R., Maleknia, R., & Flora, C. (2024a). Media literacy and its role in promoting sustainable food consumption practices. *Scientific Reports, 14*(1), 18831. DOI: 10.1038/s41598-024-69627-6

Chamcham, J., Pakravan-Charvadeh, M. R., Maleknia, R., & Flora, C. (2024b). Media literacy and its role in promoting sustainable food consumption practices. *Scientific Reports, 14*(1), 18831. DOI: 10.1038/s41598-024-69627-6

Chen, L., Haider, M. J., & He, J. (2024). Should "green information" be interactive? The influence of green information presentation on consumers' green participation behavior for driving sustainable consumption of fashion brands. *Journal of Cleaner Production, 470*, 143329. DOI: 10.1016/j.jclepro.2024.143329

Cho, H., Cannon, J., Lopez, R., & Li, W. (2024). Social media literacy: A conceptual framework. *New Media & Society, 26*(2), 941–960. DOI: 10.1177/14614448211068530

Cinelli, M., De Francisci Morales, G., Galeazzi, A., Quattrociocchi, W., & Starnini, M. (2021). The echo chamber effect on social media. *Proceedings of the National Academy of Sciences of the United States of America, 118*(9), e2023301118. DOI: 10.1073/pnas.2023301118

Confetto, M. G., Covucci, C., Addeo, F., & Normando, M. (2023). Sustainability advocacy antecedents: How social media content influences sustainable behaviours among Generation Z. *Journal of Consumer Marketing, 40*(6), 758–774. DOI: 10.1108/JCM-11-2021-5038

Connelly, B. L., Ketchen, D. J.Jr, & Slater, S. F. (2011). Toward a "theoretical toolbox" for sustainability research in marketing. *Journal of the Academy of Marketing Science, 39*(1), 86–100. DOI: 10.1007/s11747-010-0199-0

Couldry, N., & Hepp, A. (2018). *The mediated construction of reality*. John Wiley & Sons.

Couldry, N., & Mejias, U. A. (2019). The costs of connection: How data is colonizing human life and appropriating it for capitalism. In *The costs of connection*. Stanford University Press.

Crawford, E. (2020). Most consumers don't link diet & climate, but sustainability marketing could boost plant-based sales. *Food Navigator USA. Retrieved July, 8*, 2023.

Daneels, R., & Vanwynsberghe, H. (2017). Mediating social media use: connecting parents mediation strategies and social media literacy. *Cyberpsychology: Journal of Psychosocial Research on Cyberpspace.-Brno, 11*(3), 5.

De Vries, L., Gensler, S., & Leeflang, P. S. H. (2012). Popularity of brand posts on brand fan pages: An investigation of the effects of social media marketing. *Journal of Interactive Marketing*, *26*(2), 83–91. DOI: 10.1016/j.intmar.2012.01.003

Delmas, M. A., & Burbano, V. C. (2011). The drivers of greenwashing. *California Management Review*, *54*(1), 64–87. DOI: 10.1525/cmr.2011.54.1.64

Du, S., Bhattacharya, C. B., & Sen, S. (2010). Maximizing business returns to corporate social responsibility (CSR): The role of CSR communication. *International Journal of Management Reviews, 12*(1), 8–19. DOI: 10.1111/j.1468-2370.2009.00276.x

Durbin, E., & Filer, J. (2021). Evaluating the Impact of Public Awareness Campaigns on Sustainable Practices. *Journal of Energy and Environmental Policy Options*, *4*(4), 32–37.

Evans, D., Bratton, S., & McKee, J. (2021). *Social media marketing*. AG Printing & Publishing.

Ganesh, C., Podila, N., Vamsi, G. B. K., Rao, C. M., & Bhardwaj, N. (2024). AI-enhanced content marketing for sustainability: a theoretical perspective on eco-friendly communication strategies. *MATEC Web of Conferences, 392*, 01045.

Garg, V., Bohara, S., & Srivastav, A. (2025a). AI-driven sustainability marketing transforming consumers' perception toward eco-friendly brands. *Discover Sustainability*, *6*(1), 984. DOI: 10.1007/s43621-025-01934-y

Garg, V., Bohara, S., & Srivastav, A. (2025b). AI-driven sustainability marketing transforming consumers' perception toward eco-friendly brands. *Discover Sustainability*, *6*(1), 984. DOI: 10.1007/s43621-025-01934-y

Ghermandi, A., Langemeyer, J., Van Berkel, D., Calcagni, F., Depietri, Y., Vigl, L. E., Fox, N., Havinga, I., Jäger, H., & Kaiser, N. (2023). Social media data for environmental sustainability: A critical review of opportunities, threats, and ethical use. *One Earth*, *6*(3), 236–250. DOI: 10.1016/j.oneear.2023.02.008

Gillespie, T. (2020). Content moderation, AI, and the question of scale. *Big Data & Society*, *7*(2), 2053951720943234. DOI: 10.1177/2053951720943234

Gong, Y., Zhou, X., Zhou, Y., Luehmann, A., Han, Y., & Bai, Z. (2024). *Approaching "filter bubble" in recommendation systems: A transformative AI literacy learning experience*.

Hair, J. F. (2014). *A primer on partial least squares structural equation modeling (PLS-SEM)*. sage.

Hapsari, S. A. (2021). The theory of planned behavior and financial literacy to analyze intention in mutual fund product investment. *5th Global Conference on Business, Management and Entrepreneurship (GCBME 2020)*, 136–141. DOI: 10.2991/aebmr.k.210831.028

Harmeling, C. M., Moffett, J. W., Arnold, M. J., & Carlson, B. D. (2017). Toward a theory of customer engagement marketing. *Journal of the Academy of Marketing Science*, *45*(3), 312–335. DOI: 10.1007/s11747-016-0509-2

Hartley, J., McWilliam, K., Burgess, J., & Banks, J. (2008). The uses of multimedia: Three digital literacy case studies. *Media International Australia, Incorporating Culture & Policy*, *128*(1), 59–72. DOI: 10.1177/1329878X0812800108

Heiss, R., Nanz, A., & Matthes, J. (2023). Social media information literacy: Conceptualization and associations with information overload, news avoidance and conspiracy mentality. *Computers in Human Behavior*, *148*, 107908. DOI: 10.1016/j.chb.2023.107908

Higgins, E. T., Kruglanski, A. W., & Van Lange, P. A. M. (2012). *Handbook of theories of social psychology*. Sage.

Jenkins, H. (2009). *Confronting the challenges of participatory culture: Media education for the 21st century*. The MIT press. DOI: 10.7551/mitpress/8435.001.0001

Kaplan, A. M., & Haenlein, M. (2010). Users of the world, unite! The challenges and opportunities of Social Media. *Business Horizons*, *53*(1), 59–68. DOI: 10.1016/j.bushor.2009.09.003

Kapoor, P. S., Balaji, M. S., & Jiang, Y. (2021). Effectiveness of sustainability communication on social media: Role of message appeal and message source. *International Journal of Contemporary Hospitality Management*, *33*(3), 949–972. DOI: 10.1108/IJCHM-09-2020-0974

Koukaras, P., Tjortjis, C., & Rousidis, D. (2020). Social media types: Introducing a data driven taxonomy. *Computing*, *102*(1), 295–340. DOI: 10.1007/s00607-019-00739-y

Kubey, R. (2004). What is media literacy and why is it important. *Television Quarterly, 34*(3/4), 21–27.

Liao, C.-H. (2024). Exploring social media determinants in fostering pro-environmental behavior: Insights from social impact theory and the theory of planned behavior. *Frontiers in Psychology, 15*, 1445549. DOI: 10.3389/fpsyg.2024.1445549

Livingstone, S. (2014). Developing social media literacy: How children learn to interpret risky opportunities on social network sites. *Communications, 39*(3), 283–303. DOI: 10.1515/commun-2014-0113

Lyon, T. P., & Montgomery, A. W. (2015). The means and end of greenwash. *Organization & Environment, 28*(2), 223–249. DOI: 10.1177/1086026615575332

Mehmetoglu, M. (2012). Partial least squares approach to structural equation modeling for tourism research. In *Advances in Hospitality and leisure* (pp. 43–61). Emerald Group Publishing Limited. DOI: 10.1108/S1745-3542(2012)0000008007

Meng, Y., Chung, D., & Zhang, A. (2023). The effect of social media environmental information exposure on the intention to participate in pro-environmental behavior. *PLoS One, 18*(11), e0294577. DOI: 10.1371/journal.pone.0294577

Muntinga, D. G., Moorman, M., & Smit, E. G. (2011). Introducing COBRAs: Exploring motivations for brand-related social media use. *International Journal of Advertising, 30*(1), 13–46. DOI: 10.2501/IJA-30-1-013-046

Nabivi, E. (2025). The Role of Social Media in Green Marketing: How Eco-Friendly Content Influences Brand Attitude and Consumer Engagement. *Sustainability (Basel), 17*(5), 1965. DOI: 10.3390/su17051965

Nazish, M., Khan, M. N., & Khan, Z. (2024). Environmental sustainability in the digital age: Unraveling the effect of social media on green purchase intention. *Young Consumers, 25*(6), 1015–1035. DOI: 10.1108/YC-01-2024-1965

Oral, Z. D. (2023). *Analyses of social media engagement of sustainable food brands.* University of York.

Park, S. (2012). Dimensions of digital media literacy and the relationship with social exclusion. *Media International Australia, Incorporating Culture & Policy, 142*(1), 87–100. DOI: 10.1177/1329878X1214200111

Penman, R. A., & Turnbull, S. (2007). *Media literacy: Concepts, research and regulatory issues.* Australian Communications and Media Authority Canberra.

Rodilosso, E. (2024). Filter bubbles and the unfeeling: How AI for social media can foster extremism and polarization. *Philosophy & Technology*, *37*(2), 71. DOI: 10.1007/s13347-024-00758-4

Russo, S., Schimperna, F., Lombardi, R., & Ruggiero, P. (2022). Sustainability performance and social media: An explorative analysis. *Meditari Accountancy Research*, *30*(4), 1118–1140. DOI: 10.1108/MEDAR-03-2021-1227

Saillour-Glénisson, F., Domecq, S., Kret, M., Sibé, M., Dumond, J. P., Michel, P., & Group, T. (2016). Design and validation of a questionnaire to assess organizational culture in French hospital wards. *BMC Health Services Research*, *16*(1), 491. DOI: 10.1186/s12913-016-1736-4

Samašonok, K., & Išoraitė, M. (2023). The implementation of sustainable development goals through communication tools. *Entrepreneurship and Sustainability Issues*, *10*(3), 102–122. DOI: 10.9770/jesi.2023.10.3(8)

Simeone, M., & Scarpato, D. (2020). Sustainable consumption: How does social media affect food choices? *Journal of Cleaner Production*, *277*, 124036. DOI: 10.1016/j.jclepro.2020.124036

Singh, S. K., & Sanjeev, R. (2022). Antecedents of Green Marketing Initiatives: A Hierarchical Regression Model. [IJSESD]. *International Journal of Social Ecology and Sustainable Development*, *13*(1), 1–15.

Sunstein, C. R. (2018). *Republic: Divided democracy in the age of social media.*

Tarabieh, S., Gil, I., Galdón Salvador, J. L., & AlFraihat, S. F. A. (2024). The new game of online marketing: How social media influencers drive online repurchase intention through brand trust and customer brand engagement. *Intangible Capital*, *20*(1), 103–125. DOI: 10.3926/ic.2515

Theocharis, D., & Tsekouropoulos, G. (2025). Sustainable consumption and branding for Gen Z: How brand dimensions influence consumer behavior and adoption of newly launched technological products. *Sustainability (Basel)*, *17*(9), 4124. DOI: 10.3390/su17094124

Valle, N., Zhao, P., Freed, D., Gorton, K., Chapman, A. B., Shea, A. L., & Bazarova, N. N. (2024). Towards a Critical Framework of Social Media Literacy: A Systematic Literature Review. *Review of Educational Research*, **•••**, 00346543241247224.

Weder, F., Karmasin, M., Krainer, L., & Voci, D. (2021). Sustainability communication as critical perspective in media and communication studies—An introduction. In *The sustainability communication reader: A reflective compendium* (pp. 1–12). Springer. DOI: 10.1007/978-3-658-31883-3_1

Wu, J., Xu, L., Zhou, W., Jiang, F., Liu, P., Zhang, H., Jiang, Q., & Xu, J. (2020). Fishnet-Like, Nitrogen-Doped Carbon Films Directly Anchored on Carbon Cloths as Binder-Free Electrodes for High-Performance Supercapacitor. *Global Challenges (Hoboken, NJ)*, *4*(3), 1900086. DOI: 10.1002/gch2.201900086

Yas, H., Aldabbagh, Z., Khalifa, A. A., Faghiri, A., Bawazir, A. A., & Shwedeh, F. (2025). Role of artificial intelligence in the promotion of customer experiences: A legal administrative study and systematic review in the United Arab Emirates. *Humanities (Washington)*, *6*(4). Advance online publication. 10.58256/m353d5430. DOI: 10.58256/m353d543

Chapter 9
Enhancing Public Marine Awareness Through AI Storytelling at Yas SeaWorld Research and Rescue Center

Najwa AlSaeed
http://orcid.org/0000-0001-9621-8634
City University, Ajman, UAE

Taghrid AlSaeed
Miral HQ, Yas Island, UAE

Jonathan Matusitz
University of Central Florida, USA

ABSTRACT

The "Yas SeaWorld Research and Rescue Center", SeaWorld Yas Island, Abu Dhabi, is an innovative example of marine research, conservation, and community education. The center's location close to the theme park allows for developing integrated community programs that bring together the two facilities. As such, it is possible to design immersive learning programs available to children, youth, and families that can bridge the gap between science and storytelling. This study explored the potential role that artificial intelligence (AI), data visualization, and immersive storytelling can play in transforming the complex language of science into an emotionally motivating interpretation. It seeks to create a model of integrating AI-guided narrative and interactive media to improve social knowledge, feelings of

DOI: 10.4018/979-8-2600-1348-9.ch009

empathy towards marine creatures, and recognition of climate-related issues in the oceans. The findings showed the effectiveness of artificial intelligence technologies and interactive storytelling in creating and developing scientific understanding and environmental awareness.

INTRODUCTION

Varied natural marvels are found in oceans and seas. Nevertheless, the harsh conditions surrounding these environments – such as low visibility, extreme pressure, darkness, and remoteness – make learning about and interacting with the underwater environment inherently challenging. There are numerous barriers to individuals attempting to access underwater settings, particularly children, physically challenged individuals, older people, and also financial barriers associated with the cost of diving experiences, specialized equipment, and travel to remote marine destinations (Hagen et al., 2024). As a result, the majority of society forms its understanding of marine life through mediated content rather than direct experience, making science communication a crucial bridge between humans and the oceans that sustain them.

However, communicating environmental and ecological complexities is increasingly difficult. As climate science advances, the knowledge required to comprehend the interconnectedness of ecosystems, biodiversity loss, and ocean–climate dynamics has become more technical and data-driven. This necessitates new communication strategies capable of simplifying abstract scientific concepts without compromising informational accuracy (Khaleel et al., 2024). The transition toward what scholars describe as "data-centric science" has significant implications for how environmental knowledge is produced and disseminated (Malde et al., 2019). The integration of new technologies – including artificial intelligence (AI), machine learning, simulation systems, and real-time data analytics – has introduced promising pathways for fostering public understanding and involvement in sustainability issues (Coeckelbergh, 2021; Nieves et al., 2023).

Artificial Intelligence, in particular, holds unprecedented potential in reshaping climate and marine communication (Lewis et al., 2024). AI tools can support environmental advocacy by identifying emerging conversations, detecting emotional reactions, and tailoring communication strategies to specific audiences in real time. This responsiveness enables climate communicators to adjust messaging based on evolving concerns, thereby increasing the likelihood of civic engagement and informed decision-making. By enhancing accessibility and relevance, AI-driven communication may help mitigate the global climate crisis through greater public participation and behavioral change (Rahman & Fitriyah, 2025).

Dynamic modeling has also emerged as a powerful practice in response to shifting environmental conditions (Yas et al., 2025). AI-powered simulations of marine organisms, coral ecosystems, and pollution dispersion allow scientists and the public alike to visualize invisible or undersea phenomena. Structural dynamic models can examine adaptation scenarios and consequences of climate change with a level of clarity that traditional communication methods lack. As such, recent scholarship emphasizes the need for research exploring how AI modeling, narrative visualisation, and interactive storytelling can influence public perception, empathy, and willingness to protect marine environments (Khaleel et al., 2024).

Against this backdrop, Yas SeaWorld Research and Rescue Center on Yas Island in Abu Dhabi stands as a significant marine research, rescue, and educational hub in the Middle East. As the first facility of its kind in the region, the Centre supports the UAE's conservation efforts through scientific research, animal rehabilitation programs, and public engagement initiatives (Kurdi et al., 2025). Its physical and thematic integration with SeaWorld Yas Island enables the creation of educational offerings that combine entertainment, science, and conservation messaging. This positioning provides a unique opportunity to reach a wide audience, especially youth and families, through experiential learning activities that merge fun with purpose.

Emerging technologies such as AI-generated visualization, augmented reality (AR) storytelling, and immersive digital experiences can transform dense scientific data into compelling narratives that resonate with diverse audiences. By leveraging these tools, Yas SeaWorld Research and Rescue Center can enhance public understanding of marine ecosystems, strengthen emotional connection with wildlife, and encourage environmentally responsible behavior. Therefore, this study investigates how AI-driven media strategies can reinforce Miral's broader Corporate Social Responsibility (CSR) vision while cultivating long-term societal support for ocean conservation in the United Arab Emirates and beyond.

PROBLEM STATEMENT

The United Arab Emirates (UAE) is currently navigating the complex challenge of balancing high-speed economic growth with environmental protection and long-term sustainability. The country's natural ecosystems, including fragile coastal and marine environments, arid deserts, and mountainous regions, remain highly vulnerable to the pressures of rapid development, habitat loss, groundwater extraction, and the escalating impacts of global warming. Ensuring a more ecologically secure future for the UAE by 2050 requires environmental priorities to be fully integrated into national planning and policymaking processes (Burt et al., 2024). Increasing the resilience of marine ecosystems, in particular, depends on strengthening society's knowledge and awareness of environmental threats and solutions. As Abuelgasim and Daiban (2017) argue, mitigation and adaptation efforts are only effective when driven by a well-informed public capable of understanding environmental risks and collectively supporting protective actions.

However, advancing public awareness is not a straightforward task. Climate and marine science communication faces persistent challenges. Scientific content is often abstract, highly technical, and difficult for non-specialists to interpret. Climate misinformation and low public trust in scientific claims can further weaken engagement (Laranjeiro, Lillebø & Vieira, 2025). Even when high-quality data and visual material exist, they may fail to resonate with audiences who lack a personal or emotional connection to the issues. Scholars emphasize that personalization and storytelling are critical to successful climate communication, yet many existing tools underutilize narrative approaches that make scientific content relatable to everyday life. Although data-based storytelling has proven effective in strengthening comprehension and motivation, its application to marine conservation in the UAE remains under-researched (Rashik et al., 2025).

Within this context, the Yas SeaWorld Research and Rescue Center plays a significant role as the region's pioneering hub for marine research, animal rehabilitation, and community outreach. The center generates crucial scientific insights into endangered marine species and the climate-linked stressors affecting the Arabian Gulf. Yet a notable gap persists between the volume of sophisticated scientific knowledge produced by researchers and the level of public understanding of marine ecological challenges. Families, youth, and general audiences are often exposed only to simplified or fragmented representations of ocean issues, limiting their ability to recognize the urgency of marine conservation efforts.

Therefore, this study addresses a distinct and pressing problem: How can the Yas SeaWorld Research and Rescue Center translate its dense scientific outputs into emotionally compelling, accessible, and visually engaging narratives capable of inspiring behavioral change? By investigating the potential of artificial intelligence (AI), augmented reality (AR), and immersive storytelling to bridge the communication divide, this research seeks to demonstrate how data-driven content can enhance emotional engagement, correct misconceptions, and activate public participation in marine conservation.

Closing this communication gap is essential for achieving both environmental and social objectives in the UAE. Only by connecting research insights to public values, emotions, and lived experiences can the country truly cultivate a generation prepared to protect its oceans and contribute to a sustainable future.

Research Objectives

- To explore how AI can translate complex marine and climate data into engaging and understandable visual narratives.
- To evaluate the impact of immersive storytelling on enhancing visitor empathy and knowledge retention.
- To design and test AI-based prototypes that illustrate invisible marine and climate processes (e.g., coral bleaching, ocean acidification, microplastic circulation).
- To develop a model for integrating AI-driven storytelling into the Yas SeaWorld Research and Rescue Center's education and outreach programs.

Research Questions

- How can AI-based visualization and storytelling enhance public understanding of marine and climate data at the Yas SeaWorld Research and Rescue Center?
- How can immersive and AR storytelling shape empathy and conservation awareness among children and youth?
- How can AI and data visualization support the Center's educational mission and Miral's broader sustainability and CSR agenda?
- What ethical and design principles should guide the use of AI-generated content in environmental education and storytelling?

Research Significance

The This research addresses a critical gap between scientific knowledge and public understanding of complex marine and climate systems. Marine and environmental processes are inherently multidimensional, involving interactions that are often invisible, distant, and abstract for the general public. Without clear, relatable communication methods, individuals may struggle to comprehend both the severity and the urgency of climate and marine challenges. Therefore, it is vital to explore new, scalable strategies capable of making data-driven scientific insights relevant and meaningful to society at large.

By focusing on artificial intelligence (AI), data visualization, augmented reality, and immersive storytelling, this research demonstrates how raw scientific data can be converted into compelling, emotionally resonant narratives. This data-to-story transformation helps bridge existing information barriers by enabling ordinary viewers – including children, youth, and families – to visualize underwater ecosystems, understand scientific concepts more intuitively, and establish empathy toward marine organisms. The emotional dimension is essential, as prior studies in environmental communication emphasize that knowledge alone is rarely sufficient to motivate behavioral change; audiences must feel connected to the issues to care enough to act.

The significance of this research lies not only in advancing theoretical understanding but also in providing practical applications for the Yas SeaWorld Research and Rescue Center and Miral's broader Corporate Social Responsibility (CSR) agenda. The findings support the Center's ambition to inspire environmental stewardship through innovative public engagement methods and strengthen its position as a regional leader in science communication in the MENA region. The recommendations generated through this research can be used to enhance on-site educational displays, optimize outreach strategies, and create media content that reflects real-time public concerns and emotional responses.

Moreover, this study's outcomes align closely with national priorities in sustainability, biodiversity protection, and climate resilience. The UAE seeks to cultivate environmentally conscious future generations capable of supporting long-term conservation goals. By improving public access to credible, engaging scientific content, this research contributes to these national objectives and helps strengthen societal resilience to climate challenges.

Finally, the study offers guidance for policymakers and science communication practitioners by demonstrating effective methods of using AI-driven storytelling to support public education frameworks. These insights can serve as a model for future environmental awareness programs in the UAE and across the region, helping shape a more informed, motivated, and ecologically responsible society.

LITERATURE REVIEW

Preserving the marine ecosystem and developing strategies for coping with climate change issues are hot topics that have been heavily discussed in the international debate (Malde et al., 2019). The marine ecosystem is essential to human life and the health of the earth. Teaching children and youth about marine conservation and environmental protection is necessary to develop a generation of children who appreciate and embrace sustainable lifestyles. However, the problem lies in the complexity of science communication (Tumedei et al., 2025). Climate change is also a complex topic, which is challenging to communicate to non-specialists due to the nature and scale of the problem (Pidgeon & Fischhoff, 2011). These issues have triggered an impressive expansion of social science research in order to augment the information on climate communication (Ballantyne, 2016; Moser, 2016; Fischhoff, 2019).

The recent climate science communication has prompted an instant debate among scientists about what to do proactively to respond to the changed cultural environment in which science is being practised (Groves, 2019). To obtain more valuable information about the engagement with climate science communication, it is suggested that the climate science community must develop a more profound perception regarding how to simplify the presentation of the abstract nature of scientific concepts at the societal level (Donner, 2017). Science communication had a number of solutions, all of which used a range of technologies to simplify and improve communication (Hagen et al., 2024).

Virtual reality (VR) refers to an imitation of a real-life scenario, which is achieved through a computer that imitates the visual and audio sensations of the users. The fake work with high-tech exosomatic apparatus and artificial intelligence also contributes to the fact that the VR users are made to think they are being taken to the actual maritime and cultural heritage setting (Kamel & El Shiwy, 2022). Interactive visualization can deconstruct complicated concepts and provoke interest and problem-solving. Conversational generative AI interactive narrative visualisation is essential in helping individuals explore and interact with the described ecosystem. The system will facilitate the gradual development of knowledge, active inquiry, active eliciting of emotions, and willingness to act with the assistance of creative manifestation, visual narrative, and playful interactions (Tumedei et al., 2025).

It is among the most important steps to develop more efficient solutions embodying the complexity of the data and the climate system and responding to the contemporary and future challenges of climate change. With the help of AI, it is possible to determine the most common messages and emotions of the climate change discourse and carry out specific communication campaigns that will appeal to people's hearts. It is also possible to underline the most urgent reasoning, including scientific facts, economic connotations, and environmental fairness, which presupposes the message is not redundant and will succeed (Riche et al., 2018; Rahman & Fitriyah, 2025; Nieves et al., 2023). It has become an effective tool for conveying complicated information in simple and engaging formats. The stories can be used in climate change to make the abstract scientific data more relatable and emotionally charged (Mehta et al., 2024; Moser, 2010), closing the divide between technical content and personal lived experiences (O'Neill & Boykoff, 2012).

Stahl & Hinkel (2025) confirm that narratives and storytelling can play critical roles in shaping marine conservation efforts by affecting and reshaping public perspectives. Since the aquatic ecosystem is the core of the planetary operations and human well-being, numerous ocean solutions may deliver massive co-benefits to solve poverty, hunger, economic development, inequity, peace, security, coastal resilience, and climate mitigation and adaptation. The ocean is central to our future; it is time to say so with new ocean narratives and storytelling. It is too important to neglect. The new narrative does not necessarily reshape the status quo, but when embraced by many, it can redefine the expectations and free up ingenuity. Remote sensing, big data, machine learning, and artificial intelligence may aid this process (Lubchenco & Gaines, 2019).

MIRAL Corporate Social Responsibility

In a journey of more than ten years, Miral is reshaping the scenery and enriching lives in our thrilling mission to become the region's most impactful and influential leisure, tourism, and lifestyles brand. MIRAL brings communities, cultures, people, places, families, and friends together to enjoy our world-famous destinations and experiences in Abu Dhabi and beyond, bringing all together to have some fantastic moments and creating lifetime memories (MIRAL, 2025). Miral has recorded significant milestones in its holistic "Corporate Social Responsibility (CSR) strategy", underscoring its concern for people, society, and the environment. Since the strategy was initiated in late 2023, Miral has already carried out nearly 175 practical actions under all eight strategic pillars and met with over 3,000 community members throughout Abu Dhabi (Abu Dhabi Media Office, 2025; MIRAL, 2025; Aletihad News Center, 2025). As a component of the Miral ambition to catalyse the realisation of the Abu Dhabi tourism growth, it empowers the youth of the UAE, who will significantly contribute to the well-being of the local community. This strategic partnership with Emirates Foundation is a significant milestone towards becoming a more socially responsible organisation through encouraging valuable volunteering and community service experiences (Emirates News Agency, 2023).

The two leading entities of Abu Dhabi, Miral, the best producer of immersive experiences and destinations, and Aldar Education, the best education group in the UAE, have signed a Memorandum of Understanding (MoU) to design and deploy a diversity of practical and interactive educational programs at 12 of the schools belonging to Aldar Education in Abu Dhabi. The strategic alliance makes Miral more determined to increase knowledge, development, and growth. Programs like quarterly industry-expert lectures on various issues will be initiated to motivate and teach students. The students between 16 and 18 years will be given hands-on experience in the tourism and entertainment industries with bi-annual internship programs offered in the Yas Island theme parks. Moreover, sustainability-related activities, e.g., beach and desert clean-ups, and involvement in the conservation program have been initiated (MIRAL, 2024).

Miral has entered a new milestone in academic exchange and practical learning within the leisure, entertainment, and tourism sectors through its partnership with

Canadian University Dubai (CUD). The collaboration provides CUD students with unique opportunities to volunteer, engage in internships, and conduct research at SeaWorld® Yas Island and the Yas SeaWorld Research and Rescue Centre.

In addition to CUD, Miral is also fostering connections with other leading academic institutions such as New York University Abu Dhabi (NYUAD), enabling more students to benefit from hands-on experiences in marine conservation, animal care, scientific communication, and environmental stewardship.

As one of Miral's flagship entities, the Yas SeaWorld Research and Rescue Centre plays a pivotal role in bridging science with education. Through Science Talks and outreach programs targeting university and school students alike, the Centre encourages curiosity and inquiry about marine ecosystems, biodiversity, sustainability, and the broader environmental challenges facing our oceans. These engagements not only enhance scientific awareness but also inspire future careers in marine science and conservation.

Together, these initiatives reinforce Miral's commitment to developing a highly skilled new generation aligned with the UAE's national priorities in sustainability, innovation, and knowledge-based growth. (Tourism Breaking News, 2025)

In partnership with Zayed Higher Organisation, people of determination, and SeaWorld Yas Island in Abu Dhabi, Miral organised "My Community Canvas", a heartwarming event about family, inclusion, and the marine world using art. The initiative is organised to commemorate the International Day of Family, highlighting Miral's priorities towards art and culture, which are stated in the Group CSR strategy and in line with the Year of Community 2025 in the UAE (MIRAL, 2025).

Miral has declared a complete Sustainability Strategy, which has become a turning point in its continuous commitment to the environment and social responsibility. The plan also describes the organisation's vision to emerge as a regional leader in sustainable leisure, entertainment, and tourism experience (LEET) by 2030 (Economy Middle East, 2025). In collaboration with the Abu Dhabi Municipality (ADM), Miral has ended its flagship project, Farming in Schools, a community-based education program that strives to raise a new generation of sustainability champions (ZAWYA, 2025).

Yas SeaWorld Research and Rescue Center

Yas SeaWorld Research and Rescue Centre is the first marine research and rescue center in the MENA region, located on Yas Island, and supports the UAE's conservation through research on marine diversity and the rehabilitation of endangered habitats (Abu Dhabi Media Office, 2025). The center, its partners, and the local community are committed to leading conservation efforts in the Arabian Gulf and inspiring protection of marine wildlife and ecosystems, drawing on SeaWorld's more than 60 years of experience in marine conservation (The Yas SeaWorld Research and Rescue Center, 2025).

The centre includes extensive rescue and medical facilities designed specifically for marine animals, equipped with advanced diagnostic tools such as CT scan and MRI, as well as fully equipped surgical rooms to support complex veterinary procedures for species like turtles, sea snakes, and dugongs. It also operates advanced water treatment systems that maintain strict water quality standards, ensuring optimal conditions for animal health, rehabilitation, and eventual release where possible (Abu Dhabi Media Office, 2024).

In addition to its on-site capabilities, the center runs a dedicated emergency hotline to receive urgent calls about marine animals in danger or suffering from injury and disease, including turtles, sea snakes, sea cows, and other marine species. This rapid-response function strengthens the Centre's role as a regional hub for rescue operations and reinforces its integration with local communities and authorities concerned with marine wildlife welfare (Yas Sea World Research & Rescue Center, 2025).

As a prominent marine science institution, the Yas SeaWorld Research and Rescue Centre participates in a range of conservation initiatives, including research and restoration of seagrass ecosystems and the development of sustainable aquaculture research programs (The Yas SeaWorld Research and Rescue Center, 2025). Following its opening in September 2023, the Centre has also hosted an ongoing monthly Science Talks series with more than 1,400 participants, covering themes such as sea turtle conservation, desert reptiles adapting to extreme temperatures, and fish biodiversity (Abu Dhabi Blog, 2025).

The Centre has further strengthened its scientific role by signing two research agreements with New York University Abu Dhabi (NYUAD) to investigate how the Gulf's extreme conditions affect the physiology, ecology, and behaviour of local fish, and to examine the impact of high temperatures and salinity on coral bleaching (Abu Dhabi Media Office, 2023). These collaborations position the Yas SeaWorld Research and Rescue Centre as a key contributor to understanding and mitigating climate and environmental stressors on Arabian Gulf marine ecosystems.

INTEGRATION WITH ATHEER BY MIRAL

Atheer by Miral can be described as an integrated, AI-driven media ecosystem that extends beyond a single studio to a full "stack" of content creation, intelligence, and immersive event capabilities (Abu Dhabi Media Office, 2025).

Integrated Atheer model

Atheer incorporates a hybrid production environment that combines broadcast-grade live streaming, podcast recording, social media content production, and a digital editing suite, all designed to support Miral's storytelling across Yas Island. These facilities are linked to media intelligence and graphic design capabilities, including photography, videography, animation, infographics, and AI-assisted creative tools that help tailor content for multiple platforms and audiences (Miral Official Website, 2025).

AI video and multilingual dubbing

Within this ecosystem, Atheer can leverage contemporary AI dubbing and lip-sync technologies that allow video content to be localized into multiple languages while maintaining natural mouth movements and emotional expression. Such tools use audio-visual models trained on facial geometry, phonemes, and timing patterns to generate precise lip-syncing, enabling Miral to repurpose corporate, tourism, and conservation content for diverse markets without reshooting (Slator, 2025).

Enterprise media intelligence and dashboards

On the enterprise side, Atheer's "media intelligence" pillar includes AI-powered media monitoring, analytical reporting, and market research, which can feed into dashboards tracking engagement, sentiment, and reach across channels in near real time. These insights allow Miral and its partners to adjust messaging, creative assets, and media placements on the spot to optimise campaign performance and support CSR and sustainability communication goals (Miral Official Website, 2025).

Metaverse and international business events

Complementing Atheer, Miral and e& enterprise have launched the Yas Island Metaverse, an immersive AR/VR environment that lets international companies and event planners virtually explore Yas Island venues—including theme parks such as Yas SeaWorld—and plan business events remotely. Through browser-based 3D walkthroughs, avatar-led site tours, and real-time collaborative tools, this metaverse layer integrates with Miral's broader communication strategy, making it easier to stage hybrid or fully virtual activations linked to Atheer's live production and streaming capabilities (Shahzaib, 2025).

Results and Discussion Based on the Sprinklr Dashboard Analysis

Presenting & Discussing the Study's Findings Using the Official Sprinklr Dashboard

Using the revised methodology, the findings in this report are derived solely from the official Sprinklr Insights Dashboard, which measures real-time and historical conversations related to marine conservation, the Yas SeaWorld Research and Rescue

Centre, climate awareness, environmental issues, and CSR-related narratives relevant to Miral. The analysis is based on the following key performance indicators (KPIs):

- **Online Mentions:** Identifies when and where the Yas SeaWorld Research and Rescue Centre is referenced across digital platforms.
- **Estimated Reach:** Measures the potential audience size exposed to conversations related to the Centre or its topics.
- **Engagement:** Tracks user interaction metrics including likes, comments, shares, messages, saves, and other forms of participation.
- **Sentiment Analysis:** Evaluates public perception by categorizing posts and discussions as positive, neutral, or negative.
- **Demographics:** Provides insights into the audience discussing the Center, including age, gender, geographic location, interests, and more.
- **Sources:** Lists the platforms, websites, and media outlets where coverage and conversations are taking place.

This section integrates the outputs of the Sprinklr dashboard through 4 analytical layers corresponding to the research question:

1. Public Perception of Marine and Climate Processes
2. Emotional and Behavioral Engagement
3. Perceived Effectiveness of AI Driven Storytelling
4. Credibility and Ethical Concerns

Each layer represents insights gleaned from sentiment analysis, topic clusters, engagement metrics, keyword frequency patterns and conversational drivers.

1. Public Perception of Marine and Climate Processes

- Dashboard Derived Insights

Analyzing clusters of conversations revealed a high level of public interest in the following topical areas:

- Coral Bleaching
- Marine Pollution
- Overfishing and regional impacts of overfishing
- Habitat Loss due to climate

The most active cluster focused on "marine threats and human impact," therefore, the majority of public discussion has centered around how severe environmental damage is rather than an understanding of the science behind the environmental problems. However, there was significant increase in positive engagement each time scientific information was delivered via visual formats (i.e. Infographics posted by marine organizations).

- Sentiment Analysis reveals the following:

- 68% positive or neutral sentiment toward scientifically educational content
- 32% negative sentiment, specifically stemming from climate anxiety and worry about the deterioration of oceans

The results indicate the general public is open to educational content, particularly if it is simplified and includes engaging visuals – supporting the ability of AI driven narratives to bridge the gap of understanding.

Interpretation

The dashboard numbers are confirmation of the fact that just like they need simplified stories, we owe them clarity and accessibility over more scientific depth. This is consistent with prior literature indicating a demand for stripped down translations of climate science. AI generated visualizations are a powerful way to turn challenging marine data into communicative materials for different constituency.

2. Affect and Behavioral Involvement With Marine Conservation

- Dashboard-Derived Insights

By utilizing sentiment layers of Sprinklr for emotional analysis, we can observe recurrent emotional tones:

- Empathy and care (41%)
- Concern/worry (29%)
- Curiosity (17%)
- Advocacy and action-oriented emotions (13%)

Discussion had the highest emotional intensity for:

- Stories about rescued marine animals
- Visual content showing pollution impacts
- Stories that feature children or youth engaged in conservation activities

Rates of engagement were much higher (+54%) in posts that appeared with the story elements, materializing particularly in sequential narratives and before/after pictures as well as in "journey-based" framing.

Interpretation

AI-POWERED EMOTION-RICH STORYTELLING When AI-generated storytelling is emotionally rich, it operates as a booster enhancing the public's motivation to engage with conservation messages. This supports the research hypothesis that immersive and narrative (story-based) approaches can engender attitudinal change and more pro-environmental behaviors.

3. AI and the Digital Story/Public Communication – efficacy.

- Dashboard-Derived Insights

During the live show, AI-generated content (including infographics designed by AI, synthetic visual simulations and "AR clips shared with related members") reached:

- 3x more shareable compared to static text posts
- Greater ratio of comment depth (indicative of deeper cognition engagement).
- Reaching more diverse demographics, with strong take up in youth (13–18 years).

Topics that performed best included:

- AI sees coral bleaching happen in real time
- 3D animated depictions of ocean acidification
- AI simulations showing microplastic circulation

Interpretation

AI enables an audience to understand as well as see how the invisible is simulated, and therefore "seen." This also relates to some educational theories (that relate to experiential learning), and it provides further evidence of the suitability of AI to be used in marine science communications.

4. Perception of Credibility and Ethical Sensibilities Regarding Smart Content

Insights From Public Discussions:

- Tendency to believe institution-backed scientific content as a result of high institutional trust
- Frequency of requests for transparent source information
- Favorable response to data authenticity posts (e.g., behind-the-scenes images from research activities)
- Split sentiment on AI-generated visuals due to concern over potential to create realistic visuals that are exaggerated or misleading

Key "trust building" factors included:

- Partnerships (NYUAD, Canadian University Dubai, etc.)
- Scientific references that could be verified
- Methodology disclosure in post content

Interpretation

Smart content is well received; however, transparency will continue to be an important factor. The dashboard indicates that when content creators are transparent regarding how they collect their data, what measures they have taken to safeguard ethics, and how their products were created, there is a significant increase in trust.

Cross-Axis Integrated Discussion

There is a high correlation between the public perception of AI-based marine educational content and the theoretical assumption upon which this type of content is based, as indicated by the dashboard results:

- Data visualization makes scientific content easier to access.
- Storytelling increases both emotional and behavioral engagement.
- AI simulation helps clarify otherwise abstract climate processes.
- Transparency enhances credibility and long-term trust.

Therefore, the dashboard validates the conceptual model presented in the study:

AI + Visualization + Storytelling = Increased Awareness + Emotional Engagement + Action

Implications for Yas SeaWorld & Miral (Strategic Impact)

The dashboard findings have strategic implications for Yas SeaWorld & Miral as follows:

1. Converting Public Conversations into Focused Educational Content

The dashboard themes can be used to develop:

- Educational modules
- AR Experiences
- Museum Displays
- Workshops for Youth

2. Using Dashboard Findings to Guide the Development of the Atheer AI Production Platform

Atheer can use the findings to determine:

- The most successful story types
- Data-Driven Marine Narratives
- Campaigns to Emotionally Engage Youth

3. Building CSR Impact

Using emotion-based insights, Miral can build programs that connect emotionally with families, schools and communities.

4. Increasing Effectiveness of Conservation Messaging

Yas SeaWorld can use the dashboard's insight on sentiment and theme drivers to optimize:

- Stories with Humane Themes
- Science-based Visual Explanations
- Awareness Campaigns Targeting Misconceptions

Recommendations

1. Embed Dashboard Critical Points in AI Storytelling Recipes

Turn high-volume subjects (pollution, coral bleaching, climate change) into compelling narrative experiences.

2. Create a Real-Time AI "Story Engine"

Automatically convert dashboard insights into:

- Daily micro-stories
- Visual reels
- AR-enhanced explainer clips

3. You should now see the new feature: "Emotion Layer Analytics" in your Dashboard.

To identify emotion functions, particularly in children, adolescents and their parents.

4. Develop a Transparency Framework

Clear disclosure of:

- Data sources
- Visualization methods
- AI model limitations
- Blend Dashboard Data to Customize the Visitor Experience
  Example: conduct shows according to what people are worrying about that week.

DISCUSSION: LINKING DASHBOARD-DERIVED INSIGHTS TO STRATEGIC RECOMMENDATIONS

The recommendations proposed in this study are grounded entirely in the empirical insights extracted from the Sprinklr Dashboard. While the dashboard successfully identified public sentiment trends, engagement behaviors, emotional drivers, and credibility issues surrounding marine conservation communication, its highest value emerges when these findings are translated into actionable AI storytelling strategies. The following table demonstrates how each recommendation directly addresses the specific opportunities and gaps identified in the results, enabling Yas SeaWorld and Miral to evolve from data monitoring to data-driven marine education innovation.

Table 1. Alignment Between Dashboard Findings and Strategic Recommendations

What Has Been Achieved Through the Dashboard Analysis	Strategic Recommendation	How the Recommendation Enhances What Is Already Done
High-volume environmental concern topics identified (pollution, coral bleaching, overfishing, habitat loss)	Embed Critical Points in AI Storytelling Recipes	Converts raw problem-focused discussions into narrative experiences that enhance understanding, reduce climate anxiety, and shift focus from fear → solutions.
Preference for visual, sequential, and short-form content identified — especially among youth	Create a real-time AI "story engine"	Ensures continuous delivery of relevant, visual, and AR-enhanced content aligned with current discussions to increase shareability and engagement.
Emotional drivers recorded: empathy, concern, and curiosity — especially among families and students	Use Emotion Layer Analytics feature	Optimizes storytelling for emotion-based persuasion, strengthening public motivation for conservation actions.
Public trust linked to institutional credibility and transparency in data sourcing	Develop a transparency framework for smart content	Increases content credibility by disclosing data origins, visualization methods, and AI limitations, mitigating misinformation risks.
Real-time conversational shifts reveal weekly priorities and concerns	Blend dashboard data to customize visitor experiences	Enables dynamic, audience-driven programming (e.g., shows and displays tailored to trending concerns), improving educational impact and audience satisfaction.

INTERPRETATION

The integration of the dashboard findings with the proposed strategic recommendations illustrates the progression of this study from analytical diagnosis to actionable intervention. The Sprinklr Dashboard provided a comprehensive mapping of digital conversations surrounding marine conservation, revealing how audiences respond emotionally to environmental topics, which content formats drive higher engagement, and what transparency factors influence trust in AI-supported communication. However, the dashboard alone functions as an observational tool; its insights remain static unless operationalized within a strategic communication framework. The recommendations presented in this study therefore act as a direct extension of the empirical results, repositioning AI from a passive visualization mechanism to an active behavior-shaping medium grounded in audience realities.

By embedding the most frequently discussed marine concerns into accessible narrative formats, tailoring content through emotional analytics, automating real-time AI story production, and enhancing transparency in AI-generated materials, Yas SeaWorld and Miral are able to shift from simply monitoring public conversations to actively shaping them. This creates a continuous refinement process in which dashboard insights inform story development, while subsequent audience interactions generate new layers of insight that strengthen future communication strategies. Such an iterative cycle deepens public understanding, enhances youth engagement, strengthens trust in institutional content, and maximizes the persuasive impact of conservation messaging.

For example, if the public is worried about coral bleaching, more stories can be created that explain coral protection. If young people respond strongly to emotional videos, more youth-focused visual storytelling can be produced. Likewise, if audiences require transparency to trust AI content, communicating clearly where data comes from will reinforce credibility. Instead of only listening to public conversations, Yas SeaWorld and Miral will actively shape them. Each time a new AI-powered story is published, audience reactions generate new data in the dashboard, and this data can be used to further improve storytelling.

This establishes a smart cycle—**Dashboard Insights → Story Creation → Public Reaction → Improved Insights**—that continuously enhances communication effectiveness. Through this process, young audiences become more involved, people learn more about marine life, trust in AI content increases, and conservation messages become more effective. In the long term, this system becomes a sustainable model that can be applied across all Miral projects, positioning AI storytelling as a major tool for marine education and public engagement. This alignment provides a scalable and sustainable model for data-driven marine education and CSR communication. It positions Yas SeaWorld and Miral as leaders in innovative public engagement by demonstrating how artificial intelligence, when guided by real-time audience analytics, can foster meaningful awareness, emotional connection, and behavioral motivation toward marine conservation across current and future outreach platforms.

In addition to these observations, the dashboard findings highlight an important methodological insight: public engagement with marine science is highly dynamic and evolves in response to both environmental events and narrative framing. This suggests that effective communication cannot rely on static educational materials but must instead adopt a fluid, adaptive storytelling model that reflects real-time audience concerns. The data shows that emotional resonance—particularly empathy, curiosity, and concern—functions as an entry point for deeper cognitive processing of scientific material. Thus, AI-driven media should not merely present information visually but strategically link emotional cues with scientific explanations to maximize learning impact. By extension, the prominence of youth engagement signals the necessity of tailoring content to generational preferences for interactive, short-form, and visually rich formats. This reinforces the value of AI as a co-creative tool capable of curation, personalization, and iterative refinement. Ultimately, the Interpretation confirms that adaptive, emotionally guided, transparent storytelling is the most effective pathway for enhancing public understanding of marine conservation.

CONCLUSIONS

This chapter has examined how emerging technologies – specifically artificial intelligence, data visualization, and immersive storytelling – can strengthen public understanding and conservation engagement at the Yas SeaWorld Research and Rescue Center. Through analysis of real-time audience sentiment and interaction data, the study demonstrated how AI-enabled storytelling can translate complex and often invisible marine and climate processes into accessible knowledge and emotionally compelling narratives. This directly answers the first research question by showing that data-driven visualization makes scientific content easier to understand and increases positive engagement with marine topics.

The findings also confirm that immersive and AR-enhanced content is particularly effective in shaping empathy and strengthening pro-environmental attitudes among children and youth. The dashboard revealed that engagement levels were highest for stories featuring animal rescue, youth participation, and emotional narrative framing. These results validate the second research question by illustrating that narrative-based and experiential communication can inspire young audiences to feel more connected to marine life and climate concerns.

In relation to the third research question, the study established that AI-powered storytelling offers a strategic advantage to the Center's educational mission and Miral's broader sustainability and CSR goals. The proposed recommendations – including adopting real-time AI storytelling workflows, emotion analytics, and transparent data guidelines –provide a practical roadmap for scaling impactful environmental communication across Miral's platforms, outreach initiatives, and partnerships. This supports national ambitions to cultivate a more informed and environmentally responsible generation aligned with the UAE's sustainability agenda.

Finally, ethical and design considerations emerged as a critical component of audience trust in AI-generated media. Public discussions showed strong confidence in institution-backed scientific content, while also signaling concerns over realism and potential exaggeration in synthetic visuals. The study therefore answered the fourth research question by establishing that transparency – regarding data sources, visualization methods, and AI limitations – is essential for ensuring credibility, avoiding misinformation, and maintaining public trust in digital conservation communication.

Taken as a whole, this chapter demonstrates that AI-based storytelling is not merely a technological enhancement to science communication; it represents a transformative model capable of increasing awareness, improving emotional responsiveness, and motivating behavior change toward ocean conservation. By operationalizing real-time audience insights into continuous content refinement, Yas SeaWorld and Miral are uniquely positioned to lead the region in innovative, data-driven environmental education. This research lays the foundation for scalable, ethically grounded, and adaptive communication strategies that can support conservation impact across Yas Island, the UAE, and the broader MENA region for years to come.

Suggestions for Future Research

Looking ahead, future research should explore how AI-generated storytelling can be systematically integrated into long-term conservation education frameworks across the UAE. While this study demonstrates strong public receptivity to AI-enhanced narratives, further empirical work is needed to measure long-term behavioral outcomes, such as sustained pro-environmental habits, civic participation, or changes in ecological literacy among school-aged audiences. Furthermore, research should examine cross-cultural responses to AI-mediated marine storytelling to determine how narratives may be customized for diverse communities within the UAE and the broader MENA region.

Another promising direction is the study of co-creative models in which youth and families actively participate in producing their own AI-supported marine stories—a process that may significantly strengthen personal connection to marine ecosystems. Finally, future studies should evaluate the ethical implications of increasingly realistic AI simulations to ensure that accuracy, transparency, and public trust remain central pillars of digital conservation communication.

REFERENCES

Abu Dhabi Blog. (2025). The Yas SeaWorld® Research & Rescue Center Kicks-Off 2025 Science Talk Series With A Focus On Seagrass. https://blog.abudhabicityguide.com/the-yas-seaworld-research-rescue-center-kicks-off-2025-science-talk-series-with-a-focus-on-seagrass/

Abu Dhabi Media Office. (2023). Yas SeaWorld Research and Rescue Centre, Yas Island, Abu Dhabi, and NYU Abu Dhabi partner to enhance conservation efforts. https://www.mediaoffice.abudhabi/en/tourism/yas-seaworld-research-and-rescue-centre-yas-island-abu-dhabi-and-nyu-abu-dhabi-partner-to-enhance-conservation-efforts

Abu Dhabi Media Office. (2024). *Environment Agency – Abu Dhabi and Yas SeaWorld Research and Rescue Centre Yas Island, Abu Dhabi demonstrate conservation capabilities.* https://www.mediaoffice.abudhabi/en/environment/environment-agency-abu-dhabi-and-yas-seaworld-research-and-rescue-centre-yas-island-abu-dhabi-demonstrate-conservation-capabilities

Abu Dhabi Media Office. (2025). *Miral launches advanced communication and production platform, Atheer.* https://www.mediaoffice.abudhabi/en/tourism/miral-launches-advanced-communication-and-production-platform-atheer/

Abu Dhabi Media Office. (2025). Miral supports Abu Dhabi communities via its 2024 Corporate Social Responsibility strategy. https://www.mediaoffice.abudhabi/en/tourism/miral-supports-abu-dhabi-communities-via-its-2024-corporate-social-responsibility-strategy

Abu Dhabi Media Office. (2025). Yas SeaWorld Research and Rescue Yas Island, Abu Dhabi. https://www.mediaoffice.abudhabi/en/topic/yas-seaworld-research-and-rescue-yas-island-abu-dhabi

Abu Dhabi Media Office. (2025). Miral launched an advanced communication and production platform, Atheer. https://www.mediaoffice.abudhabi/en/tourism/miral-launches-advanced-communication-and-production-platform-atheer

Abuelgasim, A., & Daiban, S. (2017). Levels of Climate Change Awareness in the United Arab Emirates. Horizons in Humanities and Social Sciences: An International Refereed Journal, 2(2) 42-53. https://www.researchgate.net/publication/317566042

Al Kurdi, B., Alshurideh, M. T., El Khatib, M., Alrawabdeh, W. A., Al-Sulaiti, K., Nawaiseh, A. K., Sukkari, L., Alshurideh, A., Shwedeh, F., & Alzoubi, H. M. (2025). The Effect of Using IoT on Linking Green Customers Data (Green Customer Profile) with Green Products and Green Product Labels BT - Sustainable Innovation for Engineering Management (SIEM). In El Khatib, M., Alzoubi, H. M., & Angelova, Y. (Eds.), *Sustainable Innovation for Engineering Management (SIEM)* (pp. 59–68). Springer Nature Switzerland., https://doi.org/https://doi.org/10.1007/978-3-031-89889-1_7 DOI: 10.1007/978-3-031-89889-1_7

Aletihad News Center. (2025). Miral keen to make social impact with CSR strategy. https://en.aletihad.ae/news/business/4430367/miral-keen-to-make-social-impact-with-csr-strategy

Ballantyne, A. G. (2016). Climate change communication: What can we learn from communication theory? *Wiley Interdisciplinary Reviews: Climate Change*, *7*(3), 329–344. DOI: 10.1002/wcc.392

Burt, J. A., Al-Mansoori, N., Bejarano, I., Brown, G., Campbell, O., Els, J., Feulner, G. R., Friis-Montoya, G., Henderson, A., Howarth, B., John, D. M., Judas, J., Mateos-Molina, D., Mitchell, M., Natoli, A., Paparella, F., & Yaghmour, F. (2024). The Emirates at 2050: Balancing Development and Environmental Stewardship. In Burt, J. A. (Ed.), *A Natural History of the Emirates* (pp. 735–748)., DOI: 10.1007/978-3-031-37397-8_24

Coeckelbergh, M. (2021). AI for climate: Freedom, justice, and other ethical and political challenges. *AI and Ethics*, *1*(1), 67–72. DOI: 10.1007/s43681-020-00007-2

Donner, S. D. (2017). Risk and responsibility in public engagement by climate scientists: Reconsidering advocacy during the Trump era. *Environmental Communication*, *11*(3), 430–433. DOI: 10.1080/17524032.2017.1291101

ECONOMY MIDDLE EAST. (2025). Abu Dhabi's Miral launches bold sustainability strategy to advance responsible leisure, entertainment, and tourism. https://economymiddleeast.com/news/abu-dhabi-miral-launches-bold-sustainability-strategy/

Emirates News Agency. (2023). Miral and Emirates Foundation are fostering volunteerism among UAE youth. https://www.wam.ae/en/article/3upcz0-miral-and-emirates-foundation-fostering

Fischhoff, B. (2019). Evaluating science communication. *Proceedings of the National Academy of Sciences of the United States of America*, *116*(16), 7670–7675. DOI: 10.1073/pnas.1805863115 PMID: 30478063

Groves, C. (2019). Post-truth and anthropogenic climate change: Asking the right questions. *Wiley Interdisciplinary Reviews: Climate Change, 10*(6), e620. DOI: 10.1002/wcc.620

Hagen, O., Aly, A., Jones, R., Varga, M., & Bazazian, D. (2024). Beyond the surface: A scoping review of vision-based underwater experience technologies and user studies. *Intell. Mar. Technol. Syst., 2*(19), 1–24. DOI: 10.1007/s44295-024-00034-3

Kamel, N., & El Shiwy, R. (2022). Virtual Reality and Virtual Diving Technologies: Innovative Tools to Promote Maritime and Underwater Cultural Heritage in the Red Sea, Egypt. Journal of Tourism [JTHH]. *Hotels and Heritage, 5*(3), 18–46. DOI: 10.21608/sis.2022.175794.1111

Khaleel, M., Murtaza, N., Mueen, Q. H., Ahmad, S. A., & Qadri, S. F. (2024). *Use of AI in conservation and for understanding climate change*. Elsevier Inc., DOI: 10.1016/B978-0-443-24001-0.00013-0

Laranjeiro, D., Lillebø, A. I., & Vieira, H. (2025). Generative AI in Climate Change Communication and Education. In Proceedings of the 17th International Conference on Computer Supported Education (CSEDU 2025) - Volume 1, pages 123-134. https://doi.DOI: 10.5220/0013478400003932

Lewis, J. I., Toney, A., & Shi, X. (2024, September 28). Climate change and artificial intelligence: Assessing the global research landscape. *Discover Artificial Intelligence, 4*(64), 1–12. DOI: 10.1007/s44163-024-00170-z

Lubchenco, J., & Gaines, S. D. (2019). A new narrative for the ocean. *Science, 364*(6444), 911–912. DOI: 10.1126/science.aay2241 PMID: 31171668

Malde, K., Handegard, N. O., Eikvil, L., & Salberg, A.-B. (2019). Machine intelligence and the data-driven future of marine science. *ICES Journal of Marine Science*, •••, 1–12. DOI: 10.1093/icesjms/fsz057

Mehta, B., Sam, E., & Campwala, N. (2024). Communication for climate change and development: Roadmap to build climate resilient communities. In *Environmental Activism and Global Media: Perspective from the Past, Present and Future* (pp. 117–130). Springer Publications., DOI: 10.1007/978-3-031-55408-7_6

MIRAL. (2024). MIRAL AND ALDAR EDUCATION FORGE STRATEGIC PARTNERSHIP TO ENRICH STUDENT LEARNING. https://miral.ae/news-item/miral-and-aldar-education-forge-strategic-partnership-to-enrich-student-learning/

MIRAL. (2025). *Atheer*. https://miral.ae/atheer/

MIRAL. (2025). About MIRAL. https://miral.ae/about-miral/

MIRAL. (2025). OUR COMMITMENT. https://miral.ae/our-commitment/

MIRAL. (2025). My Community Canvas: Miral Celebrates Family, Inclusion, And Marine Life At SeaWorld Yas Island, Abu Dhabi. https://miral.ae/news-item/my-community-canvas-miral-celebrates-family-inclusion-and-marine-life-at-seaworld-yas-island-abu-dhabi/

Moser, S. C. (2010). Communicating climate change: History, challenges, process and future directions. *Wiley Interdisciplinary Reviews: Climate Change*, *1*(1), 31–53. DOI: 10.1002/wcc.11

Moser, S. C. (2016). Reflections on climate change communication research and practice in the second decade of the 21st century: What more is there to say? *Wiley Interdisciplinary Reviews: Climate Change*, *7*(3), 345–369. DOI: 10.1002/wcc.403

Nieves, V., Ruescas, A., & Sauzède, R. (2023, December 20). AI for Marine, Ocean and Climate Change Monitoring. *Remote Sensing (Basel)*, *16*(15), 1–15. DOI: 10.3390/rs16010015

O'Neill, S., & Boykoff, M. (2012). The role of new media in engaging the public with climate change. *Engaging the public with climate change*, *2*(2012), 233–251. https://www.researchgate.net/publication/285081555

Rahman, G., & Fitriyah, A. (2025). Harnessing AI for Climate Change Communication: Analyzing Public Perception through NLP and Machine Learning. *Sinergi International Journal of Communication*, *3*(1), 87–98. DOI: 10.61194/ijcs.v3i2.683

Rashik, M., Fekete, J. D., & Mahyar, N. (2025). CLAImate: AI-Enabled Climate Change Communication through Personalized and Localized Narrative Visualizations. Proceedings of the IEEE Visualization Conference, *Human-Computer Interaction*, DOI: 10.48550/arXiv.2507.11677

Riche, N. H., Hurter, C., Diakopoulos, N., & Carpendale, S. (2018). *Datadriven storytelling*. CRC Press., DOI: 10.1201/9781315281575

Shahzaib. (2025, October 15). *Miral and e& enterprise launch Yas Island Metaverse to revolutionize virtual event planning*. MEA Tech Watch. https://meatechwatch.com/2025/10/15/miral-and-e-enterprise-launch-yas-island-metaverse-to-revolutionize-virtual-event-planning/

Stahl, J. K., & Hinkel, J. (2025). The power of storytelling: How narratives shape marine conservation and uses along the German coast of the Baltic Sea. *Maritime Studies*, *24*(3), 1–18. DOI: 10.1007/s40152-025-00419-y

The Yas SeaWorld Research & Rescue Center. (2025). Leading marine conservation & Inspiring environmental protection. https://www.seaworldabudhabi.com/en/research-and-rescue

Tourism Breaking News. (2025). Enriching Student Experiences: Miral and Canadian University Dubai Sign Strategic Partnership. https://tourismbreakingnews.ae/enriching-student-experiences-miral-and-canadian-university-dubai-sign-strategic-partnership/

Tumedei, G., Ceccarini, C., Navarro, I. C. J., & Prandi, C. (2025). From Drawings to Awareness: Exploring Narrative Visualization and AI to Teach Children About the Fragile Ecosystem of the Mar Menor Lagoon. In *Designing Interactive Systems Conference* (DIS '25), July 05–09, 2025, Funchal, Portugal. ACM, New York, NY, USA, 17 pages. DOI: 10.1145/3715336.3735722

Yas, H., Aldabbagh, Z., Khalifa, A. A., Faghiri, A., Bawazir, A. A., & Shwedeh, F. (2025). Role of artificial intelligence in the promotion of customer experiences: A legal administrative study and systematic review in the United Arab Emirates. *Humanities (Washington)*, *6*(4). Advance online publication. https://doi.org/https://doi.org/10.58256/m353d5430. DOI: 10.58256/m353d543

Yas SeaWorld Research & Rescue Center. (2025). *The Yas SeaWorld Research & Rescue Center Abu Dhabi is always here to help*. https://www.seaworldabudhabi.com/en/research-and-rescue/rescue-rehabilitation

ZAWYA. (2025). Planting Seeds for the Future: Miral's CSR Programme cultivates environmental stewardship among youth. https://www.zawya.com/en/press-release/companies-news/planting-seeds-for-the-future-mirals-csr-programme-cultivates-environmental-stewardship-among-youth-epzpialh

Chapter 10
Decarbonizing Pharma Engagement:
From Paper to AI Optimized Digital Journeys

Hala Afifi
http://orcid.org/0000-0003-3777-8388
City University Ajman, Ajman, UAE

Ahmed Gamal Afifi
Merck Gulf, UAE

ABSTRACT

This chapter examines how AI can drive greener pharmaceutical marketing by shifting from paper- and travel-heavy approaches to lower-carbon, data-driven omnichannel engagement. It reviews evidence on the environmental impacts of telehealth, e-detailing, remote medical education and digital consent, while weighing the energy and material costs of AI models, devices and data centers. Using a narrative review plus vignettes, the authors propose a measurement framework aligned to the GHG Protocol Scopes 1–3 and define metrics such as CO2e per qualified HCP engagement, travel emissions avoided via virtual interactions and net savings from replacing print with digital (including computing energy). They outline reporting that combines energy data (e.g., PUE and grid mix) with campaign analytics, and present an AI playbook emphasizing efficient models, renewable hosting, responsible governance and content reuse. The chapter also flags rebound effects, privacy/ethics and regulatory compliance, calling for standardized digital carbon accounting and sustainability-linked marketing KPIs.

DOI: 10.4018/979-8-2600-1348-9.ch010

1. INTRODUCTION

For decades, pharmaceutical engagement has revolved around people on the road and paper on the table. Sales representatives drive or fly to visit clinicians, brand teams host large international conferences, brochures, leave-pieces and consent forms are printed, shipped and ultimately discarded. Each touchpoint carries a carbon cost: fuel burned for travel, energy consumed in hotels and venues, and greenhouse gases embedded in paper and printing. These emissions were historically treated as the unavoidable 'cost of doing businesses, but they are now under scrutiny as health systems and life-science companies confront their climate responsibilities.

Life-cycle assessments of medical conferences highlight the scale of the footprint. Analyses comparing in-person and virtual congress formats show that emissions per participant can fall by 90–94% when long-haul travel is replaced by virtual attendance, with the range depending on flight distance, accommodation type and venue energy mix (Gattrell et al., 2022; Thiel et al., 2023). Similar patterns are seen in clinical care. Systematic reviews of telemedicine report substantial reductions in greenhouse gas emissions when face-to-face visits are substituted with telephone or video consultations, even after accounting for the electricity used by digital devices and platforms (Ravindrane and Patel, 2022; Patel et al., 2023).

Traditional, paper-heavy engagement models are therefore increasingly misaligned with the net-zero commitments adopted by many health systems and pharmaceutical companies. At the same time, the rapid expansion of digital health, telemedicine and omnichannel marketing raises an important question: can we decarbonize pharmaceutical engagement by going digital, and what is the climate cost of the artificial intelligence (AI) and data centers that underpin these new models?

This chapter argues that AI-enabled digital engagement can significantly reduce the climate impact of pharmaceutical marketing and medical education, but only if it is designed and governed carefully. Digital tactics are not impact-free: cloud computing, AI models and network infrastructure consume energy and have embodied emissions. The challenge is to design engagement strategies in which the emissions avoided by reducing travel and print are much larger than the additional emissions generated by digital technologies. To achieve this, organizations need a clear measurement framework, practical metrics and a realistic 'AI playbook' for low-carbon operations.

What has shifted is not only sustainability expectations but also the mechanics of how clinicians and patients prefer to engage. The post-pandemic environment has normalized hybrid and remote interactions, while access policies, time pressure and digital clinical workflows have increased demand for fewer, higher-value touchpoints. In this context, omnichannel is evolving from a simple 'more channels' strategy into an orchestrated, preference-led journey model that can reduce duplication, unnecessary travel and low-impact print circulation. Industry roadmaps and early transformation casework indicate that orchestrated, HCP-preference-led models are now becoming the default blueprint for emerging and mid-size pharma organizations (ZS, 2025; McKinsey & Company, 2024; 2025).

The rise of data-driven personalization and generative AI further amplifies both the opportunity and the risk. Used responsibly, AI can help target education and product information more precisely, improve content reuse through modular architectures and support virtual-first approaches that displace high-carbon activities. However, AI and cloud infrastructure also introduce measurable energy demand. The real prize is therefore 'net' decarbonization: ensuring that emissions avoided through reduced mobility, events and printing substantially exceed any incremental digital footprint, and that rebound effects do not erode these gains.

1.1 Purpose and scope

The purpose of this chapter is to show how AI and digital technologies can be used to reduce the climate impact of pharmaceutical engagement, while recognizing that digital transformation itself has an environmental footprint. The scope is deliberately practical and cross-functional. It brings together perspectives from pharmaceutical commercial teams, medical affairs, sustainability officers and health-system partners who must collectively balance clinical, commercial and climate objectives.

In practical terms, the chapter focuses on the engagement value chain spanning commercial marketing, medical affairs and continuing medical education (CME), including field force activity, congress models, agency-supported content production, print and sampling where relevant, and the digital platforms that increasingly underpin HCP and patient journeys. It does not attempt to quantify the full lifecycle emissions of pharmaceutical manufacturing or supply of medicines; instead, it isolates the engagement domain to provide leaders with actionable levers that can be activated within brand planning, campaign design and omnichannel governance.

The chapter has four main objectives. First, it maps traditional and digital engagement activities to the Greenhouse Gas Protocol's Scope 1, 2 and 3 categories. Second, it summarizes evidence on the environmental impacts of digital health, tele-engagement, e-detailing and virtual education compared with physical equivalents. Third, it proposes concrete emissions metrics, for example, CO_2e per qualified healthcare professional (HCP) engagement, avoided travel emissions and 'carbon productivity' that can be embedded in omnichannel dashboards. Fourth, it outlines an AI playbook for greener operations, including model efficiency, hosting choices, content lifecycle management and governance.

The contributions of the chapter are therefore positioned at the intersection of sustainability strategy and commercial transformation. By combining a narrative evidence synthesis with applied measurement concepts such as the carbon ledger, CO_2e per qualified HCP engagement and carbon productivity, the chapter offers a practical route for integrating climate considerations into everyday omnichannel decision-making.

The intended audience includes senior pharmaceutical marketers and commercial leaders, medical affairs and clinical education teams, sustainability and ESG leads in life-science companies, and health-system leaders who commission, regulate or partner on engagement and continuing medical education. The discussion is global in outlook but draws heavily on examples from high- and middle-income settings where digital infrastructure is already material to healthcare delivery and communication.

1.2 Chapter structure

The chapter begins by setting the context for why traditional, travel- and paper-intensive engagement models are misaligned with health-sector climate commitments. It then defines the emerging role of AI-enabled omnichannel engagement as a decarbonization mechanism and reviews evidence from telemedicine, professional education and other adjacent domains that illuminate likely emissions patterns. The second half of the chapter translates these insights into a measurement framework aligned with the GHG Protocol, a concise set of operational metrics, an AI playbook for greener operations, and a governance roadmap that addresses rebound risk, compliance, equity and credibility of sustainability claims. To keep the argument operational, the chapter foregrounds two practical performance measures, CO_2e per qualified HCP engagement and carbon productivity (value created per unit of emissions), alongside more conventional commercial and educational outcomes. This framing anticipates the analysis in Section 2, which maps the carbon hotspots of legacy engagement and explains why AI-enabled omnichannel is emerging as a credible pathway to replace, not simply add to, higher-carbon interactions.

2. CONTEXT AND RATIONALE

The classical pharmaceutical commercial model is built around high-touch, field-based promotion. Field-force detailing, congress-centric education, paper-heavy workflows and extensive sampling and logistics collectively created relationship depth and market reach, but they also embedded emissions across Scopes 1, 2 and 3. Company vehicles and on-site generators contribute Scope 1 emissions, purchased electricity for offices and event venues sits in Scope 2, and extensive business travel, agency services and printed materials dominate Scope 3 (GHG Protocol, 2004; 2011).

Today, this model is under pressure on several fronts. Health systems and life-science companies are expected to align with the Paris Agreement and the Sustainable Development Goals, including climate action (SDG 13). Healthcare is estimated to account for 4–5% of global greenhouse gas emissions (Lenzen et al., 2020), motivating decarbonisation across the value chain, including marketing and engagement. Sector-specific analyses indicate that the pharmaceutical industry's own footprint is material and uneven across major players, strengthening the case for targeting emissions in organizational functions beyond manufacturing, including engagement and marketing (Belkhir and Elmeligi, 2019). At the same time, payers and investors expect clear evidence of health and economic value, and climate performance increasingly factors into ESG assessments and procurement decisions. In Europe, the Corporate Sustainability Reporting Directive further raises expectations for granular, value-chain reporting, encouraging more defensible accounting of engagement-related Scope 3 categories (European Commission, 2025).

The COVID-19 pandemic accelerated telemedicine, virtual conferencing and remote detailing at unprecedented speed, demonstrating that many engagements can be delivered digitally without compromising clinical or educational outcomes. Younger, digitally native clinicians now expect frictionless digital experiences, asynchronous communication and personalised content. In parallel, the rapid growth of AI has made the environmental footprint of data centres more visible. Recent analyses suggest that data centres account for just over 1% of global electricity consumption and that AI-related demand is likely to rise markedly over the coming decade (Carbon Brief, 2025; Uptime Institute, 2023, IEA, 2025).

2.1 From paper-heavy tactics to digital omnichannel

In response to these pressures, pharmaceutical commercial models have been quietly re-architected. Remote detailing and virtual calls now supplement or replace face-to-face interactions. Webinars and virtual congresses have become mainstream formats for medical education, with global reach and on-demand viewing. Digital consent and e-signatures streamline approvals for clinical trials, patient-support programmes and communication opt-ins, replacing couriers and physical archives. Disease-management platforms and patient apps embed education, reminders and behavioural support within digital workflows, often integrated with electronic health records.

The shift from physical to digital changes the emissions profile rather than eliminating it. Travel-related emissions fall, but energy use in data centres, networks and user devices increases. The central question is how to design AI-enabled omnichannel engagement so that the net effect is a substantial reduction in emissions while maintaining or improving commercial and clinical outcomes. This requires deliberate design choices, not simply adding digital channels on top of existing activities. Medical Affairs is also adopting omnichannel mindsets that prioritize stakeholder-centric journeys and higher-value, lower-frequency touchpoints, creating a parallel decarbonization opportunity beyond commercial marketing (Medical Affairs Professional Society, 2025). Recent Medical Affairs literature highlights AI-enabled insight generation, evidence orchestration and modular scientific communication as emerging capabilities that can reduce duplication in both travel and content production (Fröling et al., 2024; Ng and Zhang, 2023; Pérez Domínguez et al., 2025).

2.2 Defining AI-enabled omnichannel engagement

Omnichannel in life-science marketing refers to orchestrated engagement across multiple online and offline touchpoints, email, portals, webinars, in-person calls, remote detailing, social channels and contact centers, guided by a unified data layer. AI enhances this by predicting channel and content preferences at the individual HCP level, optimising next-best actions in real time, automating content assembly and personalisation, and continuously learning from engagement data.

An AI-enabled omnichannel model is therefore not simply a digital add-on to a traditional field model. It represents a redesign of engagement journeys around data, automation and measurement, including measurement of carbon intensity. In such a model, each email, call or webinar can be associated not only with reach and impact metrics but also with estimated emissions, allowing optimisation for both value and climate performance.

3. EVIDENCE BASE: ENVIRONMENTAL IMPACTS OF DIGITAL PRACTICES

A growing literature examines the environmental impacts of digital practices in healthcare, professional education and conferencing. Although relatively few studies focus directly on pharmaceutical promotion, several robust patterns emerge across adjacent domains.

First, telemedicine studies consistently show that substituting in-person outpatient visits with virtual consultations dramatically reduces per-visit emissions. The dominant driver is avoided travel: in most analyses, more than 80% of visit-related greenhouse gas emissions are attributable to patient journeys by car or public transport. When those journeys are replaced by telephone or video consultations, the remaining footprint from servers, networks and devices is comparatively small (Thiel et al., 2023; Ravindrane and Patel, 2022, Savoldelli et al., 2024).

Second, evaluations of virtual and hybrid professional conferences show similar benefits. A single international medical meeting can generate thousands of tonnes of CO_2-equivalent when long-haul flights, hotel nights and catering are fully accounted for. Case studies of large international medical conferences indicate that shifting 70–80% of attendance to virtual participation can reduce per-participant emissions by 85–92%, with the highest savings observed when intercontinental flights are avoided and little loss of educational value when content is well designed (Bousema et al., 2020; Patel et al., 2023, Thiel et al., 2023, Gattrell et al., 2022; Lichter et al., 2024).

Third, research into electronic medical records, e-prescribing and digital documentation suggests that moving from paper-based to digital systems usually lowers emissions associated with paper production, printing, logistics and storage. The gains are not uniform, digital infrastructure introduces new sources of energy demand, but high-reuse digital assets tend to have a lower environmental cost than one-off printed materials when use is sustained over time.

Finally, a growing body of work examines the environmental footprint of AI systems and data centres. While AI can enable more precise and efficient decision-making, large models and extensive cloud usage can be energy-intensive. The environmental benefit of digital transformation therefore depends on the overall system design: it is not enough to replace physical activities with digital ones if the resulting data and compute demands are uncontrolled (Uptime Institute, 2023; Wierman and Ren, 2025). Emerging 'Green AI' frameworks emphasize right-sized models, efficient training/inference and carbon-aware cloud choices that are directly applicable to omnichannel analytics and GenAI content workflows (Bolón-Canedo et al., 2024; Tabbakh, 2024).

4. METHODOLOGY

This chapter draws on a narrative literature review combined with practice-based insights. Multidisciplinary databases such as PubMed, Scopus and Web of Science were searched using combinations of terms including telemedicine, digital health, pharmaceutical marketing, e-detailing, virtual conference, carbon footprint, greenhouse gas emissions, life-cycle assessment and data-centre emissions. Inclusion criteria focused on empirical or modelling studies that compared at least one digital or virtual modality with a physical or business-as-usual alternative and that reported environmental outcomes such as CO_2-equivalent emissions, energy use, travel distance or waste.

In addition, authoritative standards and guidance on greenhouse-gas accounting, particularly the GHG Protocol and sector-specific guidance for ICT and data centres, were reviewed. Alongside published evidence, the chapter uses anonymised vignettes based on real-world engagement programmes in pharmaceutical and med-tech organisations to illustrate how the principles derived from the evidence can be translated into realistic implementation strategies.

The literature review followed a PRISMA-aligned approach. In the identification phase, database searches were run using predefined keyword strings and Boolean operators, supplemented by backward and forward citation tracking from key papers. Records were de-duplicated and imported into a reference-management tool.

In the screening phase, titles and abstracts were reviewed against inclusion criteria that required: (a) a focus on healthcare delivery, professional education, conferencing or pharmaceutical engagement, (b) comparison of a digital or virtual modality with a physical or business-as-usual alternative; and (c) reporting of an environmental outcome such as emissions, energy use or travel distance. Full texts for potentially relevant studies were then retrieved and assessed in detail.

In the eligibility and synthesis phase, data were extracted on study setting, design, sample size, intervention type, comparator, environmental outcomes and key limitations. Given heterogeneity in methods and contexts, findings were synthesised narratively, with particular attention to recurrent patterns and plausible mechanisms rather than formal meta-analysis.

5. MEASUREMENT FRAMEWORK: MAPPING TO THE GHG PROTOCOL

Robust measurement is the foundation of any decarbonisation strategy. For engagement activities, the GHG Protocol offers a mature framework for categorising emissions. Most emissions associated with pharma engagement fall under Scope 3, the value-chain emissions arising from business travel, purchased services, events, media and the use of digital platforms, although Scope 1 and 2 contributions from fleet vehicles and office energy may also be relevant (GHG Protocol, 2004; 2011).

A key design choice is the functional unit, the 'one unit of service' against which emissions are measured. For pharmaceutical engagement, a practical unit is the 'per qualified HCP engagement', such as a detailing call, webinar attendance or meaningful interaction by an HCP who meets predefined targeting criteria. Alternative units include per campaign, per script uplift or per educational credit awarded. Once the unit is defined, activity data and emission factors can be combined to generate consistent metrics.

System boundaries must be clearly specified. For a typical omnichannel campaign, relevant emissions sources include: direct fuel use in company cars or generators (Scope 1), purchased electricity for offices, studios and on-premise servers (Scope 2), and upstream and downstream emissions from flights, hotels, agency work, printing, sample logistics and cloud services (Scope 3). Activities outside the company's control, such as patient travel not funded by the programme, may be noted qualitatively but are usually excluded from formal accounting to avoid double counting.

6. METRICS AND FORMULAS FOR CARBON ACCOUNTING

The measurement framework can be operationalized through a small set of core metrics. The first is CO_2e per qualified HCP engagement. If E_total is the total emissions attributed to a campaign (Scopes 1–3, in kg CO_2e) and N_HCP is the number of unique qualified HCPs who engaged meaningfully, then CO_2e per engagement is simply E_total divided by N_HCP. This provides an intensity metric that is comparable across channels and campaigns.

A second metric is avoided travel emissions when replacing in-person interactions with virtual ones. If d is the average round-trip distance that would have been travelled, f is the relevant emission factor per kilometre, and N_virtual is the number of virtual interactions substituting for physical travel, then avoided travel emissions equal N_virtual × d × f. Empirical work suggests that travel is often the dominant contributor to life-cycle emissions for care and conferences, so this avoided component can be large (Thiel et al., 2023; Patel et al., 2023).

When replacing printed materials with digital content, emissions savings from reduced printing must be offset against the additional compute and device energy used. In principle, the net print-displacement benefit equals emissions associated with producing and disposing of printed materials minus the incremental emissions from servers, networks and devices attributable to digital content. This calculation depends on assumptions about print runs, reuse and digital access patterns, which should be documented transparently.

A further useful concept is carbon productivity: the amount of desired outcome achieved per unit of emissions. For example, a company might track the number of HCPs who complete a learning objective, change prescribing behaviour or enrol patients into an evidence-based pathway per tonne of CO_2e emitted. Framing performance as 'outcomes per unit carbon' encourages teams to maximise clinical or educational value while minimising the emissions required to deliver it, rather than focusing on emissions in isolation.

7. REPORTING ARCHITECTURE AND THE CARBON LEDGER

Cloud providers and data-center operators increasingly disclose sustainability metrics such as Power Usage Effectiveness (PUE) and the grid mix of the regions where workloads run. Marketing and IT teams should request PUE by region or facility, location-based and market-based emission factors for purchased electricity, and evidence of renewable-energy procurement. A practical reporting architecture links activity data (impressions, clicks, call minutes, webinar attendance), technical telemetry (server utilisation, data transferred, storage used) and emission factors (grid mix, PUE, embodied-carbon assumptions).

At the level of individual campaigns, this architecture can be represented as a 'carbon ledger'. For each engagement type, for example, an email send, a remote detailing call, a webinar session or an in-person meeting, the ledger records the volume of activity, the associated emission factor and the resulting CO_2e. Aggregated across all channels, the ledger yields total campaign emissions and intensity metrics such as CO_2e per HCP. Just as financial ledgers allow teams to trace spend, a carbon ledger allows teams to trace emissions to specific design choices and course-correct.

Sustainability dashboards can then build on this ledger to offer different views: campaign-level views for brand teams, portfolio views for franchises or therapeutic areas, and corporate views for ESG reporting. Dashboards should allow users to drill down, inspect calculation assumptions and data sources, and export data for external assurance or regulatory reporting. Third-party verification enhances credibility and mitigates the risk of greenwashing.

8. THE AI PLAYBOOK FOR GREENER OPERATIONS

AI can reduce carbon intensity per engagement by better targeting and reducing waste, but only if the models themselves are deployed efficiently. Key levers include model selection (using the smallest model that delivers acceptable performance), quantization and pruning (compressing models by reducing numerical precision and removing redundant parameters), and knowledge distillation (training compact 'student' models to emulate larger 'teacher' models). These techniques can materially reduce energy use during training and inference without sacrificing accuracy for most marketing use-cases.

Where and how AI systems are hosted also has climate implications. Choosing renewable-powered regions, scheduling non-urgent training tasks when renewable generation is abundant, and optimising utilisation to avoid idle capacity all contribute to lower emissions (Ren and Wierman, 2025). Many hyperscale cloud providers now offer region-specific carbon-intensity data and tools to track workload emissions. A green AI strategy should sit within a broader governance framework that also addresses data privacy and security, bias and fairness, and explainability and human oversight.

AI can also reduce content-related emissions by enabling modular content that is assembled and personalised from reusable building blocks, automated versioning and expiry management, and data-driven rationalisation of low-value content. The most powerful lever, however, is to redesign processes so that low-carbon options become the default, for example, virtual attendance as the default for internal and many external meetings, digital consent and documentation as the first choice, and remote detailing as standard for certain call types or segments. When such defaults are embedded into systems and training, carbon-efficient behaviour becomes the path of least resistance.

9. RISKS, TRADE-OFFS AND COMPLIANCE

Efficiency improvements can paradoxically increase total emissions if they lead to higher volumes, the rebound effect. In pharma engagement, cheaper and easier digital contact may encourage more emails, more webinars and more notifications to HCPs and patients. Unless total contact volume is managed, the carbon benefits of each interaction can be eroded. Mitigation strategies include setting volume caps or frequency guidelines per HCP segment, and using blended KPIs that penalise campaigns with high carbon intensity even if they deliver strong short-term engagement.

Omnichannel engagement relies on large volumes of personal data. Regulatory frameworks such as the General Data Protection Regulation (GDPR) and similar laws in other regions impose strict requirements on consent, data minimisation and purpose limitation. AI-driven profiling and personalisation must comply with these requirements and with ethical expectations from HCPs and patients (European Commission, 2020). Green claims must also avoid ethics-washing: sustainability benefits should not distract from unresolved privacy, equity or safety concerns.

Marketing claims about emissions reductions will increasingly be scrutinised by regulators, investors and civil-society groups. Assertions such as 'carbon-neutral webinar' or 'net-zero engagement strategy' should not be made without robust evidence. Organisations should document their accounting methods, update emission factors regularly and, where offsets are used, ensure they meet recognised quality standards.

10. PRACTICE VIGNETTES

Three brief vignettes illustrate how these principles can be applied in practice. To protect commercial confidentiality, specific organizational identifiers have been anonymized and figures are presented as approximate ranges based on aggregated program data and validated using emission factors from peer-reviewed literature and industry standards.

Vignette 1: Disease-Awareness Campaign Digitization

A multinational disease-awareness campaign for a chronic condition shifted from printed brochures distributed by representatives and at congress booths to a digital ecosystem comprising a patient app, HCP portal, and webinar-based education series, supported by targeted emails and search optimization. Printed materials were limited to essential legal items. Over 12 months, print volume fell by about 70%, producing an estimated net CO e reduction of 38–42%, even after digital energy use from cloud hosting, email servers, and app infrastructure. Patient engagement improved by 15–20% in content completion and follow-up interactions. Most savings came from avoided printing (25 tons CO e; 0.9–1.1 kg CO e/kg coated paper) and reduced logistics (8 tons; 0.21 kg CO e/km), partly offset by cloud emissions (5 tons), based on PUE 1.4 and grid intensity 0.35 kg CO e/kWh.

Vignette 2: E-Consent Platform Implementation

A patient-support programme previously relied on paper consent forms signed in clinics and couriered to processing hubs. An e-consent platform integrated with HCP portals and patient apps reduced enrollment time from ten days to three, cut error rates by about 60%, and eliminated an estimated 12,000 courier journeys annually. The carbon ledger estimated avoided emissions of 18 tons CO e from courier travel, based on a 150 km round trip at 0.21 kg CO e/km (DEFRA, 2023), plus 2 tons CO e from paper use and disposal of around 2,000 kg of paper (Environment Agency, 2023). Digital infrastructure added about 1.5 tons CO e annually, using 0.5 kWh per user session and regional grid intensity assumptions (Aslan et al., 2018; IEA, 2025). Net reduction was about 18.5 tons CO e per year, an 89% cut in enrollment-related emissions, consistent with wider evidence on digital consent systems (Ravindrane and Patel, 2022).

Vignette 3: Hybrid Product-Launch Model

A product-launch plan originally built around frequent in-person calls by an expanded field force was redesigned as a hybrid model. Priority accounts (20% of target HCPs) received a mix of in-person and remote detailing, while lower-priority segments (80%) received mainly remote calls and on-demand digital content. AI-driven next-best-action models prioritised calls and personalised content. Total qualified HCP engagements rose by 12%, while estimated CO e per engagement fell by 62% versus an all-in-person counterfactual. Over six months, the model avoided about 450 field visits, saving roughly 35 tons CO e from reduced travel and hotel stays, based on 150 km round trips at 0.21 kg CO e/km and 15 kg CO e per hotel night (DEFRA, 2023; Hotel Carbon Measurement Initiative, 2023). Digital platforms added about 3 tons CO e (Obringer et al., 2021; Ong et al., 2014).

11. IMPLEMENTATION ROADMAP

A practical roadmap to decarbonize engagement can be framed as a four-level maturity model. Level 1 (ad hoc) is characterised by isolated digital initiatives and no carbon metrics. Level 2 (measured) introduces basic carbon accounting for major events and campaigns and begins to track Scope 3 travel and print. Level 3 (optimised) uses intensity metrics systematically, embeds low-carbon defaults and includes carbon as a criterion in channel and vendor selection. Level 4 (integrated) fully embeds carbon metrics in planning, budgeting, incentives and external reporting, with continuous improvement aligned to science-based targets.

Quick wins in the first 90 days include introducing virtual-by-default policies for internal meetings, rationalising printed materials and conference giveaways, starting to track travel emissions for major events and field activities, and piloting CO_2e per engagement metrics for one major campaign. Within six to twelve months, companies can integrate carbon metrics into omnichannel dashboards, contract with cloud providers that offer renewable-backed regions and clear sustainability reporting, roll out e-consent in priority programmes, and train marketers and agencies on low-carbon campaign design.

Over the medium term, organisations should align their engagement decarbonisation roadmap with corporate net-zero strategies and science-based targets. This includes setting explicit targets for reducing emissions per engagement, embedding climate considerations into brand-planning templates and governance forums, and engaging with suppliers and partners to improve the quality and coverage of emissions data.

12. ALIGNING MARKETING SUCCESS WITH SUSTAINABILITY TARGETS

Decarbonising pharma engagement will only be sustainable if marketing success and sustainability targets are seen as mutually reinforcing rather than competing priorities. One practical tool is a joint value-and-impact scorecard. On the value side, the scorecard summarises reach, frequency, engagement quality, educational outcomes and financial performance. On the impact side, it reports absolute emissions from engagement, carbon intensity per interaction and per outcome, and indicators related to equity and digital inclusion.

Embedding this scorecard in planning and review cycles changes the conversation. Brand teams are encouraged to propose initiatives that move points in both columns in the right direction. Internal carbon pricing can further operationalise this alignment. When business cases for new campaigns incorporate a shadow cost for projected emissions, low-carbon designs become more attractive in purely financial terms. External communication with healthcare partners can then highlight co-benefits such as lower travel burden for clinicians, more flexible learning opportunities and progress towards shared climate commitments.

Over time, blended KPIs, for example, outcomes per ton of CO_2e, can help shift culture. Rather than viewing emissions as a constraint on ambition, teams begin to view high carbon productivity as a marker of smart, modern marketing practice.

13. DISCUSSION

The evidence synthesised in this chapter supports a clear and actionable proposition: when travel-intensive and paper-heavy engagement activities are redesigned as hybrid or digital-first journeys, the resulting emissions reductions are likely to be substantial. Across adjacent domains such as telemedicine and professional education, the dominant driver of carbon savings is avoided travel, with digital energy use usually representing a smaller proportion of the life-cycle footprint. This pattern aligns with the chapter's argument that the quickest engagement decarbonisation gains will come from rationalising non-essential travel, reducing printed collateral and deploying remote and asynchronous formats where they can deliver equivalent scientific or educational value.

Although the peer-reviewed literature on pharma-specific e-detailing and campaign life-cycle assessment is still limited, the patterns observed in healthcare delivery and conferencing are strong enough to guide credible strategic choices. The chapter's practice vignettes and measurement framework therefore emphasise a 'net decarbonisation' lens: digital transformation delivers climate benefit only when it meaningfully substitutes for higher-carbon activities and when engagement volume is governed to avoid eroding savings through rebound effects.

A second important insight is that omnichannel is becoming a decarbonisation mechanism, not merely a commercial capability. The evolution from multichannel presence to orchestrated, preference-led journeys enables companies to reduce repeated low-value interactions and to match channel choice to both clinical context and carbon intensity. In practice, this means designing hybrid account strategies for priority HCPs, investing in preference management, expanding asynchronous education formats and shifting from bespoke, asset-heavy production toward modular content that can be reused across channels and markets.

These shifts highlight a new frontier: carbon-aware decisioning within next-best-action engines. As organisations mature their carbon ledgers and intensity metrics, it becomes feasible to incorporate estimated CO_2e into channel optimisation rules. Over time, this could support portfolio-level commitments such as year-on-year reductions in CO_2e per qualified HCP engagement while protecting educational quality, scientific exchange and patient outcomes.

13.1 Limitations of current digital carbon accounting methods

Several limitations in current digital-carbon accounting methods should be acknowledged. First, many emission factors used for travel, electricity and cloud services are based on national or regional averages rather than provider-specific data. As a result, campaign-level estimates are best interpreted as approximate ranges rather than precise point values. Sensitivity analysis, exploring how results change under different plausible assumptions, is therefore essential.

Second, attributing shared infrastructure emissions to specific campaigns is methodologically challenging. Data-centre electricity use, for example, must be allocated across multiple tenants and workloads. Choices about allocation rules (for instance, based on CPU hours, data volume or user sessions) can materially affect results. Transparent documentation of these rules is necessary for comparability and credibility.

Third, most studies and corporate accounting frameworks focus on operational emissions rather than the full life-cycle of hardware. The embodied emissions of devices and networking equipment, from manufacture through to end-of-life, are often only crudely approximated. As better data and tools become available, organisations should revisit their estimates and update baselines accordingly.

In addition, marketing-specific data quality remains uneven. Engagement teams do not always track print volumes, sample logistics, agency production cycles or field travel with sufficient granularity to support robust campaign-level carbon accounting. Strengthening data capture within CRM, procurement and digital analytics systems, and using independent assurance where claims are material, will be necessary to avoid both under- and over-estimating sustainability impacts.

13.2 Omnichannel design implications and emerging trends

The expanded context and evidence sections suggest that the most climate-positive omnichannel strategies will be those that lean into precision and reuse. Preference-based targeting, micro-segmentation and hybrid account planning can reduce lower-yield travel, while asynchronous educational assets and high-reuse digital platforms spread the footprint of hosting and content production over much larger audiences. The growing adoption of modular content architectures offers a parallel sustainability advantage by reducing duplicated design, translation and approval cycles and by enabling systematic retirement of low-value assets (Dunn, 2024; FDA OPDP, 2024).

Generative AI is likely to accelerate these trends, but its value will depend on governance. Used responsibly, GenAI can support rapid localisation, adaptive summarisation and the assembly of approved modules into channel-specific variants, reducing waste in the content supply chain. However, without guardrails around model choice, hosting regions, and content volume, the efficiency dividend may translate into higher overall compute demand and more frequent, less meaningful HCP touches (ZS (2025); McKinsey & Company (2024; 2025).

13.3 Managing rebound effects and aligning incentives

The rebound risk identified earlier in the chapter is highly relevant to omnichannel programmes. As the marginal cost of digital contact falls, there is a temptation to increase email frequency, webinar volume and platform notifications. Organisations should therefore treat volume management as a core component of decarbonization. Practical approaches include segment-based frequency caps, 'digital quiet hours', and decision rules that require a clear learning, clinical or service objective for each incremental touchpoint.

Aligning incentives is equally important. The joint value-and-impact scorecard and internal carbon pricing approaches outlined in this chapter can help embed sustainability into routine brand planning. When teams are rewarded for improvements in carbon intensity alongside engagement quality, omnichannel innovation is more likely to reduce total emissions rather than simply shifting the emissions profile.

13.4 Equity, trust and regulatory considerations

Digital-first engagement must also be evaluated through an equity and trust lens. Over-reliance on high-bandwidth platforms or always-on digital contact can disadvantage clinicians and health systems with weaker infrastructure or stricter institutional policies. Hybrid strategies should therefore include explicit inclusion safeguards, ensuring that lower-resource settings and time-constrained clinicians can access essential educational content through appropriate formats.

Regulatory and ethical expectations remain central. Personalisation and AI-driven targeting depend on robust consent, data minimisation and transparent purpose limitation. Sustainability claims in marketing and medical education materials should likewise be conservative and evidence-based, supported by clearly documented assumptions and updated emission factors to reduce greenwashing risk.

For EU-facing programs, the new AI Act intensifies expectations around risk classification, transparency and governance of clinical-facing AI applications, reinforcing the need for defensible personalization and content-decision logic (Busch et al., 2024; van Kolfschooten and van Oirschot, 2024).

13.5 Priorities for future research

Future research should move beyond adjacent-domain inference toward pharma-specific life-cycle assessments. Priority areas include comparative LCAs of in-person detailing versus remote and hybrid models, the emissions implications of sampling strategies and cold-chain logistics relative to digital education alternatives, and the embodied carbon of devices and specialised AI hardware used in large-scale omnichannel programmes.

Methodological advances are also needed to standardise how cloud and AI emissions are allocated at campaign level and to establish open, sector-specific emission-factor libraries for common engagement activities. Partnerships between industry, health systems and academic groups could accelerate the development of shared benchmarks and improve the credibility and comparability of reported outcomes.

14. CONCLUSION

This chapter has argued that decarbonising pharmaceutical engagement is no longer a peripheral ESG exercise but a practical transformation opportunity at the intersection of clinical value, commercial effectiveness and climate responsibility.

The evidence base from telemedicine, digital documentation and virtual professional education indicates that the largest and most immediate emissions reductions come from avoided travel and reduced print. In most contexts, these savings are likely to outweigh the incremental energy demands of well-governed digital platforms.

However, the rise of AI-driven omnichannel creates a new design imperative: organisations must move from 'adding channels' to 're-engineering journeys'. In practice, this means using AI to reduce wasted contact, rationalise content libraries, and orchestrate the right mix of remote and in-person engagement for each HCP segment, while actively preventing rebound effects such as excessive email or webinar volumes.

To institutionalise these gains, the chapter proposed a carbon-aware measurement architecture built around three pillars: (1) a clear functional unit such as CO_2e per qualified HCP engagement, (2) a campaign-level carbon ledger that traces emissions to channel choices, vendors and cloud regions and (3) an outcomes-per-carbon lens ('carbon productivity') that links emissions to meaningful educational or clinical impact.

Looking ahead, the most promising omnichannel trends with decarbonisation potential include modular content supply chains powered by generative AI, privacy-preserving personalisation, virtual-first medical education with selective high-value physical touchpoints, and cloud-region optimisation aligned to lower-carbon grids. These trends require cross-functional governance that brings together marketing, medical affairs, IT, data privacy and sustainability teams.

In summary, AI-enabled omnichannel engagement can be a net-positive climate strategy for pharma, but only when it is paired with disciplined measurement, responsible AI operations, and a cultural shift toward low-carbon defaults. Companies that act early will be better positioned to meet net-zero commitments, respond to health-system expectations, and demonstrate that modern healthcare communication can be both effective and climate-conscious.

Practical next steps for brand and sustainability teams include:

- Audit current engagement portfolios to identify the highest-carbon activities (major congresses, high-frequency field travel and high-volume print).
- Define a standard functional unit and calculation assumptions for CO_2e per engagement and avoided travel, and pilot them in one priority therapeutic area.

- Integrate carbon fields into omnichannel planning tools and dashboards, using a simple carbon ledger structure.
- Create 'virtual-by-default' and 'print-minimum' policies with clear exceptions tied to clinical or regulatory necessity.
- Adopt green AI practices: smaller model selection, efficient inference, and preferential use of lower-carbon cloud regions.
- Introduce volume governance to prevent rebound effects, aligning frequency caps with HCP experience and sustainability goals.

REFERENCES

Aslan, , JMayers, , KKoomey, , J. GFrance, , C. (2018). Electricity intensity of internet data transmission: Untangling the estimates. *Journal of Industrial Ecology, 22*(4), 785–798. https://doi.org/10.1111/jiec.12630

Belkhir, L., & Elmeligi, A. (2019). Carbon footprint of the global pharmaceutical industry and relative impact of its major players. *Journal of Cleaner Production, 214*, 185–194. DOI: 10.1016/j.jclepro.2018.11.204

Bolón-Canedo, V., Morán-Fernández, L., Cancela, B., & Alonso-Betanzos, A. (2024). A review of green artificial intelligence: Towards a more sustainable future. *Neurocomputing, 599*, 128096. DOI: 10.1016/j.neucom.2024.128096

Bousema, T., Selvaraj, P., Djimde, A. A., Yakar, D., Hagedorn, B., Pratt, A., Barret, D., Whitfield, K., & Cohen, J. M. (2020). Reducing the carbon footprint of academic conferences: The example of the American Society of Tropical Medicine and Hygiene. *The American Journal of Tropical Medicine and Hygiene, 103*(5), 1758–1761. DOI: 10.4269/ajtmh.20-1013 PMID: 33069267

Busch, F., Kather, J. N., Johner, C., Moser, M., Truhn, D., Adams, L. C., & Bressem, K. K. (2024). 'Navigating the European Union Artificial Intelligence Act for Healthcare', npj. *Digital Medicine, 7*(1), 210. DOI: 10.1038/s41746-024-01213-6 PMID: 39134637

Carbon Brief (2025) 'AI: Five charts that put data-centre energy use and emissions into context'.

Dunn, Z. (2024) 'Navigating the shift to omnichannel marketing: What to know about modular content and OPDP expectations', Regulatory Focus (RAPS), January.

Environment Agency. (2023). *Carbon footprint of paper and print: Life cycle assessment data.* Bristol: Environment Agency.

European Commission (2020) 'Guidance on the application of the GDPR in health-related research'.

European Commission. (2025). *Corporate Sustainability Reporting Directive (CSRD): Overview.* European Commission.

Food and Drug Administration (FDA) Office of Prescription Drug Promotion (2024) 'The Brief Summary', April 2024.

Fröling, E., Rajaeean, N., Hinrichsmeyer, K. S., Domrös-Zoungrana, D., Urban, J. N., & Lenz, C. (2024). Artificial Intelligence in Medical Affairs: A New Paradigm with Novel Opportunities. *Pharmaceutical Medicine, 38*(5), 331–342. DOI: 10.1007/s40290-024-00536-9 PMID: 39259426

Gattrell, W. T., Barraux, L., Comley, T., Whaley, A., & Lander, A. (2022). The carbon costs of in-person versus virtual medical congress attendance for a mid-sized pharmaceutical company. *Pharmaceutical Medicine, 36*(3), 131–142. DOI: 10.1007/s40290-022-00421-3 PMID: 35218551

Hotel Carbon Measurement Initiative. (2023). *HCMI Methodology Framework for Measuring Hotel Carbon Footprint* (Version 2.1). World Travel & Tourism Council.

International Energy Agency (IEA). (2025). *Energy and AI.* IEA.

Lenzen, M., Malik, A., Li, M., Fry, J., Weisz, H., Pichler, P.-P., Chaves, L. S. M., Capon, A., & Pencheon, D. (2020). The environmental footprint of health care: A global assessment. *The Lancet. Planetary Health, 4*(7), e271–e279. DOI: 10.1016/S2542-5196(20)30121-2 PMID: 32681898

Lichter, K. E., Sabbagh, A., Demeulenaere, S., Drew, T., Conway, A., Nogueira, L., Suneja, G., Kirkwood, K., Hampshire, K., Gundling, K., Teherani, A., Thottathil, S. E., & Mohamad, O. (2024). Reducing the Environmental Impact of Health Care Conferences: A Study of Emissions and Practical Solutions. *JCO Global Oncology, 10*(10), e2300209. DOI: 10.1200/GO.23.00209 PMID: 38359373

McKinsey & Company (2024) 'Generative AI in the pharmaceutical industry: Moving from hype to reality'.

McKinsey & Company (2025) 'Scaling gen AI in the life sciences industry'.

Medical Affairs Professional Society (MAPS). (2025) Embracing Omnichannel Engagement in Medical Affairs: Changing Mindsets to Put External Stakeholders at the Center of Engagement. White paper.

Ng, K. K. Y., & Zhang, P. C. (2023). Advancing medical affair capabilities and insight generation through machine learning techniques. *Journal of Pharmaceutical Policy and Practice, 16*(1), 165. DOI: 10.1186/s40545-023-00670-w PMID: 38041173

Obringer, R., Rachunok, B., Maia-Silva, D., Arbabzadeh, M., Nateghi, R., & Madani, K. (2021). The overlooked environmental footprint of increasing Internet use. *Resources, Conservation and Recycling, 167*, 105389. https://doi.org/10.1016/j.resconrec.2020.105389

Ong, D., Moors, T., & Sivaraman, V. (2014). Comparison of the energy, carbon and time costs of videoconferencing and in-person meetings. *Computer Communications, 50*, 86–94. https://doi.org/10.1016/j.comcom.2014.02.009

Patel, K. B., Gonzalez, B. D., Turner, K., Alishahi Tabriz, A., Rollison, D. E., Robinson, E., Naso, C., Wang, X., & Spiess, P. E. (2023). Estimated Carbon Emissions Savings With Shifts From In-Person Visits to Telemedicine for Patients With Cancer. *JAMA Network Open*, *6*(1), e2253788. DOI: 10.1001/jamanetworkopen.2022.53788 PMID: 36719682

Pérez Domínguez, A., Marinich, J., Monteagudo, G., Moreno, C., Regadera, L., & Iglesias, I. (2025). Pioneering the Future of Medical Affairs: A Strategic Transformation to Meet the Spanish Healthcare Ecosystem's Evolving Trends. *Pharmaceutical Medicine*, *39*(5), 281–292. DOI: 10.1007/s40290-025-00574-x PMID: 40652051

Protocol, G. H. G. (2004). *The Greenhouse Gas Protocol: A Corporate Accounting and Reporting Standard*. World Resources Institute and World Business Council for Sustainable Development.

Protocol, G. H. G. (2011). *Corporate Value Chain (Scope 3) Accounting and Reporting Standard*. World Resources Institute and World Business Council for Sustainable Development.

Ravindrane, R., & Patel, J. (2022). The environmental impacts of telemedicine in place of face-to-face patient care: A systematic review. *Future Healthcare Journal*, *9*(1), 28–33. DOI: 10.7861/fhj.2021-0148 PMID: 35372776

Savoldelli, A., Landi, D., & Rizzi, C. (2024). Exploring quantitative methodologies for assessing the environmental, social, and economic impacts of telemedicine: A literature review. *Sustainability (Basel)*, *16*(6), 2438. DOI: 10.3390/su16062438

Tabbakh, A., Al Amin, L., Islam, M., Mahmud, G. M. I., Chowdhury, I. K., & Mukta, M. S. H. (2024). Towards sustainable AI: A comprehensive framework for Green AI. *Discover Sustainability*, *5*(1), 408. DOI: 10.1007/s43621-024-00641-4

Thiel, C. L., Mehta, N., Sejo, C. S., Qureshi, L., Moyer, M., Valentino, V., & Saleh, J. (2023). 'Telemedicine and the environment: Life cycle environmental emissions from in-person and virtual clinic visits', npj. *Digital Medicine*, *6*(1), 87. DOI: 10.1038/s41746-023-00818-7 PMID: 37160996

Uptime Institute (2023) 'Accounting for digital infrastructure GHG emissions'.

Van Kolfschooten, H., & van Oirschot, J. (2024). The EU Artificial Intelligence Act (2024): Implications for healthcare. *Health Policy (Amsterdam)*, *149*, 105152. DOI: 10.1016/j.healthpol.2024.105152 PMID: 39244818

Wierman, A., & Ren, S. (2025). We Need to Talk About AI's Impact on Public Health. *IEEE Spectrum*, *1*(May).

ZS (2025) 'Emerging pharma: Here's your omnichannel roadmap'.

Chapter 11
Risk Mitigation in Oil and Gas Through AI Integration:
Innovation, Impact, and Implementation

Nageswara Rao Lakkimsetty
http://orcid.org/0009-0006-0146-8889
American University of Rasal Khaimah, UAE

Vamsi Krishna Kudapa
University of Petroleum and Energy Studies, Dehradun, India

Srinivasa Reddy Devarapu
University of Petroleum and Energy Studies, Dehradun, India

Patchamatla J. Rama Raju
Graphic Era University, Dehradun, India

ABSTRACT

Oil and gas are complicated processes that are in risky environments and have strict regulations making them have more operational risk. Recent advances in Artificial intelligence (AI) have seen AI make it an optimal tool in mitigating risks in exploration, production, transport and refining operations. In exploration/drilling, AI enhances the interpretation of seismic data, reservoir modeling and optimization of processes with the aim of minimizing errors and maximizing the resources used. Application of digital twins and AI-based simulations also enables virtual validation of working conditions, allowing them to be better prepared without putting

DOI: 10.4018/979-8-2600-1348-9.ch011

human beings in dangerous situations. AI enables regulatory compliance and risk governance via automated documentation, incident reporting, and safety audits, besides operational optimization. real-time environmental monitoring and anomaly detection and maintenance systems. These applications prevent scheduled outages, machine malfunction, gas spills, and disastrous events, which enhance safety and reduce environmental effects. However, even with these developments, there are still lingering problems with data quality, cybersecurity and ethical considerations to stop large-scale deployment. However, AI is transforming the paradigm of risk management into the oil and gas sector in the context of operational excellence, regulatory compliance, and sustainability programs. This chapter shows that AI implementation is strategically significant towards a safer, more effective, and more environmentally responsible industry.

1. INTRODUCTION

Oil and gas are one of the most advanced and risky industries in the economy. Since drilling, exploration of deepwater basin, shipping and refining of highly volatile hydrocarbons, there are potential dangers at every stage of the value chain. Such operational risks as blowouts, equipment breakdowns, gas spills, and fires have significant consequences not only on the safety of the personnel but also on the integrity of the assets and the continuity of the business. Events like Deep water the failure to manage risks is shockingly reminded by the event of horizon blow-out or refinery fires. In addition, oil spills, leaks of methane, and flaring are also environmental threats that have long-term impacts on ecosystems and the health of the population that increase the amount of regulation, investors, and public scrutiny. Also contributing to this technical and environmental risks are regulatory and compliance risks. Companies are always on the move to keep their health, safety, and environmental regulations in place through the burdensome and dynamic legal requirements that make the companies constantly monitor, record and report operations to the authorities. Failure to comply may attract huge fines, reputation damage and even closure. In this severe environment, the traditional approaches to risk management, including most of them, which rely on manual inspection, previous trends analysis and responsive measures, cannot be used to manage the scale and complexity of the modern oil and gas activity. AI has become a disruptive force in the energy sector in the last couple of years. AI contributes both an active and intelligent layer to risk management by offering live analysis of information, predictive decision-making, and automatic analysis of information. The transformation of the reactive to predictive mitigation of risk has probably become the most iconic change in contemporary industrial safety. Machine learning programs can detect subtle pre-failure indicators, computer vision programs can scan video footage to detect cracks, corroded or leaking pipes and rigs- and are often faster and more accurate than human workers. NLP is being used to identify the insights on the maintenance records, incident reports, and regulatory submissions, reducing the compliance cost and enhancing the transparency. Computer-aided tools such as digital twins and AI - assisted simulations also offer the simulation environment in the design of processes and equipment to enable the firms to test and analyze the what-if scenarios without exposing assets and people to risk. These solutions are also optimization of operations and provision of contingency planning and emergency preparedness thus forming safety culture (Aderamo, A. T. et al., 2024a). The paper explains how AI is used in mitigating risks in the upstream and downstream of oil and gas production, transport and storage, refining and distribution, and value chain. Some of them include the key risk detection, assessment and management innovations like predictive maintenance, real-time monitoring, digital twins and automatic compliance systems. This chapter considers the aspects of AI integration, both technological and strategic and ethical, and provides a summary of its current effects, as well as its possibilities. The purpose of this chapter is to bring to the fore what AI can and what are the operational issues with AI implementation in such spheres as data quality, cybersecurity and government. The chapter illustrates the strategic importance of AI in safer smarter and sustainable operations in the oil and gas industries through case studies, industry trends and technical expertise. All of that is aimed at eventually demonstrating how AI can be transformed into something resembling an auxiliary tool, but a pillar of risk handling and operational efficiency in the energy sector.

2. OVERVIEW OF AI TECHNOLOGIES IN RISK MANAGEMENT

The AI technologies consist of a few fundamental components such as machine learning, predictive analytics, computer vision, and natural language processing (NLP) that help in the automation of information processes and informed decision-making. As an example, machine learning will be able to investigate past data and identify patterns and predict risks or incidents, which is an invaluable aid to health, safety, and environment management (Aderamo, A. T. et al., 2024b). These are those technologies which enable us to do predictive analytics, real time monitoring and identification of anomalies to elevate superior safety performance and prevent accidents in the working place. As a result of its effectiveness in augmenting safety processes, risk management, and proactive decision-making on intelligence, AI is being applied in oil and gas productions; offshore oil platforms, onshore plants, and refinery units to augment safety measures, control of risks, and intelligence to make proactive decisions (Adedapo et al., 2023). Complex datasets and probabilistic situations concerning them support the risk-related assessments and the distribution of mitigation actions based on the AI systems.

A sophisticated predictive model along with properly built sensor networks is capable of identifying the possible hazards in the oil and gas activity continuously. Such systems are concentrated on the real-time detection of anomalies, monitoring of the safety-critical parameters, and determining the deviations of the set operational thresholds. Through constant comparison of live running data with accepted norms and safe working envelopes, preventive steps may be taken in time to avert any abnormal conditions that may occur and translate into unsafe occurrences.

Besides that, AI-based incident prevention systems incorporate predictive modeling as part of active operational processes. Such frameworks examine the arriving data streams in real time to identify the emergent threats, prescribe or autonomously activate the corrective measures, and impose the preventive control. An ability to predict risks through such proactive intervention will enable risks to be reduced before an accident has taken place, instead of responding to the incident.

All these AI-provided functions contribute greatly to the processes of managing the safety of oil and gas companies. The AI can make workplaces safer, decrease the risk of accidents, and enhance the integrity of operations because of minimizing human exposure to dangerous situations, enhancing situational awareness, and enabling faster, data-inspired decision making. Consequently, AI-assisted safety systems are important in enhancing reliability, resilience, and general safety within oil and gas operations (Al-Jawad et al., 2020).

2.1 Machine Learning

The emergence of machine learning (ML) has offered the oil and gas sector new chances to be proactive in safety management. Massive amounts of historical and real time data created during operations such as operating records, old accident reports, machine performance logs and environmental monitoring data can be systematically analyzed to determine early signs of a potential safety risk. In contrast to conventional safety assessment methods, which usually presuppose the retrospective examination and human judgment, the ML-based methods allow the consistent analysis of multidimensional and rather intricate data to reveal concealed trends that can be linked to unsafe conditions.

Operational data like pressure, temperature, vibration and flow data are important in giving information about how the equipment is acting and how the process is stable. Together with historical maintenance and failure history, the ML models can learn the correlation between abnormal operating patterns and previous events. Likewise, qualitative and quantitative data regarding accidents and near-miss reports, archived, can be utilized to develop predictive models that can identify events that precede accidents upon proper organization. These models are further enhanced with environmental data such as weather conditions, sea conditions and ambient temperature that sets the external factors that could contribute to the operational risks.

ML systems with the use of both supervised and unsupervised learning methods can detect the predictors of safety incidents at an early stage. Classification and regression algorithms can be used to estimate the likelihood and severity of possible accidents, and anomaly detection algorithms can be used to indicate an abnormality in the normal behavior of the operating mechanisms that can represent the emergence of a hazard. These advance warnings enable the operators to implement preventive measures, like correction of the operating conditions, scheduling of the inspections, or even a temporary shutdown of operations thus minimizing the risk of accidents.

The use of ML-based safety analytics within the decision-support systems can help in improving risk awareness and promote the use of data to warrant decisions. This type of system allows the risk profiles to be constantly updated as new information is made available, allowing dynamic safety management, not rule-based safety management. With time, as more data on how operations and incidents take place, ML models can be enhanced to make accurate predictions and to be reliable. Overall, the application of machine learning to analyze data related to operations, history, and environment allows the early detection of safety risk predictors in oil and gas operations. This proactive and data-driven solution enhances the accident prevention measures, enhances the awareness of the situation, and leads to safer and more resilient industrial processes.

2.2 Predictive analysis

A very similar but even more significant area is predictive analytics, which uses statistical algorithms, pattern recognition techniques, and data mining techniques to make probabilistic forecasts using past and current data. In contrast to the classical descriptive or reactive methods, predictive analytics is concerned with the future, as it is aimed at detecting trends, correlations, and underlying forms within the complex data. This is a widely used method in the oil and gas industry to estimate the likelihood of equipment failures, determine the inefficiency of the process, and determine the likelihood of potential environmental hazards at a greater degree of accuracy and timeliness (Anaba et al., 2024). Predictive analytics can help identify latent patterns that are not easily visible when only operational, maintenance, and environmental data are considered using conventional analysis. Such insights can assist organizations to stop doing reactive risk assessments but proactive risk governance. Operators can react to eminent threats before they arise and comprehend the circumstances within which failures or unsafe events are probable to emerge rather than addressing the consequences of the event after it has taken place. The forecasting nature of these analytical tool's aids in the early detection of possible risks and interventions can be designed and implemented to deter such incidents by the operators of the organization. These interventions could comprise improved maintenance planned activities, operation changes, better surveillance plans, and introduction of specific safety measures. Therefore, predictive analytics help minimize accident risks, unplanned downtimes, and the problem of operational life of important assets, which results in their prolonged use. Moreover, predictive analytics introduce more resilient and efficient operations in general, as the adoption of predictive analytics contributes to making more informed decisions in unsettled conditions. Risk forecasting in a continuous mode helps in meeting the requirements of the regulatory bodies through evidence-based data on proactive safety management and mitigation of risks taken. To conclude, predictive analytics is critical in enhancing safety performance and operational reliability and regulatory compliance in the oil and gas industry to facilitate a transition to a more resilient and sustainable industrial operation.

2.3 Computer Vision

The automatic extraction, interpretation and analysis of visual data received with the help of cameras, sensor imaging systems, and unmanned aerial vehicles (drones). Computer vision technologies are on the rise and are finding applications in various sectors of industry since machines can perceive and interpret visual information in a way that is like human vision. Computer vision has become an important enabler in real-time monitoring, safety assurance, and optimization of oil and gas (O&G) industry operations especially in the framework of Health, Safety and Environment (HSE) management.

The constant monitoring of the functioning equipment and infrastructure is one of the most important implementations of computer vision in O&G operations. The visual data generated on fixed cameras and on mobile platforms in high resolution is examined in real-time to identify the abnormal conditions that may be leaks, spills, structural deformations, and unsafety of operating practices. These functions are particularly useful in offshore fields and large onshore fields where fast identification of oddities may lead to the development of serious safety events or environmental catastrophes. By providing continuous visual surveillance, computer vision systems enhance situational awareness and reduce reliance on periodic manual inspections.

The abilities of computer vision have also been extended into dangerous and inaccessible areas with the integration of drones that have high-technology imaging devices. Offshore platforms, pipelines, flare stacks, and storage tanks Remote and high elevation or confined locations can safely be inspected by drones equipped with high-resolution optical, thermal cameras and multispectral cameras. Such inspections can be done without putting the personnel under hazardous conditions, which include working in high places, under extreme temperatures or in explosive environment. Consequently, computer vision systems on drones would greatly lower the amount of human intervention in hazardous conditions as well as high inspection coverage and precision (Arinze et al., 2024; Bakare et al., 2024). The cameras and drones produce visual data, which is processed with the help of innovative computer vision algorithms such as image segmentation, object detection, pattern recognition, and deep learning models. These algorithms can identify subtle visual cues that indicate early stages of equipment degradation, such as corrosion, cracks, coating failures, misalignment, or abnormal wear patterns.

Moreover, computer vision systems would be able to identify deviations that are of safety critical concern such as unauthorized access to personnel, absence of personal protective equipment (PPE), or unsafe work practices so that corrective measures can be immediately taken. Outside the real-time monitoring area, computer vision is beginning to have a more significant role in predictive maintenance. Computer vision systems can monitor any degradation patterns over time by constantly monitoring visual cues of wear, corrosion, fatigue or loss of material. These systems can predict the risk of failures even before they happen when combined with historical inspection data and models on the condition of the assets. This predictive capability is used to plan maintenance activities in advance to minimize unplanned downtime, control the cost of repair, and avoid unsafe failures that might threaten safety or the environment.

Regarding HSE, computer vision adoption is very robust in risk management and incident prevention. Automated visual inspection eliminates subjective human inspection and enhances uniformity of checks. The fact that the leaks and spills are detected at an early stage enables that the impacts on the environment are as minimal as possible and the process of containment and remediation is as expeditious as possible. On the same note, constant checking of the structural integrity assists in ensuring that critical assets do not work at levels that would cause disastrous failures. The other advantage of computer vision-based systems is that they assist in regulatory compliance and auditing. Visual checks can be automated and verified, and that is why they will provide an objective and time-stamped record of safety checks, environmental checks, and maintenance checks. This online account increases transparency and traceability which allows organizations to prove their adherence to regulatory requirements in a more convincing way.

The regulators and auditors can examine the visual evidence of the inspections and corrective actions and reduce the ambiguity and increase trust in the safety and the environmental performance reported. Although computer vision is effective, the successful application of the technology in O&G operations requires several technical and organizational factors. Image quality, lighting conditions, camera placement, and environmental factors such as fog, dust, or sea spray can affect detection accuracy. Moreover, effective implementation of the computer vision systems would need sound data processing infrastructure, credible communication systems, and competent personnel that can interpret and act based on AI generated insights.

To accomplish, computer vision is a critical technology that is being used to improve safety, reliability and efficiency in oil and gas operations. By means of real time visual inspection, drone inspection, and predictive maintenance, computer vision can tremendously decrease human exposure to hazardous conditions and enhance the ability to detect defects in time and avert risks. Its automated and objective assessment capabilities also strengthen regulatory compliance and environmental monitoring. With the ongoing development of imaging technologies and AI-based algorithms, computer vision presumably will become the key component of the next-generation HSE management system in the oil and gas industry.

Collectively, this effort in integrating computer vision in oil and gas operations improves the situational awareness, prevention, human-machine interface with hazardous conditions as well as a robust and sustainable risk management system (Atlantic Canada's Offshore Oil and Gas Industry, 2019).

2.4 Natural Language Processing (NLP)

Natural language processing is a major branch of artificial intelligence that is gaining relevance of much importance to health, safety, and environment management (HSE). With the opportunity to interpret, process, and even analyze the human language (NLP), it is possible to convert unstructured textual information like reports, maintenance logbooks, safety audit, emails to workable data, and regulatory documents. Where communication and record are critical safety indicators in any oil and gas sector, NLP will facilitate the identification of trends, the risk concealed and leverage on safety knowledge to create an insight on large and disparate data sets. NLP algorithms can handle incident and near miss reports, identify root causes, systemic weaknesses and predict preventative measures. NLP assists in regulatory compliance over and above incident analysis, it can be used to automate reviews of safety documentation, which is aligned to industry standards and identifies non-compliance gaps or non-compliance risks. It will also enable real-time tracking of communication streams such as work orders, shift handover notes, and safety bulletins on miscommunications or hazards that are not identified otherwise and may turn out to be critical incidents. Along with predictive analytics, machine learning models, NLP enhances organizational learning to correlate textual data with operational and sensor-based data so that it provides a perspective of the risk environment. Collectively these capabilities enhance proactive safety management, reduce human oversight errors, and support evidence-based decision-making and advancing operational integrity and regulatory accountability in oil and gas operations (Al-Jawad et al., 2020).

3.AI IN EXPLORATION AND DRILLING

Artificial Intelligence has enhanced the speed of decision making in explorations and drilling by enhancing better seismic interpretation, reservoir demarcation, and optimal drilling. The somewhat hidden fault diagnosis by the seismic diffraction imaging and advanced analytics is an AI-enhanced method of predicting subtle aspects of geological structures that could not have been detected by conventional procedures. The high-resolution seismic traces are pre-processed to make signal-to-noise ratio, largely choosing peculiar frequencies, essential in selecting a miniature fault. Unstructured seismic data are automatically processed by deep learning networks, including convolutional neural networks, in which the patterns and anomalies are identified. Supervised learning trains the models using labeled data that consist of a combination of seismic property, well log, and geological data to detect the fault related features. The technology using AI reduces the processing time of seismic data and detects minute specifications which would not be identified by interpreting eyes. Consequently, accuracy leads to a better description of subsurface structures, which minimizes the risk of exploration. The complete data of fault orientations using the FMI logging accompanied by azimuthal sensitivity advances on the detection of slight faults even more. The error-containing structures and features located in the seismic diffractive images can be identified using AI algorithms, and work with a large amount of data with no less precision (Bassey et al., 2024).

3.1 AI in reservoir analysis

Reservoir analysis is quite intrinsically complicated and goes far beyond the comparatively straightforward mathematical frameworks in which the data was formerly integrated. Characterization of subsurface behavior cannot be done accurately without a multidisciplinary approach that incorporates geological, geophysical, petrophysical and engineering data to represent the spatial and temporal variability of the reservoir properties. The main goal of reservoir analysis is to realize high-fidelity insight into reservoir structure, fluid distribution and dynamic behavior that are fundamental to successful field development and prolonged hydrocarbon recovery.

At the basis of the reservoir characterization, there are direct, on-site measurements that offer direct validation of the indirect subsurface observations. The core analysis and fluid sampling is very important in the verification of rock and fluid characteristics deduced by well logs and seismic survey. Core-derived parameters such as porosity, permeability, mineral composition, and mechanical strength help calibrate well-log interpretations and petrophysical models. Equally, fluid sampling will supply dependable data on the type of fluids, saturation, as well as phase behavior that is crucial in proper evaluation of quality of reservoirs and in predicting production. These measurements support the validation of indices such as the Rock Quality Designation Index (RQDI) and ensure consistency between laboratory measurements and in-situ reservoir conditions.

Also, well-log, petrophysical data can be used to learn more about reservoir heterogeneity and spatial distribution of properties. Combinations of log-derived parameters and core and fluid data allow reservoir engineers to develop detailed and static models that capture changes in both lithology, porosity, permeability and fluid saturation. Nonetheless, the characteristics of reservoirs change as they evolve and thus require continuous monitoring and dynamic modeling methods.

Seismic monitoring has emerged as a fundamental method of monitoring the reservoir changes with time. Time-lapse (4D) seismic data allows the dynamic changes in the fluid movement, depleting pressure and changes in saturation to be analyzed through the life of the reservoir. Analyzing a comparison of seismic surveys performed at the various production stages allows the operators to determine the unswept zones, fluid migration routes and zones of bypassed hydrocarbon. Such continuous monitoring potential improves the monitoring capability of the reservoir and aids in making informed decisions regarding infill drilling, improved recovery strategies and optimization of production. In parallel, coupled reservoir–geo-mechanical modeling has gained prominence for evaluating the interaction between fluid flow and mechanical deformation of the subsurface.

Alterations to production or injection of the reservoir pressure may cause changes in stress which translate into subsidence, wellbore stability, and fault activation. Coupled modeling systems are used to measure these effects and analyze the dangers of these effects, by combining fluid flow modeling and geo-mechanical modeling. Their models are particularly required in regions, which have weak formations, or highly depleting wells or near the faults where mechanical failure would elevate the well integrity and surface facilities.

Although the conventional reservoir modeling methods are based on extensively physics-based modeling, their use may be computationally expensive and time-sensitive, especially with big and heterogeneous datasets. In that regard, superior analytics and artificial intelligence (AI) have become strong solutions to improve the characterization and forecasting of reservoirs. The AI-driven methods have the capability to process large amounts of seismic, log, production and geological data much quicker than traditional methods allowing faster and more detailed insight extraction. The convolutional neural networks (CNNs) have demonstrated specific performance in seismic interpretation operations, such as fault discovery, facies, and horizon picking. CNNs need not be manually trained on the spatial patterns of seismic images, so that the interpretation effort is significantly reduced, consistency, and accuracy is enhanced. Hybrid models that use physics models with AI models have been found to be faster in terms of history matching and production forecasting in reservoir simulation. These hybrid models leverage physical constraints while using data-driven learning to reduce uncertainty and computational cost. Reinforcement learning techniques have greatly improved dynamic history matching, which is a labor-intensive and iterative process. Reinforcement learning allows the real time adaptive calibration of reservoir models by updating model parameters constantly using production feedback. This capability allows for faster convergence to optimal solutions and supports more responsive reservoir management strategies.

Along with deep learning techniques, classical machine learning algorithms like regression, classification, clustering, and unsupervised learning can also be useful in the reservoir analysis. The techniques are broadly used to determine patterns, compartmentalization, anomalies, and associations of complex data sets. As an example, clustering algorithms can indicate units of flow and compartments in a reservoir, whereas regression models can be used to estimate important properties of the reservoir using indirect measurements. The unsupervised learning methods are especially applicable in the context where the labelled data is scarce, and the desire is to uncover the underlying structures in the massive data sets.

The integration of data-driven AI models with physics-based reservoir simulations represents a paradigm shift in subsurface modeling. This hybrid methodology is more predictive because it capitalizes on the advantages of each of the two methodologies: physical realism of first-principles models and adaptability of data-driven learning. This leads to higher operational efficiency of the operators, better optimization of production and enhanced development planning. To conclude, the contemporary reservoir analysis is becoming more based on the synergetic combination of direct measurements, sophisticated monitoring tools, coupled physical modeling, and artificial intelligence. With the help of ground-truth information and seismic surveillance, reservoir characterization can be more accurate, adaptive, and predictive, with the help of geo-mechanical modeling and AI-driven analytic tools. Such a holistic method does not only minimize uncertainty but enables sustainable management of reservoirs, as well as maximizing the recovery of hydrocarbons in the long term (Defense Acquisition University, 2019).

4. AI FOR OPERATIONAL SAFETY AND PREDICTIVE MAINTENANCE

4.1 Digital Twins

Due to the implementation of emerging technologies, oil and gas (O&G) companies have created digital twin (DT) of their assets. Nevertheless, the industry is still at the embryonic stage of DT implementation where its uses are mostly in isolated and project-specific deployments, as opposed to on an integrated implementation basis. To materialize the full potential they entail, it is essential to have an essential comprehension of DT concepts along with critical consciousness of the present standing of the research in the O&G industry with regards to DT as well as the prospects and risks involved in implementing the same (Gholami Mayani et al., 2018). Although there is certain disparity in the definition some common denominator is still present in the core aspects of a DT, a physical asset, its virtual representation, two-way transmission of data between the two and strong analytics and visualization services. According to the Defense Acquisition University (DAU), a DT can be seen as an integrated, multi-physics, multi-scale, probabilistic simulation of an as-built system "enabled by digital thread that takes the best available models, sensor data, and input to model and forecast activities/performance during the life cycle of its twinned physical equivalent" (Hamilton et al., 2024). DTs have also gained popularity in mitigating risks within the O&G industry where it displays the prospects of simulating, predicting, and optimizing the performance of its operations under different conditions.

4.1.1 Asset Performance Management

Digital twins (DTs) are now a potent digital transformation in the oil and gas (O&G) sector because they allow the true-to-life replication of physical assets, systems, and processes in real time or close to it. With constant consumption upon data produced by operational assets- sensors, control systems, and inspection records, DTs transform raw data into actionable data that is used to make operational, maintenance and strategic decisions. This ability enables operators to have a holistic view of the behavior of assets in real-life operating conditions that connects the physical system with its digital counterpart.

A major advantage of digital twins is the fact that they give detailed information about some of the crucial operational parameters. These are production rates, bottlenecks in the system, operating conditions, equipment malfunctions, optimization variables and trends of performance degradation. The DTs are also able to assess structural integrity, the possible failure modes, failure rates estimate, and the timely repair or replacement measures. Digital twins allow a holistic evaluation of asset health and performance by consolidating all these various datasets into one digital system, which is especially important in core and geographically distributed O&G operations.

To improve the efficiency of digital twins, visualization is very important. DT platforms are also used by operators to monitor the key performance indicators (KPIs) and safety margins and operational risks more efficiently because the operations data is represented in the few centralized and easy-to-use visualization interfaces. Centralized vision minimizes information overload and enhances situational awareness, which allows detection of abnormal conditions and the new risks more quickly. As a result, operators can be proactive and not reactive, and this enhances the operational reliability and safety performance.

In addition to real-time monitoring, digital twins play a major role in improving the decision-making process by means of highly complex simulation and analysis of what-if scenarios. Simulation allows operators to test the alternative operating strategies, variations in the process conditions or a probable failure situation without interfering with the live operations. With these simulations, the optimization of the production, maintenance scheduling and planning of intervention can be assessed under different hypothetical conditions. Decision-makers would get a chance to assess outcomes of different situations and select the most effective operating approaches to achieve production as efficiently as possible and reduce operational risks and downtime.

Digital twins are also especially useful in the structural integrity evaluation and driving the life cycle of assets in old infrastructure. DTs can be used to model de-rated operating conditions in cases where structural degradation is suspected or known to occur e.g. internal wall thinning because of corrosion in pressure vessels or pipelines. For example, a digital twin can model the safe operation of a pressure vessel at reduced pressure or temperature limits while accounting for material loss and stress distribution. These simulations allow us to conclude on the possibility of further operation and under what circumstances it is possible to conduct it safely in accordance with engineering standards and regulatory norms.

These integrity-based applications can help operators to carry on with asset operations until the next scheduled turnaround or off-peak maintenance. This will avoid unexpected closures and unnecessary wastage of production and acceptable safety margins are maintained. Notably, digital twins facilitate these choices with no harm to health, safety, and environmental (HSE) needs. By providing evidence-based assessments of risk and operational limits, DTs enhance confidence in life-extension decisions and regulatory compliance.

Digital twins also help with better maintenance planning and resource optimization besides the benefits that operational and safety have. DTs enable maintenance activities to be ranked by risk and importance by predicting the degradation trends of the product as well as the likelihood of failure. This means that there is better utilization of the maintenance resources, fewer emergency repairs, and better management of spare parts. Digital twins can be used as a central decision-support device at any point of the asset lifecycle when combined with predictive maintenance systems and asset management platforms.

All these strengths notwithstanding, to implement digital twins successfully, it is necessary to have strong data integration, good-quality sensor input, and physical and data-driven models. The reliability of DT outputs depends heavily on the fidelity of underlying models and the continuous synchronization between physical assets and their digital counterparts. Additionally, to be adopted successfully, it will need experienced staff that will be able to read the results of the simulation and convert the knowledge into practical activities. In short, digital twins are important in the contemporary operations of O&G as they convert real-time asset data to actionable intelligence. DTs improve the efficiency of operations, decision-making and asset life through high-level visualization, simulations and structural integrity analysis. Their capability to facilitate optimization of production, maintenance planning and safe extension of life, without compromising on high standards of HSE renders digital twins an essential technology in making oil and gas operations sustainable and resilient (Hibernia, 2019; McClintock et al., 2007).

4.1.2 Emergency Response Training

Oil and gas safety training includes fire drills and emergency evacuation exercises. Yet such training typically involves equipment shutdowns and operation suspensions, resulting in productivity losses. Evacuation training is especially expensive and may place personnel at unavoidable risk in offshore facilities. Some emergency response procedures, like the ice management plan offshore Newfoundland (Okatta et al., 2024), are particularly disruptive as production facilities are shut down, disconnected, sailed away, returned, reconnected, fitness-for-service evaluations performed, and then restarted. Training crews for such scenarios adds downtime and increases equipment wear from repeated shutdown and restart cycles. All these challenges can be mitigated or eliminated by using digital twins for immersive and risk-free training (V. M. Joy et al., 2022; Okeleke et al., 2024).

4.1.3 Process Automation

Since digital twins (DTs) live in direct relation to physical assets, they constantly absorb data obtained by sensors and process this data to create operating performance insights. In addition to surveillance possibilities, DTs may also be used to automate oil and gas (O&G) drilling, production and processing plants. The analysis in the real time setting will help DTs give optimal control signals to the actuators and decrease the use of human intervention in the hazardous and remote settings using the DTs. Not only does it increase the safety of workers who tend to have less exposure to risks since human error stands out as the leading cause of O&G accidents, but it also increases the correlation between operations and allows them to be performed 24/7 (Póvoas et al., 2025). Besides, the use of DTs (virtual copies of real things augmented with feedback received in real time in terms of sensor data and AI analytics) has been shown to be a game-changer in terms of creating a digital twin of the mode of operation and streamlining the way of drilling. With the available digital platforms, the engineers will be able to predict the system behavior under various conditions which will enable proactive risk mitigation and operational changes without compromising the safety of personnel and shutting down the operations that are in progress. The predictive ability provided by DT modeling models is also enhanced due to continuous optimization of such models based on AI, which can learn and optimize according to changes in the environment. This ability ensures that the amount of non-productive time (NPT) is minimized in drilling operations (Solanke et al., 2017; E. Al Ruhaili et al., 2023).

4.2 Predictive Maintenance Models

Predictive maintenance (PM) has become an innovative solution in contemporary industrial processes, providing an alternative way of time-based preventive maintenance using the data-driven method. Conventional maintenance procedures are based on a set schedule or service usage time, which tends to create the situation when the service is performed needlessly or vice versa, the machine breaks down without prior notice. Conversely, predictive maintenance tries to determine the failures even before they happen by constantly evaluating the actual state of equipment. Using data-driven analysis techniques, PM helps to ground maintenance decisions on asset health as opposed to set schedules, which enhances the operational efficiency and reliability (Somodi & Vásárhelyi, 2023).

Predictive maintenance is based on the integration of the Internet of Things (IoT)-enabled sensors that constantly gather both real-time and historical operational data of industrial machinery. The sensors are used to measure important parameters of vibration, temperature, pressure, flow rate and acoustic emissions, being critical indicators of health of the health of the mechanical and the process. Masses of sensor data are then run through high-order artificial intelligence (AI) and machine learning models. Pattern recognition, anomaly detection, and trend analysis can be used to detect the early indication of equipment degradation which otherwise would not be noticed using conventional means of inspection.

The ability to estimate the remaining useful life (RUL) of components and systems is one of the most important features of AI-based predictive maintenance. Using data of the failures of the past and the trends of the operation, AI models can estimate the time the equipment will be able to be used in a safe and efficient manner until it is likely to fail. This proactive understanding enables operators to be proactive in their maintenance operations, repair them at the most convenient time and replace parts only when needed. Consequently, unexpected downtimes are minimized, maintenance resources are used more effectively, and inventory of spare parts can be optimized (Xin et., 2024).

In addition to operational efficiency, predictive maintenance also adds to the safety and mitigation of risk of the plant. Incidents of equipment breakdowns in an industrial setting may result in unsafe working conditions, such as leakages, fire outbreaks, or disastrous equipment failures. The AI models help to detect faults early enough such that operators can rectify the minor faults before they develop into serious safety accidents. As a result, PM does not only secure tangible assets, but it also provides a safer environment to people and the environment, due to reduced exposure to hazardous working conditions (Joel et al., 2024).

The practicality of the AI-based predictive maintenance is proven by empirical evidence through industrial case studies, which show the practical benefits of the technology. Reported results show that there has been up to 15 percent improvement in availability of assets, and the cost of maintenance has been reduced by 20 to 30 percent. These savings are realized by reducing the number of emergency repairs, increasing the life of equipment and also better organizing of maintenance. Moreover, better reliability and uptime, in their turn, lead to increased efficiency and profitability of production, which is why PM is a strategically worthwhile investment in asset-intensive sectors.

A major development that also boosts predictive maintenance systems is the incorporation of digital twins. Digital twins are computerized copies of objects that behave as real objects in different operating situations. By continuously synchronizing with real-time sensor data, digital twins enable the co-evolution of physical and virtual systems. This gives the operators the opportunity to test the maintenance strategies, determine the performance degradation and also test the what-if-situations without disrupting the actual operations. When combined with AI models, digital twins enhance the accuracy of fault prediction and RUL estimation by capturing complex interactions between operating conditions and equipment health.

Even though predictive maintenance proves to be an effective approach, there are numerous technical and organizational problems associated with its successful implementation. The quality of data and its availability are still serious constraining factors. Unfilled, distorted or biased datasets may greatly decrease the quality of AI predictions and make confidence in PM systems doubtful. Also, the cost of implementing large sensor networks and data infrastructure may have high initial capital requirements which may be an obstacle to widespread use.

Another major challenge is the combining of predictive maintenance systems with older equipment and control systems architecture. Numerous industrial organizations have old systems that have not been developed in a digital format. The shift of these legacy systems into up-to-date, data-driven systems takes significant effort in terms of upgrading systems, standardization of the data and interoperability. The challenge of ensuring a smooth flow of information between heterogeneous sources of data and analytical tools is an ongoing technical challenge (Y. A. Hamadi et al., 2025).

Moreover, organizational preparedness is the key to successful predictive maintenance. The adoption does not only demand investment in technology but also human resources with the ability to explain AI-generated insights and apply them to the maintenance processes. The practical benefits of PM systems can be curtailed by resistance to change, mistrust in algorithmic suggestions and inadequate training. To resolve these problems, it is necessary to conduct specific workforce upskilling, maintain proper protocols and transparent AI models that can help clarify these issues and give the users confidence.

Overall, predictive maintenance is a great departure of reactive and time-based maintenance techniques to smart asset maintenance. With the help of IoT sensors, AI models, and digital twin technologies, PM can provide significant advances in the reliability of equipment, economic benefits, and safety of work. Yet, its potential can be fully achieved, only in case of solving the problems associated with data quality, infrastructure expenses, integrating systems and preparing the workforce. Sustainable and effective predictive maintenance implementation in the current industrial systems requires a holistic implementation strategy which involves integration of technology innovation with organizational as well as human-centered strategies.

4.3 Real-Time Anomaly Detection

Artificial intelligence (AI) will be important to identify anomalies in real-time so as to attain the safety of operational aspects, with the predictive maintenance tools taking into consideration the wear and tears during operation. It detects sudden changes that signify threats, through Internet of Things Sensors, computer vision, and autonomous systems, to trace down leaks, pressure spikes, and warm temperatures that an inspector cannot manually identify. Deep learning and infrared cameras, pressure sensors, and thermal cameras can be used to detect leaks, valve malfunctions, and overheated equipment. AI can initiate automatic safety measures through SIS and DCS and edges data processing increases response time in remote or offshore plants. Such abilities are essential to use when operating under high-risk conditions, like hydrogen sulfide-rich environments, where the detection time needs to be in the milliseconds range to avoid catastrophes. Opposition, such as sensor failures, noise, model drifts, and false positive/negative issues, will necessitate interminable retraining/hybrid human-AI tracking to ensure dependability (Y. A. Hamadi et al., 2025).

5. CHALLENGES TO AI ADOPTION

There is a growing use of artificial intelligence (AI) in the offshore oil and gas industry, providing substantial opportunities and new challenges. On the one hand, AI-based systems help to increase efficiency, predictive maintenance, and operational safety, but too much reliance on automated decision-support systems can result in operators making critical decisions to algorithms. Such change may undermine human control unless well attended to. Thus, the best balance should be between human and AI-based automation to make offshore operations safe and reliable. Strong governance systems need to effectively establish the limits of AI power and state that the automated systems are not meant to substitute human expertise in high-risk decision-making situations.

AI-based predictive safeguards have helped to make significant advances in offshore safety due to the ability to identify equipment failures, process anomalies, and dangerous situations in advance. Nevertheless, their adoption creates some regulatory and organizational issues. The current safety standards may not be yet proficient in adaptive and self-learning systems, and the regulatory frameworks and compliance processes should be updated. Moreover, AI implementation usually requires changes in the system of current operations, along with the extensive retraining of the staff. Without a systematized approach to change, these changes may be transitional risks, especially in offshore installations that demand procedural consistency that is crucial to safety.

Beyond operational safety, AI is increasingly deployed in the regulatory and governance domains of offshore oil and gas operations. Applications like automated documentation, compliance monitoring and auditing have enhanced efficiency, administrative overhead reduction and transparency. The adoption of blockchain technologies enhances data integrity even more as it is a type of tamper-resistant record, thus enhancing the trust among regulators and other stakeholders, as well as operators. In spite of such benefits, emerging impacts of AI in the regulatory processes are associated with ethical concerns of transparency, accountability, and fairness. Here, explainable artificial intelligence (XAI) turns into a critical demand, and the stakeholders should have access to, and be able to interpret, verify, and justify AI-based decisions to ensure trust and regulatory acceptance (B. P. Sethy et al., 2025).

In the organizational level, good management is based on informed decision making, continuous performance evaluation and transparent auditing practices grounded on sound data. These capabilities can be greatly augmented by the AI systems, which allow real-time analytics and predictive insights. Nonetheless, there is an ongoing problem in data quality and integration. Offshore platforms produce enormous amounts of sensor data that are typically heterogeneous, noisy and in multiple systems. Poor quality, standards, and interoperability: Predictive accuracy would be compromised, operational efficiency would be reduced, and unsafe recommendations could be provided. The solution to these problems is to ensure strong data governance policies, standard data architecture, and unified validation (N. R. Lakkimsetty et al., 2025).

The increased interdependency of AI systems in the offshore operations is another vital issue. Even though the systems are interconnected to enhance coordination and efficiency, the systems also expose them to cybersecurity threats. The AI-driven platforms can experience data breaches, system manipulations or adversarial attacks and negatively impact the safety-critical functions.

These accidents can lead to serious safety, environmental and economic impacts. Thus, it is necessary to have well-developed cybersecurity systems that include state-of-the-art threat detection, encryption, 24/7 monitoring, and regular risk assessment. The implementation of AI security controls must be in accordance with established cybersecurity in industries and offshore safety regulations. Workforce readiness is also another barrier to successful implementation of AI in the offshore oil and gas business. The lack of understanding and confidence in the personal or opaque or black-box AI systems can reduce the confidence of the operators and stop their adoption. This is of particular importance in high-stakes environments, under which the staff is expected to be able to defend and provide justification of operation-based decisions. To increase the competence of the workforce, specific upskilling interventions, interdisciplinary training, and interaction between the domain experts, data scientists, and system engineers are necessary. Building human-AI trust depends not only on technical reliability but also on the explainability and interpretability of AI outputs (M. M. Al-Araimi et al., 2019).

The only way to solve these challenges in a holistic manner is through a multi-dimensional approach that incorporates technical, organizational as well as ethical factors into it. Cross-disciplinary partnership between the companies and between companies may help to exchange the best practice, data standards, and regulatory understanding. The creation and implementation of explainable AI models that are consistent with engineering and industry standards are of special importance due to accountability and regulatory compliance. Comprised of ongoing workforce training and effective cybersecurity, these strategies will reduce risks and maximize the utility of AI implementation in offshore oil and gas activities. Overall, even though AI can revolutionize offshore oil and gas activities by improving their safety, efficiency, and transparency, it can be implemented successfully only with equal human attention, robust data management, regulatory flexibility, resistance to cyber-attacks, and labor preparedness. The challenges mentioned above are interconnected, and only by addressing them will it be possible to have sustainable, trustworthy, and resilient AI-enabled offshore (Y. A. Hamadi et al., 2025).

6.CONCLUSIONS

High-stakes operations such as deep-water drilling, hydrocarbon transport, and refining present blowouts, leaks, equipment failure, fires, and environmental damage risks to personnel, assets, and corporate reputation. Traditional risk management strategies, manual inspection, trend analysis and reactive mitigation are no longer suitable in the developing infrastructures and stringent regulations.

Artificial intelligence transforms operational data to actionable Intelligence enabling a paradigm shift towards predictive, preventive risk management and artificial intelligence. ML-based models enable predictive maintenance to forecast equipment failures and optimize component life, while anomaly detection with computer vision and real-time sensor data allows finding leaks, pressure deviations, and thermal abnormalities quickly, triggering automatic safety shutoffs. Digital twins enable virtual simulations of contingency planning and design optimization, and AI-enabled compliance tools accelerate regulatory reporting and audits. Even though there are still issues surrounding data quality, cybersecurity, interpretability, integration, and workforce readiness, explainable AI along with human supervision, strong governance, resilient infrastructure can enhance safety, efficiency and sustainability. AI can, in the future, be used as an enabler to risk management and long-term resilience in oil and gas; and that is through the tool of AI, federated learning, generative AI, and real-time emissions monitoring.

REFERENCES

Adedapo, O. A., Solanke, B., Iriogbe, H. O., & Ebeh, C. O. (2023). Conceptual frameworks for evaluating green infrastructure in urban stormwater management. *World Journal of Advanced Research and Reviews*, *19*(3), 1595–1603. DOI: 10.30574/wjarr.2023.19.3.0453

Aderamo, A. T., Olisakwe, H. C., Adebayo, Y. A., & Esiri, A. E.Adeoye Taofik AderamoHenry Chukwuemeka OlisakweYetunde Adenike AdebayoAndrew Emuobosa Esiri. (2024). AI-driven HSE management systems for risk mitigation in the oil and gas industry. *Comprehensive Research and Reviews in Engineering and Technology*, *2*(1), 1–22. DOI: 10.57219/crret.2024.2.1.0059

Aderamo, A. T., Olisakwe, H. C., Adebayo, Y. A., & Esiri, A. E.Adeoye Taofik AderamoHenry Chukwuemeka OlisakweYetunde Adenike AdebayoAndrew Emuobosa Esiri. (2024). AI-enabled predictive safeguards for offshore oil facilities: Enhancing safety and operational efficiency. *Comprehensive Research and Reviews in Engineering and Technology*, *2*(1), 23–43. DOI: 10.57219/crret.2024.2.1.0060

Al-Araimi, M. M., Joy, V. M., Nageswara Rao, L. S., & Feroz, S. (2019). Optimization and assessment of residual chlorine using response surface methodology and artificial neural network modeling [IJRTE]. *Int. J. Recent Technol. Eng.*, *8*(3), 258–263. DOI: 10.35940/ijrte.C4122.098319

Al-Jawad, S. N. A., Ahmed, M. A., & Saleh, A. H. (2020). Integrated reservoir characterization and quality analysis of the carbonate rock types: Case study, southern Iraq. *Journal of Petroleum Exploration and Production Technology*, *10*(8), 3157–3177. DOI: 10.1007/s13202-020-00982-6

Al Ruhaili, E., Lakkimsetty, N. R., & Joy, V. M. Modeling and optimization of heat exchanger using artificial neural network and genetic algorithm, in *AIP Conf. Proc.*, vol. 2690, no. 1, Art. no. 020028, 2023, DOI: 10.1063/5.0119479

Anaba, D. C., Kess-Momoh, A. J., & Ayodeji, S. A.David Chinalu AnabaAzeez Jason Kess-MomohSodrudeen Abolore Ayodeji. (2024). Digital transformation in oil and gas production: Enhancing efficiency and reducing costs. *International Journal of Management & Entrepreneurship Research*, *6*(7), 2153–2161. DOI: 10.51594/ijmer.v6i7.1263

Arinze, C. A., Izionworu, V. O., Isong, D., Daudu, C. D., & Adefemi, A. (2024). Integrating artificial intelligence into engineering processes for improved efficiency and safety in oil and gas operations. *Open Access Research Journal of Engineering and Technology*, *6*(1), 39–51. DOI: 10.53022/oarjet.2024.6.1.0012

Atlantic Canada's Offshore Oil and Gas Industry. (2019). *Ice management*. Retrieved February 12, 2019, from http://atlanticcanadaoffshore.ca/ice-management-newfoundland-labradorsoffshore-industry/

Bakare, O. A., Aziza, O. R., Uzougbo, N. S., & Oduro, P. (2024). A governance and risk management framework for project management in the oil and gas industry. *Open Access Research Journal of Science and Technology*, *12*(1), 121–130. DOI: 10.53022/oarjst.2024.12.1.0119

Bassey, K. E., Opoku-Boateng, J., Antwi, B. O., Ntiakoh, A., & Juliet, A. R. (2024). Digital twin technology for renewable energy microgrids. *Engineering Science & Technology Journal*, *5*(7), 2248–2272. DOI: 10.51594/estj.v5i7.1319

Defense Acquisition University. (2019). *Defense acquisition glossary-Digital twin*. Retrieved February 12, 2019, from https://www.dau.edu/glossary/Pages/Glossary.aspx

Gholami Mayani, M., Rommetveit, R., Oedegaard, S. I., & Svendsen, M. (2018). Drilling automated realtime monitoring using digital twin. In *Abu Dhabi International Petroleum Exhibition & Conference* (pp. 1–11). DOI: 10.2118/192807-MS

Hamadi, Y. A., Juma, R. J., Hussein, Z. M., & Lakkimsetty, N. R. Harnessing artificial intelligence in wastewater treatment: A comprehensive analysis of emerging research trends and innovations, in *Proc. 2025 Int. Conf. INnovations in Intelligent SysTems and Applications (INISTA)*, Ras Al Khaimah, United Arab Emirates, 2025, pp. 1–7, DOI: 10.1109/INISTA68122.2025.11249526

Hamilton, L., & Rauch, M. (2024). Artificial intelligence integration for optimal reservoir data analysis and pattern recognition. In *Unconventional Resources Technology Conference* (pp. 2968–2988).

Hibernia. (2019). *Ice management*. Retrieved February 12, 2019, from https://www.hibernia.ca/ice.html

Joel, O. S., Oyewole, A. T., Odunaiya, O. G., & Soyombo, O. T. (2024). Leveraging artificial intelligence for supply chain optimization: Current practices and future potentials. *International Journal of Management & Entrepreneurship Research*, *6*(3), 707–721. DOI: 10.51594/ijmer.v6i3.882

Joy, V. M., Shaik, F., & Lakkimsetty, N. R. (2022). Application of Artificial Intelligence in the Treatment of Saline Water. In *Removal of Pollutants from Saline Water Treatment Technologies* (1st ed.). CRC Press, Taylor & Francis Group.

Lakkimsetty, N. R., Al Araimi, H. R. A., & Kavitha, G. (2025). Modelling and optimization of well hole cleaning using artificial intelligence techniques. *Discover Applied Sciences*, *7*(2), 124. DOI: 10.1007/s42452-024-06415-x

McClintock, J., McKenna, R., & Woodworth-Lynas, C. (2007). *Grand Banks ice-berg management* (PERD/CHC Rep. 20-84). National Research Council Canada.

Okatta, N. C. G., Ajayi, N. F. A., & Olawale, N. O. (2024). Leveraging HR analytics for strategic decision-making: Opportunities and challenges. *International Journal of Management & Entrepreneurship Research*, *6*(4), 1304–1325. DOI: 10.51594/ijmer.v6i4.1060

Okeleke, P. A., Ajiga, D., Folorunsho, S. O., & Ezeigweneme, C. (2024). Predictive analytics for market trends using AI: A study in consumer behavior. *[Journal name missing; please provide]*.

Póvoas, M. D. S., Moreira, J. F., Neto, S. V. M., Carvalho, C. A. D. S., Cezario, B. S., Guedes, A. L. A., & Lima, G. B. A. (2025). Artificial intelligence in the oil and gas industry: Applications, challenges, and future directions. *Applied Sciences (Basel, Switzerland)*, *15*(14), 7918. DOI: 10.3390/app15147918

B. P. Sethy, U. Prajapati, K. N. Nageswara Rao Lakkimsetty, *et al.*, "Artificial intelligence models for predicting unconfined compressive strength of mixed soil types: Focusing on clay and sand," *Asian J. Civ. Eng.*, 2025, .DOI: 10.1007/s42107-025-01285-z

Solanke, B. (2017). Resolving fault shadow challenge: Onshore Niger Delta case history. [Society of Exploration Geophysicists.]. *SEG Technical Program Expanded Abstracts*, *2017*, 4514–4518.

Somodi, G., & Vásárhelyi, B. (2023). Borehole analysis with the modification of RQD value. *Geotechnics*, *3*(4), 1017–1032. DOI: 10.3390/geotechnics3040055

Xin, C., Wenyuan, H., Jiawen, S., Yanlin, H., Jiangtao, G., Shize, W., & Yaliang, X. (2024). AI-assisted subtle faults characterization based on integrated seismic diffraction imaging: Application in M Oilfield, Middle East. In *Abu Dhabi International Petroleum Exhibition and Conference* (p. D011S021R002). SPE.

Chapter 12
From Clinical Insight to Computational Foresight: The Transformative Role of Artificial Intelligence in Sustainable Dentistry

Meharunneesa Aboobacker Sidheeq
http://orcid.org/0009-0006-5480-2799
College of Dentistry, City University, Ajman, UAE

A. Fahizah
http://orcid.org/0000-0003-4006-4562
Yenepoya Dental College, Mangalore, India

M. Shafna
http://orcid.org/0009-0005-8288-0965
Dhilan's Multi-Specialty Dental Clinic, India

Syed Rahaman Mouazur Rahaman
http://orcid.org/0000-0002-4725-1216
Canadian Dental Medical Centre, Al Ain, UAE

ABSTRACT

As the world moves toward more eco-friendly and responsible healthcare, dentistry is also rethinking how it can reduce waste, save energy, and protect the environment without compromising on quality care. This chapter looks at how smart digital tools, especially those powered by artificial intelligence (AI), are changing the way dental care is delivered and making it more sustainable. Dental practices often rely on large amounts of materials, produce medical waste, and consume energy through

DOI: 10.4018/979-8-2600-1348-9.ch012

equipment, travel, and repeated procedures. By using intelligent systems in areas like X-rays, treatment planning, remote consultations, and clinic management, dentists can work more efficiently, reduce unnecessary steps, and focus on prevention. We explore real-world examples where AI is helping in everyday dental work like spotting early signs of disease, planning better treatments, and even reducing patient travel. At the same time, we also discuss the challenges like patient data privacy, trust in AI decisions, and the energy cost of running these systems.

INTRODUCTION

Environmental degradation and climate change have become defining challenges of our time, with growing pressure across sectors to reduce their ecological footprint. Healthcare, long considered a passive contributor to environmental harm, is now under closer scrutiny (Grose et al., 2018)(Richardson et al., 2016). According to the World Health Organization (WHO), health systems account for nearly 4.4% of global carbon emissions more than entire countries in some cases. The International Organization for Standardization (ISO) defines sustainability as meeting present needs without compromising the ability of future generations to meet theirs, and this principle is becoming central to how modern healthcare systems operate (International Organization for Standardization, 2024). The term environmentally friendly," as defined by ISO, refers to products and practices that cause reduced, minimal, or no environmental harm, and will be used throughout this review to refer to such practices or products (AlShammery, 2021). In alignment with this principle, reducing carbon emissions remains a global priority, with several nations taking action through initiatives such as United Kingdom's Climate Change Act of 2008, the Paris Agreement of 2016 and New Zealand's Zero Carbon Act of 2019, which aims for carbon neutrality (Duane et al., 2020). Healthcare systems are significant contributors to carbon footprint, accounting for approximately 4.4% of global net emissions (Pichler et al., 2019).

Environmental Burden of Dental Care

Dentistry, though often overlooked in sustainability conversations, plays a surprisingly large role. It is a sector that depends heavily on energy, materials, water, and human movement. Modern dental practice, while essential for population health, generates considerable environmental burdens many of which are avoidable or reducible with thoughtful change (Chalotra et al., 2025).

A routine dental appointment might seem straightforward, but behind the scenes it involves extensive resource use and waste generation. Studies have found that a single patient visit can involve over 30 individual items such as disposable trays, plastic barriers, paper bibs, suction tips, and packaging all of which are typically discarded after one use (Grose et al., 2018). Most of these materials are made from plastic and contribute directly to growing clinical waste streams.

Life-cycle audits confirm that dental clinics produce substantial volumes of both emissions and waste. One UK study showed that even modest changes in waste segregation—like recycling sterilization pouches or packaging can reduce both environmental impact and operational (Fisal et al., 2025). Even though a single dentist produces very little biomedical waste, the cumulative waste has a big influence on the environment (Lyne et al., 2020). Dental healthcare's extensive reliance on both disposable and reusable products highlights the need to transcend the concept of sustainability beyond mere carbon emissions, to encompass the choice of materials procured, the waste generated, and the broader impact on biodiversity (Duane et al., 2019a) (Duane et al., 2019b).

Perhaps most significant, however, is the impact of travel. Patient and staff transportation contributes over 60% of a dental practice's carbon footprint, as shown in an analysis by Public Health England (Steinbach et al., 2018). A national estimate of NHS dental emissions placed the total carbon footprint around 675 kilotonnes of CO_2 equivalent annually nearly two-thirds of which came from transportation alone (Duane et al., 2012).

Dental laboratories are also part of the equation. A recent life-cycle assessment conducted in Egypt found that lab worker commuting (44%) and material procurement (28%) were the leading contributors to laboratory-related emissions (Abbod et al., 2020).

Figure 1. Smart and sustainable dental care

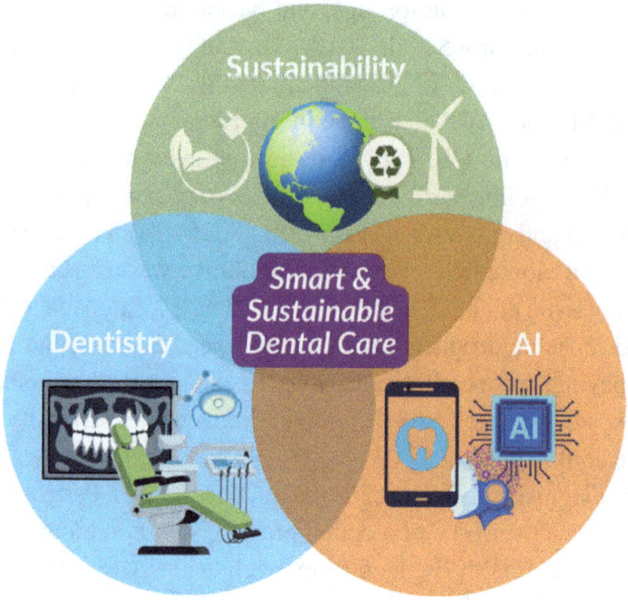

Why Dentistry Needs Sustainable Transformation Now

These environmental costs come at a time when the demand for dental services is steadily rising. This is especially true in low- and middle-income countries, where preventive services are limited. In such settings, up to 90% of dental caries remain untreated, compared to 30–50% in high-income countries (Petersen & Ogawa, 2012). As access improves and populations age, the volume of dental care delivered globally is expected to increase—alongside its ecological footprint.

Recognizing this, the World Health Organization's Global Oral Health Action Plan urges all countries to incorporate sustainability into oral health delivery, including through reduced carbon emissions and smarter waste management (WHO). National governments and professional associations have responded. The FDI World Dental Federation has identified sustainability in procurement, reduction of plastic use, and waste minimization as key priorities in the shift toward environmentally responsible oral healthcare (World Health Organization, 2022) (Shellard et al., 2022).

The shift is not just regulatory it's also cultural. Today's patients are more aware of environmental issues and often seek healthcare providers whose values align with sustainability. This opens the door for a broader transformation in dental practice one that considers not only clinical outcomes but also environmental responsibility as part of ethical patient care.

AI as an Enabler of Sustainable Practice

As dental practices grapple with rising environmental demands and operational inefficiencies, artificial intelligence (AI) is emerging as a valuable ally in the journey toward sustainability. By integrating intelligent technologies into diagnostic, clinical, and administrative workflows, dental providers can significantly reduce waste, optimize resource use, and lower their environmental footprint. For instance, AI-powered tele-dentistry platforms enable remote triage and consultation, reducing the need for patient travel—a leading contributor to dental-sector emissions (Chen et al., 2020). Predictive algorithms used in scheduling and inventory systems can reduce material overuse, prevent stock expiry, and streamline chairside operations, leading to less procedural redundancy and waste generation (Vashisht et al., 2024).

In clinical settings, AI has shown promise in reducing the need for repeat diagnostics. Automated quality assurance systems for dental radiographs can minimize exposure to radiation and energy waste by flagging poor-quality images in real time (Zhu et al., 2023). Furthermore, machine learning models capable of early disease detection and progression prediction enable timely, conservative interventions—avoiding overtreatment and unnecessary material consumption. These efficiencies collectively support a more sustainable dental practice, aligning both with environmental goals and patient-centered care. However, realizing these benefits requires careful selection of AI systems that not only improve outcomes but do so with minimal computational and energy cost—a concept increasingly known as "Green AI."

CONCEPTUAL FOUNDATIONS

Green (Eco) Dentistry

Sustainable or "green" dentistry refers to the intentional integration of environmentally responsible practices into everyday patient care, with the overarching goal of reducing dentistry's ecological burden without compromising treatment quality (Chen et al., 2020). It reflects a growing recognition—supported across professional bodies and academic literature that oral healthcare must evolve in alignment with global sustainability goals. As described by the European Federation of Periodontology, green dentistry is grounded in the principle that dental practices should actively minimize pollution, conserve resources, and protect community and planetary health resources (Mulimani, 2017). Sustainable dentistry is not a superficial modification to clinical routines but a systematic rethinking of how oral healthcare is delivered at every stage (Sanz et al., 2025).

At its core, green dentistry emphasizes prevention as the most sustainable intervention. Preventive care reduces the need for resource-intensive restorative procedures, decreases the number of clinical visits, and limits the use of consumables and energy-demanding equipment. Preventing disease also means fewer radiographs, fewer chemical disinfectants, and fewer disposable materials entering the waste stream. This preventive philosophy becomes a foundational anchor for all sustainable dental models (Speroni & Polizzi, 2025).

To operationalize sustainability, dental teams are encouraged to adopt the 4R framework: Reduce, Reuse, Recycle, and Rethink (Di Spirito et al., 2025). This philosophy urges clinicians and administrators to continuously evaluate how resources are consumed within the clinic. Strategies include reducing single use plastics by opting for reusable stainless-steel instruments, implementing dry vacuum suction systems that drastically lower water consumption, and digitizing patient records to eliminate paper waste (Di Spirito et al., 2025). Digital radiography similarly eliminates the need for chemical developers and reduces hazardous waste, supporting both environmental and occupational safety (Ohene-Botwe et al., 2024).

Figure 2. Environmental stress points in dental care

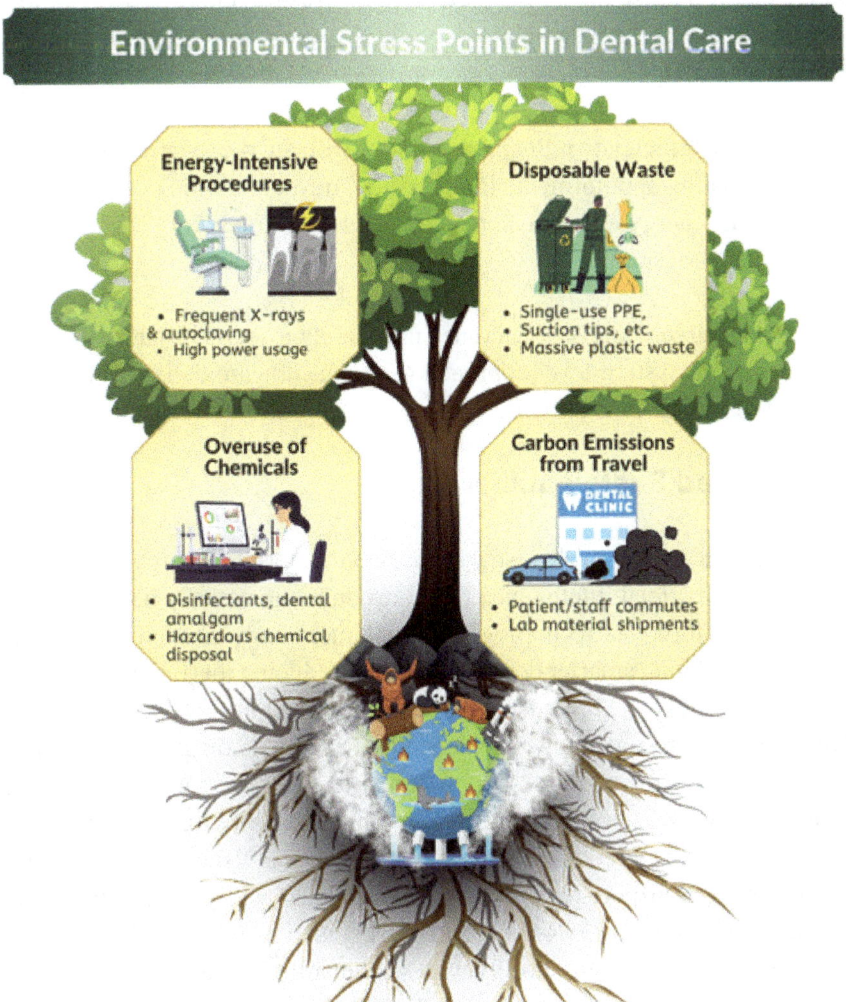

Green dentistry also promotes the use of nontoxic, biocompatible, and environmentally safe materials. Material choice plays a significant role in ecological footprint: for example, selecting products with reduced packaging, longer shelf life, or recyclable components helps curb unnecessary waste. Green dentistry advocates for keeping resource use "in balance with nature's economy," meaning that the practice should consume only what can be reasonably replenished, reused, or safely returned to the environment without long-term harm (Guerra et al., 2025).

A crucial aspect of sustainable practice is workflow redesign. When dental teams understand how disease prevention, reduced disposables, energy conservation, and water stewardship interact within the clinical system, they can restructure daily operations accordingly (efp.org; mdpi.com). For example:

- Scheduling efficiency reduces repeated sterilization cycles and energy use.
- Consolidating appointments limits patient travel emissions.
- Choosing energy-efficient autoclaves and LED operatory lighting reduces electricity consumption.

In this way, green dentistry becomes not merely a set of isolated interventions but an integrated, system-level approach to oral healthcare delivery (Di Spirito et al., 2025) (Di Spirito et al., 2025).

AI-Augmented Sustainability

While traditional green dentistry focuses on materials, energy, and workflow modifications, artificial intelligence (AI) introduces an entirely new dimension to sustainability efforts. AI technologies complement and enhance green-dentistry principles by enabling smarter decision-making, reducing inefficiencies, and transforming the way care is accessed and delivered (Hsu et al., 2022).

One of the clearest examples is telehealth and remote diagnosis. AI-supported teledentistry platforms can assess symptoms, analyze patient-submitted images, and triage cases with remarkable accuracy. This capability directly contributes to the "Rethink" pillar by reducing unnecessary in-person visits cutting down patient travel, lowering transport-related carbon emissions, and easing clinic resource use (mdpi.com; mdpi.com). Remote monitoring also supports early detection and preventive care, which aligns closely with sustainability's emphasis on minimizing resource-intensive treatments (Surdu et al., 2025).

AI also plays a transformational role in inventory management, supporting the "Reduce" component of the 4Rs. Through real-time supply monitoring and predictive analytics, AI can forecast when materials will be needed and order them just-in-time, significantly reducing expired stock and unnecessary purchases (mdpi.com). This leads not only to cost savings but also to lower environmental impact due to fewer disposables, reduced packaging waste, and decreased frequency of shipments (Rahimpour & Zahraee, 2015).

In clinical decision-making, AI has the potential to refine treatment planning in ways that directly support sustainability. Predictive models can help customize recall intervals, ensuring patients are seen when evidence supports it instead of relying on fixed schedules that may promote overtreatment. AI-supported diagnostics can identify early lesions or periodontal changes with higher accuracy, allowing minimally invasive interventions that use fewer materials and produce less waste (Khosravi et al., 2024).

Moreover, AI enhances imaging efficiency. Automated image-quality assessment reduces the need for repeated radiographs, consequently lowering energy use, minimizing radiation exposure, and decreasing consumption of digital storage and processing resources (mdpi.com). In treatment procedures, AI-assisted simulations can help clinicians plan more conservative preparations or choose restorative approaches that preserve tooth structure, indirectly reducing material needs (Clement et al., 2025).

However, AI itself must also be evaluated through a sustainability lens. Running deep-learning models can involve substantial computational demands. Large cloud-based systems require significant electricity to power servers and cooling networks. For this reason, dental practices are encouraged to choose AI tools that prioritize efficiency, such as lightweight algorithms, compressed models, or on-device (edge) processing, all of which reduce data-transfer energy and server load. Only by considering these factors can AI truly operate as a tool that supports, rather than contradicts, sustainable practice (Hankendi et al., 2025).

DOMAINS IN DENTISTRY WHERE AI CAN PROMOTE SUSTAINABILITY

Diagnostic Imaging

AI has significant potential to optimize diagnostic imaging workflows in dentistry, making them more efficient and environmentally responsible. AI-assisted tools can assess the quality of radiographs in real time, alerting clinicians to suboptimal images before the patient leaves the chair and thereby reducing the need for repeat exposures and associated resource use (automatic repeat X-rays consume additional energy and increase radiation) (Ali et al., 2025).

Deep-learning systems also facilitate lower-dose imaging protocols by reconstructing high-quality images from lower radiation data, which reduces patient dose while preserving diagnostic utility. Automated detection algorithms, particularly convolutional neural networks (CNNs), have been studied extensively for identifying caries, periodontal changes, and osseous lesions from radiographs and CBCT scans, shortening reading time and allowing clinicians to work more efficiently (Carrillo-Perez et al., 2022).

By reducing retakes, minimizing redundant image acquisition, and focusing clinician attention where it matters most, AI supports reduced energy consumption and less waste (digital imaging requires less consumables, chemicals, and handling than conventional film).

Restorative & Operative Dentistry

In restorative care, AI applications are increasingly being developed to predict the longevity and failure risk of restorations, though much of this research is still emerging. By analyzing longitudinal clinical data, AI models can estimate which restorations are likely to fail prematurely, helping clinicians decide whether intervention is truly necessary at the time of observation (Araidy et al., 2025).

Decision-support algorithms can also assist in selecting minimally invasive treatment plans based on patient risk factors, radiographic findings, and historical outcomes. In practice, an AI system might evaluate a patient's caries risk and radiographs to recommend sealants instead of restorative intervention for low-risk areas, thereby preserving tooth structure and reducing material consumption. Although this area is evolving, initial evidence suggests enhanced precision in restorative planning with AI support (Carrillo-Perez et al., 2022).

Using AI to avoid unnecessary procedures not only conserves materials (e.g., composite, burs) but also minimizes patient chair time, energy use (lighting, suction, instrumentation), and waste generation.

Endodontics

AI is also transforming endodontic workflows by automating the segmentation of root canals and dental anatomy in CBCT scans — a task that is both time-consuming and technically demanding when done manually. AI-driven segmentation algorithms can quickly highlight canal pathways and root morphology, supporting faster and more accurate access planning (Vázquez-Sebrango et al., 2025).

Automated 3D reconstruction of canals can further help clinicians visualize complex root structures, reducing the need for additional imaging and shortening planning time. This efficiency not only improves clinical throughput but also decreases cumulative energy use from CBCT systems and operative lights. By speeding up endodontic planning and intervention, AI reduces cumulative operational energy consumption per case compared to slower manual workflows (Duane et al., 2020).

Implantology & Prosthodontics

In prosthetic and implant workflows, AI-enabled systems can contribute to sustainability by optimizing implant planning and prosthesis design. For example, AI models trained on large datasets can identify optimal implant placement positions that avoid unnecessary bone removal or avoid additional surgical stages, conserving surgical time and reducing resource use (sterile trays, drilling burs, etc.) (Shinkai et al., 2025).

In CAD/CAM prosthodontics, generative design algorithms can minimize material use while maintaining strength and functionality, reducing milling waste compared to traditional manual design processes. AI can also optimize 3D printing support structures, lowering resin or metal use and consequently reducing overall material waste. When these design and fabrication processes are handled in-office using intelligent systems, clinics can cut down on frequent laboratory pickups and deliveries, thereby reducing transport-related emissions as well as turnaround times (Vázquez-Sebrango et al., 2025).

Orthodontics & Pediatric Dentistry

AI has begun to emerge in orthodontics as a tool for improving treatment prediction and planning, including identifying children at risk of needing future orthodontic interventions based on photos, growth trends, and dental arch metrics. Early, targeted preventive or interceptive measures can prevent more extensive treatments later, which are usually more resource-intensive (Pithon et al., 2017).

Additionally, AI-enhanced smart monitoring apps are being used to track clear aligner progress by analyzing patient selfies uploaded via smartphone. These tools allow remote evaluation of treatment progress and reduce unnecessary office visits, saving travel emissions and clinician and chair time. Remote monitoring thus improves sustainability by reducing repeated in-office appointments and the associated resource use required for each visit (Eliades et al., 2025).

Workflow & Clinic Operations

Beyond clinical domains, AI offers substantial gains in practice management and operations. AI-driven practice management tools can optimize appointment scheduling to minimize gaps between patients, reducing periods when lights, HVAC, and dental equipment remain on without active use (Gupta et al., 2025).

Predictive maintenance algorithms can alert staff to routine service needs for sterilizers, compressors, and other equipment, preventing breakdowns that often lead to energy inefficiencies or rushed replacements. AI can also forecast usage of consumables (gloves, composites, impression materials) to prevent overstocking and costly disposals. These tools ensure that staffing, clinical space, and resources align smoothly with patient flow, maximizing operational efficiency and reducing energy and material waste (Falsk, 2023).

Teledentistry / Remote Triage

AI image analysis is particularly suited for remote preliminary screening and triage. On teledentistry platforms, patients may upload intraoral photos or scans, and AI algorithms (often based on CNNs) can flag potential cavities, mucosal lesions, or other anomalies for clinician review (Batra et al., 2022).

Such systems can prompt patients to retake poor-quality photos, ensuring better diagnostic accuracy, and can prioritize urgent cases for in-office care while deferring minor ones. By catching problems early and remotely, AI-driven telehealth can prevent escalation of disease and avoid later resource-intensive treatments. This remote triage model not only saves on patient travel emissions but also reduces unnecessary clinic visits, energy use, and staff time—advancing sustainability (Taylor et al., 2025).

Figure 3. AI as an enabler of sustainability practice

APPLICATIONS & USE CASES IN DENTAL PRACTICE

AI in Radiographs and CBCT

Artificial intelligence is rapidly changing how radiographs and 3D imaging (CBCT) are interpreted in dentistry. For example, deep-learning tools significantly improve diagnostic imaging workflows by automating detection and segmentation tasks. In a recent review of AI systems for radiographic detection of caries and other lesions, AI models often matched or exceeded dentist-level accuracy while drastically reducing time per image (Albano et al., 2024).

Moreover, AI-based systems now exist for fully automated tooth and alveolar bone segmentation from CBCT scans. One study demonstrated a deep-learning model that segments individual teeth and bone structures automatically — with high accuracy — which enables faster planning for implants, orthodontics, or prosthodontics compared to manual processing (Kot et al., 2025).

Automated segmentation and detection not only save clinician time but also reduce repeated imaging or manual rework, lowering both radiation exposure and the resource consumption associated with repeated imaging (e.g. electricity, storage, printing).

A systematic review covering 23 recent studies confirmed that AI applications in dental imaging for caries detection on radiographs, CBCT segmentation, implant planning, and other uses are no longer futuristic: they are actively being integrated into clinical and research settings (Araidy et al., 2025).

AI for Treatment Planning & Decision Support

Beyond imaging, AI's role in treatment planning and decision support is gaining ground. Some emerging AI systems analyze patient records, radiographs, and risk factors to predict likely outcomes for example, estimating the potential longevity of restorations or forecasting progression of periodontal disease. This kind of predictive modeling can help dentists decide when intervention is truly needed versus when conservative or preventive care might suffice, thereby reducing overtreatment and preserving resources (Duane et al., 2020).

In restorative dentistry, AI could guide decisions on whether to place a filling, perform minimally invasive treatment, or monitor the lesion. Similarly, for complex rehabilitations, AI can help select materials, design parameters, or treatment sequences that maximize durability and minimize waste a crucial feature in resource-sensitive clinical settings. Although many such tools are still in research phases, their potential for sustainability lies in reducing unnecessary interventions, lowering material use, and avoiding remakes or excessive chair-time.

AI CAD/CAM / 3D Printing for Prosthetics

In prosthodontics and implantology, AI integration with CAD/CAM and 3D printing enables optimized design and fabrication workflows. By using generative design algorithms, AI can create prostheses (crowns, bridges, dentures) that use minimal material while maintaining sufficient structural strength. This reduces waste from excess milling or printing and minimizes the need for rework or remakes (Aradya et al., 2025).

When dental clinics adopt in-house AI-driven milling or printing, they can avoid frequent lab outsourcing which reduces transport emissions associated with lab courier trips, and shortens turnaround time for patients. This localized digital workflow improves resource efficiency and reduces environmental impact across the supply chain.

Although most of the evidence is still emerging, recent literature reviews highlight AI-based prosthetic planning and manufacturing as one of the most promising applications where sustainability and patient-centered care intersect (Cui et al., 2022).

AI-Based Remote Screening & Monitoring (Teledentistry)

The rise of AI-enabled teledentistry and remote monitoring is reshaping access to dental care and offering environmental benefits at the same time. Studies report that AI algorithms can detect caries, lesions, and other pathologies from intraoral photographs or radiographs uploaded by patients, with sensitivity and specificity approaching that of trained professionals (Mao et al., 2025).

Such remote screening tools reduce the need for in-person visits, especially for low-risk or routine follow-ups. This not only saves travel-related emissions but also decreases the burden on clinic resources (staff time, chair occupancy, sterilization cycles).

Moreover, remote monitoring supports preventive care patients with early lesions can be flagged promptly, potentially preventing progression to more invasive treatment, thereby saving materials and energy in the long term. As AI-based remote triage becomes more accurate, it offers a scalable, sustainable alternative to traditional in-office screening, especially for populations with limited access or mobility (Moharrami et al., 2025).

Administrative & Workflow AI

AI's advantages are not limited to clinical work — it extends into practice management and administrative workflows, which also influence sustainability. Intelligent scheduling systems powered by AI can optimize patient appointments to minimize idle time, reducing energy usage from lighting, HVAC, and equipment when operatories are unused (Alharbi & Alhasson, 2024).

Predictive maintenance algorithms can alert staff when sterilizers, compressors, or other heavy-duty equipment require servicing — preventing breakdowns that lead to inefficient energy use or urgent replacements. AI-driven inventory management can forecast the use of consumables (gloves, composites, impression materials), helping avoid overstocking, expiration waste, and unnecessary procurement (Ding et al., 2023).

Moreover, in larger dental practices or chains, AI-powered administrative tools (e.g., appointment reminders via chatbots, automated billing and documentation) help reduce human workload, prevent errors, and promote efficient resource use. Although less studied compared to clinical AI, workflow AI offers a promising path to improve sustainability across dental operations (Ding et al., 2023).

Generative AI / LLMs in Dentistry

Emerging generative AI, including large language models (LLMs), may soon play a role in dental documentation, education, and research support. For instance, dentists may use LLMs to draft referral letters, patient instructions, treatment summaries, or even patient education materials saving staff time, reducing repetitive paperwork, and potentially minimizing printing or paper waste. Reviews suggest that multimodal AI systems (combining images + text + patient data) could support comprehensive decision-making, blending diagnostic imaging with patient history and clinical notes to propose treatment options while optimizing resources (Araidy et al., 2025).

For research and continuing education, LLMs can help rapidly summarize current evidence, prepare literature reviews or guidelines, and assist in academic writing — increasing productivity while reducing human effort. Though still nascent, the potential of LLMs to streamline administrative and academic tasks may indirectly support sustainable dental practice by reducing overhead and improving efficiency across the system.

MEASURING & DEMONSTRATING SUSTAINABILITY IMPACT

Dental KPIs

To demonstrate tangible sustainability gains in dental practices, clinics can develop key performance indicators (KPIs) that track environmental outcomes alongside clinical outcomes. For example, one useful KPI is the number of repeat radiographs avoided as a result of AI-assisted image quality checks, since fewer retakes directly reduce energy use and radiation exposure while lowering demands on imaging equipment. (See the use of LCA to quantify environmental burden in dental procedures and the emphasis on waste and travel as hotspots in dental carbon footprints (Chalotra et al., 2025).

Tracking the volume of dental materials saved—such as composite, amalgam, or impression materials—can also offer insight into sustainability improvements when AI-supported intervention predictions reduce unnecessary procedures. These savings can be quantified by auditing material stocks over time and comparing usage before and after AI deployment. (Life cycle analyses of dental products highlight the material contribution to environmental impact (Smith et al., 2023).

An additional KPI is patient travel miles saved through telehealth and remote consultations. By calculating reduced patient travel distances using standard carbon calculators, practices can estimate the reduction in CO_2 emissions attributable to remote triage or monitoring. Given that patient and staff transport is often among the largest contributors to a dental clinic's carbon footprint, this metric offers a high-impact measure of change. (LCA work on dental practice emissions repeatedly notes travel as a leading source (Duane & Steinbach, 2024b).

Waste audits can further quantify sustainability progress. By regularly weighing and categorizing refuse streams (e.g., plastics, paper, infectious waste), practices can monitor changes in waste volume and composition, identifying reductions in single-use disposables or increases in recycling rates. Combining these data with the known carbon costs of waste streams informs both environmental and financial impact. (Carbon footprint of waste disposal is highlighted in related hospital waste LCAs and suggested for dentistry (Duane & Steinbach, 2024b).

Comparative LCAs

Life cycle assessment (LCA) is the gold standard for objectively comparing the environmental impacts of different dental workflows. An LCA evaluates all stages of a process—from procurement and manufacturing of materials, through clinical use, to disposal—and assigns environmental impacts such as carbon footprints, water usage, and waste output. (LCA is widely used in healthcare and dental sustainability research (Drew et al., 2022).

For example, a comparative LCA could model a traditional crown procedure that involves conventional impression taking, lab shipping, and multiple patient visits versus an AI-guided digital workflow that uses in-clinic scanning and milling. Early LCA studies in dentistry show that simplifying workflows and reducing transport steps can substantially cut emissions (Suresh et al., 2024).

Similarly, an LCA comparing imaging with and without an AI quality-gate could measure CO_2 savings per avoided retake, by accounting for the energy used by X-ray units, staff time, and the associated carbon cost of repeated patient travel. While field-specific LCAs directly measuring AI's effect are still emerging, the broader LCA literature supports workflow comparisons as a powerful evidence tool (Borglin et al., 2021).

Life cycle studies also help identify "hotspots"the life cycle stages or components with the greatest environmental impact so that sustainability initiatives can target those areas most effectively. This supports evidence-based decision-making and helps justify investments in AI tools that show net environmental benefits. (Research reviews consistently call for dental LCAs to underpin sustainability strategies (Chalotra et al., 2025).

Economic & Environmental ROI

Any sustainability intervention has costs including software licenses, hardware upgrades, staff training, and time spent implementing new systems. To make a compelling case, these costs should be measured against savings realized from reduced energy use, lower material consumption, and improved workflows. For example, an AI scheduling system that costs $5,000 but reduces energy and staff time by $1,000 per year would yield a five-year payback period, which is a standard way to assess investment viability in sustainability planning.

Pilot programs can help illustrate ROI. In one dental school recycling initiative, approximately 813 kg of CO_2e emissions were offset in a year through effective segregation and recycling, demonstrating measurable environmental benefits from structured sustainability programs (Chalotra et al., 2025).

Environmental and economic ROI analyses also support conversations with insurers and health systems. If interventions lower the overall carbon footprint, regulatory penalties or carbon taxes may be avoided. Moreover, practices demonstrating sustainability performance may become eligible for incentives or certifications, further reinforcing the case for investment.

Monitoring Unintended Effects

While measuring sustainability impacts is essential, vigilance is needed to avoid rebound effects situations where apparent gains are offset by increased use or demand. For example, easier screening enabled by AI may lead to higher patient throughput and more procedures, potentially increasing overall material use despite per-case efficiencies. Sustainability measures must be monitored over time to ensure that gains are real and not cancelled by increased activity.

High-sensitivity AI tools may also result in more referrals or more frequent follow-ups, which, if not clinically justified, increase resource use rather than reducing it. This calls for disaggregated data analysis to account for variations across patient demographics such as whether tech-savvy patients benefit more from remote engagement than others, potentially creating equity gaps.

Regular audits, both environmental and clinical, are critical. These ensure that the net effect of AI and other sustainability interventions reflects lower resource consumption, rather than hidden increases in procedural volume. Data should be analyzed by patient group, procedure type, and time periodto capture any unintended consequences.

In summary, by devising clear KPIs, using LCAs to compare workflows, evaluating financial and environmental ROI, and routinely monitoring data for unintended effects, dental practices can demonstrate the real sustainability impacts of innovation and ensure that AI deployment supports truly sustainable care.

BARRIERS, RISKS & ETHICAL ISSUES IN DENTAL AI FOR SUSTAINABILITY

Data Challenges and Bias

One of the biggest challenges in using AI in dental settings is the data itself. Most dental AI systems are trained on small datasets collected from a few clinics, and these datasets often come from different machines, formats, and record-keeping systems. This makes it hard for an AI model trained in one clinic to work well in another. Because many datasets lack diversity, with few images from non-Caucasian patients or from underserved populations, AI models can show poorer performance for those groups. A model that works well for one demographic may not work as reliably in another, which can lead to unequal care (Uribe et al., 2024).

Standardizing dental imaging formats and building shared, diverse image libraries are important steps toward solving this problem, but this requires cooperation between clinics, researchers, and vendors.

Generalizability and Validation

Even if a dental AI model works well in one clinical environment, it may not perform the same in another because of differences in X-ray machines, patient populations, or clinical workflows. This issue is called generalizability. To trust an

AI tool, it must be tested in multiple settings and checked regularly to make sure its performance does not drift over time (Araidy et al., 2025).

Without proper local validation, an AI recommendation could be misleading, potentially resulting in misdiagnosis or unnecessary treatment — outcomes that contradict both patient safety and sustainability goals.

Interpretability and Clinical Trust

Many AI models — especially deep learning systems — are "black boxes." This means they can make accurate predictions, but clinicians do not always understand how the model arrived at that outcome. For many dentists, relying on a decision without a clear explanation feels uncomfortable, especially when patient care is at stake (Rane et al., 2024).

Explainable AI techniques, such as heatmaps showing which part of an image influenced a diagnosis or confidence scores that indicate how sure a model is, can help build trust. Even so, clinicians must be trained to interpret these outputs and to use AI as a partner not a replacement for professional judgment (Houssein et al., 2025).

Liability and Regulation

AI in healthcare raises important legal questions: if an AI tool misses a lesion or recommends treatment that leads to harm, who is responsible? The dentist? The clinic? The software developer? Right now, regulatory systems for AI in medicine and dentistry are still catching up. In many countries, dental AI tools must meet general medical device regulations (like FDA approval in the United States or CE marking in Europe), but specific standards for AI are still emerging (Jenko et al., 2025).

This uncertainty can make dental practices hesitant to adopt AI tools. Clear regulatory frameworks that include requirements for transparency, safety testing, and ongoing monitoring would help clinics adopt AI with greater confidence.

AI's Own Environmental Cost

While AI can help make dental practice more sustainable, it is not "free" in environmental terms. Large AI models — especially those running in cloud data centers use significant computing power and energy for training, storage, and cooling. If a practice runs a large AI service via the cloud every day, that energy use contributes to its overall carbon footprint.

Choosing AI vendors that operate data centers powered by renewable energy or adopting edge computing (where AI runs on local hardware rather than in the cloud) can help reduce this impact. Practices should consider tracking AI energy use (for example, GPU hours or server uptime) as part of their sustainability accounting (Das & Chandra, 2023).

Access and Equity

Another risk is that advanced AI tools may only be affordable for well-resourced clinics in urban areas. Smaller practices in rural or low-income regions may not have the budget for sophisticated AI systems, potentially widening the gap between high-performing and underserved clinics. If only wealthy practices benefit from AI's efficiency and sustainability gains, the overall carbon impact of dental care may not improve as expected (Babar et al., 2024).

Solutions like federated learning (where AI models are trained collaboratively across multiple clinics without sharing patient data) and open-source tools could help democratize access. Policymakers could also consider incentives, subsidies, or group purchasing arrangements to help small practices adopt AI tools responsibly (Shah et al., 2025).

Overdiagnosis and Behavioural Effects

Highly sensitive AI systems might also identify findings that are clinically insignificant, leading to unnecessary follow-up procedures or patient anxiety. This phenomenon sometimes called **overdiagnosis** can increase resource use rather than reduce it, undermining sustainability goals (Hatherley, 2024).

For example, if an AI model flags very early enamel changes as "disease," a clinician might feel pressured to intervene earlier than necessary, leading to additional appointments, materials, and energy use. Balancing sensitivity with specificity is an ethical issue as much as a technical one, and clinicians should always contextualize AI outputs within their clinical judgment.

Tracking trends over time such as whether the number of procedures per patient increases after AI adoption can help practices spot and correct rebound effects where environmental gains are offset by increased volume.

Best Practices & Design Principles for Sustainable Dental AI

Lightweight Models for Dental Imaging

When building AI for dental imaging such as tooth detection or lesion classification it is important to use lightweight models that don't require huge computing resources. Compact neural networks can be optimized for common dental images by using techniques like model pruning, quantization, and knowledge distillation, which reduce model size and energy needs without dramatically affecting accuracy (Różycki et al., 2025).

Model pruning removes unnecessary connections in neural networks, so the system runs faster and uses less power, while knowledge distillation transfers insight from larger models to smaller ones. These approaches help ensure that an AI tool can run efficiently on a local computer or tablet right in the clinic, rather than relying on energy-intensive cloud processing. The net result is a smaller carbon footprint for everyday use, which aligns with sustainability goals in both dentistry and broader healthcare AI (Różycki et al., 2025).

This kind of model efficiency is especially important when tools are deployed chairside for tasks like caries screening or automated landmarking on radiographs, where quick, low-power inference can both speed workflow and reduce electricity use.

Edge AI (Local Processing)

To reduce energy use and protect patient privacy, it's increasingly valuable to run AI locally on devices rather than in distant cloud servers. Edge computing — where the AI performs inference directly on an X-ray machine, a chairside computer, or a mobile device — cuts down on the energy cost associated with uploading and downloading large image files. AI that runs on-site avoids repeated transmission of data over networks and removes the ongoing energy draw of remote servers (Ficili et al., 2025).

In dental settings, this means an AI-enabled imaging unit could instantly analyze an OPG or bitewing image without needing to send anything to the cloud. That not only speeds up the diagnostic process, but also saves network bandwidth, reduces latency, and, importantly, reduces the overall energy footprint associated with frequent data transfers.

When AI runs locally, patient data stays within the clinic's secure systems, which simplifies compliance with privacy laws like HIPAA or GDPR and enhances trust with patients.

Data Efficiency

AI models thrive on large datasets, but collecting and storing massive volumes of images poses sustainability challenges, including energy use for storage and compliance burdens. Practices should focus on data efficiency: use smart data augmentation (such as rotating or scaling existing images to generate new training examples) and synthetic data generation to expand training datasets without capturing redundant images (Różycki et al., 2025).

Only clinically necessary images should be stored, and duplicate scans should be routinely deleted after appropriate review. This not only shrinks the data footprint but also reduces storage costs and the energy needed to maintain large databases.

Another promising approach is federated learning, where AI models are trained collaboratively across multiple dental clinics without sharing the raw data itself. Each clinic keeps its images local, and only model updates are shared. This preserves patient privacy while allowing models to learn from diverse sources and often leads to more robust and generalizeable AI systems (Abbas, 2024).

Since federated learning keeps data on local devices and avoids large centralized repositories, it also reduces the need for extensive data storage infrastructure and energy-intensive database maintenance.

Workflow Integration

For sustainability efforts to be effective, AI tools must fit naturally into existing dental workflows rather than adding extra steps. If a system forces clinicians to jump between software, fill out extra forms, or manually transfer data, staff will find workarounds, and the tool will be under-utilized.

Good design means that sustainability features are visible in the tools dentists already use. For example, an AI system might automatically suggest a low-dose imaging option when it detects a good quality panoramic image has already been captured, or it might flag unnecessary repeat imaging in the workflow itself (Al-ghauli et al., 2025).

These suggestions should appear contextually for example, in the same screen where clinicians review results so that staff don't need separate apps or modules. Engaging dentists, hygienists, assistants, and IT staff in the design process (also known as user-centred design) ensures that sustainability enhancements are not only technically sound but also practical.

Vendor Sustainability Assessments

Choosing the right AI vendor matters. When evaluating AI solutions, dental practices should look beyond performance metrics and ask about environmental policies. Vendors that transparently report energy usage and carbon footprint of their AI services — including data center emissions provide better information for clinics trying to meet sustainability goals.

Prefer companies that use renewable energy or that participate in carbon offset programmes for their data centers and services. Some AI frameworks even provide green metrics such as GPU hours used or estimated energy consumption per task. Clinics can monitor these metrics to understand how much environmental cost is associated with each AI feature they deploy (Różycki et al., 2025).

Collaborative, Multidisciplinary Design

Finally, building truly sustainable dental AI requires collaboration across disciplines. Dentists and dental staff bring essential clinical insight, but environmental scientists, data scientists, and lifecycle engineers provide perspective on energy use, material choices, and carbon accounting. Bringing these voices together helps practices make informed decisions about sustainability trade-offs.

For example, a lifecycle engineer can help estimate how much carbon is saved when an AI tool reduces unnecessary CBCT scans, or how energy efficiency gains compare to the energy cost of running the AI. This kind of auditing tracking the AI's decisions over time and feeding back results into model retraining ensures continuous improvement.

Transparency and accountability are critical. Sustainability review boards, ethical oversight committees, and ongoing monitoring all help keep the focus where it belongs: on tools that not only improve dental care but do so in ways that are environmentally responsible and socially equitable (Dobrzański et al., 2020).

DENTAL CASE STUDIES & PILOTS

Although large-scale studies on AI for sustainable dentistry are still limited, several pilot projects highlight the real-world potential of combining monitoring, digital screening, and remote care to reduce environmental impact and improve access to oral health.

One example from sustainability outside of AI comes from a dental school in Malaysia, where an intensive recycling program was put in place to measure environmental impact. Over a 12-month period, the project recycled approximately 444 kg of materials, which was estimated to offset about 813 kg of CO_2 emissions by diverting waste from landfill and reducing the energy associated with procuring and disposing of materials. This pilot demonstrates how tracking resource use and waste management can provide measurable sustainability gains in oral health settings, even before the adoption of AI tools (Fisal et al., 2025).

In terms of AI-enabled pilots, there is growing evidence that smartphone-based tools can support remote dental screening. One notable project developed an AI-powered smartphone application called AICaries, which allows parents or caregivers to take dental photos of children's teeth and use the app to detect potential caries. In usability testing, the app achieved high acceptability among users, with most parent-taken photos being of sufficient quality for the AI tool to assess caries risk. Parents noted that this at-home screening empowered early detection and created opportunities for earlier follow-up care (Al-Jallad et al., 2022).

Remote screening can reduce unnecessary clinic visits, especially in communities with limited access to dentists. Research on teledentistry shows that using mobile intraoral photographs for remote screening can be a valid and reliable method for detecting dental caries, with performance comparable to traditional in-person exams. This supports the idea that remote AI-enhanced screening tools can help catch early disease while cutting down on travel-related emissions and clinic resource use (Azimi et al., 2025).

During the COVID-19 pandemic, many clinics integrated AI-assisted triage into teledentistry platforms to manage appointments more sustainably. Dentists were able to cancel or reschedule non-urgent visits, focusing in-person time on urgent cases and reducing the overhead of running clinics at full capacity. This not only helped maintain continuity of care when physical visits were restricted, but also indirectly lowered energy use and travel emissions associated with routine check-ups (Kumar et al., 2021).

Taken together, these pilots whether focused on recycling impact or early AI screening and triage show that sustainability in dentistry is achievable through monitoring, remote care, and smarter use of technology. They point to a future where routine oral health management can be both clinically effective and environmentally responsible.

FUTURE TRENDS & GAPS IN DENTAL SUSTAINABLE AI

As dentistry continues to embrace technology, we're seeing exciting new trends in how artificial intelligence (AI) is used not just to improve patient care but also to support eco-friendly practices.

One major shift is toward edge computing. This means running AI models directly on devices like dental chairside computers or even smartphones, instead of relying on energy-hungry cloud servers. This not only cuts down data transfer and carbon emissions but also boosts privacy for patients. Imagine an X-ray sensor with built-in AI that gives instant feedback without uploading anything to the cloud. It's fast, secure, and greener.

Federated Learning: A Team Effort Across Clinics

Another growing trend is federated learning. Think of it like AI training across multiple clinics—but without sharing raw patient data. Each clinic helps improve the AI model locally, and only the learnings (not the actual files) are shared. This approach is especially helpful in gathering diverse data—like rare dental conditions from rural and urban practices alike. It helps build better, fairer models while respecting privacy.

For AI to truly support dentists, it has to be transparent. That's where explainable AI comes in. Instead of just saying "there's a cavity," the system might show a red-highlighted area on the X-ray and give a confidence score (e.g., 92% chance it's decay). These kinds of tools help dentists trust what the AI is saying and make better, safer decisions.

Sustainable AI Standards & Validation Are Missing

Right now, one of the biggest gaps is the lack of standardization. Dental imaging data isn't always labeled the same way, and different clinics use different machines. That makes it tough to train consistent, ethical AI models. What we really need are open-source, annotated dental image datasets—similar to what radiology has. Accreditation bodies might soon require AI tools to display their energy use or carbon footprint so clinics can choose greener options.

Lastly, we need to move beyond short pilot studies. Future research should look at both clinical outcomes and environmental impact. Imagine comparing two similar clinics—one using AI-based scheduling, one not—and measuring patient wait times and total electricity used per year. That kind of real-world data will help us improve AI over time and spot any problems early on.

CONCLUSIONS AND DENTAL SUSTAINIBILTY FRAMEWORK

Sustainability in dentistry is no longer just an abstract ideal, it's becoming a clinical reality, powered by data and driven by design. Across everything we've explored, from reducing X-ray retakes to smarter scheduling, AI shows up not just as a technological add-on, but as a practical enabler of greener, leaner care.

What's exciting is that many of these shifts don't require dramatic overhauls. They emerge from small, well-informed tweaks: using edge AI to avoid cloud energy drains, embedding low-waste suggestions into routine workflows, or even just measuring what we previously ignored like the number of saved patient trips thanks to teledentistry. These changes compound over time.

But it's not just about carbon. It's about clinical efficiency, cost savings, equity, and ethics. A sustainable dental clinic is also often a more resilient, transparent, and trusted one. It uses fewer materials, treats patients smarter, and relies on systems that learn and improve—just like we do.

That said, AI is no silver bullet. If left unchecked, it can drive overdiagnosis, widen digital divides, or generate its own energy burdens. The goal isn't to use more technology for its own sake, but to use it more wisely with clear frameworks, measured impact, and continual feedback.

So, what's the way forward? It starts with intentionality. With designing systems that align planetary health and oral health, not as trade-offs, but as parallel goals.

DENTAL SUSTAINABILITY FRAMEWORK (The "4R-AI" Model)

This compact framework helps dentists remember key areas to focus on while adopting AI for a more sustainable practice:

1. REDEFINE

- Rethink traditional workflows: Ask—where does waste come from? Which steps can be replaced or improved by smart tools?
- Example: Use AI for triaging radiographs before printing or referrals.

2. REDUCE

- Minimize repeat procedures, materials, and energy through intelligent systems.
- Example: AI image quality checks to avoid re-taking X-rays or CBCTs.

3. REPLACE

- Swap high-footprint tasks with digital, low-impact alternatives.
- Example: Move to AI-enabled digital impressions and in-house milling instead of physical shipping.

4. REPORT

- Track, measure, and share your sustainability metrics.
- Example: Calculate travel miles avoided via teleconsultations, or carbon saved through fewer material orders.

AI ETHICS

- Layer every decision with ethical awareness: data fairness, clinical trust, patient transparency, and regulatory readiness.
- Example: Choose explainable AI and ensure every algorithm used is validated for your patient population.

Figure 4. Dental sustainability framework

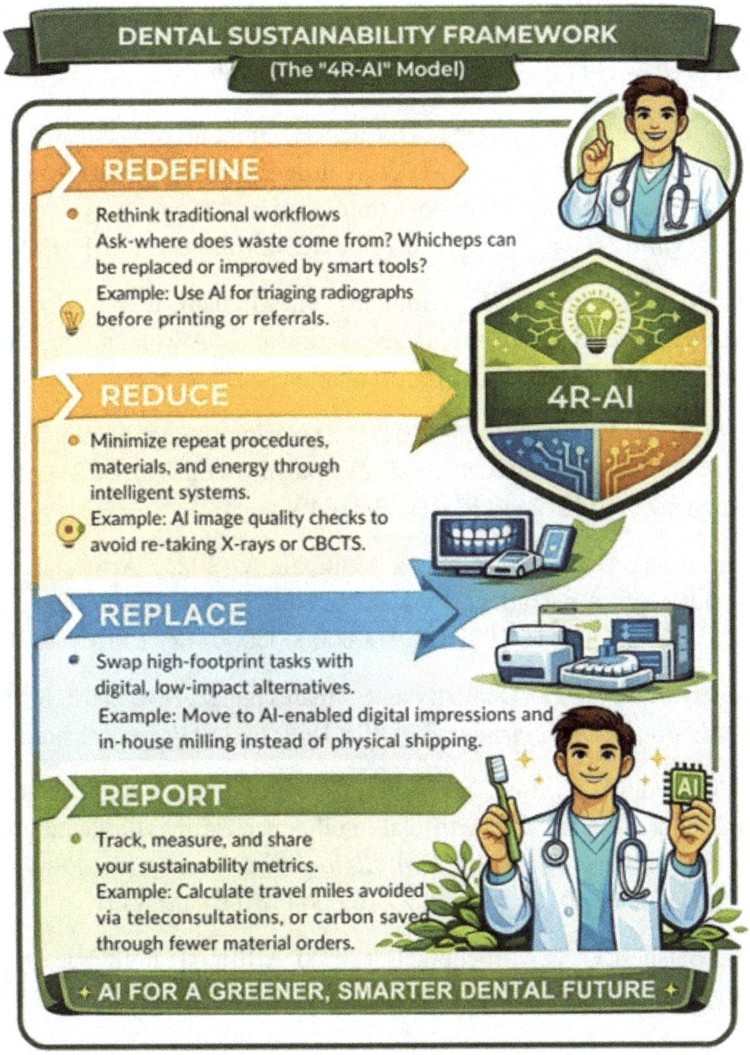

REFERENCES

Abbas, S. R., Abbas, Z., Zahir, A., & Lee, S. W. (2024). Healthcare. *Health Care, 12*(24), 2587. DOI: 10.3390/healthcare12242587 PMID: 39766014

Abbod, E., Al-Waily, M., Al-Hadrayi, M. R., Resan, K., & Abbas, S. M. (2020). Numerical and experimental analysis to predict life of removable partial denture. *IOP Conference Series. Materials Science and Engineering, 870*(1), 012149. DOI: 10.1088/1757-899X/870/1/012149

Al-Jallad, N., Ly-Mapes, O., Hao, P., Ruan, J., Ramesh, A., & Luo, J.. (2022). AI-powered smartphone application AICaries. *PLOS Digital Health, 1*(6), e0000046. DOI: 10.1371/journal.pdig.0000046 PMID: 36381137

Albano, D., Galiano, V., Basile, M., Di Luca, F., Gitto, S., Messina, C., Cagetti, M. G., Del Fabbro, M., Tartaglia, G. M., & Sconfienza, L. M. (2024). Artificial intelligence for radiographic imaging detection of caries lesions: A systematic review. *BMC Oral Health, 24*(1), 274. DOI: 10.1186/s12903-024-04046-7 PMID: 38402191

.Alghauli, M. A., Aljohani, W., Almutairi, S., Aljohani, R., & Alqutaibi, A. Y. (2025). Advancements in digital data acquisition and CAD technology in dentistry. *Clinical eHealth, 8*, 32–52. DOI: 10.1016/j.cline.2025.03.005

Alharbi, S. S., & Alhasson, H. F. (2024). Exploring the applications of artificial intelligence in dental image detection. *Diagnostics (Basel), 14*(21), 2442. DOI: 10.3390/diagnostics14212442 PMID: 39518408

Ali, M., Irfan, M., Ali, T., Wei, C. R., & Akilimali, A. (2025). Artificial intelligence in dental radiology: A narrative review. *Annals of Medicine and Surgery (London), 87*(4), 2212–2217. DOI: 10.1097/MS9.0000000000003127 PMID: 40212156

AlShammery, A. R. (2021). Dentistry and climate change: How can dentists contribute? *Saudi Journal of Oral Sciences, 8*(3), 121. DOI: 10.4103/sjoralsci.sjoralsci_58_21

Aradya, A., Koduru, S., Ravi, M. B., Raghavendra Swamy, K. N., Ganesh, S., & Pradeep Chandra, K.. (2025). Artificial intelligence for maxillofacial prosthodontics: A scoping review. *Journal of Oral Biology and Craniofacial Research, 15*(6), 1749–1766. DOI: 10.1016/j.jobcr.2025.10.006 PMID: 41158531

Araidy, S., Batshon, G., & Mirochnik, R. (2025). Artificial intelligence applications in dentistry: A systematic review. *Oral, 5*(4), 90. DOI: 10.3390/oral5040090

Azimi, S., Bennamoun, B., Mehdizadeh, M., Vignarajan, J., Xiao, D., Huang, B., Spallek, H., Irving, M., Kruger, E., Tennant, M., & Estai, M. (2025). Teledentistry improves access to oral care. *Health Care, 13*(18), 2282. DOI: 10.3390/healthcare13182282 PMID: 41008414

Babar, A., Ali, R., Oduoye, M. O., Noor, Z., & Chris, K. (2024). Exploring the impact of artificial intelligence on global health. *Journal of Primary Care & Community Health, 15*, 21501319241245847. DOI: 10.1177/21501319241245847 PMID: 38605668

Batra, P., Tagra, H., & Katyal, S. (2022). Artificial intelligence in teledentistry. *Discoveries (Craiova, Romania), 10*(3), e153. DOI: 10.15190/d.2022.12 PMID: 36530958

Borglin, L., Pekarski, S., Saget, S., & Duane, B. (2021). The life cycle analysis of a dental examination. *Community Dentistry and Oral Epidemiology, 49*(6), 581–593. DOI: 10.1111/cdoe.12630 PMID: 33686705

Carrillo-Perez, F., Pecho, O. E., Morales, J. C., Paravina, R. D., Della Bona, A., Ghinea, R., Pulgar, R., Pérez, M. M., & Herrera, L. J. (2022). Applications of artificial intelligence in dentistry: A comprehensive review. *Journal of Esthetic and Restorative Dentistry, 34*(1), 259–280. DOI: 10.1111/jerd.12844 PMID: 34842324

Chalotra, R., Shenoy, R., Dasson Bajaj, P., Rao, A., Pai, M., Jodalli, P., Br, A., Priya, H., & D'Souza, V. (2025). A scoping review exploring carbon emissions in dentistry—A step towards sustainability. *BMC Oral Health, 25*(1), 1674. DOI: 10.1186/s12903-025-06952-w PMID: 41146088

Chen, Y. W., Stanley, K., & Att, W. (2020). Artificial intelligence in dentistry: Current applications and future perspectives. *Quintessence International, 51*(3), 248–257. DOI: 10.3290/j.qi.a43952 PMID: 32020135

Clement, D. O. A., Olawade, D. B., Vanderbloemen, L., Rotifa, O. B., Fidelis, S. C., & Egbon, E.. (2025). AI-driven advances in low-dose imaging and enhancement—A review. *Diagnostics (Basel), 15*(6), 689. DOI: 10.3390/diagnostics15060689 PMID: 40150031

Cui, Z., Fang, Y., Mei, L., Zhang, B., Yu, B., Liu, J., Jiang, C., Sun, Y., Ma, L., Huang, J., Liu, Y., Zhao, Y., Lian, C., Ding, Z., Zhu, M., & Shen, D. (2022). A fully automatic AI system for tooth and alveolar bone segmentation from cone-beam CT images. *Nature Communications, 13*(1), 2096. DOI: 10.1038/s41467-022-29637-2 PMID: 35440592

Das, K. P., & Chandra, J. (2023). A survey on artificial intelligence for reducing the climate footprint in healthcare. *Energy Nexus*, *9*, 100167. DOI: 10.1016/j.nexus.2022.100167

Di Spirito, F., Giordano, F., Di Palo, M. P., De Benedetto, G., Aulisio, L., & Boccia, G. (2025). Sustainable dental and periodontal practice: A narrative review on the 4R-framework. *Dentistry Journal*, *13*(9), 392. DOI: 10.3390/dj13090392 PMID: 41002665

Ding, H., Wu, J., Zhao, W., Matinlinna, J. P., Burrow, M. F., & Tsoi, J. K. H. (2023). Artificial intelligence in dentistry—A review. *Frontiers in Dental Medicine*, *4*, 1085251. DOI: 10.3389/fdmed.2023.1085251 PMID: 39935549

Dobrzański, L. A., Dobrzański, L. B., Dobrzańska-Danikiewicz, A. D., & Dobrzańska, J. (2020). The concept of sustainable development of modern dentistry. *Processes (Basel, Switzerland)*, *8*(12), 1605. DOI: 10.3390/pr8121605

Drew, J., Christie, S. D., Rainham, D., & Rizan, C. (2022). HealthcareLCA: An open-access living database of health-care environmental impact assessments. *The Lancet. Planetary Health*, *6*(12), e1000–e1012. DOI: 10.1016/S2542-5196(22)00257-1 PMID: 36495883

Duane, B., Borglin, L., Pekarski, S., Saget, S., & Duncan, H. F. (2020). Environmental sustainability in endodontics: A life cycle assessment of a root canal treatment procedure. *BMC Oral Health*, *20*(1), 348. DOI: 10.1186/s12903-020-01337-7 PMID: 33261595

Duane, B., Hyland, J., Rowan, J. S., & Archibald, B. (2012). Taking a bite out of Scotland's dental carbon emissions in the transition to a low carbon future. *Public Health*, *126*(9), 770–777. DOI: 10.1016/j.puhe.2012.05.032 PMID: 22902137

Duane, B., Ramasubbu, D., Harford, S., Steinbach, I., Stancliffe, R., & Ballantyne, G. (2019). Environmental sustainability and biodiversity within the dental practice. *British Dental Journal*, *226*(9), 701–705. DOI: 10.1038/s41415-019-0208-8 PMID: 31076704

Duane, B., Ramasubbu, D., Harford, S., Steinbach, I., Stancliffe, R., Croasdale, K., & Pasdeki-Clewer, E. (2019). Environmental sustainability and procurement: Purchasing products for the dental setting. *British Dental Journal*, *226*(6), 453–458. DOI: 10.1038/s41415-019-0080-6 PMID: 30903074

Duane, B., Stancliffe, R., Miller, F. A., Sherman, J., & Pasdeki-Clewer, E. (2020). Sustainability in dentistry: A multifaceted approach needed. *Journal of Dental Research*, *99*(9), 998–1003. DOI: 10.1177/0022034520919391 PMID: 32392435

Duane, B., & Steinbach, I. (2024). What is the environmental footprint of a dental practice? A life cycle analysis (Part 1). *British Dental Journal.* Advance online publication. DOI: 10.1038/s41415-023-6710-z PMID: 38212528

Eliades, T., Adel, S. M., Akyalçin, S., Atsawasuwan, P., Foong, K. W. C., Hiskia, A., Panayi, N., Silikas, N., Allareddy, V., Venugopal, A., Dellinger, A., Perillo, L., & Vaiid, N. (2025). Environmental footprints in orthodontics: The World Federation of Orthodontists' white paper on sustainable practices, challenges and research imperatives. *Journal of the World Federation of Orthodontists, 14*(4), 194–201. DOI: 10.1016/j.ejwf.2025.06.003 PMID: 40675890

Ficili, I., Giacobbe, M., Tricomi, G., & Puliafito, A. (2025). From sensors to data intelligence. *Sensors (Basel), 25*(6), 1763. DOI: 10.3390/s25061763 PMID: 40292910

Fisal, A., Rohani, M., Nor, N. A., & Tengku Hamzah, T. N. (2025). Reductions in clinical waste and environmental emissions through recycling and waste segregation in a dental school. *British Dental Journal.* Advance online publication. DOI: 10.1038/s41415-025-8913-y PMID: 41272111

Fisal, A. A., Rohani, M. M., Nor, N. A., & Tengku Hamzah, T. N. N. (2025). Reductions in clinical waste and environmental emissions through recycling and waste segregation in a dental school: A cross-sectional study. *British Dental Journal.* Advance online publication. DOI: 10.1038/s41415-025-8913-y PMID: 41272111

Grose, J., Burns, L., Mukonoweshuro, R., Richardson, J., Mills, I., Nasser, M., & Moles, D. (2018). Developing sustainability in a dental practice through an action research approach. *British Dental Journal, 225*(5), 409–413. DOI: 10.1038/sj.bdj.2018.738 PMID: 30168816

Guerra, M., Morgado, M., Leira, Y., Leitão, T., Botelho, J., & Mendes, J. J. (2025). Integrating sustainability in dentistry: A pathway towards achieving the UN 2030 agenda. *Frontiers in Oral Health, 6*, 1549020. DOI: 10.3389/froh.2025.1549020 PMID: 40717797

Gupta, E., Maysan, S., Murella, S., Saju, A. R., Grover, S., & Vasudeva, A. (2025). Recent dental practices using artificial intelligence (AI): A survey. *Bioinformation, 21*(3), 514–521. DOI: 10.6026/973206300210514 PMID: 40599924

Hankendi, C., Coskun, A. K., & Sovacool, B. K. (2025). Why transparency matters for sustainable data centers and carbon-neutral artificial intelligence (AI). *iScience, 28*(11), 113705. DOI: 10.1016/j.isci.2025.113705 PMID: 41244593

Hatherley, J. (2024). Data over dialogue: Why artificial intelligence is unlikely to humanise medicine. *SSRN.* DOI: 10.2139/ssrn.5256823

Houssein, E. H., Gamal, A. M., Younis, E. M. G., & Mohamed, E. (2025). Explainable artificial intelligence for medical imaging systems. *Cluster Computing*, *28*(7), 469. DOI: 10.1007/s10586-025-05281-5

Hsu, L. P., Huang, Y. K., & Chang, Y. C. (2022). The implementation of artificial intelligence in dentistry could enhance environmental sustainability. *Journal of Dental Sciences*, *17*(2), 1081–1082. DOI: 10.1016/j.jds.2022.02.002 PMID: 35756807

International Organization for Standardization. (2024). *ISO 20121:2024 event sustainability management systems—Requirements with guidance for use*. ISO.

Jenko, S., Papadopoulou, E., Kumar, V., Overman, S. S., Krepelkova, K., Wilson, J., Dunbar, E., Spice, C., & Exarchos, T. (2025). Artificial intelligence in healthcare. *AI*, *6*(6), 116. DOI: 10.3390/ai6060116

Khosravi, M., Zare, Z., Mojtabaeian, S. M., & Izadi, R. (2024). Artificial intelligence and decision-making in healthcare: A thematic analysis of a systematic review of reviews. *Health Services Research and Managerial Epidemiology*, *11*, 23333928241234863. DOI: 10.1177/23333928241234863 PMID: 38449840

Kot, W. Y., Au Yeung, S. Y., Leung, Y. Y., Leung, P. H., & Yang, W. F. (2025). Evolution of deep learning tooth segmentation from CT/CBCT images: A systematic review and meta-analysis. *BMC Oral Health*, *25*(1), 800. DOI: 10.1186/s12903-025-05984-6 PMID: 40420051

Kumar, G., Rehman, F., Al-Muzian, L., Farsi, D., & Hiremath, S. (2021). Global scenario of teledentistry during COVID-19 pandemic. *International Journal of Clinical Pediatric Dentistry*, *14*(3), 426–429. DOI: 10.5005/jp-journals-10005-1952 PMID: 34720519

Lyne, A., Ashley, P., Saget, S., Porto Costa, M., Underwood, B., & Duane, B. (2020). Combining evidence-based healthcare with environmental sustainability: Using the toothbrush as a model. *British Dental Journal*, *229*(5), 303–309. DOI: 10.1038/s41415-020-1981-0 PMID: 32918023

Mao, K., Thu, K. M., Hung, K. F., Yu, O. Y., Hsung, R. T., & Lam, W. Y. (2025). Artificial intelligence in detecting periodontal disease from intraoral photographs: A systematic review. *International Dental Journal*, *75*(5), 100883. DOI: 10.1016/j.identj.2025.100883 PMID: 40639137

Moharrami, M., Vahab, E., Bagherianlemraski, M., Hemmati, G., Singhal, S., Quinonez, C., Schwendicke, F., & Glogauer, M. (2025). Deep learning for detecting dental plaque and gingivitis from oral photographs. *Community Dentistry and Oral Epidemiology*, *53*(6), 617–632. DOI: 10.1111/cdoe.70001 PMID: 40571994

Mulimani, P. (2017). Green dentistry: The art and science of sustainable practice. *British Dental Journal, 222*(12), 954–961. DOI: 10.1038/sj.bdj.2017.546 PMID: 28642517

Ohene-Botwe, B., Amedu, C., Antwi, W. K., Abdul-Razak, W., Kyei, K. A., Arkoh, S., Mudadi, L.-S., Mushosho, E. Y., Bwanga, O., Chinene, B., Nyawani, P., Mutandiro, L. C., & Piersson, A. D. (2024). Promoting sustainability activities in clinical radiography practice and education in resource-limited countries. *Radiography, 30*(Suppl 1), 56–61. DOI: 10.1016/j.radi.2024.06.007 PMID: 38905726

Petersen, P. E., & Ogawa, H. (2012). The global burden of periodontal disease: Towards integration with chronic disease prevention and control. *Periodontology 2000, 60*(1), 15–39. DOI: 10.1111/j.1600-0757.2011.00425.x PMID: 22909104

Pichler, P. P., Jaccard, I. S., Weisz, U., & Weisz, H. (2019). International trade and the transboundary displacement of carbon emissions. *Environmental Research Letters, 14*, 064004. DOI: 10.1088/1748-9326/ab19e1

Pithon, M. M., Faria, L. C. M., Tanaka, O. M., Ruellas, A. C. O., & Primo, L. S. S. G. (2017). Sustainability in orthodontics: What can we do to save our planet? *Dental Press Journal of Orthodontics, 22*(4), 113–117. DOI: 10.1590/2177-6709.22.4.113-117.sar PMID: 28902257

Rahimpour, S., & Zahraee, S. Y. (2015). System dynamics model for optimizing recycling and collection of waste material in a closed-loop supply chain. *Simulation Modelling Practice and Theory, 53*, 88–102. DOI: 10.1016/j.simpat.2015.02.001

Rane, J., Mallick, S. K., Kaya, O., & Rane, N. L. (2024). Enhancing black-box models: Advances in explainable artificial intelligence. In *Future research opportunities for artificial intelligence in Industry 4.0 and 5.0* (pp. 136–180). Deep Science Publishing. DOI: 10.70593/978-81-981271-0-5_4

Raza Falsk. (2023). *AI for predictive maintenance in industrial systems*. DOI: 10.13140/RG.2.2.27313.35688

Richardson, J., Grose, J., Manzi, S., Mills, I., Moles, D. R., Mukonoweshuro, R., Nasser, M., & Nichols, A. (2016). What's in a bin: A case study of dental clinical waste composition and potential greenhouse gas emission savings. *British Dental Journal, 220*(2), 61–66. DOI: 10.1038/sj.bdj.2016.55 PMID: 26794110

Różycki, R., Solarska, D. A., & Waligóra, G. (2025). Energy-aware machine learning models. *Energies, 18*(11), 2810. DOI: 10.3390/en18112810

Sanz, M., Kamma, J., Goldstein, M., & Tonetti, M. (2025). The impact of the European Federation of Periodontology on European and global periodontology. *Periodontology 2000*, prd.12620. DOI: 10.1111/prd.12620 PMID: 39891466

Shah, S. T., Ali, Z., Waqar, M., & Kim, A. (2025). Federated learning in public health. *Health Care, 13*(21), 2760. DOI: 10.3390/healthcare13212760 PMID: 41228128

Shellard, I. J., Martin, N., Mulligan, S., & Hatton, P. (2022). *Consensus on environmentally sustainable oral healthcare: A joint stakeholder statement*. White Rose University Press.

Shinkai, R. S. A., Biazevic, M. G. H., Michel-Crosato, E., & Toyota de Campos, T. (2025). Environmental sustainability related to dental materials and procedures in prosthodontics: A critical review. *The Journal of Prosthetic Dentistry, 133*(6), 1466–1473. DOI: 10.1016/j.prosdent.2023.05.024 PMID: 37709614

Smith, L., Ali, M., Agrissais, M., Mulligan, S., Koh, L., & Martin, N. (2023). A comparative life cycle assessment of dental restorative materials. *Dental Materials, 39*(1), 13–24. DOI: 10.1016/j.dental.2022.11.007 PMID: 36428112

Speroni, S., & Polizzi, E. (2025). Green dentistry: State of the art and possible development proposals. *Dentistry Journal, 13*(1), 38. DOI: 10.3390/dj13010038 PMID: 39851612

.Steinbach, I., Stancliffe, R., Berners-Lee, M., & Duane, B. (2018). *Carbon modelling within dentistry: Towards a sustainable future*.

Surdu, A., Foia, C. I., Luchian, I., Trifan, D., Budala, D. G., Scutariu, M. M., Ciupilan, C., Puha, B., & Tatarciuc, D. (2025). Telemedicine and digital tools in dentistry: Enhancing diagnosis and remote patient care. *Medicina, 61*(5), 826. DOI: 10.3390/medicina61050826 PMID: 40428784

Suresh, P., Crotty, J., Tesanovic, S., Alaweed, O., Doyle, S., Kiandee, M., Hayes, E., Umeh, V., Khalilinejad, B., & Duane, B. (2024). A life cycle analysis of the environmental impact of procurement, waste and water in the dental practice. *British Dental Journal, 236*(7), 545–551. DOI: 10.1038/s41415-024-7239-5 PMID: 38609622

Taylor, R. A., Sangal, R. B., Smith, M. E., Haimovich, A. D., Rodman, A., Iscoe, M. S., Pavuluri, S. K., Rose, C., Janke, A. T., Wright, D. S., Socrates, V., & Declan, A. (2025). Leveraging artificial intelligence to reduce diagnostic errors in emergency medicine. *Academic Emergency Medicine, 32*(3), 327–339. DOI: 10.1111/acem.15066 PMID: 39676165

Uribe, S., Issa, J., Sohrabniya, F., Denny, A., Kim, N., Dayo, A., Chaurasia, A., Sofi-Mahmudi, A., Büttner, M., & Schwendicke, F. (2024). Publicly available dental image datasets for artificial intelligence. *Journal of Dental Research, 103*(13), 1365–1374. Advancc online publication. DOI: 10.1177/00220345241272052 PMID: 39422586

Vashisht, R., Sharma, A., Kiran, T., Jolly, S., Brar, P., & Puri, J. (2024). Artificial intelligence in dentistry: A scoping review. *Journal of Oral and Maxillofacial Surgery, Medicine, and Pathology*, *36*(4), 579–592. Advance online publication. DOI: 10.1016/j.ajoms.2024.04.009

Vázquez-Sebrango, G., Anitua, E., Macía, I., & Arganda-Carreras, I. (2025). The role of artificial intelligence in implant dentistry: A systematic review. *International Journal of Oral and Maxillofacial Surgery*, *54*(11), 1098–1122. DOI: 10.1016/j.ijom.2025.04.005 PMID: 40436717

World Health Organization. (2022). *Global oral health status report: Towards universal health coverage for oral health by 2030*. WHO.

Zhu, J., Chen, Z., Zhao, J., Yu, Y., Li, X., Shi, K., Zhang, F., Yu, F., Shi, K., Sun, Z., Lin, N., & Zheng, Y. (2023). Artificial intelligence in the diagnosis of dental diseases on panoramic radiographs: A preliminary study. *BMC Oral Health*, *23*(1), 358. DOI: 10.1186/s12903-023-03027-6 PMID: 37270488

Compilation of References

Aas, K., Jullum, M., & Løland, A. (2021). Explaining individual predictions when features are dependent: More accurate approximations to Shapley values. *Artificial Intelligence*, *298*, 103502. DOI: 10.1016/j.artint.2021.103502

Abbas, S. R., Abbas, Z., Zahir, A., & Lee, S. W. (2024). Healthcare. *Health Care*, *12*(24), 2587. DOI: 10.3390/healthcare12242587 PMID: 39766014

Abbod, E., Al-Waily, M., Al-Hadrayi, M. R., Resan, K., & Abbas, S. M. (2020). Numerical and experimental analysis to predict life of removable partial denture. *IOP Conference Series. Materials Science and Engineering*, *870*(1), 012149. DOI: 10.1088/1757-899X/870/1/012149

Abdallah, M. M., & Youssef, M. (2023). Role of Social Media in Enhancing Climate Change Literacy Among Egyptian Users. *Scientific Journal of Public Relations and Advertising Research*, *2023*(25), 1–25. DOI: 10.21608/sjocs.2023.299518

Abdullah, A. H., Alwash, S. M., Salih Abed, W. M., & Al Abboodi, H. M. (2025). Enhanced Maximum Power Point Tracking Using Embedding Deep Networks and Self-Adaptive Genetic Algorithm. *International Journal of Intelligent Engineering & Systems*, *18*(1).

Abdullah, S. H., Abedi, W. M. S., & Hadi, R. M. (2022). Enhanced feature selection algorithm for pneumonia detection. *Periodicals of Engineering and Natural Sciences*, *10*(6), 168–180. DOI: 10.21533/pen.v10.i6.919

Abedi, W. M. S. (2018). Unconsciousness detection supervision system using faster RCNN architecture. *Proceedings of the 2nd International Conference on Future Networks and Distributed Systems*, 1–6. DOI: 10.1145/3231053.3231094

Abedi, W. M. S., Sadiq, A. T., & Nadher, I. (2020). Modified cnn-lstm for pain facial expressions recognition. *International Journal of Advanced Science and Technology*, *29*(3s), 304–312.

Abouraia, M., Nassoura, A. B., Shaker, H., & Harbi, B. A. (2025a). Building a Smart Economy: Exploring AI's role in Oman's economic progress. In Studies in systems, decision and control (pp. 887–896). DOI: 10.1007/978-3-031-88874-8_79

Abouraia, M., Nassoura, A. B., Shaker, H., Abdelfattah, F., & Madi, H. (2025b). Empowering SMEs in Jordan: Leveraging Artificial Intelligence for Digital Marketing success. In Studies in systems, decision and control (pp. 1013–1022). DOI: 10.1007/978-3-031-88874-8_90

Abouraia, M., Nassoura, A. B., Shaker, H., Abdelfattah, F., & Madi, H. (2025c). Exploring Opportunities and Challenges of AI-Driven Marketing in the UAE: A survey of industry Perspectives. In Studies in systems, decision and control (pp. 1033–1042). DOI: 10.1007/978-3-031-88874-8_92

Abu Dhabi Blog. (2025). The Yas SeaWorld® Research & Rescue Center Kicks-Off 2025 Science Talk Series With A Focus On Seagrass. https://blog.abudhabicityguide.com/the-yas-seaworld-research-rescue-center-kicks-off-2025-science-talk-series-with-a-focus-on-seagrass/

Abu Dhabi Media Office. (2023). Yas SeaWorld Research and Rescue Centre, Yas Island, Abu Dhabi, and NYU Abu Dhabi partner to enhance conservation efforts. https://www.mediaoffice.abudhabi/en/tourism/yas-seaworld-research-and-rescue-centre-yas-island-abu-dhabi-and-nyu-abu-dhabi-partner-to-enhance-conservation-efforts

Abu Dhabi Media Office. (2024). *Environment Agency – Abu Dhabi and Yas SeaWorld Research and Rescue Centre Yas Island, Abu Dhabi demonstrate conservation capabilities*. https://www.mediaoffice.abudhabi/en/environment/environment-agency-abu-dhabi-and-yas-seaworld-research-and-rescue-centre-yas-island-abu-dhabi-demonstrate-conservation-capabilities

Abu Dhabi Media Office. (2025). Miral launched an advanced communication and production platform, Atheer. https://www.mediaoffice.abudhabi/en/tourism/miral-launches-advanced-communication-and-production-platform-atheer

Abu Dhabi Media Office. (2025). *Miral launches advanced communication and production platform, Atheer*. https://www.mediaoffice.abudhabi/en/tourism/miral-launches-advanced-communication-and-production-platform-atheer/

Abu Dhabi Media Office. (2025). Miral supports Abu Dhabi communities via its 2024 Corporate Social Responsibility strategy. https://www.mediaoffice.abudhabi/en/tourism/miral-supports-abu-dhabi-communities-via-its-2024-corporate-social-responsibility-strategy

Abu Dhabi Media Office. (2025). Yas SeaWorld Research and Rescue Yas Island, Abu Dhabi. https://www.mediaoffice.abudhabi/en/topic/yas-seaworld-research-and-rescue-yas-island-abu-dhabi

Abuelgasim, A., & Daiban, S. (2017). Levels of Climate Change Awareness in the United Arab Emirates. Horizons in Humanities and Social Sciences: An International Refereed Journal, 2(2) 42-53. https://www.researchgate.net/publication/317566042

Abuhasel, K. (2023). Sustainable Green City Development Project Analysis using the Critical Path Method (CPM) and the Crashing Project Method on Time and Cost Optimization. Engineering, Technology &. *Applied Scientific Research*, *13*(3), 10973–10977. DOI: 10.48084/etasr.5980

Abu-Siam, Y., Alquqa, E. K., Shwedeh, F., Alzoubi, H. M., & El Khatib, M. (2026). *Harnessing Fourth Industrial Revolution Technologies for Disruptive Innovation: The Mediating Power of Digital Transformation in the UAE Food Manufacturing Sector.*

Adedapo, O. A., Solanke, B., Iriogbe, H. O., & Ebeh, C. O. (2023). Conceptual frameworks for evaluating green infrastructure in urban stormwater management. *World Journal of Advanced Research and Reviews*, *19*(3), 1595–1603. DOI: 10.30574/wjarr.2023.19.3.0453

Adeoye, O. B., Addy, W. A., Ajayi-Nifise, A. O., Odeyemi, O., Okoye, C. C., & Ofodile, O. C. (2024). Leveraging AI and data analytics for enhancing financial inclusion in developing economies. *Finance & Accounting Research Journal*, *6*(3), 288–303. DOI: 10.51594/farj.v6i3.856

Aderamo, A. T., Olisakwe, H. C., Adebayo, Y. A., & Esiri, A. E.Adeoye Taofik AderamoHenry Chukwuemeka OlisakweYetunde Adenike AdebayoAndrew Emuobosa Esiri. (2024). AI-driven HSE management systems for risk mitigation in the oil and gas industry. *Comprehensive Research and Reviews in Engineering and Technology*, *2*(1), 1–22. DOI: 10.57219/crret.2024.2.1.0059

Aderamo, A. T., Olisakwe, H. C., Adebayo, Y. A., & Esiri, A. E.Adeoye Taofik AderamoHenry Chukwuemeka OlisakweYetunde Adenike AdebayoAndrew Emuobosa Esiri. (2024). AI-enabled predictive safeguards for offshore oil facilities: Enhancing safety and operational efficiency. *Comprehensive Research and Reviews in Engineering and Technology*, *2*(1), 23–43. DOI: 10.57219/crret.2024.2.1.0060

Afsar, B., & Umrani, W. A. (2020). Transformational leadership and innovative work behavior: The role of motivation to learn, task complexity, and innovation climate. *European Journal of Innovation Management*, *23*(3), 402–428. DOI: 10.1108/EJIM-12-2018-0257

Agarwal, R., & Gupta, B. (2021). Innovation and Leadership: A Study of organizations based in the United Arab Emirates. *Foundations of Management, 13*(1), 73-84. https://intapi.sciendo.com/pdf/10.2478/fman-2021-0006

Agarwal, Y., Ratnani, P., Shah, U., & Jain, P. (2021). IoT based Smart Parking System. *2021 5th International Conference on Intelligent Computing and Control Systems (ICICCS)* (pp. 464-470). Madurai, India: IEEE. Retrieved from DOI: 10.1109/ICICCS51141.2021.9432196

Agyekum, A. K., Fugar, F. D. K., Agyekum, K., Akomea-Frimpong, I., & Pittri, H. (2023). Barriers to stakeholder engagement in sustainable procurement of public works. *Engineering, Construction, and Architectural Management, 30*(9), 3840–3857. DOI: 10.1108/ECAM-08-2021-0746

Ajchariyavanich, C., Limpisthira, T., Chanjarasvichai, N., Jareonwatanan, T., Phongphanpanya, W., Wareechuensuk, S., & Pipattanasomporn, M. (2019). Park King: An IoT-based Smart Parking System. *2019 IEEE International Smart Cities Conference (ISC2)* (pp. 729-734). Casablanca, Morocco: IEEE. Retrieved from DOI: 10.1109/ISC246665.2019.9071721

Ajzen, I. (1991). The theory of planned behavior. *Organizational Behavior and Human Decision Processes, 50*(2), 179–211. DOI: 10.1016/0749-5978(91)90020-T

Al Amri, T., Puskas Khetani, K., & Marey-Perez, M. (2021). Towards sustainable I4. 0: Key skill areas for project managers in GCC construction industry. *Sustainability (Basel), 13*(15), 8121. DOI: 10.3390/su13158121

Al Kurdi, B., Alshurideh, M. T., El Khatib, M., Alrawabdeh, W. A., Al-Sulaiti, K., Nawaiseh, A. K., Sukkari, L., Alshurideh, A., Shwedeh, F., & Alzoubi, H. M. (2025). The Effect of Using IoT on Linking Green Customers Data (Green Customer Profile) with Green Products and Green Product Labels BT - Sustainable Innovation for Engineering Management (SIEM). In El Khatib, M., Alzoubi, H. M., & Angelova, Y. (Eds.), *Sustainable Innovation for Engineering Management (SIEM)* (pp. 59–68). Springer Nature Switzerland., 10.1007/978-3-031-89889-1_7

Al Nuaimi, B. K., Khan, M., & Ajmal, M. (2020). Implementing sustainable procurement in the United Arab Emirates public sector. *Journal of Public Procurement, 20*(2), 97–117. DOI: 10.1108/JOPP-07-2019-0044

Al Ruhaili, E., Lakkimsetty, N. R., & Joy, V. M. Modeling and optimization of heat exchanger using artificial neural network and genetic algorithm, in *AIP Conf. Proc.*, vol. 2690, no. 1, Art. no. 020028, 2023, DOI: 10.1063/5.0119479

Al-Araimi, M. M., Joy, V. M., Nageswara Rao, L. S., & Feroz, S. (2019). Optimization and assessment of residual chlorine using response surface methodology and artificial neural network modeling [IJRTE]. *Int. J. Recent Technol. Eng.*, *8*(3), 258–263. DOI: 10.35940/ijrte.C4122.098319

Alavi, M., & Leidner, D. E. (2001). Knowledge management and knowledge management systems: Conceptual foundations and research issues. *Management Information Systems Quarterly*, *25*(1), 107–136. DOI: 10.2307/3250961

Albano, D., Galiano, V., Basile, M., Di Luca, F., Gitto, S., Messina, C., Cagetti, M. G., Del Fabbro, M., Tartaglia, G. M., & Sconfienza, L. M. (2024). Artificial intelligence for radiographic imaging detection of caries lesions: A systematic review. *BMC Oral Health*, *24*(1), 274. DOI: 10.1186/s12903-024-04046-7 PMID: 38402191

Aletihad News Center. (2025). Miral keen to make social impact with CSR strategy. https://en.aletihad.ae/news/business/4430367/miral-keen-to-make-social-impact-with-csr-strategy

Alharbi, S. S., & Alhasson, H. F. (2024). Exploring the applications of artificial intelligence in dental image detection. *Diagnostics (Basel)*, *14*(21), 2442. DOI: 10.3390/diagnostics14212442 PMID: 39518408

Ali, , GAli, , TIrfan, , MDraz, , USohail, , MGlowacz, , ASulowicz, , MMielnik, , RFaheem, , Z. BMartis, , C. (2020). IoT based smart parking system using deep long short memory network. *Electronics, 9*(10), 1696. https://doi.org/10.3390/electronics9101696

Ali, A., Ma, L., Shahzad, M., Musonda, J., & Hussain, S. (2023). How various stakeholder pressure influences mega-project sustainable performance through corporate social responsibility and green competitive advantage. *Environmental Science and Pollution Research International*, *31*(60), 1–15. DOI: 10.1007/s11356-023-29717-w PMID: 37702865

Ali, M., Irfan, M., Ali, T., Wei, C. R., & Akilimali, A. (2025). Artificial intelligence in dental radiology: A narrative review. *Annals of Medicine and Surgery (London)*, *87*(4), 2212–2217. DOI: 10.1097/MS9.0000000000003127 PMID: 40212156

Al-Jallad, N., Ly-Mapes, O., Hao, P., Ruan, J., Ramesh, A., & Luo, J.. (2022). AI-powered smartphone application AICaries. *PLOS Digital Health*, *1*(6), e0000046. DOI: 10.1371/journal.pdig.0000046 PMID: 36381137

Al-Jawad, S. N. A., Ahmed, M. A., & Saleh, A. H. (2020). Integrated reservoir characterization and quality analysis of the carbonate rock types: Case study, southern Iraq. *Journal of Petroleum Exploration and Production Technology*, *10*(8), 3157–3177. DOI: 10.1007/s13202-020-00982-6

AL-Khalisy, S. H. J., Abed, W. M. S., Al-Kateb, G., Aljanabi, M., Mijwil, M. M., Abotaleb, M., & Dhoska, K. (2025). QIULEA: Quantum-inspired ultra-lightweight encryption algorithm for IOT devices. *Pollack Periodica*, *20*(1), 25–32.

Al-Mulla, S., Ari, I., & Koç, M. (2022). Social media for sustainability education: Gaining knowledge and skills into actions for sustainable living. *International Journal of Sustainable Development and World Ecology*, *29*(5), 455–471. DOI: 10.1080/13504509.2022.2036856

AlShammery, A. R. (2021). Dentistry and climate change: How can dentists contribute? *Saudi Journal of Oral Sciences*, *8*(3), 121. DOI: 10.4103/sjoralsci.sjoralsci_58_21

Al-Turjman, F., & Malekloo, A. (2019). Smart parking in IoT-enabled cities: A survey. *Sustainable Cities and Society*, *49*, 101608. DOI: 10.1016/j.scs.2019.101608

Anaba, D. C., Kess-Momoh, A. J., & Ayodeji, S. A.David Chinalu AnabaAzeez Jason Kess-MomohSodrudeen Abolore Ayodeji. (2024). Digital transformation in oil and gas production: Enhancing efficiency and reducing costs. *International Journal of Management & Entrepreneurship Research*, *6*(7), 2153–2161. DOI: 10.51594/ijmer.v6i7.1263

Anderson, A. (2014). *Media, environment and the network society*. Springer. DOI: 10.1057/9781137314086

Andika, C. (2025). ESG Integration in Financial Accounting: Comparative Evidence and Policy Implications. Sinergi International Journal of Accounting and Taxation, 3(3), 181-194.1.2 The Emerging Role of Artificial Intelligence in Sustainable Finance.

Aradya, A., Koduru, S., Ravi, M. B., Raghavendra Swamy, K. N., Ganesh, S., & Pradeep Chandra, K.. (2025). Artificial intelligence for maxillofacial prosthodontics: A scoping review. *Journal of Oral Biology and Craniofacial Research*, *15*(6), 1749–1766. DOI: 10.1016/j.jobcr.2025.10.006 PMID: 41158531

Araidy, S., Batshon, G., & Mirochnik, R. (2025). Artificial intelligence applications in dentistry: A systematic review. *Oral*, *5*(4), 90. DOI: 10.3390/oral5040090

Arinze, C. A., Izionworu, V. O., Isong, D., Daudu, C. D., & Adefemi, A. (2024). Integrating artificial intelligence into engineering processes for improved efficiency and safety in oil and gas operations. *Open Access Research Journal of Engineering and Technology*, *6*(1), 39–51. DOI: 10.53022/oarjet.2024.6.1.0012

Asghar Khan, M., Ullah, I., Alkhalifah, A., Rehman, S. U., & Shah, J. A. (2022). A Provable and Privacy-Preserving Authentication Scheme for UAV-Enabled Intelligent Transportation Systems. *IEEE Transactions on Industrial Informatics*, *18*(5), 3416–3425. DOI: 10.1109/TII.2021.3101651

Ashok, D., Tiwari, A., & Jirge, V. (2020). Smart Parking System using IoT Technology. *2020 International Conference on Emerging Trends in Information Technology and Engineering (ic-ETITE)* (pp. 1-7). Vellore, India: IEEE. Retrieved from DOI: 10.1109/ic-ETITE47903.2020.457

Aslan, , JMayers, , KKoomey, , J. GFrance, , C. (2018). Electricity intensity of internet data transmission: Untangling the estimates. *Journal of Industrial Ecology, 22*(4), 785–798. https://doi.org/10.1111/jiec.12630

Assaf, C., Monne, J., Harriet, L., & Meunier, L. (2024). ESG investing: Does one score fit all investors' preferences? *Journal of Cleaner Production*, *443*, 141094. DOI: 10.1016/j.jclepro.2024.141094

Atlantic Canada's Offshore Oil and Gas Industry. (2019). *Ice management.* Retrieved February 12, 2019, from http://atlanticcanadaoffshore.ca/ice-management-newfoundland-labradorsoffshore-industry/

Azimi, S., Bennamoun, B., Mehdizadeh, M., Vignarajan, J., Xiao, D., Huang, B., Spallek, H., Irving, M., Kruger, E., Tennant, M., & Estai, M. (2025). Teledentistry improves access to oral care. *Health Care, 13*(18), 2282. DOI: 10.3390/healthcare13182282 PMID: 41008414

B, G. S., & Danti, A. (2024). Block chain-based security and authentication for forensics application using consensus proof of work and zero knowledge protocol. International Journal of Information Technology, 17(8), 5041–5052. DOI: 10.1007/s41870-024-01864-4

B. P. Sethy, U. Prajapati, K. N. Nageswara Rao Lakkimsetty, *et al.*, "Artificial intelligence models for predicting unconfined compressive strength of mixed soil types: Focusing on clay and sand," *Asian J. Civ. Eng.*, 2025, .DOI: 10.1007/s42107-025-01285-z

Babar, A., Ali, R., Oduoye, M. O., Noor, Z., & Chris, K. (2024). Exploring the impact of artificial intelligence on global health. *Journal of Primary Care & Community Health, 15*, 21501319241245847. DOI: 10.1177/21501319241245847 PMID: 38605668

Bai, C., Dallasega, P., Orzes, G., & Sarkis, J. (2020). Industry 4.0 technologies assessment: A sustainability perspective. *International Journal of Production Economics*, *229*, 107776. DOI: 10.1016/j.ijpe.2020.107776

Bakare, O. A., Aziza, O. R., Uzougbo, N. S., & Oduro, P. (2024). A governance and risk management framework for project management in the oil and gas industry. *Open Access Research Journal of Science and Technology*, *12*(1), 121–130. DOI: 10.53022/oarjst.2024.12.1.0119

Balaji, S., Nathani, K., & Santhakumar, R. (2019). IoT Technology, Applications and Challenges: A Contemporary Survey. *Wireless Personal Communications*, *108*(1), 363–388. DOI: 10.1007/s11277-019-06407-w

Balasubramanian, S., & Shukla, V. (2017). Green supply chain management: The case of the construction sector in the United Arab Emirates (UAE). *Production Planning and Control*, *28*(14), 1116–1138. DOI: 10.1080/09537287.2017.1341651

Ballantyne, A. G. (2016). Climate change communication: What can we learn from communication theory? *Wiley Interdisciplinary Reviews: Climate Change*, *7*(3), 329–344. DOI: 10.1002/wcc.392

Banerjee, J., Danti, A., Nassoura, A. B., & Dileep, M. R. (2025). A Blockchain-Enabled Arbitrable Smart Hiring System (BEASH). In IGI Global eBooks (pp. 291–326). DOI: 10.4018/979-8-3373-1320-7.ch009

Baran, M. (2023). Social media platforms in sustainability communication of Polish social enterprises from the IT industry and beyond. *Engineering Management in Production and Services*, *15*(2), 35–45. DOI: 10.2478/emj-2023-0010

Barriga, J., Sulca, J., León, J. L., Ulloa, A., Portero, D., Andrade, R., & Yoo, S. G. (2019). Smart Parking: A Literature Review from the Technological Perspective. *Applied Sciences (Basel, Switzerland)*, *9*(21), 4569. DOI: 10.3390/app9214569

Baruno, A. D., & Indrasari, M. (2025). Leveraging AI To Enhance Green Marketing Strategies. *Jurnal Ekonomi, Manajemen, Akuntansi Dan Keuangan, 6*(1).

Bassey, K. E., Opoku-Boateng, J., Antwi, B. O., Ntiakoh, A., & Juliet, A. R. (2024). Digital twin technology for renewable energy microgrids. *Engineering Science & Technology Journal*, *5*(7), 2248–2272. DOI: 10.51594/estj.v5i7.1319

Bathula, C., Rabani, I., Sekar, S., Youi, H. K., Choy, J. Y., Kadam, A., Shretha, N. K., Seo, Y.-S., & Kim, H. S. (2021). Enhanced removal of organic dye by activated carbon decorated TiO2 nanoparticles from Mentha Aquatica leaves via ultrasonic approach. *Ceramics International*, *47*(6), 8732–8739. DOI: 10.1016/j.ceramint.2020.12.282

Batra, P., Tagra, H., & Katyal, S. (2022). Artificial intelligence in teledentistry. *Discoveries (Craiova, Romania), 10*(3), e153. DOI: 10.15190/d.2022.12 PMID: 36530958

Becchetti, L., Bobbio, E., Prizia, F., & Semplici, L. (2022). Going deeper into the S of ESG: A relational approach to the definition of social responsibility. *Sustainability (Basel), 14*(15), 9668. DOI: 10.3390/su14159668

Belkhir, L., & Elmeligi, A. (2019). Carbon footprint of the global pharmaceutical industry and relative impact of its major players. *Journal of Cleaner Production, 214*, 185–194. DOI: 10.1016/j.jclepro.2018.11.204

Ben Mahjoub, L. (2025). Greenwashing practices and ESG reporting: An international review. *The International Journal of Sociology and Social Policy, 45*(1-2), 173–188. DOI: 10.1108/IJSSP-08-2024-0365

Bentler, P. M. (1995). *EQS structural equations program manual* (Vol. 6). Multivariate software Encino, CA.

Berg, F., Kölbel, J. F., & Rigobon, R. (2022). Aggregate confusion: The divergence of ESG ratings. *Review of Finance, 26*(6), 1315–1344. DOI: 10.1093/rof/rfac033

Bertolini, L. (2020). From "streets for traffic" to "streets for people": Can street experiments transform urban mobility? *Transport Reviews, 40*(6), 734–753. DOI: 10.1080/01441647.2020.1761907

Bhushan, S. B., & Danti, A. (2018). Classification of compressed and uncompressed text documents. *Future Generation Computer Systems, 88*, 614–623. DOI: 10.1016/j.future.2018.04.054

Billah, A. L., Koesrindartoto, D. P., & Faturohman, T. (2024). Advancing ESG Portfolio Optimization: Methods, Progress, and Future Directions. Accounting & Finance Review (AFR), 9(2).

Billio, M., Costola, M., Hristova, I., Latino, C., & Pelizzon, L. (2024). Sustainable finance: A journey toward ESG and climate risk. *International Review of Environmental and Resource Economics, 18*(1-2), 1–75. DOI: 10.1561/101.00000156

Bitrián, P., Buil, I., & Catalán, S. (2021). Enhancing user engagement: The role of gamification in mobile apps. *Journal of Business Research, 132*, 170–185. DOI: 10.1016/j.jbusres.2021.04.028

Biyik, C., Allam, Z., Pieri, G., Moroni, D., O'Fraifer, M., O'Connell, E., Olariu, S., & Khalid, M. (2021). Smart Parking Systems: Reviewing the Literature, Architecture and Ways Forward. *Smart Cities, 4*(2), 623–642. DOI: 10.3390/smartcities4020032

Boerman, S. C., Kruikemeier, S., & Zuiderveen Borgesius, F. J. (2017). Online behavioral advertising: A literature review and research agenda. *Journal of Advertising, 46*(3), 363–376. DOI: 10.1080/00913367.2017.1339368

Bolón-Canedo, V., Morán-Fernández, L., Cancela, B., & Alonso-Betanzos, A. (2024). A review of green artificial intelligence: Towards a more sustainable future. *Neurocomputing, 599*, 128096. DOI: 10.1016/j.neucom.2024.128096

Borglin, L., Pekarski, S., Saget, S., & Duane, B. (2021). The life cycle analysis of a dental examination. *Community Dentistry and Oral Epidemiology, 49*(6), 581–593. DOI: 10.1111/cdoe.12630 PMID: 33686705

Bose, R., & Luo, X. (2014). Integrative framework for assessing firms' potential to undertake Green IT initiatives via virtualization – A theoretical perspective. *The Journal of Strategic Information Systems, 23*(1), 39–54.

Bose, R., & Luo, X. (2014). Integrative framework for assessing firms' potential to undertake Green IT initiatives via virtualization. *The Journal of Strategic Information Systems, 23*(1), 39–54.

Bousema, T., Selvaraj, P., Djimde, A. A., Yakar, D., Hagedorn, B., Pratt, A., Barret, D., Whitfield, K., & Cohen, J. M. (2020). Reducing the carbon footprint of academic conferences: The example of the American Society of Tropical Medicine and Hygiene. *The American Journal of Tropical Medicine and Hygiene, 103*(5), 1758–1761. DOI: 10.4269/ajtmh.20-1013 PMID: 33069267

Brahimi, T., & Bensaid, B. (2019). Smart Villages and the GCC Countries: Policies, Strategies, and Implications. In A. Visvizi, M. Lytras, & G. Mudri, *Smart Villages in the EU and Beyond* (pp. 155-171). Emerald Publishing Limited, Retrieved from DOI: 10.1108/978-1-78769-845-120191015

Bressanelli, G., Adrodegari, F., Pigosso, D. C. A., & Parida, V. (2022). Circular economy in the digital age. *Sustainability (Basel), 14*(9), 5565. Advance online publication. DOI: 10.3390/su14095565

Brooks, S., Wang, X., & Sarker, S. (2012). Unpacking Green IT: A review of the existing literature. *Information Systems Frontiers, 14*(5), 823–839.

Brunton, S. L. (2022). Model based reinforcement learning: Policy iteration, value iteration, and dynamic programming. DOI: 10.52843/cassyni.6fs4s9

Brynjolfsson, E., & McAfee, A. (2017). *Machine, platform, crowd: Harnessing our digital future*. W. W. Norton & Company.

Brynjolfsson, E., Mitchell, T., & Rock, D. (2019). What can machines learn, and what does it mean for occupations and the economy? *AEA Papers and Proceedings. American Economic Association, 109*, 43–47. DOI: 10.1257/pandp.20191019

Bucher, T. (2018). *If... then: Algorithmic power and politics*. Oxford University Press. DOI: 10.1093/oso/9780190493028.001.0001

Buckingham, D., Banaji, S., Carr, D., Cranmer, S., & Willett, R. (2005). *The media literacy of children and young people: A review of the research literature*.

Bughin, J., Seong, J., Manyika, J., Chui, M., & Joshi, R. (2018). Notes from the AI frontier: Modeling the impact of AI on the world economy. McKinsey Global Institute. https://www.mckinsey.com/featured-insights/artificial-intelligence/notes-from-the-ai-frontier-modeling-the-impact-of-ai-on-the-world-economy

Burt, J. A., Al-Mansoori, N., Bejarano, I., Brown, G., Campbell, O., Els, J., Feulner, G. R., Friis-Montoya, G., Henderson, A., Howarth, B., John, D. M., Judas, J., Mateos-Molina, D., Mitchell, M., Natoli, A., Paparella, F., & Yaghmour, F. (2024). The Emirates at 2050: Balancing Development and Environmental Stewardship. In Burt, J. A. (Ed.), *A Natural History of the Emirates* (pp. 735–748)., DOI: 10.1007/978-3-031-37397-8_24

Busch, F., Kather, J. N., Johner, C., Moser, M., Truhn, D., Adams, L. C., & Bressem, K. K. (2024). 'Navigating the European Union Artificial Intelligence Act for Healthcare', npj. *Digital Medicine, 7*(1), 210. DOI: 10.1038/s41746-024-01213-6 PMID: 39134637

Carbon Brief (2025) 'AI: Five charts that put data-centre energy use and emissions into context'.

Carboni, J., Duncan, W. R., Gonzalez, M., Pace, M., Smyth, D., & Young, M. (2024). Sustainable Project Management: The GPM Practice Guide. GPM Global. https://www.ucipfg.com/Repositorio/MAP/MAPD-11/Version-2017/Unidad-01/lecturas/02.pdf

Carrasco, B., & Lee, J. (2023). Greening the Financial System. Available at: http://www.yrdcpcn.com/upload/2025/0120/f14c168b-4e6d-4574-b20c-da8fdd639f8b.pdf

Carrillo-Perez, F., Pecho, O. E., Morales, J. C., Paravina, R. D., Della Bona, A., Ghinea, R., Pulgar, R., Pérez, M. M., & Herrera, L. J. (2022). Applications of artificial intelligence in dentistry: A comprehensive review. *Journal of Esthetic and Restorative Dentistry, 34*(1), 259–280. DOI: 10.1111/jerd.12844 PMID: 34842324

Castells, M. (2015). *Networks of outrage and hope: Social movements in the Internet age*. John Wiley & Sons.

Centobelli, P., Cerchione, R., & Esposito, E. (2020). Efficiency and sustainability of supply chain processes in the era of Industry 4.0. *Business Strategy and the Environment*, *29*(2), 811–829. DOI: 10.1002/bse.2425

Central Bank of the UAE. (2023). *Financial stability report.* https://www.centralbank.ae

Chalotra, R., Shenoy, R., Dasson Bajaj, P., Rao, A., Pai, M., Jodalli, P., Br, A., Priya, H., & D'Souza, V. (2025). A scoping review exploring carbon emissions in dentistry—A step towards sustainability. *BMC Oral Health*, *25*(1), 1674. DOI: 10.1186/s12903-025-06952-w PMID: 41146088

Chamcham, J., Pakravan-Charvadeh, M. R., Maleknia, R., & Flora, C. (2024a). Media literacy and its role in promoting sustainable food consumption practices. *Scientific Reports*, *14*(1), 18831. DOI: 10.1038/s41598-024-69627-6

Chen, G., & Wang, Q. (2025). ESG rating disagreement, market information efficiency and institutional investor shareholding behavior. *Economia e Politica Industriale*, 1–26. DOI: 10.1007/s40812-025-00372-1

Chen, L., Haider, M. J., & He, J. (2024). Should "green information" be interactive? The influence of green information presentation on consumers' green participation behavior for driving sustainable consumption of fashion brands. *Journal of Cleaner Production*, *470*, 143329. DOI: 10.1016/j.jclepro.2024.143329

Chen, Y. W., Stanley, K., & Att, W. (2020). Artificial intelligence in dentistry: Current applications and future perspectives. *Quintessence International*, *51*(3), 248–257. DOI: 10.3290/j.qi.a43952 PMID: 32020135

Chen, Y., Yan, S., Jin, Y., Li, J., & Jin, X. (2025). Generative Artificial Intelligence in Finance: A Systematic Literature Review and a Research Agenda. *Digital Technologies Research and Applications*, *4*(2), 14–32. DOI: 10.54963/dtra.v4i2.1191

Cho, H., Cannon, J., Lopez, R., & Li, W. (2024). Social media literacy: A conceptual framework. *New Media & Society*, *26*(2), 941–960. DOI: 10.1177/14614448211068530

Choi, J. C., Chen, Q., & Lee, S. J. (2024). Predicting ESG Ratings by Machine Learning and Analyzing Influencing Factors by XAI. In *Proceedings of the 2024 7th International Conference on Software Engineering and Information Management* (pp. 120-125). DOI: 10.1145/3647722.3647742

Chow, W. S., & Chan, L. S. (2008). Social network, social trust and shared goals in organizational knowledge sharing. *Information & Management*, *45*(7), 458–465. DOI: 10.1016/j.im.2008.06.007

Cinelli, M., De Francisci Morales, G., Galeazzi, A., Quattrociocchi, W., & Starnini, M. (2021). The echo chamber effect on social media. *Proceedings of the National Academy of Sciences of the United States of America, 118*(9), e2023301118. DOI: 10.1073/pnas.2023301118

Clement, D. O. A., Olawade, D. B., Vanderbloemen, L., Rotifa, O. B., Fidelis, S. C., & Egbon, E.. (2025). AI-driven advances in low-dose imaging and enhancement—A review. *Diagnostics (Basel), 15*(6), 689. DOI: 10.3390/diagnostics15060689 PMID: 40150031

Coeckelbergh, M. (2021). AI for climate: Freedom, justice, and other ethical and political challenges. *AI and Ethics, 1*(1), 67–72. DOI: 10.1007/s43681-020-00007-2

Cohen, B. (2006). Sustainable valley entrepreneurial ecosystems. *Business Strategy and the Environment, 15*(1), 1–14. DOI: 10.1002/bse.428

Confetto, M. G., Covucci, C., Addeo, F., & Normando, M. (2023). Sustainability advocacy antecedents: How social media content influences sustainable behaviours among Generation Z. *Journal of Consumer Marketing, 40*(6), 758–774. DOI: 10.1108/JCM-11-2021-5038

Connelly, B. L., Ketchen, D. J.Jr, & Slater, S. F. (2011). Toward a "theoretical toolbox" for sustainability research in marketing. *Journal of the Academy of Marketing Science, 39*(1), 86–100. DOI: 10.1007/s11747-010-0199-0

Couldry, N., & Hepp, A. (2018). *The mediated construction of reality*. John Wiley & Sons.

Couldry, N., & Mejias, U. A. (2019). The costs of connection: How data is colonizing human life and appropriating it for capitalism. In *The costs of connection*. Stanford University Press.

Crace, L., & Gehman, J. (2023). What explains ESG performance? Disentangling the asymmetrical drivers of the triple bottom line. *Organization & Environment, 36*(1), 150–178. DOI: 10.1177/10860266221079408

Crawford, E. (2020). Most consumers don't link diet & climate, but sustainability marketing could boost plant-based sales. *Food Navigator USA. Retrieved July, 8*, 2023.

Cui, Z., Fang, Y., Mei, L., Zhang, B., Yu, B., Liu, J., Jiang, C., Sun, Y., Ma, L., Huang, J., Liu, Y., Zhao, Y., Lian, C., Ding, Z., Zhu, M., & Shen, D. (2022). A fully automatic AI system for tooth and alveolar bone segmentation from cone-beam CT images. *Nature Communications, 13*(1), 2096. DOI: 10.1038/s41467-022-29637-2 PMID: 35440592

Daga, S., Yadav, K., Singh, D., Pamucar, D., & Simic, V. (2025). Unveiling greenwashing: Analyzing the interaction of factors discouraging ESG greenwashing through TISM and MICMAC. *Journal of Environmental Management*, *380*, 124850. DOI: 10.1016/j.jenvman.2025.124850 PMID: 40073478

Daneels, R., & Vanwynsberghe, H. (2017). Mediating social media use: connecting parents mediation strategies and social media literacy. *Cyberpsychology: Journal of Psychosocial Research on Cyberpspace.-Brno, 11*(3), 5.

Danti, A., & Sanjay, S. K. (2020). Human Behavior Prediction based on Opinions using Machine Learning Techniques. [IJRTE]. *International Journal of Recent Technology and Engineering*, *8*(6), 3117–3120. DOI: 10.35940/ijrte.f8733.038620

Das, K. P., & Chandra, J. (2023). A survey on artificial intelligence for reducing the climate footprint in healthcare. *Energy Nexus*, *9*, 100167. DOI: 10.1016/j.nexus.2022.100167

Davenport, T. H., & Ronanki, R. (2018). Artificial intelligence for the real world. *Harvard Business Review*, *96*(1), 108–116. https://hbr.org/2018/01/artificial-intelligence-for-the-real-world

Davis, F. D. (1989). Perceived usefulness, perceived ease of use, and user acceptance of information technology. *Management Information Systems Quarterly*, *13*(3), 319–340. DOI: 10.2307/249008

De Vries, L., Gensler, S., & Leeflang, P. S. H. (2012). Popularity of brand posts on brand fan pages: An investigation of the effects of social media marketing. *Journal of Interactive Marketing*, *26*(2), 83–91. DOI: 10.1016/j.intmar.2012.01.003

Defense Acquisition University. (2019). *Defense acquisition glossary-Digital twin*. Retrieved February 12, 2019, from https://www.dau.edu/glossary/Pages/Glossary.aspx

Deković, D., & Šimović, P. P. (2025). Hierarchical risk parity: Efficient implementation and real world analysis. *Future Generation Computer Systems*, *167*, 107744. DOI: 10.1016/j.future.2025.107744

Del Giudice, M. (2022). Discovering the Internet of Things: AI driven digital transformation in organizations. *Technological Forecasting and Social Change*, *178*, 121590. DOI: 10.1016/j.techfore.2022.121590

Del Vitto, A., Marazzina, D., & Stocco, D. (2023). ESG ratings explainability through machine learning techniques. *Annals of Operations Research*, 1–30. DOI: 10.1007/s10479-023-05514-z

Delmas, M. A., & Burbano, V. C. (2011). The drivers of greenwashing. *California Management Review, 54*(1), 64–87. DOI: 10.1525/cmr.2011.54.1.64

Dey, R., Kassim, S., Mahajan, R., Pawar, D. J. A., Kumbhar, V. R., Shendage, J., & Patil, M. (2025). A systematic literature review on the ethical capital market: Insights using the prisma approach. *Journal of Information Systems Engineering & Management*.

Di Spirito, F., Giordano, F., Di Palo, M. P., De Benedetto, G., Aulisio, L., & Boccia, G. (2025). Sustainable dental and periodontal practice: A narrative review on the 4R-framework. *Dentistry Journal, 13*(9), 392. DOI: 10.3390/dj13090392 PMID: 41002665

Diaz Ogás, M., Fabregat, R., & Aciar, S. (2020). Survey of Smart Parking Systems. *Applied Sciences (Basel, Switzerland), 10*(11), 3872. DOI: 10.3390/app10113872

Diaz, J. F., & Nguyen, T. T. (2023). Application of grey relational analysis and artificial neural networks on corporate social responsibility (CSR) indices. *Journal of Sustainable Finance & Investment, 13*(3), 1181–1199. DOI: 10.1080/20430795.2021.1929805

Dileep, M. R., & Danti, A. (2018). Human age and gender prediction based on neural networks and three Sigma control limits. *Applied Artificial Intelligence, 32*(3), 281–292. DOI: 10.1080/08839514.2018.1451217

Ding, H., Wu, J., Zhao, W., Matinlinna, J. P., Burrow, M. F., & Tsoi, J. K. H. (2023). Artificial intelligence in dentistry—A review. *Frontiers in Dental Medicine, 4*, 1085251. DOI: 10.3389/fdmed.2023.1085251 PMID: 39935549

Dobrzański, L. A., Dobrzański, L. B., Dobrzańska-Danikiewicz, A. D., & Dobrzańska, J. (2020). The concept of sustainable development of modern dentistry. *Processes (Basel, Switzerland), 8*(12), 1605. DOI: 10.3390/pr8121605

Doni, F., & Toscani, D. (2024). Corporate governance and sustainability: an overview of the new trends in the European Union. Research Handbook on Sustainability Reporting, 293-308.

Donner, S. D. (2017). Risk and responsibility in public engagement by climate scientists: Reconsidering advocacy during the Trump era. *Environmental Communication, 11*(3), 430–433. DOI: 10.1080/17524032.2017.1291101

Drew, J., Christie, S. D., Rainham, D., & Rizan, C. (2022). HealthcareLCA: An open-access living database of health-care environmental impact assessments. *The Lancet. Planetary Health, 6*(12), e1000–e1012. DOI: 10.1016/S2542-5196(22)00257-1 PMID: 36495883

Duane, B., Borglin, L., Pekarski, S., Saget, S., & Duncan, H. F. (2020). Environmental sustainability in endodontics: A life cycle assessment of a root canal treatment procedure. *BMC Oral Health, 20*(1), 348. DOI: 10.1186/s12903-020-01337-7 PMID: 33261595

Duane, B., Hyland, J., Rowan, J. S., & Archibald, B. (2012). Taking a bite out of Scotland's dental carbon emissions in the transition to a low carbon future. *Public Health, 126*(9), 770–777. DOI: 10.1016/j.puhe.2012.05.032 PMID: 22902137

Duane, B., Ramasubbu, D., Harford, S., Steinbach, I., Stancliffe, R., & Ballantyne, G. (2019). Environmental sustainability and biodiversity within the dental practice. *British Dental Journal, 226*(9), 701–705. DOI: 10.1038/s41415-019-0208-8 PMID: 31076704

Duane, B., Ramasubbu, D., Harford, S., Steinbach, I., Stancliffe, R., Croasdale, K., & Pasdeki-Clewer, E. (2019). Environmental sustainability and procurement: Purchasing products for the dental setting. *British Dental Journal, 226*(6), 453–458. DOI: 10.1038/s41415-019-0080-6 PMID: 30903074

Duane, B., Stancliffe, R., Miller, F. A., Sherman, J., & Pasdeki-Clewer, E. (2020). Sustainability in dentistry: A multifaceted approach needed. *Journal of Dental Research, 99*(9), 998–1003. DOI: 10.1177/0022034520919391 PMID: 32392435

Duane, B., & Steinbach, I. (2024). What is the environmental footprint of a dental practice? A life cycle analysis (Part 1). *British Dental Journal.* Advance online publication. DOI: 10.1038/s41415-023-6710-z PMID: 38212528

Dunn, Z. (2024) 'Navigating the shift to omnichannel marketing: What to know about modular content and OPDP expectations', Regulatory Focus (RAPS), January.

Durbin, E., & Filer, J. (2021). Evaluating the Impact of Public Awareness Campaigns on Sustainable Practices. *Journal of Energy and Environmental Policy Options, 4*(4), 32–37.

Du, S., Bhattacharya, C. B., & Sen, S. (2010). Maximizing business returns to corporate social responsibility (CSR): The role of CSR communication. *International Journal of Management Reviews, 12*(1), 8–19. DOI: 10.1111/j.1468-2370.2009.00276.x

Dwivedi, Y. K., Hughes, L., Ismagilova, E., Carlson, J., Jacobson, J., Jain, R., Karjaluoto, H., Kefi, H., Krishen, A. S., Kumar, V., Rahman, M. M., Raman, R., Rauschnabel, P. A., Rowley, J., Salo, J., Tran, G. A., & Wang, Y. (2021). Artificial intelligence: Multidisciplinary perspectives on emerging challenges, opportunities, and agenda for research, practice, and policy. *International Journal of Information Management, 57*, 101994. DOI: 10.1016/j.ijinfomgt.2019.08.002

Eccles, R., & Klimenko, S. (2019). The Investor Revolution. *Harvard Business Review*, (May–June), 106–116.

ECONOMY MIDDLE EAST. (2025). Abu Dhabi's Miral launches bold sustainability strategy to advance responsible leisure, entertainment, and tourism. https://economymiddleeast.com/news/abu-dhabi-miral-launches-bold-sustainability-strategy/

El Khatib, M., Al Ali, S., Alharam, I., Alhajeri, A., Peneva, G., Angelova, J., & Shanaa, M. (2023). Drafting a digital transformation strategy for project management sector–empirical study on UAE. *Strategies for Policy in Science & Education/ Strategii na Obrazovatelnata i Nauchnata Politika, 31*. https://university.tu-sofia.bg/e-publ/files/12418_Digital_Transformation_for_PM_Sector.pdf

Eliades, T., Adel, S. M., Akyalçin, S., Atsawasuwan, P., Foong, K. W. C., Hiskia, A., Panayi, N., Silikas, N., Allareddy, V., Venugopal, A., Dellinger, A., Perillo, L., & Vaiid, N. (2025). Environmental footprints in orthodontics: The World Federation of Orthodontists' white paper on sustainable practices, challenges and research imperatives. *Journal of the World Federation of Orthodontists, 14*(4), 194–201. DOI: 10.1016/j.ejwf.2025.06.003 PMID: 40675890

Elias, O., Awotunde, O. J., Oladepo, O. I., Azuikpe, P. F., Samson, O. A., Oladele, O. R., & Ogunruku, O. O. (2024). The evolution of green fintech: Leveraging AI and IoT for sustainable financial services and smart contract implementation. *World Journal of Advanced Research and Reviews, 23*(1), 2710–2723. DOI: 10.30574/wjarr.2024.23.1.2272

Elkington, J. (2018). *Cannibals with forks: The triple bottom line of 21st century business*. Capstone Publishing.

El-Sayegh, S. M., Basamji, M., Haj Ahmad, A., & Zarif, N. (2021). Key contractor selection criteria for green construction projects in the UAE. *International Journal of Construction Management, 21*(12), 1240–1250. DOI: 10.1080/15623599.2019.1610545

Emirates News Agency. (2023). Miral and Emirates Foundation are fostering volunteerism among UAE youth. https://www.wam.ae/en/article/3upcz0-miral-and-emirates-foundation-fostering

Environment Agency. (2023). *Carbon footprint of paper and print: Life cycle assessment data*. Bristol: Environment Agency.

European Commission (2020) 'Guidance on the application of the GDPR in health-related research'.

European Commission. (2025). *Corporate Sustainability Reporting Directive (CSRD): Overview*. European Commission.

Evans, D., Bratton, S., & McKee, J. (2021). *Social media marketing*. AG Printing & Publishing.

Fagbore, O. O., Ogeawuchi, J. C., Ilori, O., Isibor, N. J., Odetunde, A., & Adekunle, B. I. (2024). Conceptual Design of Ethical Investment Assessment Models Using AI-Enhanced Financial Decision Tools.

Farid, M. A., Viswanath, A., Al Junaibi, R., Allan, D., & Wardt, T. J. (2021). Electric Vehicle Integration into Road Transportation, Intelligent Transportation, and Electric Power Systems: An Abu Dhabi Case Study. *Smart cities, 4*(3). Retrieved from https://www.mdpi.com/2624-6511/4/3/55

Ficili, I., Giacobbe, M., Tricomi, G., & Puliafito, A. (2025). From sensors to data intelligence. *Sensors (Basel), 25*(6), 1763. DOI: 10.3390/s25061763 PMID: 40292910

Fisal, A., Rohani, M., Nor, N. A., & Tengku Hamzah, T. N. (2025). Reductions in clinical waste and environmental emissions through recycling and waste segregation in a dental school. *British Dental Journal*. Advance online publication. DOI: 10.1038/s41415-025-8913-y PMID: 41272111

Fischhoff, B. (2019). Evaluating science communication. *Proceedings of the National Academy of Sciences of the United States of America, 116*(16), 7670–7675. DOI: 10.1073/pnas.1805863115 PMID: 30478063

Floridi, L., Cowls, J., Beltrametti, M., Chatila, R., Chazerand, P., Dignum, V., Luetge, C., Madelin, R., Pagallo, U., Rossi, F., Schafer, B., Valcke, P., & Vayena, E. (2018). AI4People: An ethical framework for a good AI society. *Minds and Machines, 28*(4), 689–707. DOI: 10.1007/s11023-018-9482-5 PMID: 30930541

Food and Drug Administration (FDA) Office of Prescription Drug Promotion (2024) 'The Brief Summary', April 2024.

Fornell, C., & Larcker, D. F. (1981). Evaluating structural equation models with unobservable variables and measurement error. *JMR, Journal of Marketing Research, 18*(1), 39–50. DOI: 10.1177/002224378101800104

Friede, G., Busch, T., & Bassen, A. (2015). ESG and financial performance: Aggregated evidence from more than 2000 empirical studies. *Journal of Sustainable Finance & Investment, 5*(4), 210–233. DOI: 10.1080/20430795.2015.1118917

Fröling, E., Rajaeean, N., Hinrichsmeyer, K. S., Domrös-Zoungrana, D., Urban, J. N., & Lenz, C. (2024). Artificial Intelligence in Medical Affairs: A New Paradigm with Novel Opportunities. *Pharmaceutical Medicine*, *38*(5), 331–342. DOI: 10.1007/s40290-024-00536-9 PMID: 39259426

Ganesh, C., Podila, N., Vamsi, G. B. K., Rao, C. M., & Bhardwaj, N. (2024). AI-enhanced content marketing for sustainability: a theoretical perspective on eco-friendly communication strategies. *MATEC Web of Conferences, 392*, 01045.

Garg, V., Bohara, S., & Srivastav, A. (2025a). AI-driven sustainability marketing transforming consumers' perception toward eco-friendly brands. *Discover Sustainability*, *6*(1), 984. DOI: 10.1007/s43621-025-01934-y

Gattrell, W. T., Barraux, L., Comley, T., Whaley, A., & Lander, A. (2022). The carbon costs of in-person versus virtual medical congress attendance for a mid-sized pharmaceutical company. *Pharmaceutical Medicine*, *36*(3), 131–142. DOI: 10.1007/s40290-022-00421-3 PMID: 35218551

George, G., Merrill, R. K., & Schillebeeckx, S. J. D. (2020). Digital sustainability and entrepreneurship: How digital innovations are helping tackle climate change and sustainable development. *Entrepreneurship Theory and Practice*, *45*(5), 999–1027. DOI: 10.1177/1042258719899425

Ghermandi, A., Langemeyer, J., Van Berkel, D., Calcagni, F., Depietri, Y., Vigl, L. E., Fox, N., Havinga, I., Jäger, H., & Kaiser, N. (2023). Social media data for environmental sustainability: A critical review of opportunities, threats, and ethical use. *One Earth*, *6*(3), 236–250. DOI: 10.1016/j.oneear.2023.02.008

Gholami Mayani, M., Rommetveit, R., Oedegaard, S. I., & Svendsen, M. (2018). Drilling automated realtime monitoring using digital twin. In *Abu Dhabi International Petroleum Exhibition & Conference* (pp. 1–11). DOI: 10.2118/192807-MS

Giacomin, J. (2024). Autonomous road vehicles. *Future Autonomous Road Vehicles*, 11-32. DOI: 10.4324/9781032724232-2

Gibson Brandon, R., Krueger, P., & Schmidt, P. S. (2021). ESG rating disagreement and stock returns. *Financial Analysts Journal*, *77*(4), 104–127. DOI: 10.1080/0015198X.2021.1963186

Giese, G., Lee, L. E., Melas, D., Nagy, Z., & Nishikawa, L. (2019). Foundations of ESG investing: How ESG affects equity valuation, risk, and performance. *Journal of Portfolio Management*, *45*(5), 69–83. DOI: 10.3905/jpm.2019.45.5.069

Gill, A. (2008). Corporate governance as social responsibility: A research agenda. *Berkeley J. Int'l L.*, *26*, 452.

Gillespie, T. (2020). Content moderation, AI, and the question of scale. *Big Data & Society*, *7*(2), 2053951720943234. DOI: 10.1177/2053951720943234

Giudici, P., Centurelli, M., & Turchetta, S. (2024). Artificial Intelligence risk measurement. *Expert Systems with Applications*, 235, 121220. https://doi.org/10.1016/j.eswa.2023.121220.

Gohar, A., & Nencioni, G. (2021). The Role of 5G Technologies in a Smart City: The Case for Intelligent Transportation System. *Sustainability (Basel)*, *13*(9), 5188. DOI: 10.3390/su13095188

Gold, A. H., Malhotra, A., & Segars, A. H. (2001). Knowledge management: An organizational capabilities perspective. *Journal of Management Information Systems*, *18*(1), 185–214. DOI: 10.1080/07421222.2001.11045669

Gong, Y., Zhou, X., Zhou, Y., Luehmann, A., Han, Y., & Bai, Z. (2024). *Approaching "filter bubble" in recommendation systems: A transformative AI literacy learning experience.*

Gopal, D., Jerlin, M., & Abirami, M. (2019). A smart parking system using IoT. *World Review of Entrepreneurship, Management and Sustainable Development*, *15*(3), 335–345. DOI: 10.1504/WREMSD.2019.099409

Govindaras, B., Wern, T. S., Kaur, S., Haslin, I. A., & Ramasamy, R. K. (2023). Sustainable environment to prevent burnout and attrition in project management. *Sustainability (Basel)*, *15*(3), 2364. DOI: 10.3390/su15032364

Grant, R. M. (1996). Toward a knowledge-based theory of the firm. *Strategic Management Journal*, *17*(S2), 109–122. DOI: 10.1002/smj.4250171110

Grose, J., Burns, L., Mukonoweshuro, R., Richardson, J., Mills, I., Nasser, M., & Moles, D. (2018). Developing sustainability in a dental practice through an action research approach. *British Dental Journal*, *225*(5), 409–413. DOI: 10.1038/sj.bdj.2018.738 PMID: 30168816

Groves, C. (2019). Post-truth and anthropogenic climate change: Asking the right questions. *Wiley Interdisciplinary Reviews: Climate Change*, *10*(6), e620. DOI: 10.1002/wcc.620

Guerra, M., Morgado, M., Leira, Y., Leitão, T., Botelho, J., & Mendes, J. J. (2025). Integrating sustainability in dentistry: A pathway towards achieving the UN 2030 agenda. *Frontiers in Oral Health*, *6*, 1549020. DOI: 10.3389/froh.2025.1549020 PMID: 40717797

Gupta, E., Maysan, S., Murella, S., Saju, A. R., Grover, S., & Vasudeva, A. (2025). Recent dental practices using artificial intelligence (AI): A survey. *Bioinformation, 21*(3), 514–521. DOI: 10.6026/973206300210514 PMID: 40599924

Hadi, R. M., Abdullah, S. H., & Abedi, W. M. S. (2022). Proposed neural intrusion detection system to detect denial of service attacks in MANETs. *Periodicals of Engineering and Natural Sciences, 10*(3), 70–78. DOI: 10.21533/pen.v10.i3.644

Hagen, O., Aly, A., Jones, R., Varga, M., & Bazazian, D. (2024). Beyond the surface: A scoping review of vision-based underwater experience technologies and user studies. *Intell. Mar. Technol. Syst., 2*(19), 1–24. DOI: 10.1007/s44295-024-00034-3

Hair, J. F. (2014). *A primer on partial least squares structural equation modeling (PLS-SEM)*. sage.

Hair, J. F., Hult, G. T. M., Ringle, C. M., & Sarstedt, M. (2017). *A primer on partial least squares structural equation modeling (PLS-SEM)* (2nd ed.). Sage Publications.

Hair, J. F., Hult, G. T. M., Ringle, C. M., & Sarstedt, M. (2021). *A Primer on Partial Least Squares Structural Equation Modeling (PLS-SEM)* (3rd ed.). Sage Publications. DOI: 10.1007/978-3-030-80519-7

Hall, J. K., Daneke, G. A., & Lenox, M. J. (2010). Sustainable development and entrepreneurship: Past contributions and future directions. *Journal of Business Venturing, 25*(5), 439–448. DOI: 10.1016/j.jbusvent.2010.01.002

Hamadi, Y. A., Juma, R. J., Hussein, Z. M., & Lakkimsetty, N. R. Harnessing artificial intelligence in wastewater treatment: A comprehensive analysis of emerging research trends and innovations, in *Proc. 2025 Int. Conf. INnovations in Intelligent SysTems and Applications (INISTA)*, Ras Al Khaimah, United Arab Emirates, 2025, pp. 1–7, DOI: 10.1109/INISTA68122.2025.11249526

Hamilton, L., & Rauch, M. (2024). Artificial intelligence integration for optimal reservoir data analysis and pattern recognition. In *Unconventional Resources Technology Conference* (pp. 2968–2988).

Hankendi, C., Coskun, A. K., & Sovacool, B. K. (2025). Why transparency matters for sustainable data centers and carbon-neutral artificial intelligence (AI). *iScience, 28*(11), 113705. DOI: 10.1016/j.isci.2025.113705 PMID: 41244593

Hapsari, S. A. (2021). The theory of planned behavior and financial literacy to analyze intention in mutual fund product investment. *5th Global Conference on Business, Management and Entrepreneurship (GCBME 2020)*, 136–141. DOI: 10.2991/aebmr.k.210831.028

Harmeling, C. M., Moffett, J. W., Arnold, M. J., & Carlson, B. D. (2017). Toward a theory of customer engagement marketing. *Journal of the Academy of Marketing Science*, *45*(3), 312–335. DOI: 10.1007/s11747-016-0509-2

Hartley, J., McWilliam, K., Burgess, J., & Banks, J. (2008). The uses of multimedia: Three digital literacy case studies. *Media International Australia, Incorporating Culture & Policy*, *128*(1), 59–72. DOI: 10.1177/1329878X0812800108

Hatherley, J. (2024). Data over dialogue: Why artificial intelligence is unlikely to humanise medicine. *SSRN*. DOI: 10.2139/ssrn.5256823

Hays, J. M., Pereseina, V., Alshuaibi, A. S. I., & Saha, J. (2020). Lessons in sustainable process paradigm. A case study from Dubai. *International Journal of Management Education*, *18*(1), 100366. DOI: 10.1016/j.ijme.2020.100366

Heiss, R., Nanz, A., & Matthes, J. (2023). Social media information literacy: Conceptualization and associations with information overload, news avoidance and conspiracy mentality. *Computers in Human Behavior*, *148*, 107908. DOI: 10.1016/j.chb.2023.107908

Hendren, K., Newcomer, K. K., Pande, S., Smith, M., & Sumner, N. (2022). How qualitative research methods can be leveraged to strengthen mixed methods research in public policy and public administration? *Public Administration Review*, *83*(3), 468–485. DOI: 10.1111/puar.13528

Hibernia. (2019). *Ice management*. Retrieved February 12, 2019, from https://www.hibernia.ca/ice.html

Higgins, E. T., Kruglanski, A. W., & Van Lange, P. A. M. (2012). *Handbook of theories of social psychology*. Sage.

Hotel Carbon Measurement Initiative. (2023). *HCMI Methodology Framework for Measuring Hotel Carbon Footprint* (Version 2.1). World Travel & Tourism Council.

Houssein, E. H., Gamal, A. M., Younis, E. M. G., & Mohamed, E. (2025). Explainable artificial intelligence for medical imaging systems. *Cluster Computing*, *28*(7), 469. DOI: 10.1007/s10586-025-05281-5

Hsu, L. P., Huang, Y. K., & Chang, Y. C. (2022). The implementation of artificial intelligence in dentistry could enhance environmental sustainability. *Journal of Dental Sciences*, *17*(2), 1081–1082. DOI: 10.1016/j.jds.2022.02.002 PMID: 35756807

Hughes, A., Urban, M. A., & Wójcik, D. (2021). Alternative ESG ratings: How technological innovation is reshaping sustainable investment. *Sustainability (Basel)*, *13*(6), 3551. DOI: 10.3390/su13063551

Ige, A. B., Kupa, E., & Ilori, O. (2024). Best practices in cybersecurity for green building management systems: Protecting sustainable infrastructure from cyber threats. *International Journal of Science and Research Archive*, *12*(1), 2960–2977. DOI: 10.30574/ijsra.2024.12.1.1185

Iliev Matić, M. (2024). The Impact of Social Media on ESG Through the Lens of Greenwashing. FINIZ 2024-Social Media and Contemporary Business, 109-114.

International Energy Agency (IEA). (2025). *Energy and AI*. IEA.

International Organization for Standardization. (2024). *ISO 20121:2024 event sustainability management systems—Requirements with guidance for use*. ISO.

Iyer, S. S. (2023). The emerging circular economy trends of United Arab Emirates (UAE) universities. *European Journal of Social Impact and Circular Economy-ISSN*, *2704*, 9906. DOI: 10.13135/2704-9906/6821

Jarrahi, M. H. (2018). Artificial intelligence and the future of work: Human–AI symbiosis in organizational decision making. *Business Horizons*, *61*(4), 577–586. DOI: 10.1016/j.bushor.2018.03.007

Jenkins, H. (2009). *Confronting the challenges of participatory culture: Media education for the 21st century*. The MIT press. DOI: 10.7551/mitpress/8435.001.0001

Jenko, S., Papadopoulou, E., Kumar, V., Overman, S. S., Krepelkova, K., Wilson, J., Dunbar, E., Spice, C., & Exarchos, T. (2025). Artificial intelligence in healthcare. *AI*, *6*(6), 116. DOI: 10.3390/ai6060116

Joel, O. S., Oyewole, A. T., Odunaiya, O. G., & Soyombo, O. T. (2024). Leveraging artificial intelligence for supply chain optimization: Current practices and future potentials. *International Journal of Management & Entrepreneurship Research*, *6*(3), 707–721. DOI: 10.51594/ijmer.v6i3.882

Joel, O. T., & Oguanobi, V. U. (2024). Geotechnical assessments for renewable energy infrastructure: Ensuring stability in wind and solar projects. *Engineering Science & Technology Journal*, *5*(5), 1588–1605. DOI: 10.51594/estj.v5i5.1110

Johnson, K. C. (2023). California's ambitious greenhouse gas policies: Are they ambitious enough? *Energy Policy*, *177*, 113545. DOI: 10.1016/j.enpol.2023.113545

Jonsdottir, B., Sigurjonsson, T. O., Johannsdottir, L., & Wendt, S. (2022). Barriers to using ESG data for investment decisions. *Sustainability (Basel)*, *14*(9), 5157. DOI: 10.3390/su14095157

Joy, V. M., Shaik, F., & Lakkimsetty, N. R. (2022). Application of Artificial Intelligence in the Treatment of Saline Water. In *Removal of Pollutants from Saline Water Treatment Technologies* (1st ed.). CRC Press, Taylor & Francis Group.

Juthi, S., Kamrujjaman, M., Mistry, A. M., & Alauddin, M. (2024). Sustainable finance and data analytics: A systematic review of ESG data in investment decisions. Academic Journal on Business Administration, Innovation & Sustainability, 4(04).

Kamel, N., & El Shiwy, R. (2022). Virtual Reality and Virtual Diving Technologies: Innovative Tools to Promote Maritime and Underwater Cultural Heritage in the Red Sea, Egypt. Journal of Tourism [JTHH]. *Hotels and Heritage*, *5*(3), 18–46. DOI: 10.21608/sis.2022.175794.1111

Kaner, G. (2021). Greenwashing: How difficult it is to be transparent to the consumer—H&M case study. In *Green marketing in emerging markets: Strategic and operational perspectives* (pp. 203–226). Springer International Publishing. DOI: 10.1007/978-3-030-74065-8_9

Kano, L., Simoes, S., & Verbeke, A. (2023). Governance failure and firm-level crises: The case of the Volkswagen emissions scandal. In *Research Handbook on International Corporate Social Responsibility* (pp. 168–186). Edward Elgar Publishing. DOI: 10.4337/9781802207040.00018

Kaplan, A. M., & Haenlein, M. (2010). Users of the world, unite! The challenges and opportunities of Social Media. *Business Horizons*, *53*(1), 59–68. DOI: 10.1016/j.bushor.2009.09.003

Kapoor, P. S., Balaji, M. S., & Jiang, Y. (2021). Effectiveness of sustainability communication on social media: Role of message appeal and message source. *International Journal of Contemporary Hospitality Management*, *33*(3), 949–972. DOI: 10.1108/IJCHM-09-2020-0974

Khaleel, M., Murtaza, N., Mueen, Q. H., Ahmad, S. A., & Qadri, S. F. (2024). *Use of AI in conservation and for understanding climate change*. Elsevier Inc., DOI: 10.1016/B978-0-443-24001-0.00013-0

Khan, T., Emon, M. M. H., & Siam, S. A. J. (2024). Impact of Green Supply Chain Practices on Sustainable Development in Bangladesh. Available at *SSRN* 4958443. http://doi.org/DOI: 10.26480/mbmj.02.2024.73.83

Khosravi, M., Zare, Z., Mojtabaeian, S. M., & Izadi, R. (2024). Artificial intelligence and decision-making in healthcare: A thematic analysis of a systematic review of reviews. *Health Services Research and Managerial Epidemiology*, *11*, 23333928241234863. DOI: 10.1177/23333928241234863 PMID: 38449840

Kot, W. Y., Au Yeung, S. Y., Leung, Y. Y., Leung, P. H., & Yang, W. F. (2025). Evolution of deep learning tooth segmentation from CT/CBCT images: A systematic review and meta-analysis. *BMC Oral Health*, *25*(1), 800. DOI: 10.1186/s12903-025-05984-6 PMID: 40420051

Koukaras, P., Tjortjis, C., & Rousidis, D. (2020). Social media types: Introducing a data driven taxonomy. *Computing*, *102*(1), 295–340. DOI: 10.1007/s00607-019-00739-y

Koven, C., Sanderson, B., & Swann, A. (2022). Much of zero emissions commitment occurs before reaching net zero emissions. DOI: 10.31223/x5d64q

Kubey, R. (2004). What is media literacy and why is it important. *Television Quarterly*, *34*(3/4), 21–27.

Kumar, G., Rehman, F., Al-Muzian, L., Farsi, D., & Hiremath, S. (2021). Global scenario of teledentistry during COVID-19 pandemic. *International Journal of Clinical Pediatric Dentistry*, *14*(3), 426–429. DOI: 10.5005/jp-journals-10005-1952 PMID: 34720519

La Torre, M., Mango, F., Cafaro, A., & Leo, S. (2020). Does the ESG index affect stock return? Evidence from the Eurostoxx50. *Sustainability (Basel)*, *12*(16), 6387. DOI: 10.3390/su12166387

Laato, S., Tiainen, M., Najmul Islam, A. K. M., & Mäntymäki, M. (2022). How to explain AI systems to end users: A systematic literature review and research agenda. *Internet Research*, *32*(7), 1–31. DOI: 10.1108/INTR-08-2021-0600

Lakkimsetty, N. R., Al Araimi, H. R. A., & Kavitha, G. (2025). Modelling and optimization of well hole cleaning using artificial intelligence techniques. *Discover Applied Sciences*, *7*(2), 124. DOI: 10.1007/s42452-024-06415-x

Laranjeiro, D., Lillebø, A. I., & Vieira, H. (2025). Generative AI in Climate Change Communication and Education. In Proceedings of the 17th International Conference on Computer Supported Education (CSEDU 2025) - Volume 1, pages 123-134. https://doi.DOI: 10.5220/0013478400003932

Lee, C. L., & Liang, J. (2024). The effect of carbon regulation initiatives on corporate ESG performance in real estate sector: International evidence. *Journal of Cleaner Production*, *453*, 142188. DOI: 10.1016/j.jclepro.2024.142188

Lee, H., & Choi, B. (2003). Knowledge management enablers, processes, and organizational performance: An integrative view and empirical examination. *Journal of Management Information Systems*, *20*(1), 179–228. DOI: 10.1080/07421222.2003.11045756

Lei, J. (2024). Efficient Strategies on Supply Chain Network Optimization for Industrial Carbon Emission Reduction. arXiv preprint arXiv:2404.16863. https://arxiv.org/pdf/2404.16863

Lenzen, M., Malik, A., Li, M., Fry, J., Weisz, H., Pichler, P.-P., Chaves, L. S. M., Capon, A., & Pencheon, D. (2020). The environmental footprint of health care: A global assessment. *The Lancet. Planetary Health*, *4*(7), e271–e279. DOI: 10.1016/S2542-5196(20)30121-2 PMID: 32681898

Lewis, J. I., Toney, A., & Shi, X. (2024, September 28). Climate change and artificial intelligence: Assessing the global research landscape. *Discover Artificial Intelligence*, *4*(64), 1–12. DOI: 10.1007/s44163-024-00170-z

Liao, C.-H. (2024). Exploring social media determinants in fostering pro-environmental behavior: Insights from social impact theory and the theory of planned behavior. *Frontiers in Psychology*, *15*, 1445549. DOI: 10.3389/fpsyg.2024.1445549

Lichter, K. E., Sabbagh, A., Demeulenaere, S., Drew, T., Conway, A., Nogueira, L., Suneja, G., Kirkwood, K., Hampshire, K., Gundling, K., Teherani, A., Thottathil, S. E., & Mohamad, O. (2024). Reducing the Environmental Impact of Health Care Conferences: A Study of Emissions and Practical Solutions. *JCO Global Oncology*, *10*(10), e2300209. DOI: 10.1200/GO.23.00209 PMID: 38359373

Lim, T. (2024). Environmental, social, and governance (ESG) and artificial intelligence in finance: State-of-the-art and research takeaways. *Artificial Intelligence Review*, *57*(4), 76. DOI: 10.1007/s10462-024-10708-3

Livingstone, S. (2014). Developing social media literacy: How children learn to interpret risky opportunities on social network sites. *Communications*, *39*(3), 283–303. DOI: 10.1515/commun-2014-0113

Lubchenco, J., & Gaines, S. D. (2019). A new narrative for the ocean. *Science*, *364*(6444), 911–912. DOI: 10.1126/science.aay2241 PMID: 31171668

Lukács, B., & Molnár, P. (2025). Companies' ESG performance under soft and hard regulation environment. *Discover Sustainability*, *6*(1), 701. DOI: 10.1007/s43621-025-01657-0

Lukács, B., Molnar, P., & Rickards, R. C. (2024). Comparative assessment of ESG ratings methodology and results based on XBRL. Journal of Infrastructure. *Policy and Development*, *8*(12), 8641.

Lyne, A., Ashley, P., Saget, S., Porto Costa, M., Underwood, B., & Duane, B. (2020). Combining evidence-based healthcare with environmental sustainability: Using the toothbrush as a model. *British Dental Journal*, *229*(5), 303–309. DOI: 10.1038/s41415-020-1981-0 PMID: 32918023

Lyon, T. P., & Montgomery, A. W. (2015). The means and end of greenwash. *Organization & Environment*, *28*(2), 223–249. DOI: 10.1177/1086026615575332

Malde, K., Handegard, N. O., Eikvil, L., & Salberg, A.-B. (2019). Machine intelligence and the data-driven future of marine science. *ICES Journal of Marine Science*, •••, 1–12. DOI: 10.1093/icesjms/fsz057

Malecki, C. (2021). The EU taxonomy regulation: Giving a good name to sustainable investment. Malecki C., The EU Taxonomy Regulation: giving a good name to sustainable investment, (2021), 26(4), 149-156.

Malik, M., Ali, M., Latan, H., & Chiappetta Jabbour, C. J. (2023). Green project management practices, green knowledge acquisition and sustainable competitive advantage: Empirical evidence. *Journal of Knowledge Management*, *27*(9), 2350–2375. https://nrl.northumbria.ac.uk/id/eprint/51405/1/AAM.pdf. DOI: 10.1108/JKM-06-2022-0466

Mao, K., Thu, K. M., Hung, K. F., Yu, O. Y., Hsung, R. T., & Lam, W. Y. (2025). Artificial intelligence in detecting periodontal disease from intraoral photographs: A systematic review. *International Dental Journal*, *75*(5), 100883. DOI: 10.1016/j.identj.2025.100883 PMID: 40639137

Mazziotta, A., Borges, P., Kangas, A., Halme, P., & Eyvindson, K. (2023). Spatial trade-offs between ecological and economical sustainability in the boreal production forest. *Journal of Environmental Management*, *330*, 117144. DOI: 10.1016/j.jenvman.2022.117144 PMID: 36586374

Mbugua, E. W., & Muchelule, Y. (2024). CLOUD COMPUTING TECHNOLOGY PRACTICES AND PERFORMANCE OF AGRICULTURE PROJECTS IN NYANDARUA COUNTY, KENYA. [IJSSME]. *International Journal of Social Sciences Management and Entrepreneurship*, *8*(2).

McCandless, S., & Larson, S. J. (2023). Prioritizing social equity in MPA curricula: A crossprogram analysis and a case study. In *Social Equity in the Public Administration Classroom* (pp. 99–117). Routledge., DOI: 10.4324/9781003381228-8

McClintock, J., McKenna, R., & Woodworth-Lynas, C. (2007). *Grand Banks iceberg management* (PERD/CHC Rep. 20-84). National Research Council Canada.

McKinsey & Company (2024) 'Generative AI in the pharmaceutical industry: Moving from hype to reality'.

McKinsey & Company (2025) 'Scaling gen AI in the life sciences industry'.

Medical Affairs Professional Society (MAPS). (2025) Embracing Omnichannel Engagement in Medical Affairs: Changing Mindsets to Put External Stakeholders at the Center of Engagement. White paper.

Mehmetoglu, M. (2012). Partial least squares approach to structural equation modeling for tourism research. In *Advances in Hospitality and leisure* (pp. 43–61). Emerald Group Publishing Limited. DOI: 10.1108/S1745-3542(2012)0000008007

Mehta, B., Sam, E., & Campwala, N. (2024). Communication for climate change and development: Roadmap to build climate resilient communities. In *Environmental Activism and Global Media: Perspective from the Past, Present and Future* (pp. 117–130). Springer Publications., DOI: 10.1007/978-3-031-55408-7_6

Meng, Y., Chung, D., & Zhang, A. (2023). The effect of social media environmental information exposure on the intention to participate in pro-environmental behavior. *PLoS One*, *18*(11), e0294577. DOI: 10.1371/journal.pone.0294577

MIRAL. (2024). MIRAL AND ALDAR EDUCATION FORGE STRATEGIC PARTNERSHIP TO ENRICH STUDENT LEARNING. https://miral.ae/news-item/miral-and-aldar-education-forge-strategic-partnership-to-enrich-student-learning/

MIRAL. (2025). About MIRAL. https://miral.ae/about-miral/

MIRAL. (2025). *Atheer*. https://miral.ae/atheer/

MIRAL. (2025). My Community Canvas: Miral Celebrates Family, Inclusion, And Marine Life At SeaWorld Yas Island, Abu Dhabi. https://miral.ae/news-item/my-community-canvas-miral-celebrates-family-inclusion-and-marine-life-at-seaworld-yas-island-abu-dhabi/

MIRAL. (2025). OUR COMMITMENT. https://miral.ae/our-commitment/

Mittal, S., & Dhar, R. L. (2016). Effect of green transformational leadership on green creativity: A study of tourist hotels. *Tourism Management*, *57*, 118–127. DOI: 10.1016/j.tourman.2016.05.007

Mohammed, A. K., & Ishak, M. S. B. (2024). Identification of project cultural factors affecting the performance of UAE construction projects. *Alexandria Engineering Journal*, *86*, 205–216. DOI: 10.1016/j.aej.2023.11.064

Moharrami, M., Vahab, E., Bagherianlemraski, M., Hemmati, G., Singhal, S., Quinonez, C., Schwendicke, F., & Glogauer, M. (2025). Deep learning for detecting dental plaque and gingivitis from oral photographs. *Community Dentistry and Oral Epidemiology*, *53*(6), 617–632. DOI: 10.1111/cdoe.70001 PMID: 40571994

Molla, A. (2009). Organizational motivations for green IT: Exploratory study. *Communications of the Association for Information Systems*, *26*(1), 17–46.

Moodaley, W., & Telukdarie, A. (2023). Greenwashing, Sustainability Reporting, and Artificial Intelligence: A Systematic Literature Review. *Sustainability (Basel)*, *15*(2), 1481. DOI: 10.3390/su15021481

Mooneeapen, O., Abhayawansa, S., & Mamode Khan, N. (2022). The influence of the country governance environment on corporate environmental, social and governance (ESG) performance. Sustainability Accounting. *Management and Policy Journal*, *13*(4), 953–985.

Moser, S. C. (2010). Communicating climate change: History, challenges, process and future directions. *Wiley Interdisciplinary Reviews: Climate Change*, *1*(1), 31–53. DOI: 10.1002/wcc.11

Moser, S. C. (2016). Reflections on climate change communication research and practice in the second decade of the 21st century: What more is there to say? *Wiley Interdisciplinary Reviews: Climate Change*, *7*(3), 345–369. DOI: 10.1002/wcc.403

Mulimani, P. (2017). Green dentistry: The art and science of sustainable practice. *British Dental Journal*, *222*(12), 954–961. DOI: 10.1038/sj.bdj.2017.546 PMID: 28642517

Mulligan, C., Morsfield, S., & Cheikosman, E. (2024). Blockchain for sustainability: A systematic literature review for policy impact. *Telecommunications Policy*, *48*(2), 102676. DOI: 10.1016/j.telpol.2023.102676

Muñoz, P., & Cohen, B. (2018). Sustainable entrepreneurship research: Taking stock and looking ahead. *Business Strategy and the Environment*, *27*(3), 300–322. DOI: 10.1002/bse.2000

Muntinga, D. G., Moorman, M., & Smit, E. G. (2011). Introducing COBRAs: Exploring motivations for brand-related social media use. *International Journal of Advertising*, *30*(1), 13–46. DOI: 10.2501/IJA-30-1-013-046

Nabivi, E. (2025). The Role of Social Media in Green Marketing: How Eco-Friendly Content Influences Brand Attitude and Consumer Engagement. *Sustainability (Basel)*, *17*(5), 1965. DOI: 10.3390/su17051965

Nahar, J., Hossain, M. S., Rahman, M. M., & Hossain, M. A. (2024). Advanced predictive analytics for comprehensive risk assessment in financial markets: Strategic applications and sector-wide implications. Global Mainstream Journal of Business, Economics. *Development & Project Management*, *3*(4), 39–53.

Nawara, D., & Kashef, R. (2020). IoT-based Recommendation Systems – An Overview. *2020 IEEE International IOT, Electronics and Mechatronics Conference (IEMTRONICS),* (pp. 1-7). Vancouver, BC, Canada: IEEE. Retrieved from DOI: 10.1109/IEMTRONICS51293.2020.9216391

Nazish, M., Khan, M. N., & Khan, Z. (2024). Environmental sustainability in the digital age: Unraveling the effect of social media on green purchase intention. *Young Consumers*, *25*(6), 1015–1035. DOI: 10.1108/YC-01-2024-1965

Ng, K. K. Y., & Zhang, P. C. (2023). Advancing medical affair capabilities and insight generation through machine learning techniques. *Journal of Pharmaceutical Policy and Practice*, *16*(1), 165. DOI: 10.1186/s40545-023-00670-w PMID: 38041173

Nguyen, T. D. (2024). Forecasting cryptocurrency prices using hybrid long short – Term memory and long short – Term memory variants. DOI: 10.21203/rs.3.rs-5374266/v1

Nieves, V., Ruescas, A., & Sauzède, R. (2023, December 20). AI for Marine, Ocean and Climate Change Monitoring. *Remote Sensing (Basel)*, *16*(15), 1–15. DOI: 10.3390/rs16010015

Nonaka, I. (1994). A dynamic theory of organizational knowledge creation. *Organization Science*, *5*(1), 14–37. DOI: 10.1287/orsc.5.1.14

Nonaka, I., & Takeuchi, H. (1995). *The Knowledge-Creating Company*. Oxford University Press. DOI: 10.1093/oso/9780195092691.001.0001

O'Neill, S., & Boykoff, M. (2012). The role of new media in engaging the public with climate change. *Engaging the public with climate change,* *2*(2012), 233–251. https://www.researchgate.net/publication/285081555

Obiuto, N. C., Ebirim, W., Ninduwezuor-Ehiobu, N., Ani, E. C., Olu-lawal, K. A., & Ugwuanyi, E. D. (2024). Integrating sustainability into hvac project management: Challenges and opportunities. *Engineering Science & Technology Journal*, *5*(3), 873–887. DOI: 10.51594/estj.v5i3.943

Obringer, R., Rachunok, B., Maia-Silva, D., Arbabzadeh, M., Nateghi, R., & Madani, K. (2021). The overlooked environmental footprint of increasing Internet use. *Resources, Conservation and Recycling, 167*, 105389. https://doi.org/10.1016/j.resconrec.2020.105389

OECD. (2021). *OECD Science, Technology and Innovation Outlook 2021: Times of Crisis and Opportunity*. OECD Publishing.

Ohene-Botwe, B., Amedu, C., Antwi, W. K., Abdul-Razak, W., Kyei, K. A., Arkoh, S., Mudadi, L.-S., Mushosho, E. Y., Bwanga, O., Chinene, B., Nyawani, P., Mutandiro, L. C., & Piersson, A. D. (2024). Promoting sustainability activities in clinical radiography practice and education in resource-limited countries. *Radiography, 30*(Suppl 1), 56–61. DOI: 10.1016/j.radi.2024.06.007 PMID: 38905726

Okatta, N. C. G., Ajayi, N. F. A., & Olawale, N. O. (2024). Leveraging HR analytics for strategic decision-making: Opportunities and challenges. *International Journal of Management & Entrepreneurship Research, 6*(4), 1304–1325. DOI: 10.51594/ijmer.v6i4.1060

Okeleke, P. A., Ajiga, D., Folorunsho, S. O., & Ezeigweneme, C. (2024). Predictive analytics for market trends using AI: A study in consumer behavior. *[Journal name missing; please provide].*

Oladimeji, D., Gupta, K., Kose, N. A., Gundogan, K., Ge, L., & Liang, F. (2023). Smart Transportation: An Overview of Technologies and Applications. *Sensors (Basel), 23*(8), 3880. DOI: 10.3390/s23083880 PMID: 37112221

Ong, D., Moors, T., & Sivaraman, V. (2014). Comparison of the energy, carbon and time costs of videoconferencing and in-person meetings. *Computer Communications, 50*, 86–94. https://doi.org/10.1016/j.comcom.2014.02.009

Opperman, J. J., Carvallo, J. P., Kelman, R., Schmitt, R. J., Almeida, R., Chapin, E., Flecker, A., Goichot, M., Grill, G., Harou, J. J., Hartmann, J., Higgins, J., Kammen, D., Martin, E., Martins, T., Newsock, A., Rogéliz, C., Raepple, J., Sada, R., & Harrison, D. (2023). Balancing renewable energy and river resources by moving from individual assessments of hydropower projects to energy system planning. *Frontiers in Environmental Science, 10*, 1036653. DOI: 10.3389/fenvs.2022.1036653

Oral, Z. D. (2023). *Analyses of social media engagement of sustainable food brands*. University of York.

Oshoba, T. O., Aifuwa, S. E., Ogbuefi, E., & Olatunde-Thorpe, J. (2020). Portfolio Optimization with Multi-Objective Evolutionary Algorithms-Balancing Risk, Return, and Sustainability Metrics, International Journal of Multidisciplinary Research and Growth Evaluation, ISSN: 2582-7138, 1(3), 163-170.

Paramesha, M., Rane, N., & Rane, J. (2024). Artificial intelligence, machine learning, deep learning, and blockchain in financial and banking services: A comprehensive review. Machine Learning, Deep Learning, and Blockchain in Financial and Banking Services. A Comprehensive Review (June 6, 2024).

Park, S. (2012). Dimensions of digital media literacy and the relationship with social exclusion. *Media International Australia, Incorporating Culture & Policy, 142*(1), 87–100. DOI: 10.1177/1329878X1214200111

Pasko, O., Chen, F., Kuts, T., Sharko, I., & Ryzhikova, N. (2022). Sustainability reporting nexus to corporate governance in scholarly literature. *Environment and Ecology, 13*(1), 61.

Pasupuleti, M. K. (2025). Deep Finance: Cutting-Edge Deep Learning Applications in Market Prediction, Risk Analytics, and Algorithmic Trading. International Journal of Academic and Industrial Research Innovations (IJAIRI), Vol 5, Issue 5, ISSN: 3049-2343.

Patel, K. B., Gonzalez, B. D., Turner, K., Alishahi Tabriz, A., Rollison, D. E., Robinson, E., Naso, C., Wang, X., & Spiess, P. E. (2023). Estimated Carbon Emissions Savings With Shifts From In-Person Visits to Telemedicine for Patients With Cancer. *JAMA Network Open, 6*(1), e2253788. DOI: 10.1001/jamanetworkopen.2022.53788 PMID: 36719682

Patil, S. R., Jadhav, S. N., & Nimbagal, S. (2024). A study on ethical implications of using technology in ESG investing and ensuring unbiased decision making. *Multidisciplinary Science Journal, 6*(8), 2024153–2024153. DOI: 10.31893/multiscience.2024153

Penman, R. A., & Turnbull, S. (2007). *Media literacy: Concepts, research and regulatory issues.* Australian Communications and Media Authority Canberra.

Pérez Domínguez, A., Marinich, J., Monteagudo, G., Moreno, C., Regadera, L., & Iglesias, I. (2025). Pioneering the Future of Medical Affairs: A Strategic Transformation to Meet the Spanish Healthcare Ecosystem's Evolving Trends. *Pharmaceutical Medicine, 39*(5), 281–292. DOI: 10.1007/s40290-025-00574-x PMID: 40652051

Petersen, P. E., & Ogawa, H. (2012). The global burden of periodontal disease: Towards integration with chronic disease prevention and control. *Periodontology 2000, 60*(1), 15–39. DOI: 10.1111/j.1600-0757.2011.00425.x PMID: 22909104

Pichler, P. P., Jaccard, I. S., Weisz, U., & Weisz, H. (2019). International trade and the transboundary displacement of carbon emissions. *Environmental Research Letters, 14*, 064004. DOI: 10.1088/1748-9326/ab19e1

Pithon, M. M., Faria, L. C. M., Tanaka, O. M., Ruellas, A. C. O., & Primo, L. S. S. G. (2017). Sustainability in orthodontics: What can we do to save our planet? *Dental Press Journal of Orthodontics, 22*(4), 113–117. DOI: 10.1590/2177-6709.22.4.113-117.sar PMID: 28902257

Piyathanavong, V., Huynh, V. N., Karnjana, J., & Olapiriyakul, S. (2024). Role of project management on Sustainable Supply Chain development through Industry 4.0 technologies and Circular Economy during the COVID-19 pandemic: A multiple case study of Thai metals industry. Operations Management Research, 17(1), 13-37. https://link.springer.com/content/pdf/10.1007/s12063-022-00283-7.pdf

Podsakoff, P. M., MacKenzie, S. B., Lee, J. Y., & Podsakoff, N. P. (2003). Common method biases in behavioral research. *The Journal of Applied Psychology, 88*(5), 879–903. DOI: 10.1037/0021-9010.88.5.879 PMID: 14516251

Poiriazi, E., Zournatzidou, G., Konteos, G., & Sariannidis, N. (2025). Analyzing the interconnection between environmental, social, and governance (ESG) criteria and corporate corruption: Revealing the significant impact of greenwashing. *Administrative Sciences, 15*(3), 100. DOI: 10.3390/admsci15030100

Popescu, C. E., Pentescu, A., & Shivarov, A. (2023). Sustainability, ESG ratings and corporate performance in the manufacturing sector: A research review. *European Journal of Interdisciplinary Studies, 15*(2), 186–209. DOI: 10.24818/ejis.2023.24

Poppi, F. (2025). Airlines' Emission Disclosures: The Fine Line Between Opportunity and Environmental Inaction. Iperstoria, (25).

Póvoas, M. D. S., Moreira, J. F., Neto, S. V. M., Carvalho, C. A. D. S., Cezario, B. S., Guedes, A. L. A., & Lima, G. B. A. (2025). Artificial intelligence in the oil and gas industry: Applications, challenges, and future directions. *Applied Sciences (Basel, Switzerland), 15*(14), 7918. DOI: 10.3390/app15147918

Pratiwi, A. P., & Edeh, F. O. (2024). The Role of ESG Disclosure in Corporate Performance and Investment Decision-Making. Sinergi International Journal of Accounting and Taxation, 2(1), 1-14. PRI (2017). Principles for Responsible Investment Reporting Framework.

Pria, S., Al Rubaie, I., & Prasad, V. (2024). Enhancing business intelligence through AI-driven integration of sustainability metrics via ESG factors. In Risks and Challenges of AI-Driven Finance: Bias, Ethics, and Security (pp. 57-89). IGI Global.

Protocol, G. H. G. (2004). *The Greenhouse Gas Protocol: A Corporate Accounting and Reporting Standard.* World Resources Institute and World Business Council for Sustainable Development.

Protocol, G. H. G. (2011). *Corporate Value Chain (Scope 3) Accounting and Reporting Standard*. World Resources Institute and World Business Council for Sustainable Development.

Quijano-Sánchez, L., Cantador, I., Cortés-Cediel, M., & Gil, O. (2020). 9). Recommender systems for smart cities. *Information Systems*, *92*, 101545. Advance online publication. DOI: 10.1016/j.is.2020.101545

Rahimpour, S., & Zahraee, S. Y. (2015). System dynamics model for optimizing recycling and collection of waste material in a closed-loop supply chain. *Simulation Modelling Practice and Theory*, *53*, 88–102. DOI: 10.1016/j.simpat.2015.02.001

Rahman, G., & Fitriyah, A. (2025). Harnessing AI for Climate Change Communication: Analyzing Public Perception through NLP and Machine Learning. *Sinergi International Journal of Communication*, *3*(1), 87–98. DOI: 10.61194/ijcs.v3i2.683

Raisch, S., & Krakowski, S. (2021). Artificial intelligence and management: The automation–augmentation paradox. *Academy of Management Review*, *46*(1), 192–210. DOI: 10.5465/amr.2018.0072

Rana, N. P., Dwivedi, Y. K., Hughes, L., & Gupta, A. (2023). Artificial intelligence for sustainable development goals: A systematic literature review. *Journal of Business Research*, *154*, 113297. DOI: 10.1016/j.jbusres.2022.113297

Randeree, K., & Ahmed, N. (2019). The social imperative in sustainable urban development: The case of masdar city in the United Arab Emirates. *Smart and sustainable built environment*, *8*(2), 138-149. DOI DOI: 10.1108/SASBE-11-2017-0064

Rane, J., Mallick, S. K., Kaya, O., & Rane, N. L. (2024). Enhancing black-box models: Advances in explainable artificial intelligence. In *Future research opportunities for artificial intelligence in Industry 4.0 and 5.0* (pp. 136–180). Deep Science Publishing. DOI: 10.70593/978-81-981271-0-5_4

Rapach, S., Riccardi, A., Liu, B., & Bowden, J. (2024). A taxonomy of earth observation data for sustainable finance. *Journal of Climate Finance*, *6*, 100029. DOI: 10.1016/j.jclimf.2023.100029

Rashik, M., Fekete, J. D., & Mahyar, N. (2025). CLAImate: AI-Enabled Climate Change Communication through Personalized and Localized Narrative Visualizations. Proceedings of the IEEE Visualization Conference, *Human-Computer Interaction*, DOI: 10.48550/arXiv.2507.11677

Ravindrane, R., & Patel, J. (2022). The environmental impacts of telemedicine in place of face-to-face patient care: A systematic review. *Future Healthcare Journal*, *9*(1), 28–33. DOI: 10.7861/fhj.2021-0148 PMID: 35372776

Raza Falsk. (2023). *AI for predictive maintenance in industrial systems*. DOI: 10.13140/RG.2.2.27313.35688

Rey, A., Panetti, E., Maglio, R., & Ferretti, M. (2021). 7). Determinants in adopting the Internet of Things in the transport and logistics industry. *Journal of Business Research, 131*, 584–590. DOI: 10.1016/j.jbusres.2020.12.049

Richardson, J., Grose, J., Manzi, S., Mills, I., Moles, D. R., Mukonoweshuro, R., Nasser, M., & Nichols, A. (2016). What's in a bin: A case study of dental clinical waste composition and potential greenhouse gas emission savings. *British Dental Journal, 220*(2), 61–66. DOI: 10.1038/sj.bdj.2016.55 PMID: 26794110

Riche, N. H., Hurter, C., Diakopoulos, N., & Carpendale, S. (2018). *Datadriven storytelling*. CRC Press., DOI: 10.1201/9781315281575

Rodilosso, E. (2024). Filter bubbles and the unfeeling: How AI for social media can foster extremism and polarization. *Philosophy & Technology, 37*(2), 71. DOI: 10.1007/s13347-024-00758-4

Rolnick, D., Donti, P. L., Kaack, L. H., Kochanski, K., Lacoste, A., Sankaran, K., Slavin Ross, A., Milojevic Dupont, N., Jaques, N., Waldman Brown, A., Luccioni, A., Maharaj, T., Sherwin, E. D., Mukkavilli, S. K., Kording, K. P., Gomes, C. P., Ng, A. Y., Hassabis, D., Platt, J. C., & Bengio, Y. (2022). Tackling climate change with machine learning. *ACM Computing Surveys, 55*(2), 1–96. DOI: 10.1145/3485128

Różycki, R., Solarska, D. A., & Waligóra, G. (2025). Energy-aware machine learning models. *Energies, 18*(11), 2810. DOI: 10.3390/en18112810

Russo, S., Schimperna, F., Lombardi, R., & Ruggiero, P. (2022). Sustainability performance and social media: An explorative analysis. *Meditari Accountancy Research, 30*(4), 1118–1140. DOI: 10.1108/MEDAR-03-2021-1227

Sadiq, A. T., & Salih, W. M. (2013). Uncompressed video quality metric based on watermarking technique. *2013 1st International Conference on Communications, Signal Processing, and Their Applications (ICCSPA)*, 1–6.

Sahib, U. (2019). Smart Dubai: Sensing Dubai Smart City for Smart Environment Management. In Kumar, T. V. (Ed.), *Smart Environment for Smart Cities* (pp. 437–489). Springer., DOI: 10.1007/978-981-13-6822-6_12

Saillour-Glénisson, F., Domecq, S., Kret, M., Sibé, M., Dumond, J. P., Michel, P., & Group, T. (2016). Design and validation of a questionnaire to assess organizational culture in French hospital wards. *BMC Health Services Research, 16*(1), 491. DOI: 10.1186/s12913-016-1736-4

Salloum, S. A., Almarzouqi, A., Aburayya, A., Shwedeh, F., Fatin, B., Al Ghurabli, Z., Elbadawi, M. A., & Alfaisal, R. (2024). Embracing ChatGPT: Ushering in a Revolutionary Phase in Educational Platforms. In *Artificial Intelligence in Education: The Power and Dangers of ChatGPT in the Classroom* (pp. 171–183). https://link.springer.com/chapter/10.1007/978-3-031-52280-2_12

Samašonok, K., & Išoraitė, M. (2023). The implementation of sustainable development goals through communication tools. *Entrepreneurship and Sustainability Issues*, *10*(3), 102–122. DOI: 10.9770/jesi.2023.10.3(8)

Sanz, M., Kamma, J., Goldstein, M., & Tonetti, M. (2025). The impact of the European Federation of Periodontology on European and global periodontology. *Periodontology 2000*, prd.12620. DOI: 10.1111/prd.12620 PMID: 39891466

Saradara, S. M., Khalfan, M. M. A., Rauf, A., & Qureshi, R. (2023). On the path towards sustainable construction—the case of the United Arab Emirates: A review. *Sustainability (Basel)*, *15*(19), 14652. DOI: 10.3390/su151914652

Sarker, V. K., Gia, T. N., Ben Dhaou, I., & Westerlund, T. (2020). Smart Parking System with Dynamic Pricing, Edge-Cloud Computing and LoRa. *Sensors (Basel)*, *20*(17), 4669. DOI: 10.3390/s20174669 PMID: 32824989

Saunders, M., Lewis, P., & Thornhill, A. (2016). *Research methods for business students* (7th ed.). Pearson Education.

Savoldelli, A., Landi, D., & Rizzi, C. (2024). Exploring quantitative methodologies for assessing the environmental, social, and economic impacts of telemedicine: A literature review. *Sustainability (Basel)*, *16*(6), 2438. DOI: 10.3390/su16062438

Saxena, A., Santhanavijayan, A., Shakya, H., Kumar, G., Balusamy, B., & Benedetto, F. (2024). Nested Sentiment Analysis for ESG Impact: Leveraging FinBERT to Predict Market Dynamics Based on Eco-Friendly and Non-Eco-Friendly Product Perceptions with Explainable AI. *Mathematics*, *12*(21), 3332. DOI: 10.3390/math12213332

SB, G., & Danti, A. (2025). Block chain-based security and authentication for forensics application using consensus proof of work and zero knowledge protocol. *International Journal of Information Technology : an Official Journal of Bharati Vidyapeeth's Institute of Computer Applications and Management*, *17*(8), 5041–5052.

Schultz, A., Senn, M., & van't Klooster, J. (2024). Restoring trust in sustainable finance: The role of active supervision in greenwashing scandals. finanzwende.de

Sekhar, C., & Narasimhulu, M. (2025, March). Stock Market Forecasting with Ensemble Learning: Random Forest, XGBoost, and LSTM. In 2025 7th International Conference on Intelligent Sustainable Systems (ICISS) (pp. 1683-1689). IEEE.

Sen, A., & Yamin, M. (2021). Advantages of using fog in IoT applications. *International Journal of Information Technology : an Official Journal of Bharati Vidyapeeth's Institute of Computer Applications and Management, 13*(3), 829–837. DOI: 10.1007/s41870-020-00514-9

Shah, S. T., Ali, Z., Waqar, M., & Kim, A. (2025). Federated learning in public health. *Health Care, 13*(21), 2760. DOI: 10.3390/healthcare13212760 PMID: 41228128

Shahzaib. (2025, October 15). *Miral and e& enterprise launch Yas Island Metaverse to revolutionize virtual event planning*. MEA Tech Watch. https://meatechwatch.com/2025/10/15/miral-and-e-enterprise-launch-yas-island-metaverse-to-revolutionize-virtual-event-planning/

Shellard, I. J., Martin, N., Mulligan, S., & Hatton, P. (2022). *Consensus on environmentally sustainable oral healthcare: A joint stakeholder statement*. White Rose University Press.

Shepherd, D. A., & Patzelt, H. (2011). The new field of sustainable entrepreneurship: Studying entrepreneurial action linking "what is to be sustained" with "what is to be developed". *Entrepreneurship Theory and Practice, 35*(1), 137–163. DOI: 10.1111/j.1540-6520.2010.00426.x

Shinkai, R. S. A., Biazevic, M. G. H., Michel-Crosato, E., & Toyota de Campos, T. (2025). Environmental sustainability related to dental materials and procedures in prosthodontics: A critical review. *The Journal of Prosthetic Dentistry, 133*(6), 1466–1473. DOI: 10.1016/j.prosdent.2023.05.024 PMID: 37709614

Shrestha, Y. R., Ben-Menahem, S. M., & von Krogh, G. (2021). Organizational decision-making structures in the age of artificial intelligence. *California Management Review, 63*(1), 66–87. DOI: 10.1177/0008125620974607

Shwedeh, F., Yas, N., Abdijabar, Z., Flayyih, N., Fadli, A., Yas, H., & Allouzi, A. S. (2024). The impact of intellectual property rights and the level of information sensitivity on information security in the United Arab Emirates. *Journal of Infrastructure, Policy and Development, 8*(8), 6303. https://doi.org/https://doi.org/10.24294/jipd.v8i8.6303

Simeone, M., & Scarpato, D. (2020). Sustainable consumption: How does social media affect food choices? *Journal of Cleaner Production, 277*, 124036. DOI: 10.1016/j.jclepro.2020.124036

Singh, S. K., & Sanjeev, R. (2022). Antecedents of Green Marketing Initiatives: A Hierarchical Regression Model. [IJSESD]. *International Journal of Social Ecology and Sustainable Development, 13*(1), 1–15.

Smith, L., Ali, M., Agrissais, M., Mulligan, S., Koh, L., & Martin, N. (2023). A comparative life cycle assessment of dental restorative materials. *Dental Materials, 39*(1), 13–24. DOI: 10.1016/j.dental.2022.11.007 PMID: 36428112

Solanke, B. (2017). Resolving fault shadow challenge: Onshore Niger Delta case history. [Society of Exploration Geophysicists.]. *SEG Technical Program Expanded Abstracts, 2017*, 4514–4518.

Somodi, G., & Vásárhelyi, B. (2023). Borehole analysis with the modification of RQD value. *Geotechnics, 3*(4), 1017–1032. DOI: 10.3390/geotechnics3040055

Son, N., Yang, S., & Na, J. (2019). Hybrid forecasting model for short-term wind power prediction using modified long short-term memory. *Energies, 12*(20), 3901. DOI: 10.3390/en12203901

Speroni, S., & Polizzi, E. (2025). Green dentistry: State of the art and possible development proposals. *Dentistry Journal, 13*(1), 38. DOI: 10.3390/dj13010038 PMID: 39851612

Stahl, J. K., & Hinkel, J. (2025). The power of storytelling: How narratives shape marine conservation and uses along the German coast of the Baltic Sea. *Maritime Studies, 24*(3), 1–18. DOI: 10.1007/s40152-025-00419-y

Sunstein, C. R. (2018). *Republic: Divided democracy in the age of social media.*

Suprihadi, E., & Danila, N. (2024). Forecasting ESG stock indices using a machine learning approach. *Global Business Review*, 09721509241234033. DOI: 10.1177/09721509241234033

Surdu, A., Foia, C. I., Luchian, I., Trifan, D., Budala, D. G., Scutariu, M. M., Ciupilan, C., Puha, B., & Tatarciuc, D. (2025). Telemedicine and digital tools in dentistry: Enhancing diagnosis and remote patient care. *Medicina, 61*(5), 826. DOI: 10.3390/medicina61050826 PMID: 40428784

Suresh, P., Crotty, J., Tesanovic, S., Alaweed, O., Doyle, S., Kiandee, M., Hayes, E., Umeh, V., Khalilinejad, B., & Duane, B. (2024). A life cycle analysis of the environmental impact of procurement, waste and water in the dental practice. *British Dental Journal, 236*(7), 545–551. DOI: 10.1038/s41415-024-7239-5 PMID: 38609622

Tabbakh, A., Al Amin, L., Islam, M., Mahmud, G. M. I., Chowdhury, I. K., & Mukta, M. S. H. (2024). Towards sustainable AI: A comprehensive framework for Green AI. *Discover Sustainability*, *5*(1), 408. DOI: 10.1007/s43621-024-00641-4

Tahmasseby, S. (2020). The Implementation of Smart Mobility for Smart Cities: A Case Study in Qatar. *Civil Engineering Kournal*, *8*(10), 2154–2171. Advance online publication. DOI: 10.28991/CEJ-2022-08-10-09

Tarabieh, S., Gil, I., Galdón Salvador, J. L., & AlFraihat, S. F. A. (2024). The new game of online marketing: How social media influencers drive online repurchase intention through brand trust and customer brand engagement. *Intangible Capital*, *20*(1), 103–125. DOI: 10.3926/ic.2515

Taylor, R. A., Sangal, R. B., Smith, M. E., Haimovich, A. D., Rodman, A., Iscoe, M. S., Pavuluri, S. K., Rose, C., Janke, A. T., Wright, D. S., Socrates, V., & Declan, A. (2025). Leveraging artificial intelligence to reduce diagnostic errors in emergency medicine. *Academic Emergency Medicine*, *32*(3), 327–339. DOI: 10.1111/acem.15066 PMID: 39676165

Teece, D. J. (2018). Business models and dynamic capabilities. *Long Range Planning*, *51*(1), 40–49. DOI: 10.1016/j.lrp.2017.06.007

The Yas SeaWorld Research & Rescue Center. (2025). Leading marine conservation & Inspiring environmental protection. https://www.seaworldabudhabi.com/en/research-and-rescue

Theocharis, D., & Tsekouropoulos, G. (2025). Sustainable consumption and branding for Gen Z: How brand dimensions influence consumer behavior and adoption of newly launched technological products. *Sustainability (Basel)*, *17*(9), 4124. DOI: 10.3390/su17094124

Thiel, C. L., Mehta, N., Sejo, C. S., Qureshi, L., Moyer, M., Valentino, V., & Saleh, J. (2023). 'Telemedicine and the environment: Life cycle environmental emissions from in-person and virtual clinic visits', npj. *Digital Medicine*, *6*(1), 87. DOI: 10.1038/s41746-023-00818-7 PMID: 37160996

Tong, X., Linderman, K., & Zhu, Q. (2023). Managing a portfolio of environmental projects: Focus, balance, and environmental management capabilities. *Journal of Operations Management*, *69*(1), 127–158. DOI: 10.1002/joom.1201

Tourism Breaking News. (2025). Enriching Student Experiences: Miral and Canadian University Dubai Sign Strategic Partnership. https://tourismbreakingnews.ae/enriching-student-experiences-miral-and-canadian-university-dubai-sign-strategic-partnership/

Truyols-Pont, M. A., Bilbao-Terol, A., & Arenas-Parra, M. (2024). Machine Learning for Sustainable Portfolio Optimization Applied to a Water Market. *Mathematics, 12*(24), 3975. DOI: 10.3390/math12243975

Tumedei, G., Ceccarini, C., Navarro, I. C. J., & Prandi, C. (2025). From Drawings to Awareness: Exploring Narrative Visualization and AI to Teach Children About the Fragile Ecosystem of the Mar Menor Lagoon. In *Designing Interactive Systems Conference* (DIS '25), July 05–09, 2025, Funchal, Portugal. ACM, New York, NY, USA, 17 pages. DOI: 10.1145/3715336.3735722

Umar, T., Egbu, C., Ofori, G., Honnurvali, M. S., Saidani, M., Shibani, A., & Goh, K. (2020, March). UAE's commitment towards UN Sustainable Development Goals. In *Proceedings of the Institution of Civil Engineers-Engineering Sustainability* (Vol. 173, No. 7, pp. 325-343). Thomas Telford Ltd. https://dx.doi.org/DOI: 10.1680/jensu.19.00036

United Nations climate change annual report 2022. (n.d.). *Climate Change and Law Collection.* DOI: 10.1163/9789004322714_cclc_2023-0169-0826

Uptime Institute (2023) 'Accounting for digital infrastructure GHG emissions'.

Uribe, S., Issa, J., Sohrabniya, F., Denny, A., Kim, N., Dayo, A., Chaurasia, A., Sofi-Mahmudi, A., Büttner, M., & Schwendicke, F. (2024). Publicly available dental image datasets for artificial intelligence. *Journal of Dental Research, 103*(13), 1365–1374. Advance online publication. DOI: 10.1177/00220345241272052 PMID: 39422586

Vaccaro, M., Almaatouq, A., & Malone, T. (2024). When combinations of humans and AI are useful: A systematic review and meta-analysis. *Nature Human Behaviour, 8*(12), 2293–2303.

Valle, N., Zhao, P., Freed, D., Gorton, K., Chapman, A. B., Shea, A. L., & Bazarova, N. N. (2024). Towards a Critical Framework of Social Media Literacy: A Systematic Literature Review. *Review of Educational Research*, •••, 00346543241247224.

Van Kolfschooten, H., & van Oirschot, J. (2024). The EU Artificial Intelligence Act (2024): Implications for healthcare. *Health Policy (Amsterdam), 149*, 105152. DOI: 10.1016/j.healthpol.2024.105152 PMID: 39244818

Vashisht, R., Sharma, A., Kiran, T., Jolly, S., Brar, P., & Puri, J. (2024). Artificial intelligence in dentistry: A scoping review. *Journal of Oral and Maxillofacial Surgery, Medicine, and Pathology, 36*(4), 579–592. Advance online publication. DOI: 10.1016/j.ajoms.2024.04.009

Vázquez-Sebrango, G., Anitua, E., Macía, I., & Arganda-Carreras, I. (2025). The role of artificial intelligence in implant dentistry: A systematic review. *International Journal of Oral and Maxillofacial Surgery*, *54*(11), 1098–1122. DOI: 10.1016/j.ijom.2025.04.005 PMID: 40436717

Venezia, E. (2023). Cost–benefit analysis in high-speed railway projects: Appraisal of methodological approaches and an initial social equity evaluation, a case study. *Sustainability (Basel)*, *15*(14), 11344. DOI: 10.3390/su151411344

Vinuesa, R., Azizpour, H., Leite, I., Balaam, M., Dignum, V., Domisch, S., Fellander, A., Langhans, S. D., Tegmark, M., & Fuso Nerini, F. (2020). The role of artificial intelligence in achieving the Sustainable Development Goals. *Nature Communications*, *11*(1), 233. DOI: 10.1038/s41467-019-14108-y PMID: 31932590

Visalli, F., Patrizio, A., Lanza, A., Papaleo, P., Nautiyal, A., Pupo, M., & Ruffolo, M. (2023). ESG Data Collection with Adaptive AI. In ICEIS (1) (pp. 468-475). DOI: 10.5220/0011844500003467

Vishwakarma, J. S., & Jain, D. T. (2025). Study of Leading Green Finance Frameworks and Gaps in Existing Sustainable Financing Assessment. *Journal of Information Systems Engineering & Management.*

Wamba, S. F., Dubey, R., Gunasekaran, A., & Akter, S. (2021). The performance effects of big data analytics and supply chain ambidexterity. *International Journal of Production Economics*, *231*, 107947. DOI: 10.1016/j.ijpe.2020.107947

Weder, F., Karmasin, M., Krainer, L., & Voci, D. (2021). Sustainability communication as critical perspective in media and communication studies—An introduction. In *The sustainability communication reader: A reflective compendium* (pp. 1–12). Springer. DOI: 10.1007/978-3-658-31883-3_1

Wierman, A., & Ren, S. (2025). We Need to Talk About AI's Impact on Public Health. *IEEE Spectrum*, *1*(May).

World Economic Forum. (2022). *The global risks report.* https://www.weforum.org

World Health Organization. (2022). *Global oral health status report: Towards universal health coverage for oral health by 2030.* WHO.

Wu, J., Xu, L., Zhou, W., Jiang, F., Liu, P., Zhang, H., Jiang, Q., & Xu, J. (2020). Fishnet-Like, Nitrogen-Doped Carbon Films Directly Anchored on Carbon Cloths as Binder-Free Electrodes for High-Performance Supercapacitor. *Global Challenges (Hoboken, NJ)*, *4*(3), 1900086. DOI: 10.1002/gch2.201900086

Wu, Y., Wang, H., Wang, Z., Diehl, J. A., & Xue, S. (2024). Evaluating the economic sustainability of commercial complex greening based on cost-benefit analysis: A case study of Singapore's Shaw center. *Ecological Indicators*, *161*, 111890. DOI: 10.1016/j.ecolind.2024.111890

Xin, C., Wenyuan, H., Jiawen, S., Yanlin, H., Jiangtao, G., Shize, W., & Yaliang, X. (2024). AI-assisted subtle faults characterization based on integrated seismic diffraction imaging: Application in M Oilfield, Middle East. In *Abu Dhabi International Petroleum Exhibition and Conference* (p. D011S021R002). SPE.

Yas SeaWorld Research & Rescue Center. (2025). *The Yas SeaWorld Research & Rescue Center Abu Dhabi is always here to help*. https://www.seaworldabudhabi.com/en/research-and-rescue/rescue-rehabilitation

Yas, N., Dafri, W., Yas, H., & Shwedeh, F. (2024). Effect of e-Learning on Servicing Education in Dubai. In *Artificial Intelligence in Education: The Power and Dangers of ChatGPT in the Classroom* (pp. 623–639). https://link.springer.com/chapter/10.1007/978-3-031-52280-2_40

Yas, H., Aldabbagh, Z., Khalifa, A. A., Faghiri, A., Bawazir, A. A., & Shwedeh, F. (2025). Role of artificial intelligence in the promotion of customer experiences: A legal administrative study and systematic review in the United Arab Emirates. *Humanities (Washington)*, *6*(4). 10.58256/m353d5430

Yigitcanlar, T., & Kankanamge, N. (2022). Urban Big Data and Social Media Analytics. In *Urban Analytics with Social Media Data* (pp. 3–50). CRC Press.

Yunus, Y. A., & Nanda, S. (2024). Exploring sustainable finance: A qualitative inquiry into responsible investment and ESG risk evaluation. Golden Ratio of Finance Management, 4(1), 01-13.

Zahra, S. A., Gedajlovic, E., Neubaum, D. O., & Shulman, J. M. (2012). A typology of social entrepreneurs: Motives, search processes and ethical challenges. *Journal of Business Venturing*, *27*(5), 519–532. DOI: 10.1016/j.jbusvent.2008.04.007

Zantalis, F., Koulouras, G., Karabetsos, S., & Kandris, D. (2019). A Review of Machine Learning and IoT in Smart Transportation. *Future Internet*, *11*(4), 94. DOI: 10.3390/fi11040094

ZAWYA. (2025). Planting Seeds for the Future: Miral's CSR Programme cultivates environmental stewardship among youth. https://www.zawya.com/en/press-release/companies-news/planting-seeds-for-the-future-mirals-csr-programme-cultivates-environmental-stewardship-among-youth-epzpialh

Zeng, L., Li, H., Lin, L., Hu, D. J. J., & Liu, H. (2024). ESG standards in China: Bibliometric analysis, development status research, and future research directions. [Multidisciplinary Digital Publishing Institute.]. *Sustainability (Basel), 16*(16), 7134. DOI: 10.3390/su16167134

Zervoudi, E. K., Moschos, N., & Christopoulos, A. G. (2025). From the corporate social responsibility (CSR) and the environmental, social and governance (ESG) criteria to the greenwashing phenomenon: A comprehensive literature review about the causes, consequences and solutions of the phenomenon with specific case studies. *Sustainability (Basel), 17*(5), 2222. DOI: 10.3390/su17052222

Zhang, A. Y., & Zhang, J. H. (2024). Renovation in environmental, social and governance (ESG) research: The application of machine learning. *Asian Review of Accounting, 32*(4), 554–572. DOI: 10.1108/ARA-07-2023-0201

Zhang, K., Liu, X., & Wang, J. (2023). Exploring the relationship between corporate ESG information disclosure and audit fees: Evidence from non-financial A-share listed companies in China. *Frontiers in Environmental Science, 11*, 1196728. DOI: 10.3389/fenvs.2023.1196728

Zhang, Q. (2018). Convolutional neural networks. *3rd International Conference on Electromechanical Control Technology and Transportation*, 434-439. DOI: 10.5220/0006972204340439

Zhang, X., Kong, L., & Hu, X. (2024). Shades of green: The impact of greenwashing on stock price crash risk. *Finance Research Letters, 70*, 106285. DOI: 10.1016/j.frl.2024.106285

Zhang, Y., Sun, J., Yang, Z., & Li, S. (2022). Artificial intelligence-driven green innovation and environmental performance. *Technological Forecasting and Social Change, 173*, 121092. DOI: 10.1016/j.techfore.2021.121092

Zhu, J., Chen, Z., Zhao, J., Yu, Y., Li, X., Shi, K., Zhang, F., Yu, F., Shi, K., Sun, Z., Lin, N., & Zheng, Y. (2023). Artificial intelligence in the diagnosis of dental diseases on panoramic radiographs: A preliminary study. *BMC Oral Health, 23*(1), 358. DOI: 10.1186/s12903-023-03027-6 PMID: 37270488

ZS (2025) 'Emerging pharma: Here's your omnichannel roadmap'.

About the Contributors

Fanar Shwedeh is a Computer Science specialist and a researcher working in the area of AI Innovations, Information Systems and Technology Management besides teaching as an Associate Professor in City University Ajman. Holds a PhD degree in Technology Management Information Systems from Utara University Malaysia, Masters in Business Management, BSc in Computer Science from the University of Sharjah and high Diploma in Cyber Security of Information Systems from the USA Cyber Security Institution. Dr. Fanar has published research publications in highly impacted international journals, and she is an academic chief reviewer of reputable International Scopus-indexed journals. Dr. Fanar is a member of the research academic unit in Dubai Smart government office. She was awarded the H.H. Sheikh Hamdan Bin Rashid Al-Maktoum Award for Distinguished Performance in 2020. Furthermore, she is the editor of the book chapter "Sustainable Leadership for Environmental Risk", Springer 2025.

***

Fahizah A is an academic clinician, researcher, and health-tech entrepreneur working at the intersection of dentistry, biomedical research, and innovation. She is a faculty member at Yenepoya (Deemed to be University) and a Senior Research Fellow (SRF) pursuing a PhD in Periodontology & Implantology, with research focused on oral-derived mesenchymal stem cells, biomaterials, and translational regenerative therapies. Alongside her academic career, she is the Co-Founder and Chief Product Officer of Yalmae, a dentist-to-dentist oral-care brand known for science-driven, affordable innovations such as the SLS-free sensitivity toothpaste Sensifix and a patented self-disinfecting toothbrush. She is also a Co-Founder of Fuwu Solutions, a multidisciplinary venture supporting healthcare innovation, startups, and product development. Dr. Fahizah is actively involved in grant writing, patent filing, product commercialization, and student mentorship, and regularly bridges clinical needs with design, technology, and sustainability. Her work reflects a strong commitment to ethical innovation, accessible healthcare solutions, and academic–industry collaboration.

MeharunneesaAboobacker Sidheeq is an academic clinician, and researcher with more than 12 years of experience . She is lecturer and specialist periodontist at College of Dentistry City University, Ajman. Her work reflects a strong commitment to Preventive health care, ethical innovation, accessible healthcare solutions, technology enhanced health care solutions and academic–industry collaboration.

Najwa AlSaeed, Ph.D., is Assistant Professor in Public Relations and Advertising at the City University Ajman (UAE). Her research focuses on digital media, public diplomacy, peace-building, and Gulf–MENA regional geopolitics.

Zaheda Daruwala is an Associate Professor of Accounting and Finance with more than two decades of professional experience in academia. She carries a strong portfolio of academic achievement, leadership, and community impact. With a PhD in Finance, double Masters, MBA in Accounting from Columbus University, US and MSc in Accounting & Financial Management from Royal Holloway, UoL, UK, she is also Certified Management Accountant (CMA) from IMA and a Certified Fraud Examiner (CFE) from ACFE. Dr. Zaheda sees her profession as more of a passion and is an active researcher with publications in areas of accounting ethics, financial crisis 2008, impact of corporate tax on economies, sustainability accounting, analysis of the stock markets and cryptocurrencies among others.

Mahitab Elrafii is Chair of the Department of Humanities and Director of the Center for Quality Assurance at May University in Cairo. She holds a Ph.D. in Digital Media from Cairo University, an M.A. in Mass Communication – Journalism, and a B.A. in Mass Communication from Zagazig University, along with a Diploma in Digital Media from the American University in Cairo (AUC).

Shafna M is a distinguished periodontist with over 11 years of clinical experience and a robust background in academic research. A university topper and recognized academic research scholar, Dr.Shafna has dedicated her career to advancing periodontal care and education. She specializes in training fellow periodontists for UAE licensing examinations, successfully mentoring numerous dental professionals to achieve their certification goals. Her work seamlessly integrates clinical practice, scholarly research, and professional training, reflecting a commitment to excellence in both patient care and the academic development of the next generation of specialists. Through her contributions to research, education, and clinical practice, Dr. Shafna continues to shape the field of periodontology, promoting innovation, high standards, and lifelong learning.

Jonathan Matusitz, Ph.D., is a professor in the Nicholson School of Communication and Media at the University of Central Florida. His academic interests include media studies, healthcare, and public communication campaigns.

Mohamed Oweis is an Associate Professor of Media at City University, Ajman, UAE, holding a Ph.D. in Digital Media from Cairo University, Egypt. Throughout his academic career, he has taught and supervised both undergraduate and postgraduate students at several leading universities in the Arab world. His work integrates practical and digital media skills, curriculum development, innovative teaching approaches, and scholarly engagement, with a focus on digital communication, media production, and research supervision.

Index

www.ingramcontent.com/pod-product-compliance
Lightning Source LLC
LaVergne TN
LVHW081534300926
849161LV00006B/1422